THE READER
ALI SMITH

THE READER
ALI SMITH

CONSTABLE • LONDON

Constable & Robinson Ltd
3 The Lanchesters
162 Fulham Palace Road
London W6 9ER
www.constablerobinson.com

First published in the UK by Constable,
an imprint of Constable & Robinson Ltd, 2006

A copy of the British Library Cataloguing in
Publication Data is available from the British Library.

ISBN-13: 978-1-84529-311-6
ISBN-10: 1-84529-311-8

Printed and bound in the EU

1 3 5 7 9 10 8 6 4 2

CONTENTS

Introduction 1

GIRLS

JANE AUSTEN	from *Northanger Abbey*	7
MARGARET ATWOOD	The Poet Has Come Back . . .	8
DJUNA BARNES	The Terrible Peacock	9
BILLIE HOLIDAY	from *Lady Sings the Blues*	17
LAURA HIRD	from *Born Free*	22
GEORGE MACKAY BROWN	Witch	34
MARINA TSVETAYEVA	We shall not escape Hell	48
KATHLEEN JAMIE	Meadowsweet	49
STEVIE SMITH	This Englishwoman	50
PAUL BAILEY	Spunk	51
NELL DUNN	from *Up the Junction*	57
WILLIAM DOUGLAS	Annie Laurie	62
ZORA NEALE HURSTON	from *Their Eyes Were Watching God*	64
BERYL THE PERIL	Double Act	68
ANGELA CARTER	from *Wise Children*	70
MARILYNNE ROBINSON	from *Housekeeping*	76
JANE BOWLES	Everything Is Nice	78
VIRGINIA WOOLF	from *Orlando*	85

DIALOGUES

JOHN KEATS	On First Looking into Chapman's Homer	87
LYDIA DAVIS	In the Garment District	88

KASIA BODDY	On the Ward with TV, iPod and Telephone	89
JACK RILLIE	Call-girls	94
MARGARET TAIT	Elasticity	95
	To Anybody At All	95
GRACE PALEY	Wants	96
CZESLAW MILOSZ	On Angels	99
	Ars Poetica?	100
JOHN BERGER	Between Two Colmars	102
W.G. SEBALD	from *After Nature*	108
H.D. (HILDA DOOLITTLE)	The Cinema and the Classics: Beauty	111
COLETTE	Mae West	119
LEE MILLER	Colette	122
CYNTHIA OZICK	from the Preface to *Bloodshed and Three Novellas*	129
VIRGINIA WOOLF	from *A Writer's Diary*	130
EDWIN MORGAN	More Questions than Answers	136
	Instructions to an Actor	137

JOURNEYS

JOHN DONNE	The Good-Morrow	139
JOY WILLIAMS	Lu-Lu	140
KATHERINE MANSFIELD	15 December 1919	147
KATE ATKINSON	Unseen Translation	148
EDWARD THOMAS	Adlestrop	164
W.B. YEATS	The Song Of Wandering Aengus	165
JOSEPH ROTH	Passengers with Heavy Loads	166
LAVINIA GREENLAW	The Falling City	169
LOUISE BROOKS	Kansas to New York	170
LIZ LOCHHEAD	On Midsummer Common	187
A.M. HOMES	Remedy	189
FRED D'AGUIAR	Bring Back, Bring Back	219

THE WORLD

THOMAS HARDY	The Darkling Thrush	221
ALICE OSWALD	Hymn to Iris	223
TOVE JANSSON	Art in Nature	224
WALLACE STEVENS	Earthy Anecdote	230
SYLVIA PLATH	Black Rook in Rainy Weather	231
XANDRA BINGLEY	Mrs Fish	233
HUGH MACDIARMID	Bairns Arena Frightened	245
JACKIE KAY	Old Aberdeen	246
JEANETTE WINTERSON	The 24-Hour Dog	247
WILLIAM CARLOS WILLIAMS	Pastoral	256
PHILIP LARKIN	The Trees	257
NAN SHEPHERD	from *The Living Mountain*	258
ALAN SPENCE	into the sea	267
J.M. SYNGE	Prelude	268
	In May	268
GERTRUDE STEIN	On "rose is a rose is a rose"	269

HISTORIES

WILLIAM BLAKE	Infant Joy	271
	A Poison Tree	272
LEWIS GRASSIC GIBBON	from *Sunset Song*	273
ALASDAIR GRAY	Houses and Small Labour Parties	288
HELEN OYEYEMI	Independence	302
RAMONA HERDMAN	He died on Friday	310
EDWIN MUIR	The Child Dying	312
MAGGIE O'FARRELL	The House I Live In	313
JOYCE CAROL OATES	Small Avalanches	337
ANNE FRANK	Saturday, 8 July 1944	350
DILYS POWELL	Reconciliation	353
ARMANDO	Fragments, *From Berlin*	358
RACHEL SEIFFERT	Field Study	362
NICOLA BARKER	The Butcher's Apprentice	377

BELIEFS

WILLIAM SHAKESPEARE	from *Cymbeline*	385
LEONORA CARRINGTON	The Happy Corpse Story	387
AMOS TUTUOLA	from *The Palm-Wine Drinkard*	391
SIMONE DE BEAUVOIR	from *Memoirs of a Dutiful Daughter*	402
TOM LEONARD	baa baa black sheep	412
LORNA SAGE	Our Lady of the Accident	413
CLARICE LISPECTOR	from *State of Grace*	419
E.E. CUMMINGS	thing no is(of	422
MURIEL SPARK	from *The Comforters*	423
DEREK JARMAN	White Lies	428
DUBRAVKA UGRESIC	Alchemy	439
E.Y. "YIP" HARBURG	It's only a paper moon	443
COOKIE MUELLER	Fleeting Happiness	444
ITALO CALVINO	from *Six Memos for the Next Millennium*	446
RAINER MARIA RILKE	The Ninth Elegy	447
ROBERT CREELEY	End	450
About the Writers		451
Acknowledgements		462
Index of Writers		469

"Any method is right, every method is right, that expresses what we wish to express, if we are writers; that brings us closer to the novelist's intention if we are readers."

Virginia Woolf, *The Common Reader*

"As if languages loved each other behind their own façades, despite alles was man denkt darüber davon dazu. As if words fraternised silently beneath the syntax, finding each other funny and delicious in a Misch-Masch of tender fornication, inside the bombed out hallowed structures and the rigid steel glass modern edifices of the brain."

Christine Brooke-Rose, *Between*

INTRODUCTION

This book is a great idea – and one of the most interestingly frustrating things I've ever done. My friend Becky Hardie is an editor; we've known each other since we worked together at Granta Books on a collection of short stories. Listen, she said to me, what do you think of this idea? What if we take some of the favourite reading of writers, not just current but over a lifetime, and we make an anthology?

Wonderful, I said. I'd love to do that. Who wouldn't?

It stayed a wonderful idea full of possibilities and excitement, with writer after writer and piece after piece and book after book all coming together to make a book as big as a building, no, as big and various as a library, yes, a library in itself, no, several libraries, yes, a whole community of libraries all lending out books to one another so that books flew, as if with wings, from mind to mind – until Becky gave me a deadline and a page limit and a cash limit, and until I stood in the front room of my house and looked at the shelves and knew I couldn't have them all.

And even from my favourite writers or favourite books, what would I choose? How would I ever? Take Woolf, for instance, and all her books there on the shelf in front of me. How would I choose between her fiction and her criticism and her diaries and her letters? If I chose her fiction, how would I ever choose between the novels? And what about the stories? There was nothing that wasn't a compromise. Maybe this would have to be a Woolf anthology, since if I chose at all I'd have to choose that, and that, and that, and how could I not choose that?

Plus, when Becky and I had first chatted I'd got a bit excited because this was an unexpected chance to send an anthology out to sea full of writers who generally tend to get a lot less shelf space – Lee Miller, for instance, whom people know as a photographer but tend not to know as the brilliant reportage writer she was, mid-century, for *Vogue*; or Leonora Carrington, an artist now in her late eighties who's still, mysteriously, not well enough known for her painting, let alone her strange and inspired fiction. Or Nan Shepherd, the Scottish writer from the 1920s whose achievements in both fiction and nature-writing have always been overshadowed by fellow north-east writer Lewis Grassic Gibbon, himself an international bestseller when *A Scots Quair* came out in the 1930s, and who's still hugely popular in Scotland but almost unread everywhere else.

And would I include things from my childhood that I now couldn't read any more, like the pony books whose earthy, likeable heroine was called Jill? Or would it be only things that had come the whole way with me, like *Struwwelpeter*? And what's "the whole way" anyway? A book I put together now wouldn't be anything like a book I'd have put together in my twenties, or five years ago, or last year, or one I'd do in the future.

That's the thing about books. They're alive on their own terms. Reading is like travelling with an argumentative, unpredictable good friend. It's an endless open exchange.

But I had to start and stop somewhere or we wouldn't have a book at all. So. I settled for a single volume, and for a single century – more or less – the twentieth, with one or two inter-lopers who sneaked under the rope, it couldn't be helped. I settled for two days in which I'd piece it together. Here's a record of these two days in my front room with the books all over the floor. If I was doing it now, or had done it on any other day, it'd be a different book.

It would have been a different book, too, if I'd been sensible and chosen a century where the rights for published pieces had been freed up because the writers had been dead long enough. One of the reasons there are absences which should have been presences among the writers included here is permissions fees. One of the reasons is that permissions people at publishers can take months, even years, to reply, if they reply at all, when you ask them to give you permission to reprint something. One of the reasons is that sometimes when they do reply they ask for an unfeasible amount of money. These are some of the reasons that James Joyce isn't in this anthology, or, at the other end of the spectrum, Laura Ingalls Wilder, both of whom are writers I've read and loved since childhood. And they're not the only ones.

It's bound to read like a liturgy of absences to me, this book – I hope it doesn't to you. But if it does, and you're sitting there saying "but why hasn't she included Raymond Carver, or Alice Munro, or Susan Sontag, or Flannery O Connor?" – well, we tried. And any other absence that annoys you, treat it as a presence. Treat it as a nudge to go and reread the writer who's not here.

I learned to read early; I was three years old. According to my father I learned by pairing the heard names of programmes to the words in the TV listings in the paper, and I can actually remember working out the link between the spoken and written words "fine" and "woman" on the Beatles double-A sided 45, "She's a Woman / I Feel Fine". By the age of eight I'd read everything in the house; it felt fine, to read.

I was precocious, because born at the end of a family of five children, with my closest brother seven years older than me. This meant the cupboard above the bed in the bedroom, which I shared with my two much older sisters, was full of the books they and my brothers were reading, mainly secondary school set texts, I suppose now, though there were rogue copies of unexpected things, and there was certainly a lot of Georgette Heyer up there (belonging to my sister Anne, who had the ability to remove herself so deeply into a book that you could be shouting her name right next to her ear and she'd not hear you).

I wasn't much for historical romance (though I quite liked the horses in it). I ignored the piles of Heyer and read all the other books in the cupboard. It wasn't till I was in my twenties and reading for a university degree that I realized I'd read my way through a lot of Joyce, Orwell and Swift before the age of ten.

My parents quite literally had no time for reading. My mother worked in my father's tiny electrical shop; my father was, before the advent of Thatcherism and Dixons, one of the main electrical contractors in the north of Scotland, and had had more chance to read, he says now, when he was in the Navy, underage, in the middle of the sea, and recovering after the bombing of the ship he was on, in the Second World War. *And Quiet Flows The Don*, that's a great book, he says. Both my parents were clever children to whom history denied chances. Both had won scholarships for further education which neither could take up; both were made fatherless young, and were expected, of course, to go out to work at the age of thirteen or fourteen to bring money home.

Both held the notion of books in high regard, as if books were a gift from another, unthinkable, unreal universe where things would be allotted their real worth, and they tolerated my alien status with great affection, because I was impossibly bookish, more and more so as I grew older, reading H.G. Wells and D.H. Lawrence when I should be watching TV or baking or doing the dishes or going out with boys. They worried when I developed a penchant for writers who were women who, they thought, all seemed to have committed suicide. "No, only one of them did; Stevie Smith didn't commit suicide," I told my mother. "She died normally, and Muriel Spark isn't suicidal, she's still alive, she's a Catholic."

My mother was kind. She knew I wanted to buy Plath's short stories, which had just been published in a cover the bright orange sheen of which I couldn't get out of my head, and she knew there was a copy at Melvins, the local bookshop, and she knew it was a bit expensive, and she got her purse out and gave me what it cost.

I know now that all of us born here in the 1960s inhabited a time of real choice, a time when education could be nothing to do with money, and when, in my sixth year at school, more of us from my year (the school had become comprehensive a couple of years before I went, and was full of energetic, bright, generous teachers) went to university than ever before; a time when Melvins, the one bookshop, on Union Street in Inverness, had opened its basement and filled it with shiny new Penguin classics. You always met interesting people in the basement. They always loved books. If I didn't spend the £10 a week I earned serving chips in the Littlewoods cafe there, I spent it at Leakey's, a new second-hand bookstore tucked away in the Market, which my

English teacher Ann McKay had tipped me off about; you'll love it, she'd said. John Wyndham, Simone de Beauvoir, Albert Camus all mixed in together, nestling up against the different editions of *Palgrave's Golden Treasury*. There was Paris in Inverness, there was poetry from all the centuries. Sweet lovers love the spring; everyone suddenly burst out singing; yes, I remember Adlestrop. The whole world was possible, and a whole lot of other worlds eddying out beyond it.

This anthology, when I spread it all out on the floor in the front room at the beginning of the year, seemed naturally to fall into rather tenuous sections. I've given the sections nominal titles. (For instance, I've called the first section GIRLS – although there's a lot in it about boys and men too – because I have always loved the word, and because it reminds me of my mother, for whom "the girls" were always the girls, a communal power, whether they were her friends from when she was eighteen and in the WAF, or were her two friends she went out to eat lunch with once a week in the years before she died.)

I'm not going to do that introductory thing with each piece where I'm supposed to say why I love it, or where I first read it, or how I was once under a horse chestnut tree or in a bus shelter reading blah when blah happened. I don't want to get in the way of the reader.

Suffice, I hope, to single three out: to say that Beryl the Peril, drawn by this particular (and to me anonymous) artist, the one who did late 1960s and early 1970s strips in the Beryl the Peril annuals, has reduced me to crying helplessly with laughter for more than thirty years, and, I found out, still can; that Margaret Tait, the great and little-known Orcadian film-maker who published her own poems in beautiful slim volumes in the 1950s and early 1960s, has, I believe, been quite overlooked, so I'm delighted to be able to publish a couple here and I wish someone would be wise and publish them all; and that if I hadn't pulled Liz Lochhead's first book of poems, *Memo for Spring*, off the shelf at random in Ann McKay's house when I was babysitting for her at the age of sixteen, and seen the black and white photograph of

Lochhead on the cover, a woman – a girl – and realized that she was Scottish and a girl and a poet, and that such a thing was possible, and then opened it and read it straight through, a book of poems this good, in a language that was everyday, like how we all spoke, but they were poems – then I think I'd very possibly not be here now writing an introduction to a book like this.

The cover for *The Reader* has been designed by Sarah Wood and Woodrow Phoenix with Sebastian Carter of the Rampant Lions Press. The reading figure was created by Sebastian using Hellmuth Weissenborn's original printer's geometric ornaments, with which Weissenborn designed his bookplates.

I have many writers to thank for their kindness in letting me reproduce their work for not very much money. You know who you are. Big thank you.

I have a couple of writers to thank for letting me include work I love but that's not yet published elsewhere. Thank you so much.

This book is itself a thank you, and is dedicated to my father, Donald Smith, and to the memory of my mother, Ann Smith.

Ali Smith, June 2006

GIRLS

JANE AUSTEN

Northanger Abbey

Chapter 1

No one who had ever seen Catherine Morland in her infancy, would have supposed her born to be an heroine.

MARGARET ATWOOD

The Poet Has Come Back . . .

The poet has come back to being a poet
after decades of being virtuous instead.

Can't you be both?
No. Not in public.

You could, once,
back when God was still thundering vengeance

and liked the scent of blood,
and hadn't got around to slippery forgiveness.

Then you could scatter incense and praise,
and wear your snake necklace,

and hymn the crushed skulls of your enemies
to a pious chorus.

No deferential smiling, no baking of cookies,

no *I'm a nice person really.*

Welcome back, my dear.
Time to resume our vigil,

time to unlock the cellar door,
time to remind ourselves

that the god of poets has two hands:
the dextrous, the sinister.

DJUNA BARNES

The Terrible Peacock

It was during the dull season, when a subway accident looms as big as a Thaw getaway, that an unusual item was found loose in the coffee.

Nobody seemed to know whence it had come. It dealt with a woman, one greater, more dangerous than Cleopatra, thirty-nine times as alluring as sunlight on a gold eagle, and about as elusive.

She was a Peacock, said the item, which was not ill-written – a slinky female with electrifying green eyes and red hair, dressed in clinging green-and-blue-silk, and she was very much observed as she moved languorously through the streets of Brooklyn. A Somebody – but who?

The city editor scratched his head and gave the item to Karl.

"Find out about her," he suggested.

"Better put a new guy on," said Karl. "Get the fresh angle. I got that Kinney case to look after today. What about Garvey?"

"All right," said the city editor, and selected a fresh piece of gum.

Garvey was duly impressed when Karl hove to alongside his desk and flung his leg after the item onto it, for Karl was the Star.

Rather a mysterious person in a way, was Karl. His residence was an inviolable secret. He was known to have accumulated money, despite the fact that he was a newspaperman. It was also known that he had married.

Otherwise, he was an emergency man – a first-rate reporter. When someone thought best to commit suicide and leave a little malicious note to a wife who raved three steps into the bathroom and three into the kitchen, hiccuping "Oh, my God!" with each step, it got into Karl's typewriter – and there was the birth of a front-page story.

"So you're to look her up," said Karl. "She's dashed beautiful, has cat eyes and Leslie Carter hair – a loose-jointed, ball-bearing

Clytie, rigged out with a complexion like creamed coffee stood overnight. They say she claws more men into her hair than any siren living or dead."

"You've seen her?" breathed Garvey, staring.

Karl nodded briefly.

"Why don't you get her, then?"

"There are two things," said Karl judicially, "at which I am no good. One is subtraction, and the other is attraction. Go to it, son. The assignment is yours."

He strolled away, but not too late to see Garvey swelling visibly at the implied compliment and caressing his beautiful, lyric tie.

Garvey didn't altogether like the assignment, nonetheless. There was Lilac Jane, you see. He had a date with her for that very night, and Lilac Jane was exceedingly desirable.

He was at that age when devotion to one female of the species makes dalliance with any others nothing short of treason.

But – he had been allotted this work because of his fascinations for slinky green sirens! Garvey fingered the tie again and withdrew his lavender scented handkerchief airily, as an altar-boy swings a censer.

At the door he turned under the light and pushed back his cuff, and his fellow workers groaned. It was seven by his wristwatch.

Outside he paused on the corner near the chophouse. He looked up and down the gloomy street with its wilted florist-window displays and its spattering of gray house fronts, wishing there were someone with him who could be told of his feeling of competence in a world of competent men.

His eyes on the pavement, lost in perfervid dreams of Lilac Jane, he wandered on. The roaring of the bridge traffic disturbed him not, nor the shouts of bargemen through the dusk on the waterfront.

At last through the roseate visions loomed something green.

Shoes! Tiny shoes, trim and immaculate; above them a glimpse of thin, green stockings on trimmer ankles.

There was a tinkle of laughter, and Garvey came to himself, red and perspiring, and raised his eyes past the slim, green-clad body to the eyes of the Peacock.

It was she beyond question. Her hair was terribly red, even in the darkness, and it gleamed a full eight inches above her forehead, piled higher than any hair Garvey had ever seen. The moon shone through it like butter through mosquito netting.

Her neck was long and white, her lips were redder than her hair, and her green eyes, with the close-fitting, silken dress, that undulated like troubled, weed-filled water as she moved, completed the whole daring creation. The powers that be had gone in for poster effects when they made the Peacock.

She was handsome beyond belief, and she was amused at Garvey. Her silvery laugh tinkled out again as he stared at her, his pulse a hundred in the shade.

He tried to convince himself that this physiological effect was due to his newspaper instinct, but it is to be conjectured that Lilac Jane would have had her opinion of the Peacock had she been present.

"Well, young man?" she demanded, the wonderful eyes getting in their deadly work.

"I – I'm sorry – I didn't mean –" Garvey floundered hopelessly, but he did not try to escape.

"You were handing me bouquets by staring like that? That what you're trying to say?"

She laughed again, glided up to him and took his arm. "I like you, young man," she said.

"My nun-name is Garvey, and I'm on the – the *Argus*."

She started at that and looked at him sharply. "A reporter!"

But her tinkly laugh rang out again, and they walked on. "Well, why not?" she said gaily.

Then, with entire unexpectedness: "Do you tango?"

Garvey nodded dumbly, struggling to find his tongue.

"I *love* it!" declared the Peacock, taking a step or two of the dance beside him. "Want to take me somewheres so we can have a turn or two?"

Garvey swallowed hard and mentioned a well-known resort.

"Mercy!" cried the green-eyed siren, turning shocked orbs upon him. "I don't drink! Let's go to a tearoom – Poiret's." She called it "Poyrett's."

Garvey suffered himself to be led to the slaughter, and as they went she chattered lightly. He drew out his handkerchief and dabbed gently at his temples.

"Gracious!" she drawled. "You smell like an epidemic of swooning women."

Garvey was hurt, but deep within himself he decided suddenly that scent was out of place on a masculine cold-assuager.

They turned into a brightly lighted establishment where there were already a few girls and fewer men.

They found a table, and she ordered some tea and cakes, pressing her escort not to be bashful as far as himself was concerned. Garvey ordered obediently and lavishly.

Presently the music struck up, and he swung her out on the floor and into the fascinating dance.

Now, Garvey was really some dancer. But the Peacock!

She was light and sinuous as a wreath of green mist, yet solid bone and muscle in his arms.

She was the very poetry of motion, the spirit of the dance, the essence of grace and beauty.

And when the music stopped, Garvey could have cried with vexation, though he was considerably winded.

But the Peacock was not troubled at all. Indeed, she had talked on through all the dance.

Garvey had capitulated long ago. Lilac Jane? Bah! What were a thousand Lilac Janes to this glorious creature, this Venus Anadyomene – Aphrodite of the Sea-Foam?

In the bright light of the tearoom her green eyes were greener, her red hair redder, her white throat whiter. He would have given a Texas ranch for her, with the cattle thrown in.

He tried to tell her something of this, and she laughed delightfully.

"What is it about me that makes men go mad over me?" she demanded, dreamily sipping her tea.

"Do they?" He winced.

"Oh, shamelessly. They drop their jaws, propriety, and any bundles they may be carrying. Why?"

"It's the most natural thing in the world. You have hair and eyes that few women have, and a man desires the rare." He was getting eloquent.

"But – I'm not at all pretty – thinness isn't attractive, is it?"

"It is, in you," he said simply. The fact that he could say it simply was very bad indeed for Lilac Jane.

She dimpled at him and arose abruptly. "Now I've got to vanish. Oh, Lily!"

A girl, undeniably pretty, but just an ordinary girl, crossed over.

"This is Mr. – er – Garvey, Miss Jones. Keep him amused, will you? He dances very nicely." And as he struggled to his feet, attempting a protest: "Oh, I'm coming back again," and she was gone.

Garvey tried to think of some excuse to escape from the partner thus unceremoniously thrust upon him, but the girl blocked his feeble efforts by rising expectantly as the strains of "Too Much Mustard" floated on the ambient atmosphere.

There was nothing for it but to make good. And, after all, she was a nice dancer. He found himself asking what she would have at the end of the dance.

Anyhow, he reflected, he had still his assignment to cover. The Peacock was still as great a mystery as ever – more of a mystery. But she had said that she would return. So he waited and danced and ate and treated.

Half an hour later the Peacock *did* return – with another man.

To Garvey everything turned suddenly light purple. That was the result of his being green with jealousy and seeing red at the same time.

The newest victim of her lures (for such even Garvey recognized him to be) was an elderly business man, inclined to corpulency, with a free and roving eye. Garvey hated him with a bitter hatred.

The Peacock danced once with him, then abandoned him, gasping fishily, to another girl's tender mercies.

She stopped briefly at Garvey's table, gave him a smile and a whispered: "Here, tomorrow night," and vanished in a swirl of green silk – probably in search of more captives.

Garvey put in a bad night and a worse next day. Who was she? What was her little game? What would happen tomorrow night?

He didn't care. Lilac Jane was definitely deposed in favor of a green goddess whose lure quite possibly spelled destruction.

But he didn't care.

He told the city editor that the Peacock story would be available next day, and added the mental reservation, "If I haven't resigned." And he mooned through the work in a trance that made for serious errors in his "copy."

Yet he had no illusions about it, save an undefined and noble impulse to "rescue the Peacock from her degrading surroundings."

Somehow the phrase didn't quite apply, though.

Once he thought of Lilac Jane, with her warm, normal, womanly arms stretched out to him. He took her picture from his pocket and compared it with the mental picture he carried of the Peacock, then put the photograph back, face outward.

Thus Lilac Jane's flags were struck.

Directly afterward the brazen office-boy communicated to him in strident tones that a "skoit" wanted him on the phone.

For a second he thought of the Peacock; but no, Lilac Jane was due to call. Whereupon he fled ignominiously.

It may be deduced that he had not forgotten Lilac Jane after all, merely misplaced her.

Garvey fell into the elevator, the cosmic tail of the Peacock filling his existence. He threw quoits with the god of a greater wisdom, and came out of his reverie and the elevator with a pair of jet earrings dancing before him. They were the earrings of Lilac Jane.

But beneath them, as the periods beneath double exclamation points, floated a pair of green boots.

Moodily he ate, moodily he went to his room – apartment, I beg his pardon. And at six o'clock he was ready for eight.

He took out his watch and wound it until the hands quivered and it made noises inside as though it were in pain.

He stood before the mirror and motioned at his Adam's apple, prodding the lyric tie into shape and stretching his neck the while until it seemed about to snap and leave a blank space between his chin and his collar button.

A man in love ceases mentally. All his energy is devoted to his outward appearance.

If Napoleon had been in love while on the field of Austerlitz, he would not have rejoiced in his heart, but in his surtout and small clothes.

If Wellington had been so afflicted during the battle of Waterloo, the result might have been different.

Therefore, when Garvey was finally attired, he was like unto the lilies of the field that toil not, neither do they spin. He glanced at his watch when all was at last perfect, and all but sat down suddenly. It was midnight!

But then he saw that the poor watch was travelling at the rate of a mile a minute, trying to make up for that last winding. The alarm clock said seven-thirty.

Whereupon Garvey achieved the somewhat difficult feat of descending the stairs without bending his knees. Spoil the crease in his trousers? Never!

And shortly thereafter he was at the tango tearoom, looking around eagerly for the Peacock, his heart pounding harder than his watch.

The place was crowded, and the dancers were already busy to the sprightly strains of "Stop at Chattanooga."

For a space he looked in vain. Then his cardiac engine missed a stroke.

There she was – seated at a table in the far corner.

As fast as he reasonably could without danger to his immaculateness, Garvey headed Her-ward.

Yes, it was undoubtedly the Peacock. She was leaning her elbows on the table and talking earnestly – talking to – Karl!

Garvey was abreast of the table by now. He must have made some sort of a noise, for they both looked up.

The Peacock smiled sweetly, with a touch of defiance. Karl grinned amiably, with a touch of sheepishness. And both said: "Hello!"

Then said Karl: "Old man, allow me to present you to – my wife."

Garvey choked and sat down speechless.

"Might as well 'fess it," said Karl. "Only please remember that the idea was solely mine."

"It was *not!*" said the Peacock sharply. "You wouldn't *hear* of it when I suggested it."

"Well, anyhow, I have all my money invested in this tearoom. But business has been mighty dull; it looked like bankruptcy.

"Then Mrs. Karl here – she was La Dancerita before she fell for me, you see, and – well, she's been drumming up patronage."

"It was fun!" declared La Dancerita-that-was. "I nearly got pinched once, though."

"I wrote that squib at the office that got you the assignment, thinking to help the game along a little." He smiled a deep, mahogany, wrinkled smile that disarmed when it reached the blue of his eyes. "So now you know all about the Peacock."

Garvey swallowed twice and sighed once. Then he took something from his breast pocket and put it back again.

"I – er know somebody that likes to tango," he said irrelevantly.

BILLIE HOLIDAY
WITH WILLIAM DUFTY

Lady Sings the Blues

from Chapter 1: Some Other Spring

I was a woman when I was sixteen. I was big for my age, with big breasts, big bones, a big fat healthy broad, that's all. So I started working out then, before school and after, minding babies, running errands, and scrubbing those damn white steps all over Baltimore.

When families in the neighborhood used to pay me a nickel for scrubbing them down, I decided I had to have more money, so I figured out a way. I bought me a brush of my own, a bucket, some rags, some Octagon soap, and a big white bar of that stuff I can't ever forget – Bon Ami.

The first time I stood on a white doorstep and asked this woman for fifteen cents for the job, she like to had a fit. But I explained to her the higher price came from me bringing my own supplies. She thought I had a damn nerve, I guess, but while she was thinking it over I said I'd scrub the kitchen or bathroom floor for the same price. That did it. I had the job.

All these bitches were lazy. I knew it and that's where I had them. They didn't care how filthy their damn houses were inside, as long as those white steps were clean. Sometimes I'd bring home as much as ninety cents a day. I even made as high as $2.10 – that's fourteen kitchen or bathroom floors and as many sets of steps.

When I went into the scrubbing business it was the end of roller skating, bike riding, and boxing, too. I used to like boxing. In school they used to teach us girls to box. But I didn't keep it up. Once a girl hit me on the nose and it just about finished me. I took my gloves off and beat the pants off her. The gym teacher got so sore, I never went near the school gym again.

But whether I was riding a bike or scrubbing somebody's dirty bathroom floor, I used to love to sing all the time. I liked music. If there was a place where I could go and hear it, I went.

Alice Dean used to keep a whorehouse on the corner nearest our place, and I used to run errands for her and the girls. I was very commercial in those days. I'd never go to the store for anybody for less than a nickel or a dime. But I'd run all over for Alice and the girls, and I'd wash basins, put out the Lifebuoy soap and towels. When it came time to pay me, I used to tell her she could keep the money if she'd let me come up in her front parlor and listen to Louis Armstrong and Bessie Smith on her victrola.

A victrola was a big deal in those days, and there weren't any parlors around that had one except Alice's. I spent many a wonderful hour there listening to Pops and Bessie. I remember Pops' recording of "West End Blues" and how it used to gas me. It was the first time I ever heard anybody sing without using any words. I didn't know he was singing whatever came into his head when he forgot the lyrics. Ba-ba-ba-ba-ba-ba-ba and the rest of it had plenty of meaning for me – just as much meaning as some of the other words that I didn't always understand. But the meaning used to change, depending on how I felt. Sometimes the record would make me so sad I'd cry up a storm. Other times the same damn record would make me so happy I'd forget about how much hard-earned money the session in the parlor was costing me.

But Mom didn't favor her daughter hanging around the house on the corner. And especially she couldn't understand why I wasn't bringing home any loot. "I know Eleanora," she used to complain, Eleanora being the name I'd been baptized under, "and she don't work for nobody for nothing." When Mom found out I was using my hard-earned money paying rent on Alice's parlor to listen to jazz on the victrola, she nearly had a fit too.

I guess I'm not the only one who heard their first good jazz in a whorehouse. But I never tried to make anything of it. If I'd heard Louis and Bessie at a Girl Scout Jamboree, I'd have loved it just the same. But a lot of white people first heard jazz in places like Alice Dean's, and they helped label jazz "whorehouse music."

They forget what it was like in those days. A whorehouse was about the only place where black and white folks could meet in any natural way. They damn well couldn't rub elbows in the churches. And in Baltimore, places like Alice Dean's were the only joints fancy enough to have a victrola and for real enough to pick up on the best records.

I know this for damn sure. If I'd heard Pops and Bessie wailing through the window of some minister's front parlor, I'd have been running free errands for him. There weren't any priests in Baltimore then like Father Norman O'Connor of Boston, who loves jazz and now has a big radio congregation listening to his disc-jockey shows.

About the only other place you could hear music those days was at dances. So I used to go to as many dances as I could get near. Not to dance, just to listen to the band. You couldn't expect Cousin Ida to believe that, though. She accused me of staying off the dance floor so I could hang around the edges and pick up boys. So she'd beat me for that too.

She was always worried about me and boys. We lived next door to a junk shop. The junk wagon was always parked in front after making the rounds that day. The neighborhood boys used to hang around in the junk wagon shooting marbles and dice. And I used to hang around with them. I used to shoot with them and fight with them, but that's all. One day a nosy old lady hung herself out a second-story window and started shaking her finger at me. Then she came down and hollered at me, saying I was a disgrace to the neighborhood for what I was doing with the boys.

I had no eyes for sex and I was doing nothing with the boys that another boy couldn't do. I was one of the boys. So when this nosy old bitch shook her finger at me I hollered right back. "You think I'm doing that thing with them, don't you?" I asked her.

When she heard the naughty word she forgot what she was raising hell about and started hollering about my language. She thought it was terrible for me to say what she had been thinking. I didn't care about what she thought, or anybody. But I didn't want her worrying my mother. Because I knew my mother worried.

"You ain't got no father," she used to tell me. "I work so hard. Please don't make the same mistake I made."

She was always afraid I'd end up bad and there would be nothing she could say. She never hit me when she thought I was doing something bad. She would just cry, and I couldn't stand to see her cry. I didn't want to hurt her, and I didn't – until three years before she died, when I went on junk.

But back then I was worried what this old bitch might tell my mother. So when she told me she thought I was doing the thing with those boys and I wasn't, I picked up a broom and beat her until she agreed to tell my mother she had never seen me doing nothing with the boys.

The boys were doing it, though. And they were looking for some girl who would. And I could tell them who. The one who was always a sure thing was the saintliest girl on the block. She always kept saying she was going to be a great dancer; meantime she was doing it, not only with the boys but with all those women's husbands.

But she was always so damn proper and saintly, this Evelyn, she wouldn't say "Bon Ami" if she had a mouthful. But because my mother had made a mistake, everybody, including Cousin Ida, was always raising hell with me.

I went back to Baltimore a few years ago when I was playing the Royale Theatre. I drove up in my white Cadillac in front of the house where Evelyn used to live. I parked it where the junk wagon used to sit. This saintly bitch who was going to be a big dancer was still living there. She had six kids and none of them by the same father and she was still funky and greasy. The kids lined up in the street and I bought them ice cream and gave them fifty cents apiece. They thought it was a big deal and I was a big star.

Evelyn always kept a young cat in the house and she had one that day, young and brown and good-looking. He leaned out the window, pointed to one of the six kids, and said, "This one is mine." I never forgot that day. These were the people who used to worry me and Mom to death about going bad.

There were other things I missed when I went into the scrubbing business full time. I used to love to go to the five-and-dime store in Baltimore and buy hot dogs. They never used to wait on

Negroes there. But they'd sell me a hot dog because I was a kid and I guess they could use the business if nobody was looking. But if they caught me eating that hot dog before I got outside on the street, they'd give me hell for cluttering up the place.

I used to love white silk socks, too, and of course black patent-leather shoes. I could never afford them. But I used to sneak in the five-and-dime and grab the white socks off the counter and run like hell. Why not? They wouldn't let me buy them even if I did have the money.

I learned to crawl in the back way at the movies to save the dime it cost going in the front way. I don't think I missed a single picture Billie Dove ever made. I was crazy for her. I tried to do my hair like her and eventually I borrowed her name.

My name, Eleanora, was too damn long for anyone to say. Besides, I never liked it. Especially not after my grandma shortened it and used to scream "Nora!" at me from the back porch. My father had started calling me Bill because I was such a young tomboy. I didn't mind that, but I wanted to be pretty, too, and have a pretty name. So I decided Billie was it and I made it stick.

All the time Mom worked in Philly and New York she used to send me clothes given her by the white people she worked for. They were hand-me-downs, sure, but they were beautiful and I was always the sharpest kid in the block when I was dressed up.

My mother knew I didn't like it much living with my grandparents and Cousin Ida. She didn't like it any better. But the only damn thing she could do about it was work as hard as she could up North and save every nickel. So this is what she did.

After Pop went on the road with McKinney's Cotton Pickers, he just disappeared. Later he got a job with Fletcher Henderson's band. But he was always on tour, and then one day we heard that he had gotten a divorce and married a West Indian woman named Fanny.

When my mother came back to Baltimore one day she had nine hundred dollars she had saved. She bought a real fancy house on Pennsylvania Avenue in North Baltimore, the high-class part. She was going to take in roomers. We were going to live like ladies and everything was going to be fine.

LAURA HIRD

Born Free

Chapter 9: Joni

Whoever told me the Barracuda was great was a fucking liar. We had to pay to get in, bottles of K cost three times what they do in the Paki shop, and the men here are all absolutely minging. It's not fair. The two Jackies from French got off with a couple of gorgeous Norwegians here a few weeks ago. They showed us photos and, honestly, wee Jackie's one was Christian Slater's double.

Typical, the night Rosie and me decide to come, it's crap. There's hardly any other women here, and the ones that are all look like hairdressers or footballers' wives, real old boilers. They stare at us like we're open sores.

The men are mostly greasy Arab types, hanging about in wee groups, not drinking, just standing staring at everyone in a really creepy way. The few white men are all either ancient or hackit, or have indentations on their wedding fingers where their rings usually are. Honest, Rosie pointed one out to me and I've spotted about five since.

Rosie gets chatted up right, left and centre. The Arabs are round her blonde hair like flies round shite. The music's so loud, and their English is so bad. She's just sitting insulting them – "Is it against your religion to use deodorant?/Won't you get your hands chopped off for coming in a place like this?/ Do you have your own corner shop?/Do you share a bedroom with your granny and seventeen sisters?" I just sit with my drink and listen to her. It's like I have a sign on my head that says, "Please ignore me", not that I'd get off with any of these smelly bastards anyway. It'd be nice to knock someone back nonetheless.

We give it till half-ten before deciding it's not going to improve. Twenty quid down the drain and not a Norwegian in sight.

When I get outside, Rosie's got her perfume out and is spraying it all over herself.

"Fuck, these bastards don't half stink. I'll never get a bag-off smelling like this."

"So what'll we do now then? Just walk about till someone tries to get off with us?"

We try a couple of pubs opposite the ABC but they won't let me in 'cause they say I don't look 21. Rosie goes in a huff because, being a blonde, she can get in anywhere. That seems to be what it comes down to. I'd dye mine but, with my luck, I'd end up looking like Jimmy Savile.

We wander round to a pub in Bread Street, but come straight back out as it's tiny, the barmaid looks like a prostitute, and a group of drunken schemie pensioners are flirting with a topless go-go dancer.

This is getting desperate. We decide to try the Grassmarket but hear loud music coming out the Cas Rock Café on the way down and decide to give that a shot. It's more like it. A couple of Irish guys accost us almost immediately and buy us drinks. Mines is gorgeous, sort of like Sean Hughes – big Bambi eyes, beautiful pale skin. Rosie's is a skinhead – a wee bit overweight, OK-looking but no Ewan McGregor. She doesn't look too happy but, fuck it, I've just sat through two hours of the Arabian Nights. It's my turn now.

We go over to the corner and they try to chat us up over the racket of the band. I just sit smiling and agreeing with God knows what. They get us more drink. Sean's barking something in my ear but the music seems to be getting louder. The band must think they're really brilliant. I shout that I can't hear what he's saying, but he just smirks and grabs me. His kisses are nice and gentle at first but, as he gets more excited, he plunges his tongue deeper and deeper into my mouth until I can hardly breathe. I try to push him off, but it just makes him worse. I try putting my tongue in his mouth to stop his getting into mine, but he bites it and laughs.

The fat one hasn't even attempted conversation with Rosie and is trying to push her down onto the seat. She's punching his arms and telling him to fuck off. I lean over to try and help but Sean grabs me again and puts his hand right up my dress. I squeeze my legs together, really tight to try and crush his fingers, but he's much stronger. I plead with him to stop, but he just keeps probing and biting at me. It's disgusting, I can feel his slavers running down my neck.

Suddenly the table with our drinks on it collapses onto its side and Fat Boy rolls, wailing, onto the floor grabbing his balls. Bouncers start running over and Sean leaps off me and starts pegging it through the crowd. I think they'll chase him but instead they grab Rosie and me and drag us outside.

"Aw, mister, that's not fair. They fucking attacked us. They tried to rape us in the middle of the pub."

The bouncer gives us both the finger.

"Sorry, girls, we have a no-slapper policy, I'm afraid," and the door slams. Loads of folk are looking out the windows at us, laughing. I wish I had a brick to throw so the glass would splinter in their stupid faces. I'm fucking raging.

"That's fucking terrible, that. It's like *The Accused* in there."

I hear the pub door being unlocked again.

"It's OK boys, they're waiting for you," and Sean and Fat Boy are suddenly about ten feet away from us again. Fat Boy's eyes are bulging. He comes limping towards Rosie like he's going to pull her head off.

We both take off, running into the path of a car on the way across Bread Street. The driver slams on his brakes and Rosie seems to stumble for a minute, like she's been hit. I hesitate, terrified, as I see them catching up with her.

"Hurry, hurry. Fucking Rosie, c'mon," I scream. It seems to shock her back to life. We nash all the way down Bread Street, past the hotel and the paintball place, up an alleyway beside the vet's and squeeze behind a big industrial dustbin. Rosie is nearly crying and I'm so scared I'm getting a headache. Their big clumpy footsteps echo nearer and nearer, then run past. I'm really breathless but I try to hold it in, till we can't hear them any more.

"You're a fucking bitch. How could you lumber me with that fat ugly bastard?"

"I didn't know. I couldn't even hear what they were saying. My one put his hand right up my skirt. He was really slobbery. It was disgusting."

"Big deal, Five-Bellies was trying to get me to wank him off. He had his cock out in the middle of the pub. I just yanked it as hard as I could. Did you see his face?" She starts laughing and I'm relieved that we're not going to fall out in this time of great crisis. Jesus, how do guys always want Rosie to X^2 them? How do they know? It must be her suggests it, it's too much of a co-incidence otherwise. When I work up the nerve to look out from behind the bucket, the alley seems clear.

"What if they come back down again? Maybe we should just go home."

"Aw, Rosie. Dinnae be like that. Just 'cause you've already got John. What about me? Just a wee bit longer. I'll take you for a pizza."

"Where about?"

"I don't know, I've never taken anyone for a pizza before. There's loads of places round the corner though. Go on."

"One pizza, then, but that's it. I've gone off the boil now," she says, hobbling out onto Bread Street again. I notice blood running from a gash on the back of her leg but don't mention it or she'll definitely want to go home.

Instead, I grab her hand and drag her into the first place I smell garlic bread coming out of. This Italian guy with really dreamy eyes comes over and leads us to a table. He's really polite, pulling our chairs out for us, calling us madam and everything. Foreign men really know how to treat women. It's dead busy and there's this great racket of plates being clinked, diners talking, pizzas being thrown in and dragged out the oven, vegetables being chopped and meat being slapped about the place. There's hundreds of different lovely smells – garlic, peppers, steak, chips, all hanging together in the air. The waiter hands us menus, then goes over to another really nice Italian guy who's standing beside the cheesecakes. They both smile over at us.

"Look at the fucking prices. Fourteen pounds for a pizza. Ten pounds for a bottle of wine."

I check my menu. "Aye, but it won't be the same stuff we get. It'll be posh stuff. Will we get a bottle?"

"I thought you only had 20 pounds?"

"Nah, I took another 30 from Mum's electricity envelope this afternoon. There was nearly 200 quid in it. And Dad gave me money for us to go to the pictures the night."

"Won't she notice? You better not say I knew if she catches you."

"She won't catch me, she doesnae even check. I'll just blame it on Jake if she finds out."

"Can we have a starter as well, then?"

I get Rosie to do the order, as I feel really silly. It's like we're just playing at being out for a meal. He takes ages to bring the wine but, when it arrives, it's worth it. Much nicer than the cheap stuff we nick out Scotmid, really cold and refreshing. We knock back our first glasses in one, then belch in unison and start giggling.

"Oh, beamer, that nice guy beside the cheesecakes heard that . . . naw, it's OK. He's smiling over. Aye, I love you too, darling," and I blow a kiss at him. Rosie guffaws, splurting wine everywhere. A snobby older couple at the next table start giving us the evil eye. When I point this out to Rosie, it just makes us laugh all the more.

Before long I bring the conversation round to John. She's not even mentioned him since the video went missing. So much for us all living together.

"Mum's just being her normal awful self, but she's going out tomorrow and she hasnae asked him to come round yet. I don't even know if she's spoken to him. I havnae seen him."

When the waiter brings our starters, I take one look at them and tell him he's brought the wrong things. He checks his notebook.

"Wan tamat moassarailla an wanna seafoot cockteel, yuh?"

We look at our plates in confusion, then Rosie tells him it's OK.

"I thought it was going to be all gorgeous stringy melted cheese. What the fuck is this? I only like tomatoes in a sauce," she whines, picking up a bit cheese, trying to take a bite and throwing it back down on her plate in disgust. "Fuck, it's raw. It doesn't even taste of anything. It's like chewing on a rubber."

"What about me," I say, lifting something up on my fork that looks like a washing-machine part. I try to take a bite. It tastes like a washing-machine part. I spit it onto my plate. The rest of it's mussels, which I really hate, and white things that are just like big lumps of fat. There's a few prawns in there but I can't bear to go near them as they're touching the washing-machine parts.

"I don't believe this. I thought it was going to be shrimps and nice wee bits of fish."

Rosie's looking worried now.

"What'll we do. We cannae just leave it all. They'll think we're stupid. It must be real food if it's busy like this."

I hand her across my napkin. "Here, put some of the cheese in that. Heat it up in the microwave when you get home." She does as I say.

"Really, you think it's the same stuff you get on pizzas? It's in wee bits, though, is it no?"

She's actually being serious. What a dippit.

"It's grated. Wee bits . . . fuck . . ."

She stuffs it in her bag. "Aye, OK, OK. So you think I'm an idiot."

I spoon some of the yuck off my plate and under the table. Rosie yelps and grabs the spoon off me.

"Stop it. One of your intestines just hit my leg. That's fine. They surely cannae expect you to eat any more than that. It's disgusting."

The snobby couple are nebbing at us again. I wish they would just fuck off back to Corstorphine. We're paying the same for our food as they are. I nudge the waiter the next time he goes past and ask him to take our plates away. If I have to look at the entrails in front of me any longer, it'll put me off my pizza.

"Was efrything hokay?"

"Mmh, yes, lovely," we say in one of our psychic duets as we stare up at his big dreamy eyes.

The snobby man at our side grabs him and starts moaning on about having to wait 20 minutes for his pudding. The waiter tries to explain but the snobby man won't let him get a word in.

"It'll take even longer if that wanker keeps holding him up," says Rosie really loudly.

The waiter gives us both a smile. The snobby man turns to us, his face all purple and wrinkled with temper. "If I require a running commentary from a couple of inebriated Lolitas, I'll bloody ask."

It really gets us giggling again. What's he on about? Then he's back on the waiter. Eventually Cheesecake Man comes over with two absolutely enormous knickerbocker glory type creations, with sparklers showering out the top.

"Wis are comblimends."

"Fucking hell, they're giving him it for nothing," yells Rosie. "That's no fair. Our things were rubbish but we didn't go on about it and we have to pay."

I pour her some more wine, to shut her up. I can't understand the justice of it myself, but posh man looks like a bit of a nutter. We don't need another radge chasing us about.

When they bring over our main courses, it silences us completely. Rosie's ordered fish and chips. I was really embarrassed when she asked for it, y'know, it's a bit insulting to the Italian guys to order the one Scottish thing on the menu. Now it's arrived though, I'm sort of regretting getting a pizza 'cause, although mines looks great, there's just one of it. Rosie's got chips and salad and peas and bits of lemon. Desperate not to be outdone when I'm the one paying for it, I order a side portion of chips.

Oh, my God, it's absolutely the best pizza I've ever tasted. It's about twice the size of the family ones you get in Iceland. There's tons of cheese and it's really greasy and buttery on top. I see Rosie eyeing up my mozzarella a few times but since she doesn't offer me a bit fish, I just ignore her.

By the time he brings my chips, I'm stuffed. I've only eaten the cheesy bits in the middle and left the crust, but I can hardly move. Rosie's left her salad, peas, eaten the chips, and picked all the batter off the fish. It's a waste but, to be honest, it's the only bit I like myself. As soon as he realises we've finished, Cheesecake Man's over, trying to entice us with his puddings. We both lean back in our chairs and rub our bellies, but he keeps trying to

tempt us and eventually takes Rosie's hand and pulls her over to
the sweet trolley. She seems to be over there for ages. I finish the
Leibfräumilch.

When the bitch finally comes back over, she's beaming and
looking really pleased with herself.

"Did you give him a pull for a bit Black Forest Gateau?" I
mutter, emptying my glass before she has a chance to ask for
some.

"Be like that if you want. I've just arranged for us to meet them
both outside when they go on their breaks in ten minutes. If you
dinnae want to come, though, that's fine by me."

"Who, the nice waiter as well?"

"Uh huh," she grins, blowing on her nails, ". . . just call me the
queen of lurve."

God, I feel rotten for having drunk all the wine now, although
they probably both fancy Rosie. The waiter's the best-looking but
I don't know if I'd want to go out with someone as attractive as
that. I could never trust him. Cheesecake Man's a bit fat and
baldy but he's got a really kind, smiley face. He'd be much less
likely to go with other women. And he's older too, probably
about 30.

"Which one do you fancy?"

"I don't mind. Take your pick. It's my thank-you to you for
getting all the drinks tonight," she says magnanimously.

Handsome Boy brings over the bill. Fucking hell, it's 32
pounds, for the middle of a pizza and some fish batter. I didn't
even touch my chips, they'll probably just stick them in the
microwave and give them to someone else. I count the money out
onto the wee saucer. The last four pounds I have to give them in
bronze and silver. Hopefully the two Tallies'll buy us drink.

We go and stand outside. The street is absolutely teeming with
people moving on to nightclubs, well-pissed – fighting, singing,
peeing all over the place – nice. Fuck, why didn't I steal more
money? I want to go to a club. You have to pay to get in, so you
maybe don't get as many head-cases there.

"So what did Cheesecake Man say? Did he mention me?"

"Just that they wanted to meet us. He's hardly going to say, oh,
and by the way, I fancy your pal. They're Italian, for God's sake.

They're the most romantic men in the world. Shh, here they're coming. Try not to seem desperate."

"Rosie, Rosie, I've only got 90 pence left. I can't afford to get them a drink or anything."

She looks annoyed.

"Fuck, I don't even have a bus fare. You should have said before we went for the meal."

The restaurant door swings open. Cheesecake Man puts his arm round Rosie's waist. Handsome Boy and me straggle nervously behind.

"I Antonio," he announces as we turn into Morrison Street. He is so gorgeous.

"I . . . I'm Jo . . . Joni," I stammer, pathetically.

"Ah, Joni Forster, I see . . . *Silence ov Lambs.*"

What's he on about?

"Not Jodie, Joni, Joni."

"Ah Joni, Joni, OK, s'foney, you look juslike Joni Forster."

Jesus, thanks a lot. He thinks I look like a 40-year-old lesbian with a face like a bag of spanners. Cheers, pal. I knew it. He does think I'm a dog.

Walking past the pub I'm expecting to go into, Cheesecake Man leads us into the car park. Brilliant. Most romantic men in the world, right enough. Then bloody Rosie and him get into a car and just leave me and Antonio standing there. He takes my hand.

"We walk. The buildings all lit up. Ferry beautiful."

Great, I'm going to get a boring lecture on Edinburgh architecture from a man who thinks I'm a pig while Rosie gets shagged by the bloke I fancy. What's so fucking irresistible about her? Just 'cause she's got blonde hair and a strong wrist.

We walk to the back of the car park and sit down on the grass verge.

"How-long-do-you-get-for-your-break?" I say very slowly so he'll understand me.

"Fefteen minute hoanly. Then we on till two. You wait till two?"

Fuck, I've only got 90 pence left and this stunning creature wants me to meet him after work. Maybe that's why he's not making a move now. We can't possibly sit about for another two hours, though. It's getting freezing.

"We're going home soon. I could give you my phone number."

Antonio laughs and I feel really stupid. Then he pulls a huge joint from his inside jacket pocket, lights up, and I don't feel quite so bad. Ha ha, spew Rosie. He takes ages in between tokes and has about six before he hands it to me. It smells really, really strong, like I've never smelt before. He maybe has Mafia connections. Lying back on the grass, he lets out a loud, smoky groan. I take three puffs, pausing in between each like he did, and feel really pleasantly numb. It's nice to spend time with a guy who doesn't jump on you right away. Maybe Rosie and me could go and sit in a bar till two and share a Diet Coke.

We have one more hit of the joint each, then walk back towards the car. The windows look a bit steamed up as we approach. That jammy bitch better not have done it. Antonio opens the driver's door and there's a bit of a scramble within. Cheesecake Man emerges, smiling, takes a few tokes on the joint and stands on it. Rosie comes out the other side with a big grin on her face. I'm so glad she missed the spliff.

Then, with a sudden, "See yiz later, girls," they walk quickly back towards the street, deserting us. Were they taking the piss out our accents? I'm absolutely gutted. Why didn't I say I'd meet him? What a stupid bitch.

"Well?" asks Rosie as we walk through the maze of cars.

"Well, what?"

"Did anything happen? Where did youz go?"

"We just had a joint. It was amazing stuff as well, I'm fucking wasted. He wants me to meet him later."

She ignores the mention of my potential date.

"You coulda kepties a bit. Specially since I got money for more drink." She produces a tenner from her cleavage.

"Fuck, what did you do? Did you shag him?"

She looks offended.

"What, for a tenner? Cheeky cow."

"Well, what then?"

"You know."

"Know what?" I'm starting to get annoyed now.

"I gave him a gobble. I told him the meal cost more than we
thought and we'd no money left and he said if I sucked him off
he'd give me a fiver. I must've been good eh, he gave me twice
that."

I'm stunned with envy.

"But that's like being a tart."

She grabs my arm and pulls me back towards Lothian Road.

"Is it fuck. I didn't shag him or anything. We needed money
and I got us it."

"You should have shagged him. We could have gone to a club."

"I haven't got any on my face, have I?" she asks, dead cocky, as
the green man beep-beep-beeps. I ignore her. I'm going to tell
John she's two-timing him, slag. Still, at least we can afford more
drink now.

"What about the Rutland? That's pretty bag-offy, is it no?"

"Aye, if you want to share a drink and walk home. It's really
dear. And folk steal your drinks as soon as you've bought them."

"And how are you such an expert?"

"John sometimes goes there."

Oh John, see, she's rubbing it in again. How am I ever
supposed to get a boyfriend when she's got about two dozen?

"Aw, come on, I just want to go somewhere and have a seat. I
feel a bit funny."

I am feeling a bit funny. Sort of dizzy and scared and really
clammy.

"Serves you right for not leaving me any."

We stop outside Century 2000 and have a look at the posters to
see what's going on. There's a huge queue outside, though, and it
probably costs money. I try to look inside to see what it's like,
then the bouncer opens the door to let people out and suddenly
Sean Hughes and the fat skinhead are in front of us again. I
freeze for a second, as I don't believe what I'm seeing. As soon as
we make eye contact, though, it becomes very real. When I turn
round, Rosie's already bolting down past the queue. I look
behind to see if they're following us. They are, at speed.

When I get down to King Stables Road, Rosie's vanished. I
don't have time to look for her as that pair are in hot pursuit. I
just sprint through all the milling, drunken people, screaming.

When I get to the bottom of Lothian Road, I look back. The fat guy is waiting for a car to go past, Sean is only a few feet away, but suddenly trips up and falls onto the pavement. He's so pissed he keeps running. Nashing down some steps, I run away round the back of the church. I stand, panting, against the bricks for a minute, then hold my breath and listen for any sound. Nothing. Then it starts to register where I actually am – in a fucking graveyard. I'm alone, I'm wasted, it's late on a Friday night and I'm in the middle of a fucking graveyard with two mad Irishmen chasing me. They could be murdering Rosie at this very moment. Where the fuck did she go? Fuck, she's got all the money as well. I can't even afford the night bus now.

GEORGE MACKAY BROWN

Witch

And at the farm of Howe, she being in service there, we spoke directly to the woman Marian Isbister, and after laid bonds on her. She lay that night in the laird's house, in a narrow place under the roof.

In the morning, therefore, she not yet having broken fast, the laird comes to her.

LAIRD: Tell us thy name.

MARIAN: Thou knowest my name well. Was I not with thy lady at her confinement in winter?

LAIRD: Answer to the point, and with respect. Thy name.

MARIAN: I was called Marian Isbister in Christian baptism.

STEPHEN BUTTQUOY (who was likewise present and is a factor of the Earl of Orkney): And what name does thy dark master call thee?

LAIRD: What is thy age?

MARIAN: I was eighteen on Johnsmas Eve.

LAIRD: Art thou a witch?

At this, she raised her fists to her head and made no further answer.

That same day, in the afternoon, she was convoyed to Kirkwall on horseback, to the palace of the earl there. All that road she spoke not a word. There in Kirkwall a chain was hung between her arm and the stone.

Next morning came to her Andrew Monteith, chaplain to the earl.

MONTEITH: Thou needest not fear me. I am a man in holy orders.

MARIAN: I fear thee and everyone. My father should be here.

MONTEITH: Thou hast a scunner at me for that I am a man of God and thou art a servant of the devil.

MARIAN: How can I answer thee well? They keep food from me.

MONTEITH: I will speak for food to be given thee.

MARIAN: I thank thee then.

MONTEITH: Wilt thou not be plain with me?

MARIAN: All would say then, this was the cunning of the evil one, to make me speak plain. I do speak plain, for I am no witch, but a plain country girl.

MONTEITH: Thou art as miserable a wretch as ever sat against that wall.

MARIAN: I am indeed.

MONTEITH: Thy guilt is plain in thy face.

MARIAN: John St Clair should be here.

MONTEITH: What man is that?

MARIAN: The shepherd on Greenay Hill. He would not suffer thee to say such ill words against me.

MONTEITH: Is he thy sweetheart?

MARIAN: Often enough he called himself that.

That day, at noon, they gave her milk and fish and a barley cake, the which she ate properly, thanking God beforehand. They likewise provided her a vessel for the relief of nature. It was not thought well to give her a lamp at night.

So seven days passed, a total week. On the Sabbath she prayed much. She ate little that day, but prayed and wept.

On the Tuesday came to her cell William Bourtree, Simon Leslie, John Glaitness, and John Beaton, together with the chaplain, and two clerks (myself being one) to make due note of her utterances.

MONTEITH: Stand up, witch. Thou must suffer the witch test on the body.

MARIAN: I think shame to be seen naked before strange men. This will be a hard thing to endure. A woman should be near me.

They bring Janet, wife to William Bourtree.

JANET: I think none of you would have your wives and daughters, no nor the beast in your field, dealt with thus.

She kissed Marian, and then unlaced her, she making now no objection.

Then the probe was put into the said Marian's body, in order to prove an area of insensitivity, the devil always honouring his servants in that style. These parts were probed: the breast, buttocks, shoulders, arms, thighs. Marian displayed signs of much suffering, as moaning, sweating, shivering, but uttered no words. On the seventh probe she lost her awareness and fell to the ground. They moved then to revive her with water.

JANET: She suffers much, at every stab of that thin knife, and yet I think she suffers more from your eyes and your hands – all that would be matter of laughter to a true witch.

Yet they still made three further trials of the probe at that session, Marian Isbister discovering much anguish of body at each insertion.

Then they leave her.

That night she slept little, nor did she eat and drink on the day following, and only a little water on the day following that. She asked much for Janet Bourtree, but Janet Bourtree was denied access to her.

On the eleventh day of her confinement a new face appeared to her, namely Master Peter Atholl, minister of the parish, a man of comely figure and gentle in his language. He sitting companionably at the side of Marian Isbister, taketh her hand into his.

ATHOLL: Thou art in miserable estate truly.

MARIAN: I am and may God help me.

ATHOLL: I am sent to thee by my masters.

MARIAN: I have told everything about myself. What more do they want me to say?

ATHOLL: They accuse thee to be guilty of corn-blighting, of intercourse with fairies, of incendiarism, the souring of ale, making butterless the milk of good kye, and much forby.

MARIAN: No witch's mark was found on me.

ATHOLL: The point of a pin is but a small thing, and thy body a large area. Here are no cunning witch-finders who would infallibly know the spot where the finger of the devil touched thee with his dark blessing.

Whereupon, Marian Isbister answering nothing, and a sign being given by Master Atholl, three men entered the prison, of whom the first unlocked the chain at her wrist, the second brought wine in a flask, and the third a lamp which he hung at the wall.

ATHOLL: This is in celebration of thy enlargement. Thou art free. Be glad now, and drink.

Then began Marian to weep for joy and to clap her hands.

MARIAN: I have never drunk wine, sir.

ATHOLL: This is from the earl himself. I will drink a little with thee.

Then they drink the wine together.

MARIAN: And am I at liberty to walk home tonight, a blameless woman?

ATHOLL: First thou shalt put thy mark to this paper.

MARIAN: I cannot read the writing on it.

ATHOLL: That matters nothing.

But Marian withdrew her hand from the parchment and let the quill fall from her fingers.

MARIAN: I fear you are little better than the other priest, and deceive me.

ATHOLL: You deceive yourself. Sign this paper, and all that will happen to thee is that thou shalt be tied to a cart and whipped through the street of Kirkwall, a small thing, and Piers the hangman is a good fellow who uses the scourge gently. But if thou art obdurate, that same Piers has strong hands to strangle thee, and a red fire to burn thee with, and a terrible eternity to dispatch thee into.

MARIAN: I wish I had never drunk thy wine. Take thy paper away.

Then was the chain put back on Marian Isbister's wrist, and the lamp darkened on the wall, and Master Peter Atholl left her, a silent man to her from that day to the day of her death.

John Glaitness cometh to her the next morning, who telleth her she must stand her trial before the King's sheriff in the hall of Newark of the Yards, that is to say, the earl's palace, on the Monday following.

MARIAN: I am content.

And she occupied herself much in the interval with apparent prayer, and the repetition of psalms, wherein she showed sharp memory for an unlettered girl.

Howbeit, she ate and drank now with relish, as one who had little more to fear or to hope for. In the days before her trial, for food she had brose, and potage, and a little fish, and milk, ale, and water for her drink, without stint.

Two days before the commencement of her trial, there came to Earl Patrick Stewart where he was hunting in Birsay, a deputation of men from her parish, among them a few who were mentioned in the indictment as having been damaged by her machinations, namely, George Taing whose butter-kirn she had enchanted, Robert Folster whose young son she had carried to the fairies on the hill, Adam Adamson whose boat she had overturned whereby two of his three sons were drowned, these and others came to the earl at the shore of Birsay, protesting that they had never at any time laid information against Marian Isbister as having harmed them or theirs, but they knew on the contrary the charge was a devised thing by Stephen Buttquoy, a factor of the earl, for that his lustful advances to the girl Marian Isbister in the byre at Howe (Stephen Buttquoy riding round the parish at that time for the collection of his lordship's rents) had gotten no encouragement. Nor had there wanted women in the parish, and a few men also, to infect the bruised pride of Stephen Buttquoy with dark suggestions concerning the girl, out of malice and envy.

This deputation the earl heard fairly and openly, and he promised to investigate their words and allegations – "and yet," says he, "Master Buttquoy is my good and faithful servant, and I will not easily believe him to be guilty of such an essayed wrenching of justice. And, furthermore, the woman is in the hands of the law, whose end is equity and peace, and doubtless if she is innocent not a hair of her head will suffer."

The day before her trial she sat long in the afternoon with Janet Bourtree.

MARIAN: It is the common thing to be first a child, and then a maiden, and then a wife, and then perhaps a widow and an old patient woman before death. But that way is not for me.

JANET: There is much grief at every milestone. A young girl

cries for a lost bird. An old woman stands among six graves or seven in the kirkyard. It is best not to tarry overlong on the road.

MARIAN: Yet with John the shepherd I might have been content for a summer or two.

JANET: Yea, and I thought that with my barbarian.

Now they bring her to trial in the great hall of the palace. There sat in judgment upon her the Sheriff, Master Malachi Lorimer. The procurator was Master James Muir. Merchants and craftsmen of the town of Kirkwall, fifteen in number, sat at the jurors' table.

The officers had much ado to keep out a noisy swarm of the vulgar, as carters, alehouse keepers, ploughmen, seamen, indigents, who demanded admittance, using much violent and uproarious language in the yard outside. And though it was the earl's desire that only the more respectable sort be admitted, yet many of those others forced a way in also. (That year was much popular disorder in the islands, on account of the earl's recent decree concerning impressed labour, and the adjustment of weights and measures, whereby certain of the commonalty claimed to be much abused in their ancient rights and freedoms.)

Marian Isbister appeared and answered "Not guilty" to the charge in a low voice. Then began Master James Muir to list against her a heavy indictment, as burning, cursing net and plough, intercourse with devil and trow, enchanting men, cows, pigs, horses, manipulation of winds in order to extract tribute from storm-bound seamen, and he declared he would bring witnesses in proof of all.

Jean Scollite, widow in Waness, witness, said Marian Isbister walked round her house three times against the sun the night before the Lammas Market, whereby her dog fell sick and died.

Oliver Spens, farmer in Congesquoy, witness, said he was on the vessel *Maribel* crossing from Hoy to Cairston, which vessel was much tossed by storm all the way, whereby all except Marian Isbister were sick and in much fear of drowning. But the said Marian Isbister said they would all doubtless come safe to the shore.

John Lyking, farmer in Clowster, witness, said his black cow would not take the bull two years. The bull was from the farm of Howe, where Marian Isbister was in service. Yet his cow at once took the bull from the farm of Redland on the far side of the hill.

Maud Sinclair, servant lass in Howe, witness, said she had a child by Robert the ploughman there, that dwined with sickness from the age of three months, and was like to die. But as soon as Marian Isbister was taken from Howe by the earl's officers, the child began to recover.

THE SHERIFF: And is thy child well now?

MAUD SINCLAIR: It is buried these six days, and never a penny did I have from Robert the ploughman, either for the lawless pleasure he had of me, nor for the bairn's nurse-fee, nor for the laying-out and burial of the body. And but that I am told to say what I do, I have no complaint against Marian Isbister, who was ever a sweet friend to me and loving to the child.

THE SHERIFF: This is idle nonsense. Step down.

Andrew Caithness, farmer in Helyatoun, witness, said he had a fire in his haystack the very day that Marian Isbister passed that way with her black shawl coming home, from the kirk. None other had passed that way that day.

MARIAN: Yet I never did thee harm, Andrew, and never till today hast thou complained of me. And did not thy leaky lantern set fire to the heather on Orphir Hill that same spring?

ANDREW: It did that, Marian.

Ann St Clair, in Deepdale, witness, said she got no butter from her churn the day she reproved Marian Isbister for kissing lewdly at the end of the peatstock her son John who was shepherd at Greenay in Birsay.

William St Clair, spouse to the above, farmer in Deepdale, witness, said he was ill at ease whenever the prisoner came about the house, which lately was more than he could abide. He had lost three sheep, and his son was held from his lawful work, and one day, all his household being in the oatfield cutting, a thick rain fell upon his field that fell nowhere else in the parish, and with the rain a wind, so that his oats were much damaged. And one day when he reproved Marian Isbister for coming so much about the place after his son, he that same night and for a week following suffered much pain in the shoulder, that kept him from work and sleep.

John St Clair, son to the above, shepherd in Greenay, witness, stated that he was a man of normal lustihood, who before he met with Marian Isbister, had fathered three children on different women in the parish. Yet after he met Marian Isbister, he was unable through her enchantment to have fleshly dealings with her, though he felt deeper affection for her than for any other woman. And this he attributed to her bewitching of his members.

Margaret Gray, spinster in Blotchnie, witness, said she had known Marian Isbister to be a witch for seven years, ever since she made extracts from the juice of flowers for reddening the cheeks, eye brighteners, and sweetening of the breath.

SHERIFF: All country girls do this, do they not?

MARGARET GRAY: Yea, but Marian hath a particular art in it, and a proper skill to know the gathering-time of herbs and their true admixture.

Now the court was dismissed for eating and refreshment, and upon its reassembly the sheriff asked Master Muir whether he had many more witnesses to call.

PROCURATOR: Upwards of a score.

SHERIFF: There is already a superfluity of that kind of evidence.

Then he asks Marian Isbister whether she wishes to speak in her defence.

MARIAN: I wished to speak, and I had much to say, but the words of John St Clair have silenced my mouth.

JANET BOURTREE: A curse on him and all the liars that have infested this court this day!

On this Janet Bourtree was removed from the court by officers.

The Sheriff then made his charge to the jury.

SHERIFF: Gentlemen, I would have you to distinguish between witchcraft and other crimes that are brought before me in this court, and God knows I am fitter to try those other crimes than the supernatural crime we are dealing with here today, for they in a sense are crimes in the natural order – that is, they have some sensible material end in view – but witchcraft involves seduction of souls and entanglements of nature, so that I would rather, as in the old days, some doctor of divinity and not I were sitting solemnly on this bench. And furthermore this devil's work displays itself under an aspect of infernal roguishness, on the mean level of jugglers and conjurers, so that the dignity of this court is sorely strained dealing with it. Yet try the case we must.

Gentlemen, I have said that straightforward crime is an ordinary enough matter. What befalls a man who steals a sheep from his neighbour? A rope is put about his neck and he is hanged; and rightly so, for by such stealing the whole economy and social harmony of the countryside is endangered. As men of property, you appreciate that.

And what becomes of a man who murders his neighbour, by knife or gun? For him also the rope is twisted and tied, and a tree of shame prepared. And rightly so, for an assassin's blade tears the whole fabric of the community. As men who uphold the sanctities of life and property, you appreciate that.

There are worse crimes still. How do we treat the man who denies the authority of his lord and seeks to overthrow it, either by cunning or by overt force? I speak not only of treason against the sovereign. There are not wanting nearer home men who murmur against the sweet person and governance of Patrick Stewart our earl.

A VOICE: When will sweet Patrick restore our ruined weights and measures? When will he leave our women alone? Sweet Patrick be damned!

At this point was taken into custody by the court officers a smallholder, Thomas Harra, who later suffered public whipping for his insolence; though many present swore that the said Thomas Harra had not once opened his mouth.

SHERIFF: You know, gentlemen, that under God we men live according to a changeless social order. Immediately under God is the King; then the lords temporal and spiritual; then knights; then craftsmen, merchants, officers, lawyers, clergymen; then at the base (though no whit less worthy in God's sight) the great multitude of fishermen, ploughmen, labourers, hewers of wood and drawers of water. Thus society appears as an organism, a harmony, with each man performing his pre-ordained task to the glory of God and the health of the whole community. He who sets himself against that harmony is worthy of a red and wretched end indeed. As loyal citizens, you appreciate that.

Such deaths we reserve for the thief, the murderer, the rebel.

Yet these criminals, though they do the devil's work, are in a sense claimants on our pity, for they think, though perversely, that they are doing good. Your sheep-stealer thinks that perchance his ram could breed thick wool and fat mutton out of that grey fleece on his neighbour's hill. Your murderer undoubtedly thinks the world would be a quieter place for himself if his victim's tombstone were prematurely raised. Your rebel (God help him) hears in his mind, through pride and arrogance, a nobler social harmony than that which obtains, for example, under our God-appointed Patrick – a sweeter concourse of pipes and lutes.

A VOICE: A piper like Patrick would have his arse kicked black and blue from every ale-house in Orkney!

On this, three more men were ejected from the court room.

SHERIFF: Today we are dealing with another kind of crime altogether, namely witchcraft.

Gentlemen, you see standing before you what appears to be an innocent and chaste girl. She has a calm honest demeanour, has she not? She could be your daughter, or mine, and we would not be ashamed of her, would we? Are not your hearts moved to pity by what you see? You would hasten to succour any woman in such parlous danger of death and the fire as she is in, and yet here, in this young person, we observe a special sweetness, a unique openness of countenance, a right winning modesty.

Gentlemen, we will not allow ourselves to be led astray by appearances.

Further, you might say, "What is this she is accused of – changing the wind, drying the dugs of an old cow, causing a lascivious youth to be chaste? Nay (you might say) these are light derisory things, and not weighty at all in the normal scale of crime."

Yet see this thing for what it truly is.

The souls of thief, murderer, rebel are yet in the hand of God until their last breath, but the soul of a witch is forfeit irrevocably because of the pact she has made with the Adversary.

We say this of a witch, that she is a thousand times worse than those others. She is pure evil, utter and absolute darkness, an assigned agent of hell. Of her Scripture says, *Thou shalt not suffer a witch to live.*

Regarding the apparent lightness of her misdemeanours, marvel not at that. The Prince of Darkness is not always a roaring lion, an augustitude, a harrower of the souls of men, but frequently he seeks to lure and destroy with ridiculous playful actions, like the clown or the fool at a country fair, and then, when we are convulsed with that folly, off comes the disguise, and the horn, the tail, the cloven goat hoof, the unspeakable reek of damnation, are thrust into our faces.

So, in seeming simplicity and innocence, a girl lives in her native parish. Events strange, unnatural, ridiculous, accumulate round her, too insignificant one might think to take account of. These are the first shoots of a boundless harvest of evil.

Know that evil makes slow growth in the soil of a God-ordained society. But it is well to choke the black shoots early. For if we neglect them, then in the fulness of time must we eat bitter dark bread indeed – blasphemy, adultery, fratricide, tempest, flood, war, anarchy, famine.

As men of God I ask you to consider these things, and to reach now an honest verdict in the secrecy of your chamber.

It was no long time when the jury came back with the one word *Guilty*. Then rose from his place the dempster.

DEMPSTER: Marian Isbister, for this thy crime of witchcraft proven against thee in this court, thou shalt be taken tomorrow to Gallowsha, and at the stake there strangled till no breath remains in thee, and afterwards thy body shall be burnt to ashes and scattered to the winds, and this is pronounced for doom. May the Lord have mercy on thy soul.

CHAPLAIN: Amen.

Then was Marian Isbister taken down to her prison. And at once came to her William Bourtree, Simon Leslie, John Glaitness and John Beaton, with shears, razors, and pincers, who cut off her hair and afterwards shaved her skull clean, denuding her even of her eyebrows. Then one by one with the pincers John Glaitness drew out her finger-nails and toe-nails; and this operation caused her much pain.

Then they give her water but her bleeding fingers will not hold the cup.

They put their heaviest chain upon her and left her.

That night was with her Master Andrew Monteith the chaplain, and Master Peter Atholl the parish minister, from before midnight till dawn.

MONTEITH: This is thy last night on earth.

MARIAN: I thank God for it.

Then they sought with mild comforting words to prepare her for her end. By full confession of her fault it might be God would yet have mercy on her. Yet she answered only with sighs and shakings of her head.

ATHOLL: Only say, art thou guilty of witchcraft, yea or nay.

MARIAN: It needs must be.

MONTEITH: I think the devil would not love thee now, with thy skull bare as an egg.

MARIAN: I have much pain and much sorrow.

Then they read to her from the beginning of the Book, God's marvellous creation, the happiness of Adam in the Garden, Eve's temptation by the Serpent, the eating of the fruit, the angel with the flaming sword, Abel's good sacrifice and the red hand of Cain.

To these holy words she listened with much meekness.

Then said she: "Tell my father the sheep Peggy knows the path down to the cliff, and he is to keep watch on her to keep her from that dangerous place. And tell him there is a sleeve still to sew in his winter shirt, but Isabel his neighbour will see to that."

Then they read to her the ending of the Book, Revelation. And having prayed, soon after dawn they left her.

In the morning, at eight o'clock, when they came for her, she was asleep. They had to rouse her with shakings and loud callings of her name.

MARIAN: It is cold.

SIMON LESLIE: Thou will soon be warm enough.

MARIAN: Yea, and there are longer fires than the brief flame at Gallowsha.

Because her toes were blue and swollen after the extraction of the cuticles, she could not walk but with much difficulty. Therefore they bound her arms and carried her out on to the street. There was much laughter and shouting at sight of her naked head. Every alehouse in town had been open since midnight, the earl having decreed a public holiday. All night people had come into the town from the parishes and islands. There was much drunkenness and dancing along the road to Gallowsha.

As she hobbled through the Laverock with her fingers like a tangle of red roots at the end of her long white arms, and her head like an egg, some had pity for her but the voices of others fell on her in a confusion of cursing and ribaldry and mockery, so that the holy words of Master Andrew Monteith could scarcely be heard.

They came to Gallowsha by a steep ascent. There beside the stake waited Piers with a new rope in his hand. With courtesy and kind words he received Marian Isbister from her jailers, and led her to the stake.

PIERS: My hands are quick at their work. Thou hast had enough of pain. Only forgive me for what I have to do.

Marian Isbister kissed him on the hands.

At this, some of the crowd shouted, "The witch's kiss, the witch's kiss!" But Piers answered, "I do not fear that."

It is usual on such occasions for the sentence to be read out first, and thereafter ceremonially executed on the body of the criminal. But the clerk had not uttered three words when Piers secretly put the rope about the neck of Marian Isbister and made a quick end. Those standing near saw her give a quick shrug, and then a long shiver through her entire body. She was dead before the clerk had finished reading from the parchment. Most of that great crowd saw nothing of the strangling.

An ale booth had been erected near the stake. Men crowded in there till the walls bulged. Many were too drunk to get near the fire. To that burning came Neil the Juggler with his two dancing dogs, Firth with his fiddle and new ballad entitled "The Just and Dreadful End of Marian Isbister for Sorcery", Richan the hell-fire preacher, the long-haired dwarf Mans with medicine to cure consumption, palsy, the seven poxes, toothache, women's moustaches, the squinnying eye – all of whom made great uproar at Gallowsha until the time of the gathering of the ashes into a brass box, and their secret removal to the summit of the hill Wideford.

That same day, in the palace of Holy Rood, Edinburgh, King James the Sixth of Scotland, acting on private information, set his seal to a paper ordering due inquiry to be instituted into alleged defalcations, extortions, oppressions, and tortures practised by his cousin Earl Patrick Stewart on the groaning inhabitants of Orkney, whereby the whole realm was put in jeopardy and the providence of God affronted.

At midnight, in the town of Kirkwall, the dancing was still going on.

MARINA TSVETAYEVA

We shall not escape Hell, my passionate
sisters, we shall drink black resins –
we who sang our praises to the Lord
with every one of our sinews, even the finest,

we did not lean over cradles or
spinning wheels at night, and now we are
carried off by an unsteady boat
under the skirts of a sleeveless cloak,

we dressed every morning in
fine Chinese silk, and we would
sing our paradisal songs at
the fire of the robbers' camp,

slovenly needlewomen, (all
our sewing came apart), dancers,
players upon pipes: we have been
the queens of the whole world!

first scarcely covered by rags,
then with constellations in our hair, in
gaol and at feasts we have
bartered away heaven,

in starry nights, in the apple
orchards of Paradise.
– Gentle girls, my beloved sisters,
we shall certainly find ourselves in Hell!

KATHLEEN JAMIE

Meadowsweet

Tradition suggests that certain of the Gaelic
women poets were buried face down.

So they buried her, and turned home,
a drab psalm
hanging about them like haar,

not knowing the liquid
trickling from her lips
would seek its way down,

and that caught in her slowly
unravelling plait of grey hair
were summer seeds:

meadowsweet, bastard balm,
tokens of honesty, already
beginning their crawl

toward light, so showing her,
when the time came,
how to dig herself out –

to surface and greet them,
mouth young, and full again
of dirt, and spit, and poetry.

STEVIE SMITH

This Englishwoman

This Englishwoman is so refined
She has no bosom and no behind.

PAUL BAILEY

An Immaculate Mistake: scenes from childhood and beyond

Spunk

Where had I read that this was the hour of the damned, when the tormented are startled out of quiet slumber? I remember asking myself that literary question as I lay awake in a state much like terror early one morning in my fifteenth year. I had just masturbated, in my brown-skinned idol's imagined embrace. Thoughts of pleasure were succeeded by feelings of shame and guilt. I sat up in bed, in the absolute darkness of the long hour that only ends with dawn, and realized I was among the lost.

Three years before, in pre-spunk times, I had known desire of the kind other boys knew. I could speak of it, if I wanted to, with the voice of experience. On that memorable Saturday evening, my parents told me I would have to sleep with the two girls who lived on the ground floor. My mother and father were having a party and some of the guests would be staying the night. There was no room for me upstairs.

"You can lie between us," said the older girl, who was well into adolescence. I was under orders, and obeyed. She and her sister pulled back the bedclothes and made a space for me. In clean pyjamas, with my face freshly scrubbed, my teeth brushed and hair neatly combed, I had passed my mother's test for immaculacy: "You've washed behind your ears, for once. Miracles will never cease."

I wonder, now, who were the more innocent – the four trusting parents, or their three apparently guileless children. Into the bed I went, with no anticipation of the bliss that was to ensue. I had been instructed to go off to sleep as quickly as possible, and, when the girls' mother wished us sweet dreams and turned out the light, I closed my eyes and kept them closed.

They opened, in surprise, when the older girl guided my right hand to her large, round breasts, which seemed to grow larger and rounder at the touch. I was soon aware that one hand was insufficient to cope with the abundance of flesh I was being offered. She pushed me aside, asked me to wait a minute, and then made her nightdress ride up until it was like a vast collar round her throat. I had complete access to the swollen beauties, and pressed and squeezed them while she whispered that I should try to be more gentle and not be so rough. She then commanded me to kiss her nipples, which I did. From kissing I progressed to sucking and licking. In the meantime, the younger sister, determined to join in the fun, had lowered my pyjama trousers from the rear and now held my throbbing penis in a firm grip. It was still in her possession when I had the first "moment" – for such was the name I gave it – of my life. I trembled with delicious excitement as it happened. At the age of eleven, I was too young to leave incriminating stains on the sheet.

"Semen" and "sperm" were unknown words to us. It was "spunk" we talked of, in and out of class. The more extroverted boys held competitions in the lavatories to see who could produce most and who could send it flying farthest. We were spunk-obsessed, in our differing ways, in the spring of 1950. The sticky stuff had us in its thrall.

"You're getting through rather a lot of handkerchiefs," observed my suspicious mother. "Yet you don't seem to have the sniffles."

There were not many advantages in being immaculate, but this was one of them. Every morning throughout my schooldays, my mother folded a clean handkerchief into the breast pocket of my blazer, above the arms and motto of the school's founder: "Rather Deathe than False of Faythe." I rarely had colds, thanks to my love of oranges, and seldom sneezed, but now I could use what she called the sniffles as the reason for the stiffened squares of cotton collecting under my pillow.

"You never took a hanky to bed with you before."

Often, during the night, guessing that she was awake in the next room, I pretended to sneeze at the moment of ejaculation. Cunning and deceit can be born of guilt, I discovered.

There was a boy in our year, I recall, who knew neither shame nor deception. He masturbated whenever he needed to, and his need was limitless. His desk shook with him as orgasm was frantically achieved, and only subsided when he was calm again. As soon as the word went round that he was "at it", we tried not to snigger and the master tried not to notice. One teacher, and one alone, was openly amused by the spectacle. This dapper man, who wore floppy bow-ties, taught chemistry. "Today I shall communicate to the class the ideas of a certain Avogadro, who is not to be confused with a certain Ava Gardner. Those of you who wish to learn about the Italian physicist's work on gases will have pens and paper to the ready – with the exception, that is, of the single-minded student in your midst who would appear to be interested in more stimulating pursuits." He looked at the boy, whose eyes had already glazed over. Shortly afterwards, when the boy let out a resounding gasp, he diverted from the subject of Avogadro for an instant and enquired if E – was "better now"? E – replied that he was, thank you, sir. "That's good," said the teacher, and went on with the lesson.

It was always at the hour of the damned – the time when most people die – that I felt ashamed and miserable. I tried, with infrequent success, to curb the need to masturbate. Boys who indulged in self-abuse could expect fearsome manifestations of that indulgence in later life – blindness, hairy growths on the palms of the hands and complete loss of memory were but three of the promised signs.

How did I know this? We did not talk of sex at home, and, if anyone attempted to, my mother brought discussion to an abrupt halt with "Go and wash your mouth out with carbolic soap' or "I didn't bring you up to think filth". My knowledge was a common one: it was in the air, it was all about us. At school, in religious instruction, we learned that God slew Onan, the son of Judah, for spilling the seed his father had ordered him to put into Tamar, the wife of his wicked brother, Er, whom God had also dispatched. I did not view this episode, then, as yet another example of God's customary perverseness – I simply understood, as I was meant to, that Onan had committed a terrible sin, for which he was duly punished.

Seed-spilling was bad for you, morally and physically, but doing what the men of Sodom wanted to do to the two angels who put up for the night at Lot's house was infinitely worse. We had to know that "to know" in the Bible was not "to know" as we knew it. When the young and old males of that soon-to-be-destroyed city (by God, of course) demanded of Lot that he bring his visitors "unto us, that we may know them", they had something more than a friendly handshake in mind. The scribe responsible for Chapter 19 of Genesis is annoyingly vague on the subject of the methods employed by Sodom's welcome committee, and our teacher emulated his vagueness. We had to read between the lines.

My feelings of shame were founded on nonsense, on unexamined superstition. Yet they persisted long after I had sent God packing. I continued to believe that I was unnatural, though a healthy strain of arrogance in me occasionally translated this as "different". That I wasn't really ashamed of being a coward and a hypocrite is what shames me, in retrospect, for I never rose to the defence of my fellow pansies when they were insulted or mocked. I stayed silent when I should have spoken, and was even a party to the mockery.

Two events, both comic in essence, signalled the beginning of the end of shame. In the first, a congenial young woman with whom I was endeavouring to make love on a friend's divan suddenly began to giggle. I persevered. "What's the matter?" I asked, when her giggling became uncontrollable. "You are," she answered, pushing me off. "You're the matter. You're soft where you shouldn't be. You want a man, don't you?"

"Yes," I astonished myself by admitting.

"So do I," she said, without malice. "Let's go and get drunk."

Her honesty and kindliness were beneficial to me, and we remained friends for years. In the second deciding event, it was I who laughed – inwardly. I had gone to bed with an actor who had converted to Roman Catholicism in his twenties. His tiny flat, at the top of a huge Victorian house, was decorated with icons. We had eaten a sparse dinner, which he had made sure we had washed down with a surfeit of red wine. Incense was burning in the bedroom when we undressed, in the dark. He did not care for kissing, he told me. What *did* he care for? "Playing," he revealed. The play, when it took place, was not inventive. My hand having fulfilled its required duty, he moaned and turned away from me. I pretended to doze off. Some time later, when he felt certain that I was asleep, he left the bed, stealthily. Then I heard him muttering, and made out the words "forgive me", which he repeated. I opened my eyes and saw him on his knees before a crucifix. He was begging forgiveness – from Jesus, from the Virgin Mary – for wasting his seed.

In the morning, when he invited me to play again, I said, truthfully, that I was not in the mood. He demanded a reason. "I'm just not in the mood," I replied.

"Try to be," he pleaded.

"I can't. I honestly can't."

He glowered at me as I put my clothes on. I said goodbye, and thanked him for the meal and the wine and the play. I could not thank him, then, for the gift of his abjectness, which helped to release me from mine.

" 'That girl's got more spunk than any boy I've ever met' " – the sentence, encountered in a children's adventure story, caused me to stop and think. A girl, with spunk? The only spunk I was conscious of was the stuff I couldn't resist spilling, despite the example of slaughtered Onan. I consulted the *Oxford Dictionary* in the school library and was initially bewildered. Was the fictional girl a spark, a touchwood or tinder, a fungoid growth on a tree, a match or lucifer? The fifth definition made sense: "Spirit, mettle; courage, pluck." To have spunk is to have courage, I learned. This spunk is rarer, much rarer, than the other kinds, and it does not stain.

NELL DUNN

Up the Junction

The Deserted House

We are at a party in a block of LCC flats: plates of ham sandwiches, crates of brown ale and Babycham, the radiogram in the
lounge, pop-song oblivion with the volume knob turned to full:

> *I go out of my mind*
> *When you're out of my arms . . .*

Rube, face deadpan, dances the Madison, brown velvet skirt, red
patent sling-backs.

The record finishes. She whispers in my ear, "Isn't he a darlin'?
I don't half fancy a snog tonight." Her black hair hangs long and
thick. "He's a couchty-mouch. After going steady for six months
you get a bit fed up, snoggin' with the same bloke every night.
And I've noticed when we're out Terry'll start staring at some
other bird. He'll say to me, 'You all right, love?' And then his
eyes will wander off and get affixiated on some silly cow. 'What
are you lookin' at then?' I says. 'Am I so borin'?'"

The thick-set fellow comes over and holds out a hand to Rube.
"You Romeo" she says, following him onto the floor, a faint smell
of hair-oil and a brown suit.

Out on the concrete balcony dusky Fulham stretches away.

"My wife went for me this morning when I was lying in bed, hit
me on the back of the neck," says Dave. The lights of Stamford
Bridge Saturday-night football. Little rows of houses cluster
round the gasworks. "I should never have got married, I'm
not the marrying sort."

> *My heart breaks up inside*
> *With the tears that I cry*
> *And I'm out of my mind over you.*

Sylvie comes over with a bloke. "This is me mate I was telling you about."

The boys talk. "I was working on this posh flat up in Hampstead. We'd just finished the bathroom, all pink tiles, and I fancied a bath. So I goes in and I'm havin' a lovely soak when the lady whose place it is comes in to have a look around and the boys, instead of telling her I'm havin' a toilet or something lets her walk right into the bathroom and she sees me in the nude and gives a great scream . . ."

"Surprised she didn't jump on yer . . ."

"You girls like to come over the One-O-One?"

Out in the road the six of us pile into the beat-up Buick. Rube and I sit up the back on the rolled down hood.

"You don't drive a big flash car – you – on your money we can't go far."

"Shut yer mouth, Rube, you'll get a sore throat!"

"Well, I've got to open something and I can't open me legs."

The car slews to a stop. Dave lifts me off the back. We go through a bricklayers' yard and down some filthy stone steps. The club is an old cellar poshed up with hardboard and flashy paper. "Got two thousand pound' worth of gear in 'ere. There's that one-armed bandit – a hundred and fifty nicker. Them pintables, you can win fifteen pound on them – they cost a thousand. And that new American-style juke-box, that cost over a thousand."

Outside in the yard the toilet is aswim with piss. Rube blacks her eyebrows. "Terry doesn't reckon I should go out with anyone but him, but I tell him straight, "I ain't got no rings on my fingers 'cept me own!' "

"Has Dave kissed yer tonight? You wanta get him worked up. Give him a love-bite, that'll get him at it."

"Tom and Ronnie are going to do a clothes factory and get us each a new rig-out."

"Sylvie was well away in the back row at the New Vic.
They put us right up the front so we couldn't do nothin'. I was choked."

Back in the club the music blares out of the juke-box. Rube dances, hands up and down thighs.

"I haven't half studied the form on that bird."

"I reckon I'm the only one out of this lot what's at work."

"You bin swimmin', Sylv?"

"Yeah."

"I wondered why you looked so clean."

She cuffs him in the stomach and he catches her hands. "Come and dance."

The constant ring of the bells on the pin-table, the flashing lights and numbers. Dave leans back against the wall. "I got three years Borstal for me first offence. I reckon the judge didn't like the look of me. 'How much lead you took?' he says to me. 'One and a half ton', I says, 'ripped off all the roofs in the fairground'."

Rube and her Romeo join us. "Who's comin' bowlin'?"

"Ent got no money."

"I've got plenty of money." He unbuttons his pocket and shows the top of a ten-shilling note.

"Half a bleedin' quid – that's not money!"

"Comin' down to Southend this week-end? We take a crate of beer and have a right piss-up on the beach . . ."

"Me mate Johnny fell thirty feet off the scaffolding Friday. He's still unconscious. The foreman's trying to rig it, says he had a hole in his shoe and it tripped him over backwards, but really there weren't no safety rails . . ."

"Bin up the Lyceum lately, Tom?"

"I go up there Monday nights for a giggle – Continental dancing – but you offer to take a bird home and most of them live right out in the suburbs, so you find yerself walkin' home twenty miles if you haven't got a bike . . ."

"Let's go. It's dead in here."

Outside the night is soft. We pile into the Buick and cruise through the park. A smell of damp flowers and black trees against the mauve sky and the coloured beads of light trimming its neck.

Then among the houses the car stops. "What's up?" "We're going for a walk." Tom and Kath get out of the car and march off into the night. Romeo twists Rube's body round towards him.

"Let's get out," says Dave. "I can't take you home because me mum's pawned all the furniture." It is about three in the morning. The sky is navy-blue. We walk across a chaos of grass and rubble to a row of deserted houses. "This is where we lived till it got demolished – slum clearance. They moved us out to lousy Roehampton." He strikes a match and looks through a broken window. "Comin' in?"

Strewn over the torn-up wooden boards lie – a bicycle wheel, two mattresses and a pair of National Health glasses. We go upstairs. There are just two rooms, one off each side. "When I saw yer sittin' there I began to sizzle: 'I'm in it tonight', I thought. Then you began to talk and I realised you were a nice girl. I used to be a hospital porter. Cart the dead bodies about. They treat the old people like lumps of meat. When one dies they wheel him out past the others, visitors and all and never bother to screen 'em off. When they get near to dying they usually know it and start to moan all day. A queer moan and it gets on yer nerves, you have to say, 'Oh shut up you old bugger'. There's no such thing as respect for the dead.

"There are two things I'd like to have bin, a racin' driver or a test pilot, but you need money for that . . .

"Once I had eight hundred pounds. We'd just done a tobacconist – I walked into a shop – I was dressed casual like a gentleman. The salesman came up to me immediately. "Yes, sir?" "I'll have that Triumph TR3", I says and took out £725 out of me pocket. "Yes, sir", he says and I drove out in that Triumph . . .

"I've gotta terrible temper, so has my wife. I never start an argument in the kitchen with her in case she picks up a knife. If I ask her to do me a hard-boiled egg and she does it soft, then I lose me temper . . ."

"Know how an engine works? Come here, then I'll show yer . . ."

He takes a wad of paper out of his pocket and opens out an advertisement for an electric-blue Mercedes SL300. "They cost four thousand quid, you know. Your old man got four thousand quid?"

Out of the window the garden is full of tangled grass and trees.

"Let's sit down. You smell as if you never sweated in yer life . . . I don't want a girl who's bin through all what I've bin through . . ." He spreads his coat over the bare boards. Outside the dawn slides over the gasworks, slips over the rubble through the window.

"I've got to go straight now. It just ain't worth it. If they catch me I do five years. So I've got a job in a scrapyard breaking up old cars. I earn twelve pound' a week. It don't go far when you've bin used to havin' a hundred pound' in yer pocket. The trouble with me is I don't really know what I want out of life except money, but I know I want money . . . Sometimes I get a real ache inside of me when I haven't driven for a long time. Then I just have to steal a car . . . I don't go in for motor-bikes any more since me mate's accident. He hit a scaffolding lorry – one of them iron pipes went through his neck. His head was rollin' in the gutter, while his body was still on the bike racin' down the North Circular . . ."

The smell of damp from the mattress against my cheek.

"Do you ever use perfume?"

"No."

"I'll get you some."

At five in the morning a bird sang a complicated song.

"That's a thrush," he says. "I don't love my wife because I wasn't her first – she went with another bloke when she was sixteen." He combs his hair and I look at the early morning sun dappling the filth.

WILLIAM DOUGLAS

Annie Laurie

Her brow is like the snaw-drift,
Her neck is like the swan;
Her face it is the fairest
That e'er the sun shone on.
That e'er the sun shone on,
And dark-blue is her e'e;
And for bonnie Annie Laurie
I'd lay me doun and dee.

Like dew on the gowan lying
Is the fa' o' her fairy feet;
And like winds in summer sighing,
Her voice is low and sweet.
Her voice is low and sweet,
And she's a' the world to me;
And for bonnie Annie Laurie
I'd lay me doun and dee.

ZORA NEALE HURSTON

from *Their Eyes Were Watching God*

Janie saw her life like a great tree in leaf with the things suffered, things enjoyed, things done and undone. Dawn and doom was in the branches.

"Ah know exactly what Ah got to tell yuh, but it's hard to know where to start at.

"Ah ain't never seen mah papa. And Ah didn't know 'im if Ah did. Mah mama neither. She was gone from round dere long before Ah wuz big enough tuh know. Mah grandma raised me. Mah grandma and de white folks she worked wid. She had a house out in de backyard and dat's where Ah wuz born. They was quality white folks up dere in West Florida. Named Washburn. She had four gran'chillun on de place and all of us played together and dat's how come Ah never called mah Grandma nothin' but Nanny, 'cause dat's what everybody on de place called her. Nanny used to ketch us in our devilment and lick every youngun on de place and Mis' Washburn did de same. Ah reckon dey never hit us ah lick amiss 'cause dem three boys and us two girls wuz pretty aggravatin', Ah speck.

"Ah was wide dem white chillun so much till Ah didn't know Ah wuzn't white till Ah was round six years old. Wouldn't have found it out then, but a man come long takin' pictures and without askin' anybody, Selby, dat was de oldest boy, he told him to take us. Round a week later de man brought de picture for Mis' Washburn to see and pay him which she did, then give us all a good lickin'.

"So when we looked at de picture and everybody got pointed out there wasn't nobody left except a real dark little girl with long hair standing by Eleanor. Dat's where Ah wuz s'posed to be, but Ah couldn't recognize dat dark chile as me. So Ah ast, 'where is me? Ah don't see me.'

"Everybody laughed, even Mr Washburn. Miss Nellie, de Mama of de chillun who come back home after her husband dead, she pointed to de dark one and said, 'Dat's you, Alphabet, don't you know yo' ownself?'

"Dey all uster call me Alphabet 'cause so many people had done named me different names. Ah looked at de picture a long time and seen it was mah dress and mah hair so Ah said:

"'Aw, aw! Ah'm colored!'

"Den dey all laughed real hard. But before Ah seen de picture Ah thought Ah wuz just like de rest.

"Us lived dere havin' 'fun till de chillun at school got to teasin' me 'bout livin' in de white folks back-yard. Dere wuz uh knotty-head gal name Mayrella dat useter git mad every time she look at me. Mis' Washburn useter dress me up in all de clothes her gran'chillun didn't need no mo' which still wuz better'n whut de rest uh de colored chillun had. And then she useter put hair ribbon on mah head fuh me tuh wear. Dat useter rile Mayrella uh lot. So she would pick at me all de time and put some others up tuh do de same. They'd push me 'way from de ring plays and make out they couldn't play wid nobody dat lived on premises. Den they'd tell me not to be takin' on over mah looks 'cause they mama told 'em 'bout de hound dawgs huntin' mah papa all night long. 'Bout Mr Washburn and de sheriff puttin' de bloodhounds on de trail tuh ketch mah papa for whut he done tuh mah mama. Dey didn't tell about how he wuz seen tryin' tuh git in touch wid mah mama later on so he could marry her. Naw, dey didn't talk dat part of it atall. Dey made it sound real bad so as tuh crumple mah feathers. None of 'em didn'e even remember whut his name wuz, but dey all knowed de bloodhound part by heart. Nanny didn't love tuh see me wid mah head hung down, so she figgered it would be mo' better fuh me if us had uh house. She got de land and everything and then Mis' Washburn helped out uh whole heap wid things."

Phoeby's hungry listening helped Janie to tell her story. So she went on thinking back to her young years and explaining them to her friend in soft, easy phrases while all around the house, the night time put on flesh and blackness.

She thought awhile and decided that her conscious life had commenced at Nanny's gate. On a late afternoon Nanny had called her to come inside the house because she had spied Janie letting Johnny Taylor kiss her over the gatepost.

It was a spring afternoon in West Florida, Janie had spent most of the day under a blossoming pear tree in the back-yard. She had been spending every minute that she could steal from her chores under that tree for the last three days. That was to say, ever since the first tiny bloom had opened. It had called her to come and gaze on a mystery. From barren brown stems to glistening leaf-buds; from the leaf-buds to snowy virginity of bloom. It stirred her tremendously. How? Why? It was like a flute song forgotton in another existence and remembered again. What? How? Why? This singing she heard that had nothing to do with her ears. The rose of the world was breathing out smell. It followed her through all her waking moments and caressed her in her sleep. It connected itself with other vaguely felt matters that had struck her outside observation and buried themselves in her flesh. Now they emerged and quested about her consciousness.

She was stretched on her back beneath the pear tree soaking in the alto chant of the visiting bees, the gold of the sun and the panting breath of the breeze when the inaudible voice of it all came to her. She saw a dust-bearing bee sink into the sanctum of a bloom; the thousand sister-calyxes arch to meet the love embrace and the ecstatic shiver of the tree from root to tiniest branch creaming in every blossom and frothing with delight. So this was a marriage! She had been summoned to behold a revelation. Then Janie felt a pain remorseless sweet that left her limp and languid.

After a while she got up from where she was and went over the little garden field entire. She was seeking confirmation of the voice and vision, and everywhere she found and acknowledged answers. A personal answer for all other creations except herself. She felt an answer seeking her, but where? When? How? She found herself at the kitchen door and stumbled inside. In the air of the room were flies tumbling and singing, marrying and giving in marriage. When she reached the narrow hallway she was reminded that her grandmother was home with a sick headache. She was lying across the bed asleep so Janie tipped on out of the front door. Oh to be a pear tree – *any* tree in bloom! With kissing bees singing of the beginning of the world! She was sixteen. She had glossy leaves and bursting buds and she wanted to struggle with life but it seemed to elude her. Where were the singing bees for her? Nothing on the place nor in her grandma's house answered her. She searched as much of the world as she could from the top of the front steps and then went on down to the front gate and leaned over to gaze up and down the road. Looking, waiting, breathing short with impatience. Waiting for the world to be made.

Through pollinated air she saw a glorious being coming up the road. In her former blindness she had known him as shiftless Johnny Taylor, tall and lean. That was before the golden dust of pollen had beglamored his rags and her eyes.

In the last stages of Nanny's sleep, she dreamed of voices. Voices far-off but persistent, and gradually coming nearer. Janie's voice. Janie talking in whispery snatches with a male voice she couldn't quite place. That brought her wide awake. She bolted upright and peered out of the window and saw Johnny Taylor lacerating her Janie with a kiss.

"Janie!"

The old woman's voice was so lacking in command and reproof, so full of crumbling dissolution, that Janie half believed that Nanny had not seen her. So she extended herself outside of her dream and went inside of the house. That was the end of her childhood.

BERYL THE PERIL

Double Act

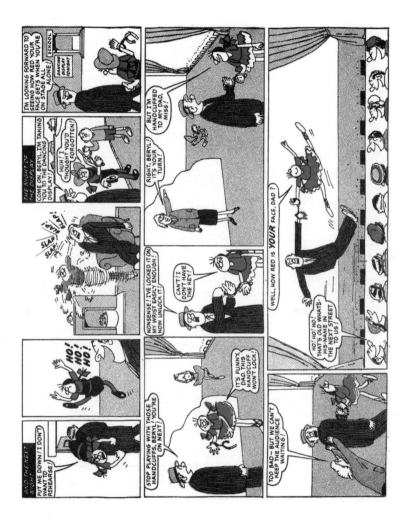

ANGELA CARTER

Wise Children

II

One, two, three, hop! See me dance the Polka.

Once upon a time, there was an old woman in splitting black satin pounding away at an upright piano in a room over a haberdasher's shop in Clapham High Street and her daughter in a pink tutu and wrinkled tights slapped at your ankles with a cane if you didn't pick up your feet high enough. Once a week, every Saturday morning, Grandma Chance would wash us, brush us and do up our hair in sausage curls. We had long, brown stockings strung up to our liberty bodices by suspenders. Grandma Chance would take firm hold of one hand of each of us, then – ho! for the dancing class; off we'd trot to catch the tram.

We always took the tram from Brixton to Clapham High Street. The stately progress of the tram, occupying by right of bulk and majesty the centre of the road, not veering to the left nor right upon its way but sometimes swaying every now and then with a sickening lurch, like Grandma, coming home from the pub.

One, two, three, hop.

Big mirrors blooming like plums with dust along the walls. I can see us now, in our vests and knickers and our little pink dancing slippers, dipping a curtsey to our reflections. Grandma sat by the door with her bag in her lap, squinting at us between the spots on her veil. She looked grieving, as if she was scared we might sprain ourselves, but this was because she was sucking on a Fox's glacier mint. Everything smelled of sweat and gas fire. The old woman thumped the piano and Miss Worthington in her droopy tutu showed us how to *fouetté*, poor thing, sixty if she was a day.

One, two, three, hop! See us cover the ground.

We did our exercises at the barre. Nora's bum in her navy-blue bloomers jiggled away in front of me like two hard-boiled eggs in a handkerchief. We'd turn around, then she could feast her eyes on mine. Outside, a tram went by with a whirr and a click, knocking out sparks from the overhead cables.

To tell the truth, we lived for that dancing class. We thought that was what the week was for, for Saturday mornings.

Then we were seven.

There was a cake with seven candles in the larder iced up to the eyebrows, its stunning pink and white beauty marred only by one little fingerprint – Nora, unable to resist. It sat in state in the larder, awaiting our return from our birthday treat, our first matinée. Our Cyn waved us off. We had our best coats on, green tweed, quite hairy, with velvet collars so the tweed didn't scratch our necks, and little hats to match. Grandma dressed us like princesses. We always had glacé kid gloves, for best.

Grandma splashed out, she got us seats in the stalls. It was almost too much for me and Nora. We were mute with ecstasy. The plaster cherubs lifting aloft gilt swags and crystal candelabra on the walls; the red plush; the floral and pastel silks of the afternoon frocks of the ladies in the stalls, from whom mingled odours of talc and scent and toilet soap arose; and the wonderful curtain that hung between us and pleasure, the curtain that, in a delicious agony of anticipation, we knew would soon rise and then and then . . . what wonderful secrets would be revealed to us, then?

"You just wait and see," said Grandma.

The lights went down, the bottom of the curtain glowed. I loved it and have always loved it best of all, the moment when the lights go down the curtain glows, you know that something wonderful is going to happen. It doesn't matter if what happens next spoils everything; the anticipation itself is always pure.

To travel hopefully is better than to arrive, as Uncle Perry used to say. I always preferred foreplay, too.

Well. Not *always*.

When the lights went down and the curtain glowed that first time of all, Nora and I gave one another a look. Our little hearts went pit-a-pat.

Up went the curtain; there were Fred and Adèle, evicted, out on the street with all their bits and pieces. She set out the chairs, she staightened the sofa, she hung a sign on the lamppost: "Bless this house". We thought that we would die of pleasure. We clung on to one another's hands like grim death, we thought we might wake up and find out we had been dreaming. Nora liked Adèle best; she liked it when she dressed up like a Mexican widow and did her Spanish dance, but it was old Fred for me, then and for ever, with his funny little nutcracker face and the Eton crop that looked painted on, it shone, so, and not a hair ever moved. Who'd have thought we'd be on "Hi, Fred," "Hi, girls" terms when we grew up?

God knows what sixth sense made Grandma pick out *Lady Be Good* for our seventh birthday treat. "I was looking for a nayce musical comedy," she said, "but nothing with that Jessie Matthews in it." She thought Jessie Matthews was common although *I* always found her a perfect lady. But *Lady Be Good* showed us the way. It was the Damascus road for us. We spent hours, at home, afterwards, in the ground-floor front, rolling back the rug, getting the numbers off pat. That finale, she in her Tyrolean costume, him like a sailor doll. We took it in turns to be the lady.

"You've got stars in your eyes, girls," said Grandma in the interval.

Then tea on a tray arrived, no expense spared. Hotel silver service, cucumber sandwiches. Grandma rolled her veil up over her nose and slipped an iced fancy in between her magenta lips. Even in those days, we always felt defiant of the world when we went out with Grandma, we knew she looked a bit of a funniosity. Just as we were brushing off the crumbs came something of a commotion in the dress circle. Grandma was handing the tray back to the waitress when she froze, the way a dog does when it sees a rabbit. The girl caught hold of the tea-things just in time; Grandma rose up and raised her hand, she pointed.

If you'd drawn a line straight from the end of her finger up into the dress circle, it would have landed on the nose of a man, a very handsome young man, a tall, dark, young man with big, dark eyes, well turned out, red rose in his buttonhole, black hair just a touch long therefore bespeaking an artistic profession. He was escorting a fair-haired lady with a sheep's profile in a chic afternoon frock of

lavender wool and they'd evidently freshly arrived, come to kill
the hour before cocktails at the smartest show in town, no doubt;
they cut a bit of a swathe as they "excused me's" their way along
the row. Glances, stares, even the odd "ooh" and "aah". They were
young and glamorous. Everybody there knew who they were but
us. The lights were going down, the band was tuning up. Grandma
still stood there, quivering.

"That man is . . . your father!"

Her revelation didn't have the force it might have had for us
because, at that age, we still weren't sure just what it was that
fathers did. Since we didn't know how to put one and one
together to make two, we didn't know we were different, either.
You'd think, wouldn't you, the neighbours would have nudged
and winked a bit but Grandma kept her lip buttoned and main-
tained the outward appearance of propriety, at least in the hours
before opening time, although if the milkman or the postie ever
peeked in through the net curtains in the middle of the morning,
they might have spotted her doing the dusting in her altogether
and *then* there would have been talk.

So when Grandma announced so dramatically, that's your
father! we dutifully took a look because she told us to but then
the curtain glowed, the overture began.

"I say, do sit down, madame," said the bloke in the row behind
so she subsided mutinously. But it ruined the second half for her.
She kept craning round, she was muttering the filthiest things
under her breath but we had been transported to a different
world, we were oblivious. For us, Fred and Adèle were everything.

There was such a press of people, at the end, and it took so long
to get our coats, and we were in such a dream because of the
dance and song that we missed them. We got out on to the
pavement as our father and his missus sailed off in a cab leaving
Grandma waving her umbrella uselessly after them.

"Damn," said Grandma. "Damn, damn, damn."

Her face told you that she meant it.

Now that the spell of the show was broken, we had time to
ponder her words.

"Grandma," said Nora. "Tell us some more about fathers."

On top of the tram, on the way home, she told us the lot. She was a naturist, she was a vegetarian, she was a pacifist; when it came to sex education, what do you expect? But we found it hard to believe, neither what she said about the prong and how it could change its shape, etc., but also what she said the prong came in handy for. We thought she made it up to tease us. To think that we girls were in the world because a man we'd never met did *that* to a girl we didn't remember, once upon a time! What we knew for certain was, our grandma loved us and we had the best uncle in the world. Although Our Cyn, the worldly one, thought that Perry was our father.

But something took root in us that afternoon, some kind of curiosity. At first it was a niggling thing. We'd spot his picture in the paper and exclaim. When we went up West to buy new dancing shoes at Freed's, we'd make a detour round Shaftesbury Avenue, to look at the photographs wherever he was playing. Over the years, the curiosity turned into a yearning, a longing. I tucked a postcard of him in ermine as Richard II into a secret place at the back of the drawer where I kept my underwear, and, it was the one thing Nora kept from me, she only told me this afternoon, she did the same with one of him as young Prince Hal on the q.t. You could say, I suppose, that we *had a crush* on Melchior Hazard, like lots of girls. You could say he was our first romance, and bittersweet it turned out to be, in the end.

Anyway, that was the first time we ever saw our father. And the first time we saw Fred Astaire. And the first time we spent a penny – that is, used a public convenience. The one at Piccadilly Circus, with white tiles and a little old lady in a white pinny to take your penny off you and put it in the lock so you wouldn' soil your hands. A child remembers these things. It was a red-letter day all round and its wonders were by no means over. When we got home, the cake had moved out of the larder on to the kitchen table, its candles were blazing and, in our absence, a packing case that took up half the kitchen had arrived. Our Cyn pointed to the label: "For my two lovely girls."

"He hasn't forgotten," she said, pleased for our sakes and also pleased for the sake of fatherhood – that Perry might be errant but did his duty, all the same. Little did she know.

In that packing case there was a toy theatre. It was a lovely one, a marvel, an antique – he'd got hold of it in Venice. In the middle of the gilt proscenium arch there they were, side by side, the comic mask, the tragic mask, one mouth turned up at the ends, the other down, the presiding geniuses – just like life. The *commedia*, that's life, isn't it?

MARILYNNE ROBINSON

Housekeeping

from Chapter 11

All this is fact. Fact explains nothing. On the contrary, it is fact that requires explanation. For example, I pass again and again behind my grandmother's house, and never get off at the station and walk back to see if it is still the same house, altered perhaps by the repairs the fire made necessary, or if it is a new house built on the old site. I would like to see the people who live there. Seeing them would expel poor Lucille, who has, in my mind, waited there in a fury of righteousness, cleansing and polishing, all these years. She thinks she hears someone on the walk, and hurries to open the door, too eager to wait for the bell. It is the mailman, it is the wind, it is nothing at all. Sometimes she dreams that we come walking up the road in our billowing raincoats, hunched against the cold, talking together in words she cannot quite understand. And when we look up and speak to her the words are smothered, and their intervals swelled, and their cadences distended, like sounds in water. What if I should walk to the house one night and find Lucille there? It is possible. Since we are dead, the house would be hers now. Perhaps she is in the kitchen, snuggling pretty daughters in her lap, and perhaps now and then they look at the black window to find out what their mother seems to see there, and they see their own faces and a face so like their mother's, so rapt and full of tender watching, that only Lucille could think the face was mine. If Lucille is there, Sylvie and I have stood outside her window a thousand times, and we have thrown the side door open when she was upstairs changing beds, and we have brought in leaves, and flung the curtains and tipped the bud vase, and somehow left the house again before she could run downstairs, leaving behind us a strong smell of lake water. She would sigh and think, "They never change."

Or imagine Lucille in Boston, at a table in a restaurant, waiting for a friend. She is tastefully dressed – wearing, say, a tweed suit with an amber scarf at the throat to draw attention to the red in her darkening hair. Her water glass has left two-thirds of a ring on the table, and she works at completing the circle with her thumbnail. Sylvie and I do not flounce in through the door, smoothing the skirts of our oversized coats and combing our hair back with our fingers. We do not sit down at the table next to hers and empty our pockets in a small damp heap in the middle of the table, and sort out the gum wrappers and ticket stubs, and add up the coins and dollar bills, and laugh and add them up again. My mother, likewise, is not there, and my grandmother in her house slippers with her pigtail wagging, and my grandfather, with his hair combed flat against his brow, does not examine the menu with studious interest. We are nowhere in Boston. However Lucille may look, she will never find us there, or any trace or sign. We pause nowhere in Boston, even to admire a store window, and the perimeters of our wandering are nowhere. No one watching this woman smear her initials in the steam on her water glass with her first finger, or slip cellophane packets of oyster crackers into her handbag for the sea gulls, could know how her thoughts are thronged by our absence, or know how she does not watch, does not listen, does not wait, does not hope, and always for me and Sylvie.

JANE BOWLES

Everything Is Nice

The highest street in the blue Moslem town skirted the edge of a cliff. She walked over to the thick protecting wall and looked down. The tide was out, and the flat dirty rocks below were swarming with skinny boys. A Moslem woman came up to the blue wall and stood next to her, grazing her hip with the basket she was carrying. She pretended not to notice her, and kept her eyes fixed on a white dog that had just slipped down the side of a rock and plunged into a crater of sea water. The sound of its bark was earsplitting. Then the woman jabbed the basket firmly into her ribs, and she looked up.

"That one is a porcupine," said the woman, pointing a henna-stained finger into the basket.

This was true. A large dead porcupine lay there, with a pair of new yellow socks folded on top of it.

She looked again at the woman. She was dressed in a haik, and the white cloth covering the lower half of her face was loose, about to fall down.

"I am Zodelia," she announced in a high voice. "And you are Betsoul's friend." The loose cloth slipped below her chin and hung there like a bib. She did not pull it up.

"You sit in her house and you sleep in her house and you eat in her house," the woman went on, and she nodded in agreement. "Your name is Jeanie and you live in a hotel with other Nazarenes. How much does the hotel cost you?"

A loaf of bread shaped like a disc flopped on to the ground from inside the folds of the woman's haik, and she did not have to answer her question. With some difficulty the woman picked the loaf up and stuffed it in between the quills of the porcupine and the basket handle. Then she set the basket down on the top of the blue wall and turned to her with bright eyes.

"I am the people in the hotel," she said. "Watch me."

She was pleased because she knew that the woman who called herself Zodelia was about to present her with a little skit. It would be delightful to watch, since all the people of the town spoke and gesticulated as though they had studied at the *Comédie Française*.

"The people in the hotel," Zodelia announced, formally beginning her skit. "I am the people in the hotel."

" 'Good-bye, Jeanie, good-bye. Where are you going?'

" 'I am going to a Moslem house to visit my Moslem friends, Betsoul and her family. I will sit in a Moslem room and eat Moslem food and sleep on a Moslem bed.'

" 'Jeanie, Jeanie, when will you come back to us in the hotel and sleep in your own room?'

" 'I will come back to you in three days. I will come back and sit in a Nazarene room and eat Nazarene food and sleep on a Nazarene bed. I will spend half the week with Moslem friends and half with Nazarenes.' "

The woman's voice had a triumphant ring as she finished her sentence; then, without announcing the end of the sketch, she walked over to the wall and put one arm around her basket.

Down below, just at the edge of the cliff's shadow, a Moslem woman was seated on a rock, washing her legs in one of the holes filled with sea water. Her haik was piled on her lap and she was huddled over it, examining her feet.

"She is looking at the ocean," said Zodelia.

She was not looking at the ocean; with her head down and the mass of cloth in her lap she could not possibly have seen it; she would have had to straighten up and turn around.

"She is *not* looking at the ocean," she said.

"She is looking at the ocean," Zodelia repeated, as if she had not spoken.

She decided to change the subject. "Why do you have a porcupine with you?" she asked her, although she knew that some of the Moslems, particularly the country people, enjoyed eating them.

"It is a present for my aunt. Do you like it?"

"Yes," she said. "I like porcupines. I like big porcupines and little ones, too."

Zodelia seemed bewildered, and then bored, and she decided she had somehow ruined the conversation by mentioning small porcupines.

"Where is your mother?" Zodelia said at length.

"My mother is in her country in her own house," she said automatically; she had answered the question a hundred times.

"Why don't you write her a letter and tell her to come here? You can take her on a promenade and show her the ocean. After that she can go back to her own country and sit in her house." She picked up her basket and adjusted the strip of cloth over her mouth. "Would you like to go to a wedding?" she asked her.

She said she would love to go to a wedding, and they started off down the crooked blue street, heading into the wind. As they passed a small shop Zodelia stopped. "Stand here," she said. "I want to buy something."

After studying the display for a minute or two Zodelia poked her and pointed to some cakes inside a square box with glass sides. "Nice?" she asked her. "Or not nice?"

The cakes were dusty and coated with a thin, ugly-colored icing. They were called *Galletas Ortiz.*

"They are very nice," she replied, and bought her a dozen of them. Zodelia thanked her briefly and they walked on. Presently they turned off the street into a narrow alley and started downhill. Soon Zodelia stopped at a door on the right, and lifted the heavy brass knocker in the form of a fist.

"The wedding is here?" she said to her.

Zodelia shook her head and looked grave. "There is no wedding here," she said.

A child opened the door and quickly hid behind it, covering her face. She followed Zodelia across the black and white tile floor of the closed patio. The walls were washed in blue, and a cold light shone through the broken panes of glass far above their heads. There was a door on each side of the patio. Outside one of them, barring the threshold, was a row of pointed slippers. Zodelia stepped out of her own shoes and set them down near the others.

She stood behind Zodelia and began to take off her own shoes. It took her a long time because there was a knot in one of her laces. When she was ready, Zodelia took her hand and pulled her along with her into a dimly lit room, where she led her over to a mattress which lay against the wall.

"Sit," she told her, and she obeyed. Then, without further comment she walked off, heading for the far end of the room. Because her eyes had not grown used to the dimness, she had the impression of a figure disappearing down a long corridor. Then she began to see the brass bars of a bed, glowing weakly in the darkness.

Only a few feet away, in the middle of the carpet, sat an old lady in a dress made of green and purple curtain fabric. Through the many rents in the material she could see the printed cotton dress and the tan sweater underneath. Across the room several women sat along another mattress, and further along the mattress three babies were sleeping in a row, each one close against the wall with its head resting on a fancy cushion.

"Is it nice here?" It was Zodelia, who had returned without her haik. Her black crepe European dress hung unbelted down to her ankles, almost grazing her bare feet. The hem was lopsided. "Is it nice here?" she asked again, crouching on her haunches in front of her and pointing at the old woman. "That one is Tetum," she said. The old lady plunged both hands into a bowl of raw chopped meat and began shaping the stuff into little balls.

"Tetum," echoed the ladies on the mattress.

"This Nazarene," said Zodelia, gesturing in her direction, "spends half her time in a Moslem house with Moslem friends and the other half in a Nazarene hotel with other Nazarenes."

"That's nice," said the women opposite. "Half with Moslem friends and half with Nazarenes."

The old lady looked very stern. She noticed that her bony cheeks were tattooed with tiny blue crosses.

"Why?" asked the old lady abruptly in a deep voice. "*Why* does she spend half her time with Moslem friends and half with Nazarenes?" She fixed her eye on Zodelia, never ceasing to shape the meat with her swift fingers. Now she saw that her knuckles were also tattooed with blue crosses.

Zodelia stared back at her stupidly. "I don't know why," she said, shrugging one fat shoulder. It was clear that the picture she had been painting for them had suddenly lost all its charm for her.

"Is she crazy?" the old lady asked.

"No," Zodelia answered listlessly. "She is not crazy." There were shrieks of laughter from the mattress.

The old lady fastened her sharp eyes on the visitor, and she saw that they were heavily outlined in black. "Where is your husband?" she demanded.

"He's traveling in the desert."

"Selling things," Zodelia put in. This was the popular explanation for her husband's trips; she did not try to contradict it.

"Where is your mother?" the old lady asked.

"My mother is in our country in her own house."

"Why don't you go and sit with your mother in her own house?" she scolded. "The hotel costs a lot of money."

"In the city where I was born," she began, "there are many, many automobiles and many, many trucks."

The women on the mattress were smiling pleasantly. "Is that true?" remarked the one in the center in a tone of polite interest.

"I hate trucks," she told the woman with feeling.

The old lady lifted the bowl of meat off her lap and set it down on the carpet. "Trucks are nice," she said severely.

"That's true," the women agreed, after only a moment's hesitation. "Trucks are very nice."

"Do *you* like trucks?" she asked Zodelia, thinking that because of their relatively greater intimacy she might perhaps agree with her.

"Yes," she said. "They are nice. Trucks are very nice." She seemed lost in meditation, but only for an instant. "Everything is nice," she announced, with a look of triumph.

"It's the truth," the women said from their mattress. "Everything is nice."

They all looked happy, but the old lady was still frowning. "Aicha!" she yelled, twisting her neck so that her voice could be heard in the patio. "Bring the tea!"

Several little girls came into the room carrying the tea things and a low round table.

"Pass the cakes to the Nazarene," she told the smallest child, who was carrying a cut-glass dish piled with cakes. She saw that they were the ones she had bought for Zodelia; she did not want any of them. She wanted to go home.

"Eat!" the women called out from their mattress. "Eat the cakes."

The child pushed the glass dish forward.

"The dinner at the hotel is ready," she said, standing up.

"Drink tea," said the old woman scornfully. "Later you will sit with the other Nazarenes and eat their food."

"The Nazarenes will be angry if I'm late." She realized that she was lying stupidly, but she could not stop. "They will hit me!" She tried to look wild and frightened.

"Drink tea. They will not hit you," the old woman told her. "Sit down and drink tea."

The child was still offering her the glass dish as she backed away toward the door. Outside she sat down on the black and white tiles to lace her shoes. Only Zodelia followed her into the patio.

"Come back," the others were calling. "Come back into the room."

Then she noticed the porcupine basket standing nearby against the wall. "Is that old lady in the room your aunt? Is she the one you were bringing the porcupine to?" she asked her.

"No. She is not my aunt."

"Where *is* your aunt?"

"My aunt is in her own house."

"When will you take the porcupine to her?" She wanted to keep talking, so that Zodelia would be distracted and forget to fuss about her departure.

"The porcupine sits here," she said firmly. "In my own house."

She decided not to ask her again about the wedding.

When they reached the door Zodelia opened it just enough to let her through. "Good-bye," she said behind her. "I shall see you tomorrow, if Allah wills it."

"When?"

"Four o'clock." It was obvious that she had chosen the first figure that had come into her head. Before closing the door she reached out and pressed two of the dry Spanish cakes into her hand. "Eat them," she said graciously. "Eat them at the hotel with the other Nazarenes."

She started up the steep alley, headed once again for the walk along the cliff. The houses on either side of her were so close that she could smell the dampness of the walls and feel it on her cheeks like a thicker air.

When she reached the place where she had met Zodelia she went over to the wall and leaned on it. Although the sun had sunk behind the houses, the sky was still luminous and the blue of the wall had deepened. She rubbed her fingers along it: the wash was fresh and a little of the powdery stuff came off. And she remembered how once she had reached out to touch the face of a clown because it had awakened some longing. It had happened at a little circus, but not when she was a child.

VIRGINIA WOOLF

from *Orlando*

"All ends in death," Orlando would say, sitting upright, his face clouded with gloom. (For that was the way his mind worked now, in violent see-saws from life to death, stopping at nothing in between, so that the biographer must not stop either, but must fly as fast as he can and so keep pace with the unthinking passionate foolish actions and sudden extravagant words in which, it is impossible to deny, Orlando at this time of his life indulged.)

"All ends in death," Orlando would say, sitting upright on the ice. But Sasha who after all had no English blood in her but was from Russia where the sunsets are longer, the dawns less sudden, and sentences often left unfinished from doubt as to how best to end them – Sasha stared at him, perhaps sneered at him, for he must have seemed a child to her, and said nothing. But at length the ice grew cold beneath them, which she disliked, so pulling him to his feet again, she talked so enchantingly, so wittily, so wisely (but unfortunately always in French, which notoriously loses its flavour in translation) that he forgot the frozen waters or night coming or the old woman or whatever it was, and would try to tell her – plunging and splashing among a thousand images which had gone as stale as the women who inspired them – what she was like. Snow, cream, marble, cherries, alabaster, golden wire? None of these. She was like a fox, or an olive tree; like the waves of the sea when you look down upon them from a height; like an emerald; like the sun on a green hill which is yet clouded – like nothing he had seen or known in England. Ransack the language as he might, words failed him. He wanted another landscape, and another tongue.

DIALOGUES

JOHN KEATS

On First Looking into Chapman's Homer

Much have I travell'd in the realms of gold,
    And many goodly states and kingdoms seen;
    Round many western islands have I been
Which bards in fealty to Apollo hold.
Oft of one wide expanse had I been told
    That deep-browed Homer ruled as his demesne;
    Yet did I never breathe its pure serene
Till I heard Chapman speak out loud and bold:
Then felt I like some watcher of the skies
    When a new planet swims into his ken;
Or like stout Cortez when with eagle eyes
    He stared at the Pacific – and all his men
Look'd at each other with a wild surmise –
    Silent, upon a peak in Darien.

LYDIA DAVIS

In the Garment District

A man has been making deliveries in the garment district for years now: every morning he takes the same garments on a moving rack through the streets to a shop and every evening takes them back again to the warehouse. This happens because there is a dispute between the shop and the warehouse which cannot be settled: the shop denies it ever ordered the clothes, which are badly made and of cheap material and by now years out of style; while the warehouse will not take responsibility because the clothes cannot be returned to the wholesalers, who have no use for them. To the man all this is nothing. They are not his clothes, he is paid for this work, and he intends to leave the company soon, though the right moment has not yet come.

KASIA BODDY

On the Ward with TV, iPod and Telephone

She arrived at the ward with a temperature of 38.2. It had been steadily rising all day, and she had felt that the dread 38, which meant hospital admission, was inevitable. It had happened twice before with this kind of chemotherapy.

"There she goes, there she goes again." (The La's)

The worst thing about the ward – well, not the worst thing – was the noise. The worst thing was how ill some people were; how, in their drugged-up state, they shouted out surreal instructions – "Help me mother, oh mother"; "No, no, Mr Harrington, let's sit in there"; "Oh darling, let's not be at war, darling" – and how sweet and resigned their husbands were. "What are you doing, Geoffrey?" "Just sitting here, sweetheart." "Well, that's bloody typical, isn't it Geoffrey? Bloody, bloody typical."

"Shouldn't have got on this flight tonight" (Joni Mitchell)

The first time she had been on the ward, she'd made friends, chatting to everyone, exchanging stories about diagnosis, prognosis and how you could fool the nurses about your temperature if you stuck your ear out of the window just before "obs" were done. She was one of the walking wounded, able to draw curtains back and forth, able to fetch a nurse or switch the lights off. She liked the sense of herself as the relatively healthy one. But after she'd been there for 12 days, the sadness of the ward began to affect her. This could be her in a couple of years was the thought to repress. But it was hard. "Do you ever feel like you can't go on anymore?" asked a usually jolly horsey woman one morning. She couldn't say, "no, I want to go on and on and on"; she didn't know what to say. But then she'd only been sick a few months, while Eileen had been in and out of hospital for 13 years. A couple of weeks later she received a letter from Eileen's husband. Eileen had died, "at home, with no pain".

"You've gotta run run run run." (The Velvet Underground)

The next time on the ward she decided to keep to herself much more and to block out the various sounds using a variety of technologies. She had a radio, a CD player to play audio books on at night (reading was impossible), and, an extravagant gift from dear, extravagant friends, an iPod. There was also the bedside TV and telephone. The 17-year-old boy who served tea said she was a big teenager, lying sprawled on her bed – bed 9 – always on the phone or watching TV or listening to music.

"Is this the way to Amarillo?
Every night I've been hugging my pillow" (Tony Christie)

The TV and music kept a lot at bay, but she couldn't escape the phone calls of her fellow patients. In fact she was fascinated at the way many of the women kept control of their domestic lives from the hospital beds. Lying there, with IV drugs pumping through them, they reported their symptoms and kept close tabs on their husbands and children. Like she did.

"It happens to be true. I only want to be with you." (Dusty Springfield)

The phone rang for bed 10: "Put her on then. No, Sharon, no, babe. You've got to go to school. No, no. I'll be home soon, sweetheart, and I'll see you this evening. That's right. You can tell me about what Miss MacKenzie did then. OK? Yes, I'm alright, babe. I'm alright. I'm fine."

The nursing assistant came to take some blood. She had "bad veins" and so they sent the expert. It still took him 4 attempts – "sharp prick", "sharp prick", "sharp prick", "sharp prick". This was at 2am. She was now awake and, needing consolation, raided her bedside stash for a KitKat and a Diet Coke. Bad idea. Fast eating and drinking while lying down gave her chest pains. Given everything else that was going on, it was easy to believe that she was having a heart attack. She imagined her family and friends at the funeral: "I can't believe it. We were so worried about the cancer, and then this." She called the nurse, who did an ECG. It was fine (of course). About 3.30, she finally went to sleep.

"I get along without you very well. Of course I do. Except . . ."
(Chet Baker)

The phone rang for bed 8: "Your shirts are on the line, darling. Let the mist clear a bit and then bring them in. Don't wait until they're completely dry – it looks like rain from here anyway – or they'll be much harder to iron. You want them a bit damp, you know."

She watched all the programmes her husband didn't like – every makeover show, every schmaltzy film. All the really good bad stuff was on the Living Channel. Was that ironic? A good sign? This is not, she thought, the way to think.

"What if Mr Right and the father of my child turn out to be
different people?" (Will and Grace, The Living Channel)

She was shivering. They took her temperature. Gone up. 39.5. One nurse said the best way to bring it down was to take all the blankets off. She shivered and shivered. Another nurse came along, gave her a paracetamol, and let her pull the blankets up.

"When I'm wearing a new bonnet, all the figures I ever knew go
right slap out of my head." (Gone with the Wind, TCM)

The phone rang for bed 11: "Listen, Roger, I only managed to half do the moussaka. Can you see the recipe book? It's on the counter, I think. Near the kettle? Great. It should be open on the moussaka page. Well, you just need to do the last bit. The

topping. Can you manage that? Honestly, Roger, it's not difficult."

"We've got to take more blood now, lovey," said the nurse. "How
about your foot this time? Maybe some better veins. Ah, bless."
All the nurses said "bless" a lot. Was it something they taught
them in nursing school? "Bless" and "Sharp prick".

*"On a Sunday morning sidewalk, wishing Lord that I was
stoned." (Kris Kristofferson)*

The phone rang for bed 12: "Oh, I'm better. Only been sick three
times this morning. Diarrhoea? Yes, about 2am and 4am, but
nothing since. I haven't eaten anything, no. Had some sips of
water. And how's Doreen?"

"Let's get away, come on let's make a get-away." (Franz Ferdinand)

The doctor said: "Well, your temperature is better but your
neutrophils are still only point one. We'll just have to wait
for the cavalry to arrive."

Lady goes to market, clippity clop, clippity clop.
Gentleman goes to market, trot trot, trot trot.
Farmer goes to market, gallopa gallopa,
And falls into a ditch!

*"Now for some jobs you can be getting on with this weekend."
(Gardeners World, BBC2)*

The phone rang for bed 8: "Oh, just leave the shirts then. For
goodness sakes. I'll do them all in half an hour. It'll take you that
for each one."

The phone rang for bed 12: "Open the freezer. Take out the blue
box. Defrost it in the fridge overnight. Turn the oven to 170 and

wait for it to heat up first. Then it'll be about 40 minutes. Is that alright? Then you'll need a plate and a knife and fork, ok? Ha ha. Only kidding, sweetie."

"It's the answer. It's" (News at Ten, BBC Text Channel)

She woke up to a Gauguin vision; a beautiful South Sea island maiden leaning over her. Many of the nurses here, she found out, were from the Philippines. There were two married couples – the women were nurses and their husbands were nursing assistants. The men took the blood. One kissed her after a belated success at finding a vein. "Sharp prick!" He was very handsome.

The phone rang for bed 10: "Are you keeping an eye on my e-bay bid? You know, the Barbie Princess duvet cover. Sharon will love it; she'll just love it. How long is left? About four hours? You've got to watch out for those last minute hustlers, you know. Give me a ring. I know it'll be late. We'll whisper."

The phone rang for bed 12: "I just had a little vomit, early in the night, so that's better. Oh, but I tell you, when I went to the loo, by the time I came back, my heart was going bang bang bang."

"We gotta get out of this place
If it's the last thing we ever do" (The Animals)

The doctor said: "Well, your temperature's been down for the last 24 hours and your neutrophils are up to 2, so I think you can go home." The cannula was out; her bag was packed. She slipped her shoes on and, as she hurried for the lift, plugged in her i-pod.

"I'm walking on sunshine, whoa oh
And don't it feel good"   *(Katrina and the Waves)*

JACK RILLIE

Call-girls

hello
HELLO
THAT YOU DAD?
that's me
HOW ARE YOU? OK?
ok you might say
THAT'S FINE IS MUM THERE?
not quite yet but approaching
OK DAD NICE TALKING TO YOU
must do it again
sometime

MARGARET TAIT

Elasticity

Think of the word, elastic.
The real elastic quality is the being able to spring back
    to the original shape,
Not the being able to be stretched.
So, metal is described as elastic
And steel is the most elastic of all metals.
It is specially manufactured to have the elastic quality
    of retaining its own shape.
Steel is so elastic you can't budge it.

To Anybody At All

I didn't want you cosy and neat and limited.
I didn't want you to be understandable,
Understood.
I wanted you to stay mad and limitless,
Neither bound to me nor bound to anyone else's or
    your own preconceived idea of yourself.

GRACE PALEY

Wants

I saw my ex-husband in the street. I was sitting on the steps of the new library.

Hello, my life, I said. We had once been married for twenty-seven years, so I felt justified.

He said, What? What life? No life of mine.

I said, O.K. I don't argue when there's real disagreement. I got up and went into the library to see how much I owed them.

The librarian said $32 even and you've owed it for eighteen years. I didn't deny anything. Because I don't understand how time passes. I have had those books. I have often thought of them. The library is only two blocks away.

My ex-husband followed me to the Books Returned desk. He interrupted the librarian, who had more to tell. In many ways, he said, as I look back, I attribute the dissolution of our marriage to the fact that you never invited the Bertrams to dinner.

That's possible, I said. But really, if you remember: first, my father was sick that Friday, then the children were born, then I had those Tuesday-night meetings, then the war began. Then we didn't seem to know them anymore. But you're right. I should have had them to dinner.

I gave the librarian a check for $32. Immediately she trusted me, put my past behind her, wiped the record clean, which is just what most other municipal and/or state bureaucracies will not do.

I checked out the two Edith Wharton books I had just returned because I'd read them so long ago and they are more apropos now than ever. They were *The House of Mirth* and *The Children*, which is about how life in the United States in New York changed in twenty-seven years fifty years ago.

A nice thing I do remember is breakfast, my ex-husband said. I was surprised. All we ever had was coffee. Then I remembered there was a hole in the back of the kitchen closet which opened into the apartment next door. There, they always ate sugar-cured smoked bacon. It gave us a very grand feeling about breakfast, but we never got stuffed and sluggish.

That was when we were poor, I said.

When were we ever rich? he asked.

Oh, as time went on, as our responsibilities increased, we didn't go in need. You took adequate financial care, I reminded him. The children went to camp four weeks a year and in decent ponchos with sleeping bags and boots, just like everyone else. They looked very nice. Our place was warm in winter, and we had nice red pillows and things.

I wanted a sailboat, he said. But you didn't want anything.

Don't be bitter, I said. It's never too late.

No, he said with a great deal of bitterness. I may get a sailboat. As a matter of fact I have money down on an eighteen-foot two-rigger. I'm doing well this year and can look forward to better. But as for you, it's too late. You'll always want nothing.

He had had a habit throughout the twenty-seven years of making a narrow remark which, like a plumber's snake, could work its way through the ear down the throat, halfway to my heart. He would then disappear, leaving me choking with equipment. What I mean is, I sat down on the library steps and he went away.

I looked through *The House of Mirth*, but lost interest. I felt extremely accused. Now, it's true, I'm short of requests and absolute requirements. But I do want *something*.

I want, for instance, to be a different person. I want to be the woman who brings these two books back in two weeks. I want to be the effective citizen who changes the school system and addresses the Board of Estimate on the troubles of this dear urban center.

I *had* promised my children to end the war before they grew up.

I wanted to have been married forever to one person, my ex-husband or my present one. Either has enough character for a whole life, which as it turns out is really not such a long time. You couldn't exhaust either man's qualities or get under the rock of his reasons in one short life.

Just this morning I looked out the window to watch the street for a while and saw that the little sycamores the city had dreamily planted a couple of years before the kids were born had come that day to the prime of their lives.

Well! I decided to bring those two books back to the library. Which proves that when a person or an event comes along to jolt or appraise me I *can* take some appropriate action, although I am better known for my hospitable remarks.

CZESLAW MILOSZ

On Angels

All was taken away from you: white dresses,
wings, even existence.
Yet I believe you,
messengers.

There, where the world is turned inside out,
a heavy fabric embroidered with stars and beasts,
you stroll, inspecting the trustworthy seams.

Short is your stay here:
now and then at a matinal hour, if the sky is clear,
in a melody repeated by a bird,
or in the smell of apples at the close of day
when the light makes the orchards magic.

They say somebody has invented you
but to me this does not sound convincing
for humans invented themselves as well.

The voice – no doubt it is a valid proof,
as it can belong only to radiant creatures,
weightless and winged (after all, why not?),
girdled with the lightning.

I have heard that voice many a time when asleep
and, what is strange, I understood more or less
an order or an appeal in an unearthly tongue:

day draws near
another one
do what you can.

Ars Poetica?

I have always aspired to a more spacious form
that would be free from the claims of poetry or prose
and would let us understand each other without exposing
the author or reader to sublime agonies.

In the very essence of poetry there is something indecent:
a thing is brought forth which we didn't know we had in us,
so we blink our eyes, as if a tiger had sprung out
and stood in the light, lashing his tail.

That's why poetry is rightly said to be dictated by a daimonion,
though it's an exaggeration to maintain that he must be an angel.
It's hard to guess where that pride of poets comes from,
when so often they're put to shame by the disclosure of their
    frailty.

What reasonable man would like to be a city of demons,
who behave as if they were at home, speak in many tongues,
and who, not satisfied with stealing his lips or hand,
work at changing his destiny for their convenience?

It's true that what is morbid is highly valued today,
and so you may think that I am only joking
or that I've devised just one more means
of praising Art with the help of irony.

There was a time when only wise books were read,
helping us to bear our pain and misery.
This, after all, is not quite the same
as leafing through a thousand works fresh from
    psychiatric clinics.

And yet the world is different from what it seems to be
and we are other than how we see ourselves in our ravings.
People therefore preserve silent integrity,
thus earning the respect of their relatives and neighbors.

The purpose of poetry is to remind us
how difficult it is to remain just one person,
for our house is open, there are no keys in the doors,
and invisible guests come in and out at will.

What I'm saying here is not, I agree, poetry,
as poems should be written rarely and reluctantly,
under unbearable duress and only with the hope
that good spirits, not evil ones, choose us for their instrument.

JOHN BERGER

Between Two Colmars

I first went to Colmar to look at the Grünewald Altarpiece in the winter of 1963. I went a second time ten years later. I didn't plan it that way. During the intervening years a great deal had changed. Not at Colmar, but, generally, in the world, and also in my life. The dramatic point of change was exactly half-way through that decade. In 1968, hopes, nurtured more or less underground for years, were born in several places in the world and given their names: and in the same year, these hopes were categorically defeated. This became clearer in retrospect. At the time many of us tried to shield ourselves from the harshness of the truth. For instance, at the beginning of 1969, we still thought in terms of a second 1968 possibly recurring.

This is not the place for an analysis of what changed in the alignment of political forces on a world scale. Enough to say that the road was cleared for what, later, would be called *normalization*. Many thousands of lives were changed too. But this will not be read in the history books. (There was a comparable, although very different, watershed in 1848, and its effects on the life of a generation are recorded, not in the histories, but in Flaubert's *Sentimental Education*.) When I look around at my friends – and particularly those who were (or still are) politically conscious – I see how the long-term direction of their lives was altered or deflected at that moment just as it might have been by a private event: the onset of an illness, an unexpected recovery, a bankruptcy. I imagine that if they looked at me, they would see something similar.

Normalization means that between the different political systems, which share the control of almost the entire world, anything can be exchanged under the single condition that nothing anywhere is radically changed. The present is assumed to be continuous, the continuity allowing for technological development.

A time of expectant hopes (as before 1968) encourages one to think of oneself as unflinching. Everything needs to be faced. The only danger seems to be evasion or sentimentality. Harsh truth will aid liberation. This principle becomes so integral to one's thinking that it is accepted without question. One is aware of how it might be otherwise. Hope is a marvellous focusing lens. One's eye becomes fixed to it. And one can examine anything.

The altarpiece, no less than a Greek tragedy or 19th century novel, was originally planned to encompass the totality of a life and an explanation of the world. It was painted on hinged panels of wood. When these were shut, those before the altar saw the Crucifixion, flanked by St. Anthony and St. Sebastian. When the panels were opened, they saw a Concert of Angels and a Madonna and Child, flanked by an Annunciation and Resurrection. When the panels were opened once again, they saw the apostles and some church dignitaries flanked by paintings about the life of St. Anthony. The altarpiece was commissioned for a hospice at Isenheim by the Antonite order. The hospice was for victims of the plague and syphilis. The altarpiece was used to help victims come to terms with their suffering.

On my first visit to Colmar I saw the Crucifixion as the key to the whole altarpiece and I saw disease as the key to the Crucifixion. "The longer I look, the more convinced I become that for Grünewald disease represents the actual state of man. Disease is not for him the prelude to death – as modern man tends to fear; it is the condition of life." This is what I wrote in 1963. I ignored the hinging of the Altarpiece. With my lens of hope, I had no need of the painted panels of hope. I saw Christ in the Resurrection "as pallid with the pallor of death"; I saw the Virgin in the Annunciation responding to the Angel as if "to the news of an incurable disease"; in the Madonna and Child I seized upon the fact that the swaddling cloth was the tattered (infected) rag which would later serve as loin cloth in the Crucifixion.

This view of the work was not altogether arbitrary. The beginning of the 16th century was felt and experienced in many parts of Europe as a time of damnation. And undoubtedly this experience *is* in the Altarpiece. Yet not exclusively so. But in

1963 I saw only this, only the bleakness. I had no need of anything else.

Ten years later, the gigantic crucified body still dwarfed the mourners in the painting and the onlooker outside it. This time I thought: the European tradition is full of images of torture and pain, most of them sadistic. How is it that this, which is one of the harshest and most pain-filled of all, is an exception? How is it painted?

It is painted inch by inch. No contour, no cavity, no rise within the contours, reveals a moment's flickering of the intensity of depiction. Depiction is pinned to the pain suffered. Since no part of the body escapes pain, the depiction can nowhere slack its precision. The cause of the pain is irrelevant; all that matters now is the faithfulness of the depiction. This faithfulness came from the empathy of love.

Love bestows innocence. It has nothing to forgive. The person loved is not the same as the person seen crossing the street or washing her face. Nor exactly the same as the person living his (or her) own life and experience, for he (or she) cannot remain innocent.

Who then is the person loved? A mystery, whose identity is confirmed by nobody except the lover. How well Dostoevsky saw this. Love is solitary even though it joins.

The person loved is the being who continues when the person's own actions and egocentricity have been dissolved. Love recognises a person before the act and the *same* person after it. It invests this person with a value which is untranslatable into virtue.

Such love might be epitomised by the love of a mother for her child. Passion is only one mode of love. Yet there are differences. A child is in process of becoming. A child is incomplete. In what he is, at any given moment, he may be remarkably complete. In the passage between moments, however, he becomes dependent, and his incompleteness becomes obvious. The love of the mother connives with the child. She imagines him more complete. Their wishes become mixed, or they alternate. Like legs walking.

The discovery of a loved person, already formed and completed, is the onset of a passion.

One recognises those whom one does not love by their attainments. The attainments one finds important may differ from those which society in general acclaims. Nevertheless we take account of those we do not love according to the way they fill a contour, and to describe this contour we use comparative adjectives. Their overall "shape" is the sum of their attainments, as described by adjectives.

A person loved is seen in the opposite way. Their contour or shape is not a surface encountered but an horizon which borders. A person loved is recognised not by attainments but by the *verbs* which can satisfy that person. His or her needs may be quite distinct from those of the lover, but they create value: the value of that love.

For Grünewald the verb was *to paint*. To paint the life of Christ.

Empathy, carried to the degree which Grünewald carried it, may reveal an area of truth between the objective and subjective. Doctors and scientists working today on the phenomenology of pain might well study this painting. The distortions of form and proportion – the enlargement of the feet, the barrel-chesting of the torso, the elongation of the arms, the planting out of the fingers – may describe exactly the *felt* anatomy of pain.

I do not want to suggest that I saw more in 1973 than in 1963. I saw differently. That is all. The ten years do not necessarily mark a progress; in many ways they represent defeat.

The altarpiece is housed in a tall gallery with gothic windows near a river by some warehouses. During my second visit I was making notes and occasionally looking up at the Angel's Concert. The gallery was deserted except for the single guardian, an old man rubbing his hands in woollen gloves over a portable oil stove. I looked up and was aware that something had moved or changed. Yet I had heard nothing and the gallery was absolutely silent. Then I saw what had changed. The sun was out. Low in the winter sky, it shone directly through the gothic windows so that on the white wall opposite, their pointed arches were printed, with sharp edges, in light. I looked from the "window lights" on the wall to the light in the painted panels – the painted window at the far end of the painted chapel where the Annunciation takes place, the light that pours down the mountainside behind the Madonna, the great circle of light like an aurora borealis round the resurrected Christ. In each case the painted light held its own. It remained light; it did not disintegrate into coloured paint. The sun went in and the white wall lost its animation. The paintings retained their radiance.

The whole altarpiece, I now realised, is about darkness and light. The immense space of sky and plain behind the crucifixion – the plain of Alsace crossed by thousands of refugees fleeing war and famine – is deserted and filled with a darkness that appears final. In 1963 the light in the other panels seemed to me frail and artificial. Or, more accurately, frail and unearthly. (A light dreamt of in the darkness.) In 1973 I thought I saw that the light in these panels accords with the essential experience of light.

Only in rare circumstances is light uniform and constant. (Sometimes at sea; sometimes around high mountains.) Normally light is variegated or shifting. Shadows cross it. Some surfaces reflect more light than others. Light is not, as the moralists would have us believe, the constant polar opposite to darkness. Light flares out of darkness.

Look at the panels of the Madonna and the Angel's Consort. When it is not absolutely regular, light overturns the regular measurement of space. Light re-forms space as we perceive it. At first what is in light has a tendency to look nearer than what is in shadow. The village lights at night appear to bring the village closer. When one examines this phenomenon more closely, it becomes more subtle. Each concentration of light acts as a centre of imaginative attraction, so that in imagination one measures *from* it across the areas in shadow or darkness. And so there are as many articulated spaces as there are concentrations of light. Where one is actually situated establishes the primary space of a ground plan. But far from there a dialogue begins with each place in light, however distant, and each proposes another space and a different spatial articulation. Each place where there is brilliant light, prompts one to imagine oneself there. It is as though the seeing eye sees echoes of itself wherever the light is concentrated. This multiplicity is a kind of joy.

The attraction of the eye to light, the attraction of the organism to light as a source of energy, is basic. The attraction of the imagination to light is more complex because it involves the mind as a whole and therefore it involves comparative experience. We respond to physical modifications of light with distinct but infinitesimal modifications of spirit, high and low, hopeful and fearful. In front of most scenes one's experience of their light is divided in spatial zones of sureness and doubt. Vision advances from light to light like a figure walking on stepping stones.

Put these two observations, made above, together: hope attracts, radiates as a point, to which one wants to be near, from which one wants to measure. Doubt has no centre and is ubiquitous.

Hence the strength and fragility of Grünewald's light.

On the occasion of both my visits to Colmar it was winter, and the town was under the grip of a similar cold, the cold which comes off the plain and carries with it a reminder of hunger. In the same town, under similar physical conditions, I saw differently. It is a commonplace that the significance of a work of art changes as it survives. Usually however, this knowledge is used to distinguish between "them" (in the past) and "us" (now). There is a tendency to picture *them* and their reactions to art as being embedded in history, and at the same time to credit *ourselves* with an over-view, looking across from what we treat as the summit of history. The surviving work of art then seems to confirm our superior position. The aim of its survival was us.

This is illusion. There is no exemption from history. The first time I saw the Grünewald I was anxious to place *it* historically. In terms of medieval religion, the plague, medicine, the Lazar house. Now I have been forced to place myself historically.

In a period of revolutionary expectation, I saw a work of art which had survived as evidence of the past's despair; in a period which has to be endured, I see the same work miraculously offering a narrow pass across despair.

W. G. SEBALD

After Nature

As the Snow on the Alps: I

Whoever closes the wings
of the altar in the Lindenhardt
parish church, and locks up
the carved figures in their casing,
on the left-hand panel
will be met by St George.
Foremost at the picture's edge he stands
above the world by a hand's breadth
and is about to step over the frame's
threshold. Georgius Miles,
man with the iron torso, rounded chest
of ore, red-golden hair and silver
feminine features. The face of the unknown
Grünewald emerges again and again
in his work, as that of a witness
to the snow miracle, a hermit
in the desert, a commiserator
in the Munich *Mocking of Christ*.
Last of all, in the afternoon light
in the Erlangen library, it shines forth
from a self-portrait, sketched out
in heightened white crayon, later destroyed
by an alien hand's pen and wash,
as that of a painter aged forty
to fifty. Always the same
gentleness, the same burden of grief,
the same irregularity of the eyes, veiled
and sliding sideways down into loneliness.
Grünewald's face reappears, too,
in a Basel painting by Holbein

the Younger of a crowned female saint.
These were strangely disguised
instances of resemblance, wrote Fraenger,
whose books were burned by the Fascists.
Indeed, it seemed as though in such works of art
men had revered each other like brothers, and
often made monuments in each other's
image where their paths had crossed.
Hence, too, at the centre of
the Lindenhardt altar's right wing,
that troubled gaze upon the youth
on the other side from the older man
whom, years ago now, on a grey
January morning I myself once
encountered in the railway station
in Bamberg. It is St Dionysius,
his cut-off head under one arm.
To him, his chosen guardian,
who in the midst of life carries
his death with him, Grünewald gives
the appearance of Riemenschneider, whom
twenty years later the Würzburg bishop
condemned to the breaking of his hands
in the torture cell. Long before that time
pain had entered into the pictures.
That is the command, knows the painter,
who on the altar aligns himself
with the scant company of the
fourteen auxiliary saints. All these,
the blessed Blasius, Achaz and Eustace;
Panthaleon, Aegidius, Cyriax, Christopher and
Erasmus and the truly beautiful
Saint Vitus with the cockerel,
each looks in a different
direction without knowing
why. The three female saints
Barbara, Catherine and Margaret on
the other hand hide at the edge

of the left panel behind the back of
St George, putting together their
uniform oriental heads for
a conspiracy against the men.
The misfortune of saints
is their sex, is the terrible
separation of the sexes, which Grünewald
suffered in his own person. The exorcised
devil that Cyriax, not only because
of the narrow confines, holds raised
high as an emblem in
the air is a female being
and, as a grisaille of Grünewald's
in the Frankfurt Städel shows in
the most drastic of fashions, derives from
Diocletian's epileptic daughter,
the misshapen princess Artemia whom
Cyriax, as beside him she kneels on
the ground, holds tightly leashed
with a maniple of his vestments,
like a dog. Spreading out
above them is the branch work
of a fig tree with fruit, one of which
is entirely hollowed out by insects.

H. D. (HILDA DOOLITTLE)

The Cinema and the Classics

Beauty

I suppose we might begin rhetorically by asking, what is the cinema, what are the classics? For I don't in my heart believe one out of ten of us highbrow intellectuals, Golders Greenites, Chautauqua lecturers, knows the least little bit about either. Classics. Cinema. The word cinema (or movies) would bring to nine out of ten of us a memory of crowds and crowds and saccharine music and longdrawn out embraces and the artificially enhanced thud-offs of galloping bronchoes. What would be our word-reaction to Classics? What to Cinema? Take Cinema to begin with, (cinema = movies), boredom, tedium, suffocation, pink lemonade, saw-dust even: old reactions connected with cheap circuses, crowds and crowds and crowds and illiteracy and more crowds and breathless suffocation and (if "we" the editorial "us" is an American) peanut shells and grit and perhaps a sudden collapse of jerry-built scaffoldings. Danger somewhere anyhow. Danger to the physical safety, danger to the moral safety, a shivering away as when "politics" or "graft" is mentioned, a great thing that must be accepted (like the pre-cinema days circus) with abashed guilt, sneaked to at least intellectually. The cinema or the movies is to the vast horde of the fair-to-middling intellectuals, a Juggernaught crushing out mind and perception in one vast orgy of the senses.

So much for the cinema. (Our "classic" word-reaction will come along in due course.) I speak here, when I would appear ironical, of the fair-to-middling intellectual, not of the fortunately vast-increasing, valiant, little army of the advance guard or the franc-tireur of the arts, in whose hands mercifully since the days of the stone-writers, the arts really rested. The little leaven. But the leaven, turning in the lump, sometimes takes it into its microscopic mind to wonder what the lump is about and why can't the lump, for its own good, for its own happiness, for its own (to use the word goodness in its Hellenic sense) *beauty*, be leavened just a little quicker? The leaven, regarding the lump, is sometimes curious as to the lump's point of view, for all the lump itself so grandiloquently ignores it, the microscopic leaven. And so with me or editorially "us" at just this moment. Wedged securely in the lump (we won't class ourselves as sniffingly above it), we want to prod our little microbe way into its understanding. Thereby having the thrill of our lives, getting an immense kick out of trying to see what it is up to, what I am up against, what we all, franc-tireurs, have to deal with.

First as I say, amazing prejudice. The movies, the cinema, the pictures. Prejudice has sprouted, a rank weed, where the growth of wheat is thickest. In other words, films that blossom here in Europe (perhaps a frail, little, appreciated flower) are swiftly cut and grafted in America into a more sturdy, respectable rootstock. Take "Vaudeville", for example, a film that I didn't particularly revel in, yet must appreciate, Zolaesque realism which succeeded admirably in its medium; was stripped (by this gigantic Cyclops, the American censor) of its one bloom. The stem is valuable, is transplanted, but the spirit, the flower so to speak of "Vaudeville" (we called it here "Variété"), the thing holding its created centre, its (as it happens) Zolaesque sincerity, is carefully abstracted. A reel or in some cases an artist or a producer, is carefully gelded before being given free run of the public. The lump heaving under its own lumpishness is perforce content, is perforce ignorant, is perforce so sated with mechanical efficiency, with whir and thud of various hypnotic appliances, that it doesn't know what it is missing. The lump doesn't know that it has been deprived of beauty, of the flower of some producer's wit and inspiration. The lump is hypnotized by the thud-thud of constant repetition until it begins to believe, like the African tribesman, that the thump-thump of its medicine man's formula is the only formula, that his medicine man is the only medicine man, that his god, his totem is (save for some neighbouring flat-faced almost similar effigies) the only totem. America accepts totems, not because the crowd wants totems, but because totems have so long been imposed on him, on it, on the race consciousness that it or him or the race consciousness is becoming hypnotized, is in danger of some race fixation; he or it or the race consciousness is so duped by mechanical efficiency and saccharine dramatic mediocrity that he or it doesn't in the least know, in fact would be incapable (if he did know) of saying what he does want.

He learns that there is a new European importation for instance of a "star"; this importation being thudded into his senses for some months beforehand, his mind is made up for him; she is beautiful. We take that for granted. There I agree, the leaven and the lump are in this at one. The lump really wants beauty or this totem of beauty would not be set up by its astute leaders. Beauty. She is beautiful. This time "she" is a northern girl, a "nordic", another word they fall for. A Nordic beauty has been acclaimed and we all want to see her. I am grateful (it was my privilege) that I, for one, saw this grave, sweet creature before America claimed her. I saw her, as I see most of my pictures, more or less by accident. At least the divine Chance or classic Fortune that more or less guides all of us, led me one day to worship. I, like the Lump, am drawn by this slogan, "Beauty", though this particular enchantress was not particularly head-lined on the provincial bill-boards. In fact, the whole cast was modestly set forth in small type along with the producer and I thought "well it looks harmless anyhow" and it was raining and so in Montreux, Switzerland, I happened (as it happened) to see my first real revelation of the real art of the cinema.

I am led a little afield in trying to realize in retrospect the vast deflowering that took place in at least one rare artist. I dare say it is a common occurrence but in this particular case particularly devastating. I saw "Joyless Street" ("Die Freudlose Gasse") in Montreux, some two or three years ago when it was first "released" from Germany to take its tottering frail way across Europe towards Paris, where it was half-heartedly received, to London, where it was privately viewed by screen enthusiasts, only last winter, at one of those admirable Sunday afternoon performances of the London Film Society. In the meantime, I had seen Greta Garbo, deflowered, deracinated, devitalized, more

than that, actively and acutely distorted by an odd unbelievable
parody of life, of beauty, we were efficiently offered (was it at the
Capitol about a year ago?) "The Torrent".

Greta Garbo in Montreux, Switzerland, trailing with frail,
very young feet through perhaps the most astonishingly consis-
tently lovely film I have ever seen ("Joyless Street") could not be,
but by some fluke of evil magic, the same creature I saw, with
sewed-in, black lashes, with waist-lined, svelte, obvious contours, with gowns and gowns, all of them almost (by some
anachronism) trailing on the floor, with black-dyed wig, obscuring her own nordic nimbus, in the later a "Torrent". The Censor,
this magnificent ogre, had seen fit to devitalize this Nordic
flower, to graft upon the stem of a living, wild camellia (if we
may be fanciful for a moment) the most blatant of obvious, crepe,
tissue-paper orchids. A beauty, it is evident, from the Totem's
stand-point, must be a vamp, an evil woman, and an evil woman,
in spite of all or any observation to the contrary, must be black-
eyed, must be dark even if it is a nordic ice-flower and Lya de
Puttiesque. Beauty is what the Lump and the Leaven alike
demand. So "beauty, here it is," says the Ogre. The Ogre knows
that the world will not be sustained, will not exist without that
classic, ancient Beauty. Beauty and Goodness, I must again
reiterate, to the Greek, meant one thing. To Kalon, the beautiful,
the good. Kalon, the mob must, in spite of its highbrow detractors, have. The Ogre knows enough to know that. But he paints
the lily, offers a Nice-carnival, frilled, tissue-paper rose in place
of a wild-briar.

Beauty was made to endure, in men, in flowers, in hearts, in
spirits, in minds. That flame, in spite of the highbrow detractors,
exists at the very centre, the very heart of the multitude. It is the
business of the Ogre, the Censor, to offer it a serpent for an egg, a
stone for bread. It is the duty of every sincere intellectual to
work for the better understanding of the cinema, for the clearing
of the ground, for the rescuing of this superb art, from its hide-
bound convention. Perseus, in other words, and the chained
Virgin. Saint George in other words, and the Totem dragon.
Anyhow it is up to us, as quickly as we can, to rescue this
captured Innocent (for the moment embodied in this Greta

Garbo) taking frail and tortuous veils of light and shadow, wandering in photogenetic guise that Leonardo would have marvelled at and Tintoretto radiantly acclaimed. Greta Garbo, as I first saw her, gave me a clue, a new angle, and a new sense of elation. This is beauty, and this is a beautiful and young woman not exaggerated in any particular, stepping, frail yet secure across a wasted city. Post-war Vienna really wrung our hearts that time; the cheap, later clap-trap of starving stage Vienna had not yet blighted and blunted our sense of proportion and reality. Before our eyes, the city was unfolded, like some blighted flower, like some modernized epic of Troy town is down, like some mournful and pitiful Babylon is fallen, is fallen. The true note was struck, the first post-war touch of authentic pathos, not over-done, not over-exaggerated, a net of finely spun tragedy, pathos so fine and so intolerable that after all, we can't wonder that the flagrant, Parisian, commercial "buyers" must disdain it. London could not (being governed also by a brother to our American Cyclops) allow this performance to be broadcast. War and war and war. Helen who ruined Troy seems to have taken shape, but this time it is Troy by some fantastic readjustment who is about to ruin Helen. Little Miss Garbo (I think of her as little; I believe from the columns of "gossip" I read dished up in various Hollywood camera news productions that "Greta Garbo is taller than John Gilbert", a thing they seem in some subtle way to have, among many other things, against her) brought into her performance of the professor's elder, little daughter in "Joyless Street", something of a quality that I can't for the life of me label otherwise than classic. As long as beauty is classic, so long beauty on the screen, presented with candour and true acumen, must take its place with the greatest masterpieces of the renaissance and of antiquity.

For there is no getting over this astonishing and indubitable fact. Beauty as it has existed in pre-Periclean Athens, in the islands of the Cyclades, in the temple of Karnak, in the frescoes of Simone Martini and the etchings of Albrecht Dürer still does find expression, still does wander veiled as with dawn, still does wait for a renaissance to hail her. Miss Garbo is a symbol, was, I should say, a symbol as I saw her in "Joyless Street". She may again become some such glorified embodiment as flung itself in its youth and its strange, statuesque abandonment across the wretched divan of Madame whatever-was-her-name's evil house. Beauty, the youth and charm, by just a fluke, wasn't tarnished in that atmosphere. The odd thing was that this story of poverty and fervid business speculation and the lady of the world and her lovers and her pearls and the young financier and their meeting in this ill-flavoured establishment and the secret murder, wasn't commonplace, wasn't trivial, partook of the most ethereal overtones of subtlety. Tragedy rang like little bells, fairy bells almost. Tragedy didn't dare, those days, to stalk openly in its ornate purple. Not in Europe, not in London or Paris or Vienna. Murder and pearls and speculation seemed perilously a part of life in those days. Tragedy was a muse whose glory was for the moment over-shadowed with an almost mystical, hardly to be expressed quality that one might possibly define as pathos. Beauty and the warrior were at rest. For the rest of us in London and Paris and Vienna, there was something different, something too subtle to be called disintegration or dissociation, but a state in which the soul and body didn't seem on good terms. Hardly on speaking terms. So it is that this fine little Greta Garbo with her youth, her purity, her straight brows and her unqualified distinction found a role to fit her. She had, it is true, appeared, I am told, creditably in other films; it was my good fortune to meet her first in this "Joyless Street" or, as it was billed in our Lake Geneva small-town, "La Petite Rue Sans Joie". The theatre, I need hardly say, was half empty. The performance began with a street (will I ever forget it) and the sombre plodding limp of a one-legged, old ruffian. No appeal to pity, to beauty, the distinguished mind that conceived this opening said simply, this is it, this is us, no glory, no pathos, no glamour. Just a long, Freudian, tunnel-like, dark street. Nothing within sight, nothing to dream of or ponder on but . . . the butcher's shop with its attendant, terrible, waiting line of frenzied women.

Life is getting something to eat said the presenter of this "Petite Rue Sans Joie". Getting it somehow, anyhow. Beauty itself must come to me, says La Petite Rue Sans Joie and one after another through sheer boredom with starvation, the "girls"

of the neighbourhood, the banal, the merely pretty, the sometimes ambitious, and the sheerly slovenly are drawn within the
portals of la Petite Rue. For in the little street there is a shop that
rivals even the butcher's for gaiety and distraction. It is neatly
disguised, yet thinly. Clothes are bought and sold by a certain
suave Madame (the performance of this entrepreneuse whose
name I have forgotten, was amazing) and the little bigger of the
little daughters of the proud, utterly destitute, brilliant, young-
ish, middle-aged professor strolls from time to time discreetly to
its portal. Madame who is so suave, so kind (will I ever forget the
subtlety of her make up, that suggested shadow of a mustache
across her sly upper lip) one day offers the little Mademoiselle a
fur coat to wear home, she needn't pay for it yet, just wear it and
keep warm, things are so hard, madame is so suave, so genuinely
sympathetic. The little lady loses her job through the insidious
gift. A fur coat. Everyone knows what that means in post-war
Vienna. The Manager of the office is pleased, didn't know this
wild-flower was a game one. He summons her, offers a rise in
salary, the usual denouement, of course, she being she, can't
possibly accept it. La Petite Rue Sans Joie seems perilously near
to swallowing our Beauty. Helen walking scatheless among
execrating warriors, the plague, distress, and famine is in this
child's icy, mermaid-like integrity. Her purity shines like an
enchanter's crown. We *know* nothing can happen to her, yet
do we? Things happen, we ourselves have known them to happen
. . . one by one, our audience (already meagre) has risen, has
blatantly stamped downstairs. I hear words, whispers, English.
"A thing like *this* . . . filthy . . . no one but a *foreigner* would dare
present it." La Petite Rue Sans Joie was a real, little street. It
was a little war-street, a little, post-war street, therefore our
little picture palace in our comparatively broad-minded Lake
Geneva town, is empty. People won't, they dare not face reality.

And beauty, among other things, is reality, and beauty once in
so many hundred years, raises a wan head, suddenly decides to
avenge itself for all the slights that it has negligently accepted,
sometimes through weariness, sometimes through sheer omnipo-
tence, sometimes through cynicism or through boredom. Simo-
netta, the famous Medician Venus (though I don't care for her),

one and one and one, all stand as witnesses that once in so often, beauty herself, Helen above Troy, rises triumphant and denounces the world for a season and then retires, spins a little web of illusion and shuffles off to forget men and their stale formulas of existence. Well beauty has been slurred over and laughed at and forgotten. But Helen of Troy didn't always stay at home with Menelaus. Beauty has been recognised and for that reason (as the world will not face reality and the ogre, the Censor, this Polyphemus knows well enough that beauty is a danger), Miss Garbo has been trained, and that with astonishing efficiency, to sway forward and backward in long skirts with pseudo-Lillian Gish affection, to pose with a distinct, parrot-like flare for the Gloria Swansonesque. Her wigs, her eye-lashes have all but eclipsed our mermaid's straight stare, her odd, magic quality of almost clairvoyant intensity. She simpers. Something has been imposed, a blatant tinsel and paper-flowers and paste-jewel exterior, yet it doesn't quite dominate this nordic ice-flower. Beauty brings a curse, a blessing, a responsibility. Is that why your Ogre, the Censor, is so intent on disguising it, on dishing it up as vamp charm, as stale, Nice-carnival beauty-as-we-get-it-in-a-beauty-contest? Greta Garbo remains Greta Garbo. Let us hope she takes it into her stupid, magic head to rise and rend those who have so defamed her. Anyhow for the present, let us be thankful that she, momentarily at least, touched the screen with her purity and glamour. The screen has been touched by beauty, and the screen, in spite of all the totems, must finally respond, Polyphemus of our latest day, to the mermaid enchantment.

COLETTE

Colette at the Movies:
Criticism and Screen Plays

Mae West

The first of the following two selections is an excerpt from "Les
Cinéacteurs," a piece written in 1934 and collected in *La Jumelle
Noire* (*Black Opera Glasses*). From the same collection comes a
1938 piece on the apparent decline of Miss West.

I

. . . I hope that we are not too quick to dismiss the astonishing
actress who has only to appear in order to convince us, to gain
our vote by means as sure as they are unexpected – I mean Mae
West. "And do you know, she's like that in real life!" If that is
so, we could rely almost solely on her private life, her author-
ial independence, her impetuosity – like a wholehearted cavalry charge – even her greediness, to keep her for us just as
we see her in *She Done Him Wrong*. However, I'm dubious; in
I'm No Angel her mastery already seems a bit mechanical. She
has not been sufficiently on her guard against the scenario,
which lacks bite; the scene with the lions leaves us unmoved.
Happily, the beautiful blonde she-devil spirits away all the
weaknesses of the film with a sway of her hips, a glance that
undermines morals, and a damnable little "hu . . . hum" on two
notes.

But I feel that she is being pulled in different directions. And
moreover – an unforgivable detail, a violation of principle – she
is a little thinner.

II

What's wrong? She's thinner. Nevertheless the film critics, who
don't mince their words, reproach her with both the mediocrity
of her latest film and her corpulence. One speaks of "fat

haunches," another calls her "the adipose beauty," a third makes fun of her age, and the fourth is indignant at her cynicism.

I wanted to see this film, which isn't good, in which Mae West is said to "kill" nobody, though she was so "killing" in *She Done Him Wrong*. But Mae West, ever since *She Done Him Wrong*, has been worth going someplace to see. She alone out of an enormous and dull catalogue of heroines, does not get married at the end of the film, does not die, does not take the road to exile, does not gaze sadly at her declining youth in a silver-framed mirror in the worst possible taste; and she alone does not experience the bitterness of the abandoned "older woman." She alone has no parents, no children, no husband. This impudent woman is, in her style, as solitary as Chaplin used to be.

Impudence is rare in the cinema. In every country, to ensure its survival it finds itself obliged to borrow the mask of simple grossness and a joviality that dishonors the dialogue. By means of such concessions, it remains an exclusively virile virtue.

If some pretty young American tries to use it for her own ends, the result is desolating. The star has only two ways, both blameworthy, of adopting impudence: to resemble a bad supporting actress in a tragedy, or to have the air of a drunken woman. When we went to see *She Done Him Wrong*, we perceived that Mae West had invented something in the acting art. Since then she has continued, with the nonchalance of a woman of wit and the obstinacy of a trader.

To enlighten my judgment, I would have liked America to send us a great deal of Mae West, since she is the *auteur* and the principal interpreter of her films. It would have interested me to know how, by being insisted upon, the best discoveries spoil, and what is the process that ankyloses and discolors a character so rich, so hardy, so un-American: the woman without scruples, the female rival of the male débauché, the brave enemy of the male, valorous enough to use the same weapons as he. Balzac, who was quick to see things, knew and showed these women warriors. Except for Madame Marneffe, he places them, as is his right and his preference, in the highest ranks of the French peerage.

For Mae West, the age of vice is not 1900 but 1907 or '08: the era of giant hats made popular by Lantelme, the clinging dresses of

Margaine-Lacroix, the straight corsets that enclosed the female body from under the arm to the knee – corsets for the sake of which Germaine Gallois stipulated in her contracts that she would not have to sit down on stage. In comparison with such rigors, 1900 was easy, and Mae West's instinct was true when it led her to barricade herself in 1907. Just think of the kind of low drama she acts almost without gestures, except for the local undulations of her backside. Think of the murdered woman, camouflaged by a great head of hair that Mae West combs as she says in her nasal voice to the man calling to her: "Wait a minute, I'm doing something I've never done before." And can you honestly name another artist, male or female, in the cinema whose comic acting equals that of this ample blonde who undulates in little waves, who is ornamented with her real diamonds, whose eye is pale and hard, whose throat swells with the coos of a professional dove?

The only trouble is that since then, due to a major *maladresse*, she is thinner. I am looking at stills of *She Done Him Wrong*. During the short and restrained hand-to-hand struggle between the two women, two breasts, white, powerful, strongly attached to her torso, all but spring nude out of Mae West's bodice. She has the short neck, the round cheek of a young blonde butcher. Her arms are athletic, the cloth of the clinging dress creases, rides up from the well-fleshed thighs onto authentic buttocks.

Through lack of inspiration or good counsel, she has rejected these "advantages" of former days, reduced them all too visibly. In her latest film she is falsely fleshy. Her princess-style dresses don't cling to her living flesh but to immobile padding. The short arms have lost their character of compelling force. The essential signification of sensuality and animality abandons the shrunken body, the face barricaded behind make-up and fearing every moment. Thus the dimples in the cheeks, thus the cruel and generous smile she once had, no longer charmingly and infallibly contradict her hard eyes. This implacable gaze, the expression of utter lack of clemency of a Mae West turned to stone – I hardly expected it to remind me, by a resemblance more of inner nature than form, of Castiglione's paralyzed Countess, who, threatened less by mankind than by time, saw her approaching death.

LEE MILLER

Colette

There is a window above the graceful arches of the Palais Royal
gardens which is pointed out as Colette's. The children, playing
hopping games and the bent, old woman who dusts off the
"paying" chairs, pause to point it out to strangers who wander
through the galleries, hunting fashionable or notorious ghosts of
the past. They watch Cocteau's, Marais' and Colette's blinds
with a reverence their prototypes a few generation ago scarcely
had for the jewellers' "fences", revolutionaries and courtesans
whose windows were equally well known.

Up the darkest staircase in Paris to press a mute, electricityless
doorbell; to pound till knuckles are numb and Pauline, the devoted
ogress-slave of Colette stumbles through a lightless corridor to peer
at and identify the visitor, and to satisfy herself that she approves;
for if Pauline doesn't approve there is no second invitation.

Against the cold light from the tall windows Colette's fuzzy
hair is a halo. The room is hot, the fur coverings of her bed,
tawny rich, and she is almost certainly telephoning. She took off
her grotesque heavy-rimmed spectacles, shifted the phone and
tugged my hand for me to sit on the side of the bed while she
continued tutoying and gently scolding a small female voice
which leaked out into the room. Finally: the typewriter would be
returned, by the small voice; she would also apply for transport
to Limoges and would come for tea, tomorrow. *A demain*!

Colette turned to me and said *"Alors, qu'est ce que vous
voulez?"* Her voice was gruff but her hand had been warm and
her kohl-rimmed eyes matched in sparkle and clarity the myriad
of crystal balls and glass bibelots which strewed the room.

Her eyes were shrewd, too; so I spoke my piece. *"Pour vous dire
bonjour et pour vous demander si je peux faire votre portrait en
photo."* *"Tiens, elle parle le français!"* and she relaxed. "Have you
just arrived?" "Oh! I've been in Paris a long time, but they said
you were in bed, ill. I hesitated to call." "But of course, I'm

always in bed. I always will be. Once in a while I go out, but . . ." and she pouted.

We chatted about America and England as well as about the big three, the cold, the black market and the vanishing end of the war. She thought it funny that I should have been transformed from Cocteau's statue in *The Blood of a Poet* to a *poilu*.

Her enthusiasm came in gusts which carried her across the room, darting here and there to choose a book or an *"objet"* – and yet she never left her bed. I was an extension of her body and she stretched her hand on my arm to reach an envelope of pictures high on a shelf but from way in her past, and from the past of her friends.

In faded ochre and sepia the parade of fifty extraordinary years was given me like flashbacks or cinema trailers. Colette as Colette. Colette, the siren, the *gamine*, the lady of fashion, the diplomat's wife, the mother, the author . . . the Legion of Honor, the Academy. Colette on top of the Chrysler building in the St. Tropez barefoot sandals which tickled the jaded shutters of New York's cheesecake ship photographers ten years ago.

There was the dandyish, vicious Monsieur Willy, her first husband. He was a very odd bird. Colette married him when she was twenty and he nearly twice her age. He was a talked-about man about town, a dazzling, successful author. She left a comfortable, petted life with her family for irregular and precarious living with a man who was irresponsible and perverted. Her life was lonesomeness, misery, neglect and ill health; and like the books make out, the lot of a cad's wife. She was ashamed to let her family know her disillusionment.

Her husband's methods of being a "best-seller" were applied to her. He was an "author" vicariously; a sort of impresario or Svengali and a cheat. Some psychological impediment of words made him impotent to write but forced him to seek authorship through what are now known as "ghostwriters". He had a series of youngsters working for him under his name and he spent more creative energy in this devious organizing than if he'd done the original work. Colette's first try, *Claudine à l'école*, embroidered memories of her schooldays, disappointed him and he pigeon-holed it in disgust.

A year later he gave it to a publisher who swooped with joy and M. Willy had the further personal frustration of not having recognized the pearl he had found. However, by the nursery method of locking her in her room until she completed a quota of pages, he sweated Colette into writing three more *Claudines.*

There were pictures of the delicately beautiful Polaire who first played *Claudine* on the stage. A picture of Colette and Polaire dressed alike being promenaded by M. Willy at the races, to provoke publicity and scandal. Pictures of Colette with ankle-length hair. Colette in music-hall costume after her divorce; in street clothes, serene and stylish. In the theater wearing the trousers and cropped curly hair which was sensational. In drapery: her beautiful feet were naughty, then. Colette when she returned to writing, especially after the success of *La Vagabonde* in 1911.

None of these pictures were in order. They piled out and slithered over each other and off the bed, each inciting a story or reminiscence. The trouble she'd had with that monstrous little dog; the quarrel after that first night. Nearly every one attracted another object or book toward the bed.

Two little pastels she'd made, her only "works of art" evoked memories of a "camp follower" trip to join her second husband, Lieutenant Henri de Juvenel, who was in Verdun during the heroic black days. She had gone with a forged pass and five kilos of black-market butter which she lost on the troop train taking her to that Leningrad of the last war. It had been evacuated and forbidden to all women, so she'd been obliged to hide from the Commandant as much as from the shells. Like a good journalist, though unofficial war correspondent, she wrote *Les Heures Longues*, based on this visit; and the understanding treatment of the war in her next few books was from this personal knowledge.

Pictures of them both, diplomats in Algeria; of a flaxen-haired daughter, Colette de Juvenel – she was the other end of the phone conversation I'd listened to, now thirty-two and ending her first visit to Paris after the liberation of her own area, where she'd been with the Maquis after several years of underground work. There were newer pictures, early Hollywood technique;

one particularly poisonous one, like a costume-ball Theda Bara. Colette seemed very fond of it. Portraits of all the cats and all the dogs which appeared in her books. Portraits of her by Man Ray, Hoyningen-Huene, and me. A photo and letters from Proust. A sheaf of school-children's watercolors, illustrating a descriptive passage in her writings, a house, a field, the stars. The paragraph itself was written out in a large scrawl of childish perfectionism which snubbed Colette's own manuscripts lying on her bed-table desk. Her own writing is a scrawl, too, which is complicated by being scratched out, rewritten, rescratched and arrowed. When the bright blue page will bear no more torture, she copies it over with larger spaces between, and starts the scraping and polishing again.

Each of her perfectly poised words has struggled for existence, each has been hammered ruthlessly into place, and each of her graceful, facile sentences has survived total warfare. Many people say that French has frozen itself into a dead language. The rules are rigid and exclusive. The famous *clarté* is the goal of French writing, but if there's only one correct way to express a thought it would be the writer with the greatest *Thesaurus* mind who could express the most thoughts, and all French Academicians of equal knowledge and the same ideas would write the same sentences, and, what's more, not be ashamed of it. Colette, in spite of her prodigious vocabulary, which is the envy of all her fellow Academicians (she was the first woman member of the Belgian Academy), somehow manages to relax the French language into an easy intimacy, which is nonetheless mechanically accurate.

The manuscripts of her first four books are in school *cahiers*, pink and blue printed covers labelled in purple ink. They looked groomed enough for a county-fair exhibition, but they were the finale of many drafts. I don't know whether it's encouraging news or defeatist propaganda to young authors to say that a brilliant professional writer, Colette, suffers the same anguish for every paragraph now, after fifty years of experience, as she did on those first four books. (Personally I'm alarmed and very despondent.)

Seven fountain pens and a couple of pencils stand in a round, blue jug. She had me write with all of them. Hard points for digging, soft, easy ones for first drafts and letters, an old, wise one she trusted when she was completely stuck. She showed me a treasure too precious to use – a package of *Pat-a-par*, which she loved and approved in theory, but had never tried. She can but doesn't cook, and has favorite recipes which she has always imposed on each new cook.

She was looking past my shoulder as she was talking, and I turned around to see a quiet man smiling indulgently at us. He was Maurice Goudeket, a journalist, Colette's husband. He spoke beautiful English and toured me round the room while Colette embarked on another telephone conversation which she interrupted with squeals to him to show me this and that: the glass-domed jars on the far bookshelves held colored glass ornaments which hung in liquid from floating buoys like mines. There were little hands and figures and ships and acrobats, votive offerings sealed in holy water and very likely cabbages and kings if I'd looked long enough. There were magical fairy-land patterns embedded in glass paper weights; last generation's snowstorms swirled in others, and the mantel was bedecked with second-sightseers' gazing-balls. All but one were icy and brittle to touch. It was glass instead of pure crystal and had become *chambré*, tattle-telling its lowly origin.

His tiny study was warm with the glow of the beautiful leather bindings of his book collections. His desk invited work, and the windows like from the big room, look treetop high on the formal statue-studded garden. I'm a bored though docile bibliophile ordinarily, but there was something in the way he handled manuscripts and letters and bindings that made me enthusiastic. The tenderness with which he showed me his complete set of first editions of Colette's work awed me. Inside the covers of his copy of *La Vagabonde* are pasted the original manuscript page and her contract with the publisher. The margins are full of notes, nearly all references to the inspiration for the scene . . . she had annotated it for him. One pointed to a paragraph and said, "At least this man was real, although I didn't know him myself." She never talks about her work, and I don't think anyone except, perhaps, Maurice Goudeket, knows which of her book people are real and which simply visit her mind.

The cocktail party by phone had stopped. We went back in to find Colette needling roses into scrim. All the chairs in the tiny flat were upholstered with tapestry she had made herself. I did a few stitches in the piece, like wielding a crowbar, and wrote my name along the side while Colette leafed through an old botany book from the case behind her head to show me the watercolors and engravings she had taken for patterns. Nearly all the books in the shelf were about animals, flowers and natural history. Her fingers are so "green" that the pictures came alive, and grew. She designed gardens in passing a page, and scolded about pigeons being the symbol of faithful love, instead of ducks or wild geese. She was a little bit deafened from a cold and it was fun to tease her by talking very low to get the flash of defiance and pique which daggered at us, apprehensive of missing something, greedy for everything that went on.

She kept trying the switch of her bed reading-lamp in hopes the electricity might have come on, pouted because the letter which arrived didn't have the proofs of the illustrations she wanted to show me, and joined in a real lover's quarrel with her husband, after these twenty years of being married, when I asked for the details of his second disappearance, which was during the battle of Paris. Shortly after the occupation of Vichy France, they had returned to Paris where Maurice was put under arrest as a "non-Aryan." Colette traced him.

The first thing a friend or relative did when someone was "taken" under his own name was to make a quick tour of all the prisons in the Paris area with packages addressed to the victim. The prison management was usually sufficiently honest or else frightened of checkups on legitimate deliveries to refuse a package if the addressee was unregistered there. Once the prisoner was located, an assessment of the possible and probable charges could be made, and from then on the grapevine echo system would know where he had been transferred to on the next shift up or down the crime and punishment scales. Not that they were by any means parallel to each other, but would be better to delay escape measures if it was a "real" case, and weak, than to precipitate the reprisals and enforced hiding of other members of the family which would follow the "guilt proving" escape of an "innocent man".

She contacted everyone, high and low: so many people that even now no one knows who it was exactly who arranged his release. In any case, all efforts to free him met indifference until Colette showed herself as writing for the German controlled French press. She wrote innocuous nostalgic pieces which added nothing to German prestige. Paris understood and forgave.

There was nothing to do about his second disappearance. He just disappeared. There were battles raging all over Paris; she was bed-ridden and all the phone calls to all the grapevine friends availed nothing. Colette was quite frantic, imagining he'd been a last-minute snatch-hostage, that he'd fallen in the street fighting. He was simply lured by curiosity, and by a rumor that the Krauts had left, into going to the Tuileries – where the battle broke out again and he found himself in the garden, the enemy surrounding him and pinned down by fire from both sides. He ducked into an air-raid shelter which he shared with an old *clochard* for two days, eating the green tomatoes off the "dig for Hun victory" vines which were just within reach. There was an hour's truce in the firing during which he got home, safe and chastened, but Colette still upbraids him for worrying her.

I'd evidently brought up an uncongenial topic or else it was a favorite scene they like replaying. Her pointed elfin face was fifty years younger while she was haranguing. Peace and order were restored to the room. The photos went back into their portfolios; the precious cats together – not to be contaminated by human beings. All the souvenirs dispersed except a sheet of notepaper with embossed lace edges and colored cut-outs like an old-fashioned valentine, which she gave me – the holiday paper of her girlhood.

It had grown dark, the electricity wasn't on yet, the last glimmers of light were imprisoned in the crystals, in the irides-cent blue of captive framed butterflies and in the glistening whites of Colette's eyes.

Pauline said "Au revoir", so I knew I could come back.

CYNTHIA OZICK

Bloodshed and Three Novellas

from the Preface

What is the difference between a novel and a story or a novella? Not length (though some say length is the only difference), but maturation. The novel is long because it commences green and ignorant. The novel is long because it is a process, like chewing the apple of the Tree of Knowledge: it takes the novel a while before it discovers its human nakedness. The short forms are short because they begin with completion – with knowledge of nakedness. If the novella is the most captivating short form of all, it is because there is nothing more interesting than beginning with the end, nothing more mysterious than heading out to seek your fortune with your destination securely in your pocket. In the fairy tale, at the very outset of his journey, the Youngest Son receives from the magical crone an ordinary handkerchief – but spread it on the ground, and all manner of sweetmeats mob it. That is what the short forms do: you are in possession of your luck before you have gone half a mile.

Why is it perilous to say out loud that you aimed for a novel and were rewarded with a story? Someone is likely to argue, "Aha, see? You can *tell* that's a novel that got turned into a story," and that will be held against the writer, like the sin of transvestism. But you cannot make a novel out of a story, or a story out of a novel. What the novel requires is not length, but recognition. What the short forms require is not brevity, but realization.

VIRGINIA WOOLF

A Writer's Diary

Sunday, July 25th 1926

At first I thought it was Hardy, and it was the parlourmaid, a small thin girl, wearing a proper cap. She came in with silver cake stands and so on. Mrs Hardy talked to us about her dog. How long ought we to stay? Can Mr Hardy walk much etc. I asked, making conversation, as I knew one would have to. She has the large sad lack-lustre eyes of a childless woman: great docility and readiness, as if she had learnt her part; not great alacrity, but resignation, in welcoming more visitors; wears a sprigged voile dress, black shoes and a necklace. We can't go far now, she said, though we do walk every day, because our dog isn't able to walk far. He bites, she told us. She became more natural and animated about the dog, who is evidently the real centre of her thoughts – then the maid came in. Then again the door opened, more sprucely, and in trotted a little puffy-cheeked cheerful old man, with an atmosphere cheerful and business-like in addressing us, rather like an old doctor's or solicitor's, saying "Well now—" or words like that as he shook hands. He was dressed in rough grey with a striped tie. His nose has a joint in it and the end curves down. A round whitish face, the eyes now faded and rather watery, but the whole aspect cheerful and vigorous. He sat on a three-cornered chair (I am too jaded with all this coming and going to do more than gather facts) at a round table, where there were the cake stands and so on; a chocolate roll; what is called a good tea; but he only drank one cup, sitting on his three-cornered chair. He was extremely affable and aware of his duties. He did not let the talk stop or disdain making talk. He talked of father: said he had seen me, or it might have been my sister but he thought it was me, in my cradle. He had been to Hyde Park Place – oh, Gate was it. A very quiet street. That was why my father liked it. Odd to think that in all these years he had never been down there again. He went there

often. Your father took my novel – *Far From the Madding Crowd.*
We stood shoulder to shoulder against the British public about
certain matters dealt with in that novel. You may have heard.
Then he said how some other novel had fallen through that was to
appear – the parcel had been lost coming from France – not a very
likely thing to happen, as your father said – a big parcel of
manuscript; and he asked me to send my story. I think he broke
all the Cornhill laws – not to see the whole book; so I sent it in
chapter by chapter and was never late. Wonderful what youth is! I
had it in my head doubtless, but I never thought twice about it. It
came out every month. They were nervous, because of Miss
Thackeray I think. She said she became paralysed and could
not write a word directly she heard the press begin. I daresay
it was bad for a novel to appear like that. One begins to think what
is good for the magazine, not what is good for the novel.

"You think what makes a strong curtain," put in Mrs Hardy
jocularly. She was leaning upon the tea table, not eating – gazing
out.

Then we talked about manuscripts. Mrs Smith had found the
MS of *F. from the M.C.* in a drawer during the war and sold it for
the Red Cross. Now he has his MSS back and the printer rubs out
all the marks. But he wishes they would leave them as they prove
it genuine.

He puts his head down like some old pouter pigeon. He has a
very long head; and quizzical bright eyes, for in talk they grow
bright. He said when he was in the Strand 6 years ago he scarcely
knew where he was and he used to know it all intimately. He told
us that he used to buy second-hand books – nothing valuable – in
Wyck Street. Then he wondered why Great James Street should
be so narrow and Bedford Row so broad. He had often wondered
about that. At this rate, London would soon be unrecognizable.
But I shall never go there again. Mrs Hardy tried to persuade
him that it was an easy drive – only 6 hours or so. I asked if she
liked it, and she said Granville Barker had told her that when
she was in the nursing home she had "the time of her life". She
knew everyone in Dorchester but she thought there were more
interesting people in London. Had I often been to Siegfried's[1]

[1] Siegfried Sassoon.

flat? I said no. Then she asked about him and Morgan, said he was elusive, as if they enjoyed visits from him. I said I heard from Wells that Mr Hardy had been up to London to see an air raid. "What things they say!" he said. "It was my wife. There was an air raid one night when we stayed with Barrie. We just heard a little pop in the distance. The searchlights were beautiful. I thought if a bomb now were to fall on this flat how many writers would be lost." And he smiled, in his queer way, which is fresh and yet sarcastic a little: anyhow shrewd. Indeed, there was no trace to my thinking of the simple peasant. He seemed perfectly aware of everything; in no doubt or hesitation; having made up his mind; and being delivered of all his work, so that he was in no doubt about that either. He was not interested much in his novels, or in anybody's novels: took it all easily and naturally. "I never took long with them," he said. "The longest was *The Dinnasts* (so pronounced)." "But that was really three books," said Mrs Hardy. "Yes; and that took me six years; but not working all the time." "Can you write poetry regularly?" I asked (being beset with the desire to hear him say something about his books; but the dog kept cropping up. How he bit: how the inspector came out; how he was ill; and they could do nothing for him). "Would you mind if I let him in?" asked Mrs Hardy, and in came Wessex, a very tousled, rough brown and white mongrel; got to guard the house, so naturally he bites people, said Mrs. H. "Well, I don't know about that," said Hardy, perfectly natural, and not setting much stock by his poems either it seemed. "Did you write poems at the same time as your novels?" I asked. "No," he said. "I wrote a great many poems. I used to send them about, but they were always returned," he chuckled. "And in those days I believed in editors. Many were lost – all the fair copies were lost. But I found the notes and I wrote them from those. I was always finding them. I found one the other day; but I don't think I shall find any more.

"Siegfried took rooms near here and said he was going to work very hard, but he left soon.

"E. M. Forster takes a long time to produce anything – 7 years," he chuckled. All this made a great impression of the ease with which he did things. "I daresay *Far from the Madding Crowd* would have been a great deal better if I had written it differently," he said. But as if it could not be helped and did not matter.

He used to go to the Lushingtons in Kensington Square and saw my mother there. "She used to come in and out when I was talking to your father."

I wanted him to say one word about his writing before we left and could only ask which of his books he would have chosen if, like me, he had had to choose one to read in the train. I had taken the *Mayor of Casterbridge*. "That's being dramatized," put in Mrs Hardy, and then brought *Life's Little Ironies*.

"And did it hold your interest?" he asked. I stammered that I could not stop reading it, which was true, but sounded wrong. Anyhow, he was not going to be drawn and went off about giving a young lady a wedding present. "None of my books are fitted to be wedding presents," he said. "You must give Mrs Woolf one of your books," said Mrs Hardy, inevitably. "Yes I will. But I'm afraid only in the little thin paper edition," he said. I protested that it would be enough if he wrote his name (then was vaguely uncomfortable).

Then there was de la Mare. His last book of stories seemed to them such a pity. Hardy had liked some of his poems very much. People said he must be a sinister man to write such stories. But he is a very nice man – a very nice man indeed. He said to a friend who begged him not to give up poetry, "I'm afraid poetry is giving up me." The truth is he is a very kind man and sees anyone who wants to see him. He has 16 people for the day sometimes. "Do you think one can't write poetry if one sees people?" I asked. "One might be able to – I don't see why not. It's a question of physical strength," said Hardy. But clearly he preferred solitude himself. Always however he said something sensible and sincere, and thus made the obvious business of compliment-giving rather unpleasant. He seemed to be free of it all; very active minded; liking to describe people; not to talk in an abstract way; for example Col. Lawrence, bicycling with a broken arm "held like that" from Lincoln to Hardy, listened at the door to hear if there was anyone there. "I hope he won't commit suicide," said Mrs Hardy pensively, still leaning over the tea cups, gazing despondently. "He often says things like it, though he has never said quite that perhaps. But he has blue lines round his eyes. He calls himself Shaw in the army. No one is to know where he is. But it got into the papers." "He promised me not to go into the air," said Hardy. "My husband doesn't like anything to do with the air," said Mrs Hardy.

Now we began to look at the grandfather clock in the corner. We said we must go – tried to confess we were only down for the day. I forgot to say that he offered L. whisky and water, which struck me that he was competent as a host and in every way. So we got up and signed Mrs Hardy's visitors books; and Hardy took my *Life's Little Ironies* off and trotted back with it signed; and Woolf spelt Wolff, which I daresay had given him some anxiety. Then Wessex came in again. I asked if Hardy could stroke him. So he bent down and stroked him; like the master of the house. Wessex went on wheezing away.

There was not a trace anywhere of deference to editors, or respect for rank or extreme simplicity. What impressed me was his freedom, ease and vitality. He seemed very, "Great Victorian" doing the whole thing with a sweep of his hand (they are ordinary smallish, curled up hands, and setting no great stock by literature; but immensely interested in facts; incidents; and somehow, one could imagine, naturally swept off into imagining and creating without a thought of its being difficult or remarkable: becoming obsessed; and living in imagination. Mrs Hardy thrust his old grey hat into his hand and he trotted us out on to the road. "Where is that?" I asked him, pointing to a clump of trees on the down opposite, for his house is outside the town, with open country (rolling, massive downs, crowned with little tree coronets before and behind) and he said, with interest. "That is Weymouth. We see the lights at night – not the lights themselves, but the reflection of them." And so we left and he trotted in again.

Also I asked him if I might see the picture of Tess which Morgan had described, an old picture: whereupon he led me to an awful engraving of Tess coming into a room from a picture by Herkomer. "That was rather my idea of her," he said. But I said I had been told he had an old picture. "That's fiction," he said. "I used to see people now and then with a look of her."

Also Mrs Hardy said to me "Do you know Aldous Huxley?" I

said I did. They had been reading his book, which she thought "very clever". But Hardy could not remember it; said his wife had to read to him – his eyes were now so bad. "They've changed everything now," he said. "We used to think there was a beginning and a middle and an end. We believed in the Aristotelian theory. Now one of those stories came to an end with a woman going out of the room." He chuckled. But he no longer reads novels. The whole thing – literature, novels etc., all seemed to him an amusement far away too, scarcely to be taken seriously. Yet he had sympathy and pity for those still engaged in it. But what his secret interests and activities are – to what occupation he trotted off when we left him – I do not know. Small boys write to him from New Zealand and have to be answered. They bring out a "Hardy number" of a Japanese paper, which he produced. Talked too about Blunden. I think Mrs Hardy keeps him posted in the doings of the younger poets.

EDWIN MORGAN

More Questions than Answers

"Can acupuncture cure pins and needles?"
Can bumbledom regalvanize the beadles?
Can the fed hand bite back what it wheedles?

Improbabilities are *de rigueur*.
Hearts are primed to heat-seek, *alles Natur*.
Pass me the ashen light, *por favor*.

You make the story as you go you make
the story even if you go you take
the story on the go and watch it break.

So far this poem does not have a focus.
The wandering locum cannot keep his locus.
Lit, sweet, hand-rolled, we're passed to friends to smoke us.

The curtains nearly meet, the iron steams.
Reality, though straining at the seams,
may still press on, hunched there in the moonbeams.

All right that's it. Make a kirk or a mill o't.
You are not like to find nothing of note.
Buy a season and don't miss the boat.

Instructions to an Actor

Now, boy, remember this is the great scene.
You'll stand on a pedestal behind a curtain,
the curtain will be drawn, and then you don't move
for eighty lines; don't move, don't speak, don't breathe.
I'll stun them all out there, I'll scare them,
make them weep, but it depends on you.
I warn you eighty lines is a long time,
but you don't breathe, you're dead,
you're a dead queen, a statue,
you're dead as stone, new-carved,
new-painted and the paint not dry
– we'll get some red to keep your lip shining –
and you're a mature woman, you've got dignity,
some beauty still in middle age, and
you're kind and true, but you're dead,
your husband thinks you're dead,
the audience thinks you're dead,
and you don't breathe, boy, I say
you don't even blink for eighty lines,
if you blink you're out!
Fix your eye on something and keep watching it.
Practise when you get home. It can be done.
And you move at last – music's the cue.
When you hear a mysterious solemn jangle
of instruments, make yourself ready.
Five lines more, you can lift a hand.
It may tingle a bit, but lift it –
slow, slow –
O this is where I hit them
right between the eyes, I've got them now –
I'm making the dead walk –
you move a foot, slow, steady, down,
you guard your balance in case you're stiff,
you move, you step down, down from the pedestal,
control your skirt with one hand, the other hand
you now hold out –

O this will melt their hearts if nothing does –
to your husband who wronged you long ago
and hesitates in amazement
to believe you are alive.
Finally he embraces you, and there's nothing
I can give you to say, boy,
but you must show that you have forgiven him.
Forgiveness, that's the thing. It's like a second life.
I know you can do it. Right then, shall we try?

JOURNEYS

JOHN DONNE

The Good-Morrow

I wonder by my troth, what thou and I
Did, till we lov'd? were we not wean'd till then?
But suck'd on country pleasures, childishly?
Or snorted we i'the seven sleepers den?
'Twas so; But this, all pleasures fancies bee.
If ever any beauty I did see,
Which I desir'd, and got, 'twas but a dreame of thee.

And now good morrow to our waking soules,
Which watch not one another out of feare;
For love, all love of other sights controules,
And makes one little roome, an every where.
Let sea-discoverers to new worlds have gone,
Let Maps to others, worlds on worlds have showne,
Let us possesse our world, each hath one, and is one.

My face in thine eye, thine in mine appeares,
And true plaine hearts doe in the faces rest,
Where can we finde two better hemispheares
Without sharpe North, without declining West?
What ever dyes, was not mixt equally;
If our two loves be one, or thou and I
Love so alike, that none doe slacken, none can die.

JOY WILLIAMS

Lu-Lu

Heather was sitting with the Dunes, Don and Debbie, beside their swimming pool. The Dunes were old. Heather, who lived next door to the Dunes in a little rented house, was young and desperate. They were all suntanned and drinking gin and grapefruit juice, trying to do their best by the prolifically fruiting tree in the Dunes's back yard. The grape-fruits were organic, and pink inside. They shone prettily by the hundreds between leaves curled and bumpy and spotted from spider mite and aphid infestation.

Before Heather and the Dunes on a glass-topped table was the bottle of gin, two thirds gone, three grapefruits, and a hand juicer. The bottle had a picture of a little old lady on the label who gazed out at them sternly. Beneath the table, their knees were visible, Heather's young dimpled ones and the Dunes's knobby ones. The knees looked troubled, even baffled, beneath the glass.

"We could take her to Mexico," Don said. "Lu-Lu would love Mexico, I bet." He was wearing a dirty blue billed cap with a fish leaping on it.

"Not Baja, though," Debbie said. Her left arm was bandaged from where she'd burnt it on the stove. "Too many RVs there. All those old geezers with nothing better to do in their twilight years than to drive up and down Baja. They'd flatten Lu-Lu in a minute."

"I've heard that those volcanic islands off Bahia Los Angeles are full of snakes," Heather said.

The Dunes looked at her, shocked.

After a moment, Debbie said, "Lu-Lu wouldn't like that at all."

"She don't know any other snakes," Don added.

He poured more gin in all the glasses.

"Do you remember tequila, my dear?" he said to Debbie. He turned his old wrinkled face towards her.

"The beverage of Mexico," Debbie said solemnly.

"On the back of each label is a big black crow," Don said. "You can see it real good when the liquor's gone."

"The Mexicans are a morbid people," Debbie said.

"What I like best about snakes," Heather said, "is the way they move without seeming to. They *move*, but they seem to be moving in *place*. Then suddenly, they're *gone*." She snapped her fingers wetly.

"That's the thing you like best about 'em?" Don said morosely. "Better things than that to like."

Heather looked at her fingers. How did they get so damp, she wondered.

"We got inquiries as far away as San Diego, did we tell you?" Don said. "San Diego wants her real bad."

Debbie raised her chin high and shook her head back and forth. The stringy tendons in her neck trembled. "Never!" she said. "People would stare and make comments." She shuddered. "I can hear them!"

"She's got second sight, Debbie has," Don confided to Heather. "It don't use her as a vehicle much though."

Debbie had shut her eyes and was wobbling back and forth in her chair. "San Diego!" She groaned. "A cement floor. A room with nothing in it but Lu-Lu. Nothing! No pictures, no plants . . . and people staring at her through the glass. There's a little sign telling about her happy life here in Tampa and a little about her personality, but not much, and her dimensions and all . . . And I can see one big fat guy holding an ice-cream sandwich in one hand and a little girl by the other and he's saying, "Why that thing weighs fifteen pounds more than Daddy!" Debbie gave a little yelp and dug in her ears with her fingers.

"Second sight's no gift," Don said.

"We're so old," Debbie wailed.

Don tapped the elbow of her good arm solicitously and nodded at her drink.

"We're so old," Debbie said, taking a sip. "Can't take care of ourselves nor the ones we love."

"And Heather here is young," Don said. "Don't make no difference."

"We live in the wrong time, just like Lu-Lu," Debbie said.

"Lu-Lu should have lived in the Age of Reptiles," Heather said slowly. Speaking seemed to present certain problems. She looked at the stern old lady on the gin bottle.

"She would have loved it," Don said.

"Those were the days," Debbie said. "Days of doomed grandeur."

"You know what I was reading about the other day," Don said. "I was reading about the Neanderthals."

Debbie looked at Don proudly. Heather scratched her tanned shoulder. The sun beat down on the crooked part in her hair. Why has love eluded me, she wondered.

"They weren't us, I read. They were a whole different species. But we're the only species that are supposed to have souls, am I right? But the Neanderthals, it turned out, buried their dead Neanderthals with bits of food and flint chips and such, and even flowers. They found the graves."

"Now how could they know there were flowers?" Debbie said.

"I forget," Don said impatiently. "I'm seventy-six, I can't remember everything." He thought for a moment. "They got ways," he said.

Debbie Dune was silent. She smoothed the little skirt of her bathing suit.

"My point is that those things might not have had souls but they *thought* they had souls."

"That's a very pretty story," Heather said slowly.

The Dunes looked at her.

"The flowers and all," Heather said.

"I don't know what you're saying, Don," Debbie said politely.

"What I'm saying," Don said, "is who's to say what's got a soul and what hasn't."

"Another thing I like about snakes," Heather said, "is the way they can occupy themselves for long stretches of time doing nothing."

"I think," Debbie said, "that what it boils down to soul-wise is simple. If things cry, they got souls. If they don't, they don't."

"Lu-Lu don't cry," Don said.

"That's right," Debbie said pluckily.

"May I get some more ice?" Heather asked.

"Oh, that's a good idea, honey. Do get some more ice," Debbie said.

Heather stood up and carefully skirting the swimming pool, made her way into the kitchen. Lu-Lu was there, drinking from a pan of milk.

"Hello, Lu-Lu," Heather said. Deaf as a post, she thought.

She opened the freezer and took out a tray of ice. She looked inside the refrigerator. There was a dozen eggs and a box of shredded wheat. I should do something for these poor old people, Heather thought. Make them a quiche or something. She nibbled on a biscuit of shredded wheat and watched Lu-Lu drink her milk. Lu-Lu stared at her as she watched.

Heather walked outside. It was hot. The geraniums growing from Crisco cans looked peaked.

"Whoops," Debbie said. "I guess we need more gin now with all this ice."

"This is a difficult day for us," Don said. "It is a day of decision."

"The gin's right on the counter there beneath the emergency phone numbers," Debbie said.

Heather went back into the kitchen. Lu-Lu was still working away at shoveling the milk in.

"Lu-Lu's eating," Heather said, outside again.

"She don't eat much," Don said.

"No, she don't," Debbie said. "But she does like her rats. You know when she swallows a rat, she keeps it in her gullet for a while and that rat is fine. That rat's snug as if it were in its own little hole."

"That rat's oblivious," Don said. "That rat thinks it might even have escaped."

"Her gullet's like a comfy little waiting room to the chamber of horrors beyond it," Debbie said.

"You know in Mexico, in that big zoo in Mexico City, once a month they feed the boas and everybody turns out to watch. They feed 'em live chickens."

"*Such* a morbid people," Debbie said.

Heather looked across the Dunes's yard into the yard of her

little rented house. Her diaphanous nightie hung on the clothes-line, barely moving. Time to go, Heather thought. She sat in her chair, chewing on her sun-blistered lip.

Lu-Lu slithered toward them. She placed her spadelike head on Debbie's knee.

"Poor dear doesn't know what's going to happen next," Debbie said.

"We know neither the time nor the hour," Don said. "None of us." He peered through the glass-topped table at Lu-Lu. "Is she clouding up again?"

"She molted less than four months ago," Debbie said. "It's your eyes that are clouding up."

"She looks kind of milky to me," Don said.

"Don't you wish!" exclaimed Debbie. She winked at Heather. "Don gets the biggest kick out of Lu-Lu shedding her skin."

Don grinned shyly. He took off his billed cap and put it back on again.

"We got her skins hanging up in the lanai," Debbie said to Heather. "Have you seen them?"

Heather shook her head. They all three got up and lurched toward the lanai, a small screened room looking out over where they had been. Lu-Lu followed behind. There, thumb-tacked double-up to the mildewed ceiling were half a dozen chevron-patterned gray and papery skins rustling and clicking in the hot breeze.

"In order to do this really right, you'd need a taller room," Debbie said. "I've always wanted a nice tall room and I've never gotten one. With a nice tall room they could hang in all their glory."

"There's nothing prettier than Lu-Lu right after she molts," Don said. "She's so shiny and new!"

Heather went over to Lu-Lu's old skins. There were Lu-Lu's big empty mouth and eyes. Heather pushed her face closer and sniffed. The skins smelled salty, she thought. Then she thought that they couldn't possibly smell like anything that she could remember.

"They got a prettier sound than those tinny wind chimes," Don said. "Anybody can buy themselves one of those. What's the sense of it?"

"I almost called Lu-Lu Draco, but I'm glad I didn't," Debbie said.

"Draco would have been a big mistake all right," Don agreed.

"You'll never guess what Don used to be," Debbie said.

Heather felt sleepy and anxious at the same time. She took several tiny, restless steps.

"He was a pastry chef," Debbie said.

Heather looked at the Dunes. Never would she have imagined Don Dune to be a pastry chef.

The disclosure seemed to exhaust Debbie. Her good arm paddled through the air toward Don. "I have to go to bed now," she said.

"My dear," Don said, crooking his elbow gallantly in her direction.

Heather followed them into their small, brown bedroom. Everything was brown. It seemed cool and peaceful. Lu-Lu remained on the lanai, wrapped around a hassock.

Heather turned back the sheets and the Dunes crawled in, wearing their bathing suits.

"When I was a little girl," Debbie said, "nothing was more horrible to me than having to go to bed while it was still light."

Don took off his cap and patted his head. "Even my hair feels drunk," he said.

"I would like to take Lu-Lu and make a new life for myself," Heather announced. "I can't wait any longer."

"It's not good to wait too much," Don said.

The Dunes lay in bed, the dark sheets pulled up to their chins.

"If you go off with Lu-Lu, you've got to love her good, because Lu-Lu's got no way of showing she loves you back," Debbie said.

"Snakes ain't demonstrative as a rule," Don added. "They've got no obvious way of showing attachment."

"She'll be able to recognize your footsteps after awhile," Debbie said.

Heather was delighted.

"Will she get into my car, do you think?" Heather asked.

"Lu-Lu's a good rider," Debbie said. "A real good rider. I always wanted to drive her into a nice big desert, but I never did."

"We'll find a desert," Heather said with enthusiasm. She wouldn't wait a moment longer.

"Debbie don't think she's ever wanted much, but she has," Don said. He sighed.

"We'd better get started," Heather said. She smoothed the sheet and tucked it in under the mattress.

"Bless you, honey," Debbie said drowsily.

"Spoon a little jelly in Lu-Lu's milk sometimes," Don said. "She enjoys that."

Heather left the bedroom and hurried across the yard to her driveway. Her car stalled several times as she coaxed it across the two lawns toward the Dunes's swimming pool. She opened all the doors to the car, and then the doors to the Dunes's house. She was rushing all around inside herself. Lu-Lu stared fixedly at her from the lanai.

"Come, Lu-Lu!" Heather cried.

Already her own house looked as if it had been left for good. The nightie dangled on the clothesline. Leave it there, she thought. Ugly nightie with its yearnings. She wondered if Lu-Lu would want dirt for their trip. She found Don Dune's shovel and threw some earth into the back seat of the car. She didn't know how she was going to get Lu-Lu in. She sat on the hood of the car and stared at Lu-Lu. Dusk was growing into dark. How do you beckon to something like this, she wondered; something that can change everything, your life.

KATHERINE MANSFIELD

Journal

15 December 1919

All these two years I have been obsessed by the fear of death. This grew and grew and grew *gigantic*, and this it was that made me cling so, I think. Ten days ago it went, I care no more. It leaves me perfectly cold.

I must put down here a dream. The first night I was in bed here, i.e. after my first day in bed, I went to sleep. And suddenly I felt my whole body *breaking up*. It broke up with a violent shock – an earthquake – and it broke like glass. A long terrible shiver, you understand – and the spinal cord and the bones and every bit and particle quaking. It sounded in my ears – a low, confused din, and there was a sense of flashing greenish brilliance, like broken glass. When I woke up I thought there had been a violent earthquake. But all was still. It slowly dawned upon me – the conviction that in that dream I died. I shall go on living now – it may be for months, or for weeks or days or hours. Time is not. In that dream I died. The *spirit* that is the enemy of death and quakes so and is so tenacious was shaken out of me. I am (December 15, 1919) a dead woman, and *I don't care*. It might comfort others to know that one gives up caring; but they'd not believe any more than I did until it happened. And, oh, how strong was its hold upon me! How I *adored* life and *dreaded* death!

I'd like to write my books and spend some happy time with Jack (not very much faith withal) and see Lawrence in a sunny place and pick violets – all kinds of flowers. Oh, I'd like to do heaps of things, really. But I don't mind if I do not do them.

KATE ATKINSON

Unseen Translation

Αρτεμιν αειδω χρυσηλακατον, κελαδεινην,
παρθενον αιδοιην, ελαφηβολον ιωχεαιραν . . .

I sing of Artemis, whose shafts are of gold, who cheers on the
hounds, the pure maiden shooter of stags, who delights in
archery.

HOMERIC HYMN TO ARTEMIS

They had managed an entire afternoon in the Bird Gallery. From
egg to skeleton, from common to extinct, from flightless to free,
Missy and Arthur were on familiar terms with the avian world.

"Can we come back and do mammals tomorrow?" Arthur
asked.

"If you like. There are a lot of them though, remember. You
might want to subdivide them into categories."

"There were a lot of birds. We didn't subdivide them."

"True."

Missy believed that knowledge was best taken in small, diges-
tible portions. Museums and galleries, in her opinion, were full
of people wandering listlessly from exhibit to exhibit, their eyes
glazed over with too much information and not enough knowledge.

"It's an established neurological fact," Missy told Arthur
(Missy believed in using long words with children wherever
possible), "that window shopping and museums are the two most
tiring activities for the brain. A chronic insomniac could probably come into the Natural History Museum and fall asleep
before he'd got past the diplodocus in the Central Hall." Arthur
yawned.

"I've noticed you're very suggestible, Arthur."

"Is that bad?"

"No, it's a good thing, it makes my job much easier. Just make

sure it's me that you take suggestions from, not someone else."
The words "like your mother" remained unspoken, but understood, between them.

The Natural History Museum was closing, already echoing
with emptiness and a promise of the secret life it led when no one
was there. Missy imagined the birds shaking out their feathers
and shuffling from one stiff leg to the other, cracking neck bones
and easing off flight muscles. Diplodocus himself gave a little
tidal tremor along the vertebrae of his huge backbone as if
warming up for a leisurely evening stroll. They took no notice
of him. Missy never bothered her charges too much with dino-
saurs. She thought children (not to mention parents) were far too
obsessed with them already.

Outside, the threat of summer rain had darkened the South
Kensington sky to an otherworldly purple.

"Are we going home?" Arthur asked, rather indifferently.

"No, we're going to Patisserie Valerie for hot chocolate and
cake. Unless you don't like that idea."

"Ha, ha."

Missy and Arthur had spent Arthur's school holidays picking
and choosing from the capital's smorgasbord of culture. This
week, for example, had begun with a short visit to the British
Museum (where they spent most of their time admiring Jennings
Dog), followed on Tuesday by a Mozart String Quartet at the
Wigmore Hall, Wednesday was Shakespeare in the Park (*As You
Like It* – "Very good" in Arthur's opinion) and yesterday it had
been the eighteenth-century rooms of the National Gallery.
Missy was pleased to find that Arthur was able to spend almost
twenty minutes in near-silent contemplation of *Whistlejacket*. It
was at that moment, as they sat companionably together con-
sidering Stubbs's huge ideal of a horse ("Essence of horse,"
Missy whispered in Arthur's ear), that Missy knew for certain
that Arthur was a superior version of an eight-year-old boy.

Unfortunately, children were usually spoilt for life by the time
Missy got her hands on them. At two years old they had acquired
all the faults that would mar them for ever and Missy had to
spend most of her time rectifying their old bad habits rather than
instilling new good ones. Of course, that was why Missy was

called in. She had a reputation, like a Jesuitical troubleshooter, a Marine Corps Mary Poppins – when all else failed, call in Missy Clark. They expected her to drop in from the skies on the end of an umbrella, like a parachutist floating into a country in the middle of a civil war, and rescue their children from bad behaviour.

Missy was tiring of this phase of her life. She was even thinking of returning to nursing, although not to the hellish half-world of the NHS. She was considering applying to a private clinic somewhere, plastic surgery perhaps – somewhere where people weren't actually ill. If she was to remain in this job beyond the age of forty (she was thirty-eight – a difficult age) then she needed a completely blank canvas on which to practise her art. A tabula rasa, untouched by another's hand. A new baby. That was what Romney Wright had offered. A baby so untouched that it wasn't even born yet.

Missy was never interviewed by an employer, she interviewed them. Not that she was looking for the perfect family – years of experience had taught her there was no such thing. All she wanted was a family capable of reformation, and failing that, then just one child in the family who could be rescued from the fate which awaited it (ordinariness). Missy made it a rule never to stay anywhere longer than two years.

"Think of me as the SAS," she said brightly, when the hugely pregnant Romney had engaged her two weeks before the birth of her second child. Romney – sometime wife of a rock star, glamour model and ironic game-show guest, "now concentrating on her acting career", but mostly famous for being famous – forgot to mention the first child until Missy was dictating her non-negotiable terms and conditions (own bedroom, kitchen, bathroom and sitting room; own car; one and a half days off a week; no nights; full-time maternity nurses for the first three months; pension allowance). In fact, it was only by chance that Arthur wandered into the room at that moment and asked Romney if anyone was going to make his tea or should he heat up some baked beans? Missy was pleased at this – she liked to see a self-sufficient child and had nothing against baked beans.

"Oh, and, of course, this is Arthur," Romney said carelessly in a grating kind of East London accent that was already beginning to annoy Missy. Hadn't elocution lessons been on the curriculum at Romney's stage school?

Missy did actually know about Arthur's existence as she had checked out Romney's (entirely tabloid) cuttings file ("My love for my little boy", "My single-parent hell", and so on) before arriving at Romney's Primrose Hill house.

"This is the new nanny, Arthur," Romney said.

"Oh," Arthur said, raising surprised eyebrows. Missy liked a child who didn't speak when he had nothing to say.

"Missy," Missy said to Arthur.

"Missy?" Romney repeated thoughtfully. "What kind of a name is that?"

"A nickname my father gave me. It stuck."

"Right. Well, Arthur's called Arthur because his dad was into like Camelot and all that stuff."

"I think it's a very good name," Missy said, smiling encouragingly at Arthur.

"It's a bit old-fashioned though, isn't it?" Romney frowned. "I mean 'Arthur Wright' sounds like your grandad or something. But that was his dad all over, thought it was funny. His dad's Campbell Wright? Lead singer with Boak? Useless piece of Scottish string. Completely debauched, the lot of them." Romney pronounced "debauched" with relish as if it was only recently learned. Arthur, a solemn, bespectacled boy, said nothing. Missy had already looked up Boak on the internet. Romney was surprisingly accurate in her choice of vocabulary. Boak were debauched. In photographs they all wore Second World War gas masks, so it was impossible to see if Arthur looked like his father. He certainly didn't resemble his mother, at least not in any major particular, perhaps in the whorl of an ear, the oval of a nostril, nothing too relevant.

"What would you have called him?" Missy asked, intrigued by the idea that you could be the mother of a child and not name it.

"Zeus," Romney said, without hesitation.

"Zeus?"

"King of the gods," Romney explained helpfully. Arthur looked at Missy with absolutely no expression on his face. Missy liked a child who kept his own counsel.

"He wears glasses, of course." Romney sighed. "Arthur, not Zeus, obviously. When I was a kid," she carried on, when neither Arthur nor Missy had anything to add to this observation, "if you wore glasses you were like 'speccy four-eyes' or 'double-glazing' but now it's cool, like because of Harry Potter. And that kid in that Tom Cruise film. Or no, maybe not him, I don't think that kid was cool, was he? Of course, Campbell was very romantic then, now he's a wanker, but you should have seen our wedding – he planned it all himself – in a ruined castle, I rode over the drawbridge on a white horse and when we were pronounced man and wife – although it wasn't really a vicar, it was more of a shaman kind of bloke – they released butterflies, hundreds of butterflies, over our heads. It was really something, I never thought – "

Missy stood up abruptly, she could see that Romney was a talker. "I have to go now," she said. "When would you like me to start?"

"Tomorrow," Arthur said promptly. Missy was pleased to hear that he spoke a more civilized form of the English language than his mother.

"He's a funny one, isn't he?" Romney said, for no particular reason.

Missy allowed Arthur two cakes with his hot chocolate. She understood that sometimes one simply wasn't enough.

"What do you think she'll call the baby?" Arthur asked.

"Who are we talking about – the cat's mother? Wipe your fingers."

"You know who I mean. I bet it's something stupid."

Romney had been delivered of a baby girl the previous day and Missy and Arthur had visited her that morning in the hospital, in the private maternity wing that was like a five-star hotel. Romney had opted to be knocked unconscious and split open rather than give birth naturally. Missy favoured natural child-birth wherever possible. She thought it was character-forming for a child to have to fight its way into existence. Missy herself was a twin and had made sure she'd elbowed her way out first, ahead of her brother.

The father of Romney's baby was a multi-millionaire, Swiss-born financier who had led an impeccably boring life until a lifelong interest in West End musicals had led him to bankroll a doomed stage version of Charlotte Brontë's *Villette* in which Romney had a small and surprisingly naked part. In a moment of champagne-and-cocaine-fuelled incontinence at the opening night party, the Swiss financier had found himself in a backstage dressing-room toilet having frantic sex with Romney – a fact which he subsequently vehemently denied when it became tabloid knowledge. (" 'I am a love god!' Otto shouted in our steamy sex session.") Romney was now looking forward to the DNA tests to see just how wealthy Otto's seed would prove.

"I'm glad it's a girl," Arthur said, finishing off his second cake (both his chosen cakes had been chocolate). "I like girls. Do you know I used to have a male nanny once?"

"And? Was he all right?"

"So-so. He was Australian."

"How many nannies have you had, Arthur?"

"Five. I think."

"Why do they leave? Not because of you, you're not a difficult child."

"Thank you."

"What about the last one, my predecessor?"

Arthur shrugged.

"What does that mean? The shrugging?"

Arthur stood up and piled their dirty plates neatly. "We should go. The tube's going to be packed."

The rain held off as they walked to the underground. Missy thought it was important for a child to use public transport, to suffer dreary queues and biting winds. Even when working for the richest families she had made a point of hauling their children around the streets of London on buses and tubes and trains. She believed stoicism was a virtue that was badly in need of reviving.

They went into a newsagent's so that Missy could replenish essentials – she was never without Elastoplasts, safety pins, first-class stamps, tissues, extra-strong mints, Nurofen, cough sweets, Calpol, bottled water. The search for tissues led them past the newspaper and magazine racks which took up one wall. All of the top shelf was occupied by glossy girls presenting their buttocks or breasts to the camera.

"Difficult though it may be for you to believe, one day, sadly, you will probably find these images attractive," Missy told Arthur. "But for now you can buy a *Beano*."

Arthur wasn't listening. "Look," he said, pointing to the rack of tabloids beneath the naked women. Nearly every newspaper had a photograph of Romney Wright on the front, posing in her hospital bed – "Romney's bundle of joy", "Love-rat leaves Romney holding the baby", "Romney keeping mum about dad" (which was hardly true). Romney had managed to adopt a pose similar to the models in the pornographic magazines – her huge, milk-swollen breasts offered to the camera like gifts. The baby itself seemed incidental, almost invisible inside its shawl cocoon. Arthur skim-read the text. "They don't mention me," he said.

"That's a good thing."

"I know." Arthur gazed at the photographs of his mother as if she was an interesting stranger. "Do you think we'll like the baby?"

"What's not to like?"

Arthur gazed at his overexposed mother. Missy liked a wise child better than anyone but she considered the expression on Arthur's face to be knowledgeable well beyond his years.

"I realize you've already had far too much chocolate today and are probably as high as a kite, which is a technical term used by nannies, but, and against my better judgement, and you will rarely hear those words from my lips, Arthur, you can have a packet of chocolate buttons. Now come on, don't dawdle."

The baby was finally named. Romney toyed with a galaxy of goddesses ("Athene? Aphrodite? Artemis?") and gave up before reaching the end of the alphas.

"What did they do?" Arthur asked as they meandered ("from the river god Maeander, by the way") through the textile rooms of the V and A.

"Well," Missy said, "Athene was smug and thought she knew everything, Aphrodite was a troublemaker, and very irritating, I might add, and only Artemis had any sense."

"What did she do?"

"Virgin, close relationship with the moon, childbirth, wolves. Oh, and the chase."

"The chase?"

"Shot stags with silver arrows, that kind of thing."

Arthur looked horrified. "Shot stags?" he echoed ("from Echo – an unfortunate nymph. Show me one that isn't").

"It's a mythic thing, no stags were actually harmed during the . . . that kind of thing."

Romney had offered the choice of name to Arthur but reneged when he opted for "Jane", a name far too plain for Romney's tastes. In the end, she went for world geography. Romney's sister Johdi had a child called Africa and her friend Lily had a baby called India so Romney decided on China for Arthur's sister. "Like collecting countries," she said to Missy. "They'll be like NATO or something when they grow up."

"It could have been much worse," Missy said to Arthur. "Belgium, Luxemburg, New Zealand, Gibraltar, Uzbekistan. The list of worse is endless. That's not grammatical, by the way."

China, although in no way Chinese, was as delicate as porcelain with creamy skin and a rosy blush on her cheeks. She was more robust than her name implied but nevertheless received round-the-clock attention from a series of maternity nurses who themselves received round-the-clock attention from the nanny-cam in the nursery. Romney had a monitor in her bedroom so that she could watch the nurse watching her baby. Otto's DNA had finally been forced to own up as the culprit ("Kraut comes clean – 'China's mine' ") much to Romney's relief, although, "He wasn't a kraut," she said indignantly.

Autumn came. The Primrose Hill household was running smoothly – Romney was sated with money and sex, the sex in the stocky form of a soap star, Arthur was as happy as an eight-year-old boy can be at school ("OK, I suppose") and China was a dream of a child. Even the tabloid photographers had stopped camping on the doorstep and Missy was looking forward to the school break and some leaf-kicking time in London's parks with

Arthur and the baby, when Romney suddenly announced that Arthur was going to visit his father for half-term.

"They have joint custody," Arthur explained over a boiled-egg tea down in the huge basement kitchen.

"And when did you last see him?"

Arthur thought for a long time. "Two years ago, I think. You have to come with me," he added matter-of-factly.

"Why?"

"Because he's on tour."

"On tour?"

"Oh yeah, didn't I say?" Romney said when Missy questioned her. "Boak are in the middle of like this huge world tour, actually I think they're always on it. Arthur's going to visit him when they're in Germany. Flying into Munich, flying out of Hamburg at the end of the week. All the arrangements have been made by his publicist, you're going too. And I tell you what, I'm going to give you your own credit card. How's that? One more thing for the kraut to pay for."

"He's Swiss," Missy reminded her.

"Same difference," Romney said.

"What about my hamster?" Arthur asked Missy.

"We'll ask Africa to look after him."

"What about the baby?"

"It's only a week," Missy said, "and babies are almost indestructible, you know." Romney, however, decided not to look after China herself but to go on a "detox meditation" in the Cotswolds with her friend Lily while China went to stay with her maternal grandmother, who had, in Romney's words, "been dying to get a shot at her".

"So China will be fine," Missy reassured Arthur. "After all, your grandmother managed to bring your mother up." Arthur gave Missy the most beautifully blank look.

"You can be very enigmatic sometimes, Arthur," Missy said ("from the Greek *ainigma*, derived from *ainos* – fable").

If they were on their way to partake of Boak's debauchery, there was no indication of it in Lufthansa business class, which was so clean and grey and lacking in decadence that Arthur, a non-chalant traveller, managed to study the Collins German phrase book that Missy had bought him in an Oxfam shop prior to the trip ("Why buy new?" she said to Arthur, "when you can buy cheap?") while Missy herself read a book about astronomy that she had taken out from the library. Missy thought it was important to use libraries. ("Why buy at all when you can borrow?") She wasn't particularly interested in astronomy but she believed an important part of her job was to impart as much general knowledge as possible to her charges, because if not her, then who?

"Did you know," Missy asked Arthur, "that they can weigh galaxies?"

"Sie führen mich an," Arthur said, consulting his phrase book.

"I'm sorry?"

"You're pulling my leg," he laughed, pleased that he knew something that Missy didn't.

Missy and Arthur were in possession of an extraordinarily detailed itinerary for the German leg of Boak's tour, prepared by the band's publicist, a girl called Lulu, who, as well as providing flight times, driver details and hotel reservations, had also given two different mobile numbers on which she could be contacted. The itinerary also informed them that they were going to travel around Germany on Boak's tour bus.

"What will that be like?" Missy asked Arthur, as the plane bumped lightly onto the runway at Munich airport. Arthur frowned, carefully searching for the right word.

"Extreme," he said finally.

There was no car to collect them at the airport, as promised by Lulu, but Missy had changed sterling into Deutschmarks at

Heathrow and they caught a taxi to the hotel with the careless abandon of people on someone else's expenses.

The Bayerischer Hof had no record of any reservation. "Two rooms? In the name of Wright?" Missy persisted, showing the receptionist Lulu's careful itinerary. The receptionist regarded it politely as if it was a document from another civilization, far away in time and space, and beyond translation.

"Are Boak actually staying here?" Missy asked, wishing they weren't called such a stupid name. At first, the receptionist thought she was trying to say "book" and then "Björk". The smile on the receptionist's face grew stiff and tired. She called the manager.

"What does boak mean, anyway?" Missy asked Arthur as they waited.

"It's Scottish for sick."

"Ill sick or vomit sick?"

"Vomit sick."

The manager appeared, smiling sadly, and said that he very much regretted but the hotel never revealed details about its guests. It was growing late by now and Missy felt an uncharacteristic reluctance for battle. Arthur was sitting on their luggage, looking like a weary refugee, and Missy decided they would take a room anyway. She offered the brand-new gold credit card Romney had given her before they left. A few minutes later the hotel manager returned it to her and said in a low murmur that he was very sorry but the card was "not acceptable". He smiled even more sadly. Missy paid for the room on her own card.

"How much money do you have?" Arthur asked.

"Quite a lot actually," Missy said truthfully. "I've been saving for years."

"But you're not supposed to be paying."

"True. But it's only for one night. I expect your father'll turn up tomorrow."

"Das ist Pech," Arthur consoled.

The room was nice, although not the "luxury suite" promised by Lulu. The floors were clean and the sheets snappy with starch.

Missy ordered cheese omelettes and apfelstrudel on room service. After they had eaten she phoned both the mobile numbers that Lulu had provided. One was completely dead, the other announced something impenetrable in a German that was well beyond the capacity of the phrase book. Missy phoned Romney's Primrose Hill number but there was no answer. On Romney's mobile a voice announced that it might not be switched on.

They filled in their breakfast cards – Arthur found this very exciting – and then watched an incomprehensible game show on television that even if they had been fluent in German they probably wouldn't have understood. They went to their beds at nine o'clock German time, eight o'clock Primrose Hill time, and they both slept as soundly as babies until the maid hammered on the door with their breakfast, long after the dawn had scattered her yellow robes across the skies.

After breakfast, which Arthur liked almost as much as the ordering of it, Missy tried all the phone numbers she had tried the previous evening, with the same result. "Es sind schlechte Zeiten," Arthur said, leafing industriously through his phrase book. "Wie schade."

Missy went down to reception and looked the sadly smiling manager in the eye in the same way that she looked at little boys when she particularly wanted them to tell her the truth.

"If you were me," she said to him, "and think about this carefully, would you stay another night in this unbelievably expensive hotel and wait for the band known, unfortunately, as Boak to turn up?"

"No," he said, "I wouldn't."

"Thank you."

"Look at it this way," Missy said to Arthur. "Our flight from Hamburg isn't for another week, we have enough money – even if it's mine – and we are in one of the great cultural cities of Western Europe in the half-term holidays, so we may as well enjoy ourselves."

They moved into a guest house on Karlstrasse, although they returned several times to the Bayerischer Hof to check that Boak

hadn't suddenly materialized. "Hat jemand nach uns gefragt?"
Arthur asked the sad manager. No, he replied, in English, they
hadn't.

They trekked to the Olympiahalle and discovered a tour poster
slashed with a banner in large red capitals, declaring that Boak's
concert was "Entfällt".

"I think that means cancelled," Arthur said without bothering
to consult the German dictionary they'd bought ("Sometimes
you have no choice but to buy"). After that, they didn't bother
returning to the Bayerischer Hof. Lulu and Romney remained
unreachable by all means.

"Perhaps we're dead," Arthur suggested, "and we just don't
know it."

"I think that's a rather fanciful explanation," Missy said.

In accord with Missy's beliefs, they visited museums and
galleries in moderation – the Forum der Technik (but only
the Planetarium), the Deutsches Museum (but only the coal
mine), the Alte Pinakothek (but only pre-sixteenth-century
paintings). Arthur stayed awake for the whole of the BMW
museum – he wasn't an eight-year-old boy for nothing – but was
asleep on his feet within minutes of going into the Residenz-
Museum. The Frauenkirche and the Peterskirche had much the
same effect on both of them. An expedition to the Schloss
Nymphenburg might have been more of a success if it hadn't
rained so much. Their favourite museum exhibit was a chance
discovery, a stuffed creature, in the oddly named Jagd- und
Fischereimuseum ("Hunting and fishing," Arthur supplied
helpfully). The "Wolpertinger" was a curious Mitteleuropean
chimera, a mix of rabbit, stag and duck, plus something less
definable and more frightening. ("Distantly related to the rare
wolfkin," Missy said.)

"Bavarian primeval creature," Arthur read from the guide-
book the sad hotel manager had given them on their last visit to
the Bayerischer Hof.

In truth, neither of them was much in the mood for history and
culture and they spent a lot of time wandering in the Englischer
Garten or drinking hot chocolate. Every day at midday they went
and stood ritualistically in front of the glockenspiel on the Neues

Rathaus and watched for all the brightly coloured figures to make their rounds.

"What did happen to your last nanny?" Missy asked as they waited for the glockenspiel to start. Arthur made a pinched sort of face.

"What," Missy encouraged, "she was murdered? She killed herself, she came back as a ghost and wandered round a lake? Fell in love with the master who had a mad wife in the attic and who became hideously disfigured in a fire?"

"You're not supposed to talk like that to eight-year-olds."

"Sorry."

"She left."

"Left?"

"Left. She said she wouldn't leave and she did. And I liked her." Arthur stuck his hands in his pockets and angrily kicked an imaginary stone on the ground. "I liked her and she promised she wouldn't leave and she did. And you'll leave." His face began to quiver and he kicked the ground harder. His shoe was getting scuffed. Missy tried to touch the small shoulders, heaving with suppressed tears, but Arthur grew suddenly hysterical and shook her off.

"You'll leave just like she did," he screamed. "You'll leave me and I hate you! I hate you, I hate you, I hate you!"

"Arthur—"

"Shut up, shut up, shut up!" he yelled, so wound up now that he could hardly breathe, and several passers-by regarded with curiosity the small English boy struggling furiously to escape his mother's grip.

"It feels as though we've been away years," Arthur said when the cab dropped them off at Munich airport.

"I know."

"Do you think anyone's missed us?"

"Can you see the Lufthansa sales desk?"

"Over there."

Arthur, Missy was relieved to see, was quite calm today, although his eyes were still red from crying – he had sobbed for hours, long after Missy had got him back to the Karlstrasse guest house, long after she had put him to bed with milk and honey cake offered by the sympathetic proprietress. "Die Kinder," she sighed, as if to be a child was the worst thing in the world. Arthur had finally fallen asleep, flushed and tear-stained, clutching onto Missy's hand. "I don't hate you, you know," he said, with a grief-stricken hiccup. "I love you really."

"I love you too," she said, kissing the top of his head, "and I promise I won't leave you and I never break promises. Ever. You'll leave me one day, though," she added softly when Arthur was asleep.

They waited in the queue at the ticket sales desk. The airport was hot and incredibly busy. So many airlines, so many destinations. Arthur read them off the departure board: "Paris, Rome, Lisbon, New York, London Heathrow."

"I think we should have bought these tickets earlier," Missy said, looking uncharacteristically distracted. Arthur yawned extravagantly. "Ich langweile mich," he said. "At least I learnt some German."

"Yes, you've done very well, Arthur," Missy said vaguely.

"Are you all right?"

"Mm."

The Lufthansa sales clerk regarded Missy's request for two single tickets to Hamburg with solemnity. She would gladly sell her them, she said, but all the Hamburg flights were full until that evening, did she still want to go?

"How about London?" Missy asked.

"I can get you on the next flight to Heathrow," the sales clerk said, "but not sitting together."

"It will be quicker for us just to go straight home," Missy said to Arthur.

"Mm," Arthur said.

Missy thought about buying a ticket for London. She thought for rather a long time so that the sales clerk grew agitated because of the long queue snaking and coiling and knotting behind Arthur and Missy.

"Arthur," Missy said finally, "have you ever been to Rome?"

"I don't think so."

"I can get you on a connecting flight to Rome leaving in half an hour," the sales clerk said hopefully.

"A lot of museums in Rome," Arthur said.

"A lot," Missy agreed.

"And there are other places too," Arthur said.

"Oh, yes," Missy agreed, "there are many places. So many places that you need never come back to where you started from."

"Which was Primrose Hill," Arthur said. He tugged at Missy's hand. "What about China?"

"China?" the sales clerk asked, looking agitated.

"Don't panic," Missy said to her ("from the Great God Pan, now dead, thank goodness"). "I don't know about China," Missy said solemnly to Arthur. "I'm afraid her fate may be to stay with Romney."

"You're going to have to hurry," the sales clerk said, "the gate will be closing soon."

They ran. They ran so fast Arthur was sure they were going to take off before they even got on the plane. Missy pulled him along by the hand and when he looked at her feet her sensible leather boots had turned into silver sandals and he wondered if that was why they were able to run so fast. The airport tannoy stopped announcing that passengers for Düsseldorf should go to the gate and instead broadcast the rousing sound of a hunting horn. For a few dizzy seconds Arthur saw the quiver of silver arrows on Missy's back, gleaming with moonshine. He saw her green, wolfish eyes light up with amusement as she shouted, "Come on, Arthur, hurry up," while a pack of hounds bayed and boiled around her silver-sandalled feet, eager for the chase.

EDWARD THOMAS

Adlestrop

Yes. I remember Adlestrop –
The name, because one afternoon
Of heat the express-train drew up there
Unwontedly. It was late June.

The steam hissed. Some one cleared his throat.
No one left and no one came
On the bare platform. What I saw
Was Adlestrop – only the name

And willows, willow-herb, and grass,
And meadowsweet, and haycocks dry,
No whit less still and lonely fair
Than the high cloudlets in the sky.

And for that minute a blackbird sang
Close by, and round him, mistier,
Farther and farther, all the birds
Of Oxfordshire and Gloucestershire.

W.B. YEATS

The Song Of Wandering Aengus

I went out to the hazel wood,
Because a fire was in my head,
And cut and peeled a hazel wand,
And hooked a berry to a thread;
And when white moths were on the wing,
And moth-like stars were flickering out,
I dropped the berry in a stream
And caught a little silver trout.

When I had laid it on the floor
I went to blow the fire aflame,
But something rustled on the floor,
And some one called me by my name:
It had become a glimmering girl
With apple blossom in her hair
Who called me by my name and ran
And faded through the brightening air.

Though I am old with wandering
Through hollow lands and hilly lands,
I will find out where she has gone,
And kiss her lips and take her hands;
And walk among long dappled grass,
And pluck till time and times are done
The silver apples of the moon,
The golden apples of the sun.

JOSEPH ROTH

What I Saw: Reports from Berlin 1920–33

Passengers with Heavy Loads (1923)

Passengers with heavy loads take their place in the very last cars of our endless trains, alongside "Passengers with Dogs" and "War Invalids." The last car is the one that rattles around the most; its doors close badly, and its windows are not sealed, and are sometimes broken and stuffed with brown paper.

It's not chance but destiny that makes a person into a passenger with heavy baggage. War invalids were made by exploding shells, whose destructive effect was not calculation but such infinite randomness that it was bound to be destructive. To take a dog with us or not is an expression of personal freedom. But being a passenger with heavy baggage is a full-time occupation. Even without a load, he would still be a passenger with heavy baggage. He belongs to a particular type of human being – and the sign on the car window is less a piece of railway terminology than a philosophical definition.

Baggage cars are filled with a kind of dense atmosphere you could cut maybe with a saw, a freak of nature, a kind of gas in a state of aggregation. The smell is of cold pipe tobacco, damp wood, the cadavers of leaves, and the humus of autumn forests. What causes the smell are the bundles of wood belonging to the occupants, who have come straight from the forests, having escaped the shotguns of enthusiastic huntsmen, with the damp chill of the earth in their bones and on their boot soles. They are encrusted with green moss, as if they were pieces of old masonry. Their hands are cracked, their old fingers gouty and deformed, resembling peculiar gnarled roots. A few leaves have caught in the thin hair of an old woman – a funeral wreath of the cheapest kind. Swallows could make nests for themselves in the tangled beards of the old men. . . .

Passengers with heavy loads don't set down their forests when they themselves sit down. Having to pick up one's load again after a half hour in which one's spine has felt free for all eternity seems to weigh heavier than an entire pine forest. I know that with us soldiers, when a few minutes' rest beckoned after hours of marching, we didn't undo our packs but continued to drag them with us like a horribly loyal misfortune, or a foe to whom we were bound in an eternal alliance. That's how these old bundle carriers sit, not so much passengers with heavy loads, as heavy loads with passengers. And that also goes to demonstrate the fatefulness of carrying loads, that it's a condition rather than an activity. And what do the forest people talk about? They speak in half sentences and stunted sounds. They keep silent not from wisdom but from poverty. They reply hesitantly, because their brains work slowly, forming thoughts only gradually, and then burying them in silent depths no sooner than they are born. In the forests where their work is, there is a vast silence unbroken by idle chatter; there the only sound is that of a woodpecker attacking a branch. In the forests they have learned that words are useless, and only good for fools to waste their time on.

But in the scraps these people do say is expressed the sorrow of an entire world. They have only to say "butter," and right away you understand that butter is something very remote and inaccessible, not something you spread with a knife on a piece of bread, but a gift from heaven, where the good things of this world pile up as inaccessibly as in a shop window. They say: "Summer's early this year" – and that means that they'll be going out into the forests looking for snowdrops, that the children will be allowed out of bed to play in the street, and that their stoves can be left unheated till the autumn.

Actors, who relate their woes in many clever sentences and with much waving of hands and rolling of eyes – they should be made to ride in the cars for passengers with heavy loads, to learn that a slightly bent hand can hold in it the misery of all time, and that the quiver of an eyelid can be more moving than a whole evening full of crocodile tears. Perhaps they shouldn't be trained in drama schools but sent to work in the forests, to understand that their work is not speech but silence, not expression but *tacit* expression.

Evening comes, an overhead light goes on. Its illumination is oily and greasy; it burns in a haze like a star in a sea of fog. We ride past lit-up advertisements, past a world without burdens, commercial hymns to laundry soap, cigars, shoe polish, and bootlaces suddenly shine forth against the darkened sky. It's the time of day when the world goes to the theater, to experience human destinies on expensive stages, and riding in this train are the most sublime tragedies and tragic farces, the passengers with heavy loads.

Of all the labels and bits of jargon, the verbose or laconic edicts that regulate the bustle of a city, providing information and instructions, offering advice, and constituting law – of all the impersonal formulations in stations, waiting rooms, and the centers of life – this one is humane, artistic, epigrammatic, concealing and revealing its huge content.

The honest man who came up with "Passengers with Heavy Loads" for practical purposes can't have known that at the same time he found a title for a great drama.

This is how poetry is made.

Berliner Börsen-Courier, March 4, 1923

LAVINIA GREENLAW

The Falling City

I was eight, I was atmosphere,
more than willing to take to the air.
The world was locked and clear.

For a moment the glass forgave me,
curved like a hand that absolutely
loved me, let me down so gently.

LOUISE BROOKS

Lulu in Hollywood

I: Kansas to New York

The Brooks family were poor English farmers who came to America on a merchant ship at the end of the eighteenth century. They settled in the mountainous northeastern part of Tennessee. During the Civil War, they fought against the slaveholders who owned plantations in western Tennessee. In 1871, my great-grandfather John Brooks, with his son Martin and Martin's young family, journeyed by covered wagon a thousand miles across Tennessee, Arkansas, and the corner of Missouri to homestead in the southeastern part of the free state of Kansas. The government let them have one hundred and sixty acres of land near the village of Burden. There they built a log cabin, ten feet by twelve, in which all twelve members of the family had to live. The Pawnee and Cherokee Indians had already been driven into a reservation in the Oklahoma Territory, to the south, while the last of the Plains Indians were then fighting hopelessly against the United States Army and Cavalry, which soon swept their survivors west into Colorado. Furthermore, by 1875 the Indians' subsistence – the millions of buffalo – had been slaughtered by the white hunters. Thereafter, homesteaders poured in.

My father, Leonard Porter Brooks, who was the second of eight children, was born in 1868, before the family left Tennessee. He became a lawyer, and in 1904, at the age of thirty-six, married my mother, Myra Rude, who was nineteen. They moved to the little town of Cherryvale, Kansas, where Father worked for the Prairie Oil Company until it was gobbled up by John D. Rockefeller. Mother bore four children: Martin, in 1905; Louise, in 1906; Theodore, in 1912; and June, in 1914.

A small, black-haired man, quiet, cheerful, and energetic, my father had only two loves throughout his life – my mother and his law practice. He dreamed of becoming a United States district judge – an unrealizable dream, because his abhorrence of boozing, whoring, and profanity made him unacceptable to the rough politicians of his day. In 1919, we moved to Wichita, where my father had a general law practice and where a common joke was that "L. P. Brooks is so honest that his secretary makes more money than he does." However, when he was nearly eighty, his integrity was rewarded by his being made an assistant attorney general of the state of Kansas. He died in 1960, at the age of ninety-two.

My mother was born in Burden, Kansas, in 1884, to Mary and Thomas Rude, who was a country doctor. Because he was the only doctor for miles around, the villagers, though they were a puritanical lot, found it necessary to condone much in him that they would never have forgiven in others – drinking, smoking, swearing, and refusing to go to church. He delivered babies, set bones, and eased the pain of the dying with morphine. When the weather was good, he drove to see his patients in a horse-and-buggy. When the weather was bad, he rode horseback. And when the weather was very bad and the horse could not find its way in the snowdrifts, he went on foot. A few of the patients paid him with money, some with pigs or sacks of corn, many with nothing at all.

As the eldest of six children borne by a tiny, withdrawn mother who "enjoyed poor health," Myra Rude had been forced to sacrifice her girlhood to the care of what she called "squalling brats." When she married, she told Father that he was her escape to freedom and the arts, and that any squalling brats she produced could take care of themselves. And that is what happened. My mother pursued freedom by writing book reviews to present at her women's club, by delivering lectures on Wagner's *Ring*, and by playing the piano, at which she was extremely talented. When my older brother and I got into a fight, my father would retire to his lawbooks and violin on the third floor, and my mother, who had a sense of the absurd which almost always reduced crime and punishment to laughter, often simply laughed. She did, however, foster my dancing career. It began when I was ten; both my mother and I hoped I would become a serious dancer. From the time I was ten, when a Mrs. Buckpitt came eight miles by train from the town of Independence to the village of Cherryvale to give me dancing lessons, I was what amounted to a professional dancer. I danced at men's clubs, women's clubs, fairs, and various other gatherings in southeastern Kansas. I was given to temper tantrums, brought on by an unruly costume or a wrong dance tempo, but my mother, who was my costumer and pianist, bore them with professional calm. My father thought I had been mutilated when Mother, in the interests of improving my stage appearance, had a barber chop off my long black braids and shape what remained of my hair in a straight Dutch bob with bangs. He called my dancing career "just silly."

After we moved to Wichita, however, I studied dancing at the Wichita College of Music, with Alice Campbell, who also taught elocution, a fancy exercise in speech which permitted her – she was from Kansas City, Missouri – to express her disdain for the entire state of Kansas. (I later learned that every state in the Union, with the exception of Nebraska, felt disdain for Kansas.) In the twenties, Isadora Duncan, Ruth St. Denis, and Ted Shawn were just beginning to give a teachable form to serious American dance. For the rest, dancing teachers around the country taught the high kicks, splits, and cart-wheels of acrobatic dancing; or tap dancing; or a flabby imitation of the technique of the Russian ballet. Miss Campbell, her plump body uniformed in a starched white middy, pleated black serge bloomers, black hose, and ballet slippers, turned out her toes in the five positions, raised her legs in arabesques, pirouetted with ladylike care. Her regional superiority could not approximate my contempt for her brazen counterfeit of an art – revealed to all Wichita when the Pavley-Oukrainsky Ballet, of Chicago, appeared with the annual Wheat Show in 1920.

Here I must confess to a lifelong curse. In December, 1940, Scott Fitzgerald touched it when he wrote to his daughter, Scotty, "Zelda is tragically brilliant in all matters except that of central importance – she has failed as a social creature." On first meeting Ernest Hemingway, in 1925, Zelda called him "bogus." Hemingway retaliated by publicizing her as "crazy" and Scott as a destructive drunk, with the result that they were banished by their friends the Gerald Murphys and consequently by the rest of the social colony on the French Riviera. A year later, my friend Townsend Martin, a screenwriter at Paramount who had gone to Princeton with Fitzgerald, and who spent a part of each summer in Paris and Antibes, gave me my first insight into the herd mentality of high society.

Returning from France in 1926, he declared that the conduct of his previously adored Fitzgeralds "has become too outrageous," and went on to say, "Nobody sees them anymore." As for my own failure as a social creature, my mother did attempt to make me less openly critical of people's false faces. "Now, dear, try to be more popular," she told me. "Try not to make people so mad!" I would watch my mother, pretty and charming, as she laughed and made people feel clever and pleased with themselves, but I could not act that way. And so I have remained, in cruel pursuit of truth and excellence, an inhumane executioner of the bogus, an abomination to all but those few who have overcome their aversion to truth in order to free whatever is good in them.

Inevitably, the time came when Miss Campbell dismissed me from her dancing class, saying that I was spoiled, bad-tempered, and insulting. It was useless for Mother to plead, "Yes, Louise *is* hard on everyone, but she is *much* harder on herself"; Miss Campbell had borne the intensity of my critical stare for the last time. My 1921 diary records, "Although Mother has gone to everybody, weeping and telling the tale, it has left me with a curiously relieved feeling. I must study, and that means away to broader fields. I've had enough of teaching my teacher what to teach me." It didn't occur to Mother that her little monster had taken shape in her own happy home, where truth was never punished. Away from his law office and the courts, my father, a peaceable man, avoided litigation at home with his children. He, like my mother, often turned our naughty deeds into jokes. At the dinner table once, when Martin confessed to having thrown me down the steep back stairs, Father suggested that next time it would be safer to throw me down to the first landing of the U-shaped front stairs. My mother nearly always had more creative uses for her energy than disciplining children. One day, while she was seated at the piano, I ran to her to confess that I had just smashed a cup belonging to her best set of Haviland china. Without looking at me, she said, "Now, dear, don't bother me when I am memorizing Bach." Never having experienced the necessity for lying at home, I went into the world with an established habit of truthfulness, which has automatically eliminated from my life the boring sameness that must be experienced by liars. All lies are alike. My parents' resolute pursuit of their own interests also accounted for my own early autonomy and my later inability, when I went to work in the Hollywood film factories, to submit to slavery.

My father and mother were examples of excellence. In his attic office, filled with calfbound lawbooks, Father worked on his briefs. At the piano, Mother spent hours mastering the difficult timing of Debussy, a composer new to the prairie in 1920. It was by watching her face that I first recognized the joy of creative effort.

The unsolved mystery of my mother's character was why, although she was such a talented pianist, she never played as a soloist in public. She gave her Wagner lectures on *The Ring*; she gave her book reviews; she even played onstage for my dances. Yet never in her sixty years of life did she so much as appear in a piano recital on her own, nor did she ever offer any reason for obscuring her art. I can still see her, in 1931, inspecting the grand piano left behind by the band leader Paul Whiteman when he rented me his Hollywood house. "My goodness, Louise, there has been enough liquor spilled in this piano to set it afloat," she said. "It can't possibly be tuned." I would gladly have rented a decent piano if she had expressed a wish for one, but she did not, and she didn't complain about doing without one for the six months we lived in Whiteman's house.

Blacklisted by Miss Campbell, I was without a dancing teacher when, in November, 1921, Ted Shawn, assisted by Martha Graham, Betty May, and Charles Weidman, appeared in a dance recital at the Crawford Theatre. After the performance, Mother took me backstage to meet Mr. Shawn. He told us that he was on his way to open a dance school in New York, and that I should come there for the summer course in 1922. Although Father loved Mother as much as he loved his law practice, it took all winter and spring for her to wheedle him into providing the Denishawn tuition of three hundred dollars, and the expense money for my summer in New York. She finally overcame his strong objection to sending "a little fifteen-year-old girl away from home alone" by finding me a chaperon, Alice Mills, a stocky, bespectacled housewife of thirty-six who, having fallen idiotically in love with the beautiful Ted Shawn at first sight, decided to study dance with him. She agreed to accompany me on the train and live with me in New York.

So it was that in the summer of 1922 poor Mrs. Mills found herself next to my hot, restless body in a double bed in a rented room in a railroad flat in a building on Eighty-sixth Street near Riverside Drive. Denishawn classes were held in the basement of a church on Broadway near Seventy-second Street. Mr. Shawn's lessons consisted of demonstrations of his matchless balance and body control in such creations as his *Japanese Spear Dance* and his *Pose Plastique*. Charles Weidman, his most experienced male dancer, took us through barre and ballet exercises. During a sweltering July and August, I went to weekday classes from ten to twelve in the morning and from one to three in the afternoon. Even in the ballet work, we danced barefoot, which was painful for unaccustomed feet on the splintering pine floor. Having gone barefoot during Kansas summers, I was spared the torn soles and blisters that tormented some of the pupils. Sweat! Sweat! Sweat! Exhausted boys stood in pools of their own sweat. Unwashed black wool bathing suits stank with stale sweat. The only sweat-free, stink-free pupil was also the only New York pupil – a sweet, lonely fat girl, who stood around waiting for one of the three boys in the class to ask her out, which none of them ever did. Most of the students were females from the Middle West, to which, like my chaperon, Alice Mills, they would return to establish Denishawn schools. Kansas-born though I was, "these hicks," with their marcelled hair, their blouses and skirts, and their flat, unsyncopated voices describing the wonders of Grant's Tomb and the Statue of Liberty, filled me with scorn.

I tolerated Mrs. Mills' provincialism because she shared my love of the theatre. Together, we saw all the Broadway shows, one of them being a favorite of mine – the *Ziegfeld Follies*. In the first act, Fanny Brice's burlesque of Pavlova's swan dance filled the New Amsterdam Theatre with laughter. In the last act, standing motionless in front of a black velvet curtain, with black velvet sheathing her exquisite figure, she broke the audience's heart with her singing of "My Man." (Three years later, I would hear this art of transmitting emotion by phrasing alone echoed in the voice of Helen Morgan singing Gershwin's "The Man I Love.") The rest of my attention was concentrated on the famous *Follies* girls. I was not impressed. Only Anastasia Reilly, with her smooth dark hair and her boyish figure set off by a pageboy costume, showed personality, that faithfulness to nature which I sought, and still seek, in all human beings. The rest of the girls wore smiles as fixed as their towering feather headdresses. I decided right then that onstage I would never smile unless I felt like it. For inside the brat who sweated four hours a day at dancing school lived the secret bride of New York whose goal was the sophisticated grace of the lovely women already seen and studied in the pages of *Harper's Bazaar* and *Vanity Fair*. In Wichita, Mother had permitted me to subscribe to those expensive magazines – magazines that so infuriated my jealous brother Martin that he would tear them up and hide the scraps behind the bookcases in the living room.

Our house back in Wichita – a fourteen-room gray frame structure – was literally falling down with books. The foundation on the right side had sunk eleven inches from the weight of the lawbooks in Father's third-floor retreat. There were new books in the bedrooms, old books in the basement, and unread books in the living room; and in the library were the books I loved. Father's was basically an English Victorian library, stocked with Dickens, Thackeray, Tennyson, Carlyle, John Stuart Mill, and Darwin. Among the American authors were Emerson, Hawthorne, and Mark Twain. Goethe was the only foreign-language genius represented. All these books I read with delight, not caring in the least that I understood little of what I read. My passion for words was born when, at the age of five, I learned to read by looking over Mother's shoulder as she read *A Child's Garden of Verses* and *Alice in Wonderland* aloud. Mother herself laughed at literature. For her book reviews, she selected such books as *Nijinsky*, written by the dancer's wife, Romola. Its strange sexual overtones set up a pleasurable creaking of the respectable matrons' chairs. Behind their backs, putting on her club-member's face, Mother would coo unctuously, "Myra Brooks is *so* cultured."

Culture, I was to learn, was not a prerequisite for becoming a sophisticated New Yorker. It was, in fact, a handicap. The rich men who before long were exhibiting me in fashionable restaurants, theatres, and nightclubs shrank like truant schoolboys from the name of Shakespeare, and they looked upon an evening spent at the Metropolitan Opera or at a concert in Carnegie Hall as unthinkable misery. Since I could not gossip about these socialites' families and friends, did not feel secure discussing the theatre and movies, and detested the vulgar game of dirty jokes and sexual innuendos, I talked scarcely at all. Years later, the dress designer Travis Banton told me that in 1925, at the Colony – the grandest restaurant in town – he watched from another table and put me in the category of "beautiful but dumb," where I remained to the end of my film career.

In 1922, then, if I was to create my dream woman, I had to get rid of my Kansas accent, to learn the etiquette of the social élite, and to learn to dress beautifully. I could not correct my speech at a fashionable girls' school. I could not learn table manners from escorts embarrassed by my social inferiority. I could not afford Fifth Avenue couturiers. Therefore, I went for my education directly to the unknown people who were experts in such matters – the people at the bottom whose services supported the enchantment at the top of New York. My English instructor was a fresh, contemptuous soda jerk at a Broadway drugstore where I went for fudge sundaes. Because he was working his way through Columbia University, because he spoke excellent English and had a fine ear for my accent, which he mimicked, I refused to let him drive me away in anger. I did not possess the appeal of a child star, but I possessed a more powerful attraction: a pupil's total attention. Nobody can learn to dance without complete attention and sustained concentration on the disposition of the head, neck, trunk, arms, legs, and feet – on the use of every muscle of the body as it moves before the eyes with the speed of motion-picture film. And not even an unwilling teacher can resist the flattery of extraordinarily close attention. One day, when the soda jerk was making the customers at the fountain laugh with a story about "mulking a kee-yow," I stopped him, saying, "Instead of making fun of me, why don't you teach me how to say it?" While he was concocting a banana split, he began to smile at the fancy of becoming my Pygmalion, and before I finished my fudge sundae our lessons had begun. "Mulk" became "milk," and "kee-yow" became "cow." Then: "Not 'watter' as in 'hotter' but 'water' as in 'daughter.' And it's not 'hep,' you hayseed – it's 'help,' 'help,' 'help'!" Within a month of fudge sundaes, this boy had picked his way through my vocabulary, eliminating the last trace of my hated Kansas accent. From the start, it had been my intention not to exchange one label for another. I didn't want to speak the affected London stage-English of the high-comedy stars, like Ina Claire and Ruth Chatterton; I wanted to speak clean, unlabeled English. My soda jerk spoke clean, unlabeled English. Mother had already lowered my childish squeals to a pleasant middle range, making me forever aware of the voice as a manipulative power.

I went on tour with Ruth St. Denis, Ted Shawn, and the Denishawn Dancers for the 1922–23 season, after which I attended a Denishawn summer school at Mariarden, a summer-theatre-school-camp near Peterborough, New Hampshire. There I became a friend of Barbara Bennett, the seventeen-year-old daughter of Richard Bennett, the famous actor. In September, when we returned to New York – Barbara to her home, I to rehearse for a second season on tour – she introduced me to the Wall Street brokers who would take me to dine at the Colony. And there I, who in Kansas had never seen a lobster, was terrorized by a bright-red lobster, which I sent away uneaten. When I questioned Barbara about lobsters, she said, "You just mess them around in butter and eat them, silly." At the Forty-second Street Public Library, after an unsuccessful hour with Emily Post's *Etiquette*, I read an advertisement in a magazine for Nelson Doubleday's *Book of Etiquette* which exactly described my plight. It showed a girl staring wild-eyed at a menu and said, "Across the table her escort smiles at her, proud of her prettiness, glad to notice that others admire, then, with surprise, he gives the waiter her order for a chicken salad. This was the third time she had ordered chicken salad while dining with him. He would think she didn't know how to order a dinner, didn't know how to pronounce those French words on the menu, didn't know how to use the table appointments as gracefully as she would have liked. Well, did she? No." That book taught me nothing, either. Evidently, I had to learn by direct contact with my instructor.

A few nights later, when I was sawing away at a squab at the Colony, it scooted off my plate. One of the captains, Ernest, whisked it away and returned with a fresh squab, which I watched him carve on the service table. From then on, indifferent to the reactions of my dinner partners, I took instructions from the waiters on how to eat everything on the menu. There was how-to-bone-a-brook-trout night, how-to-fork-snails night, how-to-dismember-artichokes night, and so on, until we came to the bottom of the menu, which included a dessert of the understanding and proper pronunciation of French words. At the dinner following my graduation, I announced to Ernest that I was at last going to order a dish I truly liked – creamed chipped beef. He sent a busboy to a Madison Avenue delicatessen for a jar of chipped beef, which was transformed into the most delicious chipped-beef-in-cream-on-toast I would ever eat.

Mrs. Bennett, the actress Adrienne Morrison, had sent Barbara to Mariarden in the hope that exercise would strengthen her long, flat feet and her long, slim legs. She shared a cabin with me and two other girls, with whom she never became friendly. She became my friend because my strange customs made her laugh. In the dining hall, she sat next to me at one of a row of long tables upon which were served what she referred to as "those disgusting country breakfasts." After several mornings of sipping coffee, nibbling toast, and watching me devour big slabs of apple pie, she began our friendship by smiling at me and saying, "Hello, Pie Face." From then on, I participated in her efforts to inject some excitement into her bored existence. Defying the nine-o'clock lights-out regulation, she invited Peterborough boys to our cabin. They brought us cigarettes and applejack. In return, although she permitted no sexual liberties, Barbara entertained the boys with an enviable collection of dirty songs and limericks. I can still remember every word of:

> In Fairy Town,
> In Fairy Town,
> They don't go up,
> They all go down.
> Even the chief of police is queer.
> Oophs, my dear,
> Listen here,
> The elevator's there they say.
> They don't go up,

Just the other way.
Holy Bejesus,
There's lots of paresis
In Fairy Town.

As she became aware of my dangerous ignorance of sexual matters and my offensive social behavior, Barbara, for perhaps the only time in her passionate, reckless life, exerted herself in another's behalf: she faced down family and friends in order to protect and instruct "that obnoxious little Brooks girl." My education in the art of dress did not begin until I returned to New York in September. Denishawn rehearsals left me plenty of time to visit the Bennett apartment on Park Avenue. One morning, the apartment door was opened by Mrs. Bennett. She looked at me as if I were a stray dog, and said, "What are you doing here at eight o'clock in the morning?" I began to cry, so she let me in and left me on a sofa, waiting for Barbara to wake up. In a gray wrapper, without makeup, how worn and unhappy Mrs. Bennett looked. Not a bit like her elegant fashion photographs in *Vogue*. And this beautiful living room was her creation – all white with dark touches, uncluttered, like a Chinese painting. It bore no resemblance to the usual crowded rooms of the rich, which repelled me. Yet, like Mrs. Bennett, the room had the look of something uncared-for and unloved.

After a while, Barbara's beautiful younger sister, Joan, came in with her schoolbooks to study at the secretary by the window. Barbara's beautiful older sister, Constance, had just started her career, but her reputation as the best-dressed and haughtiest actress in movies was already established. All the girls had Richard Bennett's wide cheekbones and finely set eyes, but in character the three daughters did not resemble one another in any way. Constance loved money. During a career that continued to the year of her death, in 1965, she demanded and received a salary equal to that of the top stars. Yet beauty, great acting ability, and a lovely voice could not compensate for the lack of the one attribute without which the rest did not matter: she did not have that generosity, that love for her audience, which makes a true star. What Joan loved was security. Her marriages to men powerful in films guaranteed a successful career. Barbara made a career of her emotions. Periods of work or marriage were terminated by her frightening, abandoned laughter of despair and failure. Only her death, in 1958, achieved in her fifth suicide attempt, could be termed a success. In the dusty white living room, Joan, who was always kind to me, was putting on her glasses to study her history book. "What I can't figure out," I said, "is how, if you can't see without your glasses, you get around without them." Joan took them off and smiled at me. "I can see something without them. For instance, your long black dress. Where did you get that funny, old-lady's dress?"

"A woman in a shop on Broadway sold it to me."

Joan laughed.

At eleven, we heard sounds of rising Bennetts. We heard Constance raging at Barbara: "If you dare to sneak out once more in my white chiffon, I am going to slit your throat." We heard Richard Bennett singing, "I love life and I want to live," followed by his entrance in a blue brocade dressing gown for a trip to the liquor cabinet. After tossing down a glass of whiskey, he turned to me, saying, "My God, Joan, where did you get that damned black dress?" Between liquor and his poor eyesight, he sometimes confused me with Joan, who had not yet changed her dark hair to blond. (Mine was black.) He had returned to his room when Constance, dressed in a perfectly tailored suit of navy blue, flew across the living room and out the front door, leaving behind the perfume of gardenias and a dirty look cast in my direction. (Among the Hollywood detestables, even I was no match for Constance, who could sit across from me at the dinner table in Marion Davies' beach house and never acknowledge my existence with so much as an icy nod.) Barbara finally appeared, wearing Constance's beige gabardine suit. We lunched on chocolate milkshakes at a drugstore, after which she took me to the smart hairdressing shop of Saveli, where Saveli himself attended to my hair. He shortened my bangs to a line above my eyebrows, shaped the sides in points at my cheekbones, and shingled the back of my head. Barbara was pleased. "As a mat-tra-fact, Pie Face," she said, "you are beginning to look almost human."

It was then that Barbara introduced me to a group of Wall Street men who made it possible for me to buy expensive clothes. These most eligible bachelors in their thirties, finding débutantes a threat, turned to pretty girls in the theatre, whose mothers weren't husband-hunting. Café society developed about this time. The theatre, Hollywood, and society mingled in the monthly Mayfair dances at the Ritz, where society women could monitor their theatrical enemies and snub them publicly. All the rich men were friends who entertained one another in their perfectly appointed Park Avenue apartments and Long Island homes. The extravagant sums given to the girls for clothes were part of the fun – part of competing to see whose girl would win the Best-Dressed title. Sexual submission was not a condition of this arrangement, although many affairs grew out of it. For a time, Barbara was kept by William Rhinelander Stewart, who gave her a square-cut emerald from Cartier. One night, when we were swimming off Caleb Bragg's houseboat, the *Masquerader*, she watched it slip off her finger into Long Island Sound. She kept this hilarious accident secret from Stewart by buying a fake-emerald ring from Denis Smith, whose jewelry business was unknown to innocent lovers. They would have been staggered to learn how many of their gifts were converted into imitations and cash. Truly, ours was a heartless racket. After receiving an ermine coat from Jaeckel's, the gift of a stockbroker named John Lock, I let him take me just once to a tea dance at the Biltmore Hotel.

In 1924, shopping on my own proved fatal. I would buy anything a persuasive salesgirl thrust upon me. A childish short pink dress was responsible for getting me thrown out of the Algonquin Hotel. In May, when the Denishawn tour ended, Barbara stuffed me into that hotel because, she said, "you will meet influential people at the Algonquin, and you don't want to spend the rest of your life on tour, washing and pressing costumes." I didn't give a damn about influential people, and I hated my dark little room, with its old-fashioned brass bedstead. The owner of the Algonquin was Frank Case, a tall, thin middle-aged man, who spent much of his time in the lobby among his guests. One afternoon, as I stepped out of the elevator, I found him waiting for me.

"How old are you, Miss Brooks?" Mr. Case asked.

"Seventeen," I said.

"Are you sure you aren't fourteen?"

"Yes."

"Does your family know you are here?"

"Yes."

"Well," said Mr. Case, walking me away from the elevator, "George Cohan just phoned to tell me that last night he came down in the elevator with a fourteen-year-old black-haired girl in a little pink dress. Where were you going at two o'clock in the morning?"

"To meet Barbara Bennett at Texas Guinan's – the El Fay Club."

"Well," said Mr. Case again, frowning down at me, "you are creating a scandal in the hotel which must stop. I have arranged for you to move to the Martha Washington, a respectable women's hotel on East Twenty-ninth Street, where you will be much better off. When can you move?"

"Right now," I said.

I felt disgusted with myself as I packed my trunk. This humiliating eviction could not have taken place if I'd been wearing a fashionable slinky dress and a hat.

The atmosphere of the Martha Washington Hotel was institutional. The women wore short hair, suits, and sensible shoes, and worked, I assumed, in offices. Two weeks after I had been assigned a cell under the roof, I went into the grim, nearly empty dining room for tea. To my amazement, sitting alone at a large table was the exotic star of the film *Java Head*, Jetta Goudal. While I ate a ham sandwich and drank iced tea, I watched her welcome to her table a group of girls, some of them bringing gifts. She was particularly pleased with a handmade shawl of white wool, which she threw over her shoulders.

"Does Jetta Goudal *live* here?" I asked my waitress.

"Yes, Miss."

"Is this her birthday?"

"No, Miss, this happens once a month. Those girls are her fans."

Before I could investigate Jetta Goudal's tea parties any further, I was asked to leave the Martha Washington, because people in a building overlooking the hotel had been shocked to see me on the roof, exercising in "flimsy pajamas." Within a month, my wearing apparel had got me kicked out of two hotels.

On my own this time, I moved to the Wentworth, an unpretentious theatrical hotel on West Forty-sixth Street.

My dress problem had become acute. I couldn't trust ordinary salesgirls, and the clothes that suited the slim, long-legged Bennetts looked dreadful on my short, dancer's body. One night, I saw in a theatre program a photograph of Marilyn Miller, the Ziegfeld star, posed in a stunning evening gown from Milgrim, a fashionable store then on Broadway at Seventy-fourth Street. The next morning, I took five hundred dollars in cash to Milgrim's and handed it to Miss Rita, a salesgirl from the Bronx, who had never before been exposed to such a straightforward confession of ignorance in dress. Neither she nor I could guess that in 1926 my photograph would advertise Milgrim in theatre programs, but she did sense an extraordinary intensity in one who appeared to be a chorus girl with a windfall. She studied my face, my figure, my movements closely, while I looked at the models showing evening clothes. After I had seen them all, she selected for me an evening gown of white crystal bugle beads, and a silver cloth evening coat with a white fox collar. When I came for my first fitting, I met an exuberant Italian woman, who, because I had small, firm breasts, slashed my evening gowns almost to the navel. My back she left bare. Sitting at a restaurant or nightclub table, I was a nearly naked sight to behold. Miss Rita chose my afternoon dresses in pastel shades of satin and silk crêpes. My suits were severely tailored by Gus, who stuck pins in me when I didn't stand still. At last, my beloved New York was able to present a Louise Brooks who was neither Kansas nor Broadway nor Hollywood nor Park Avenue but uniquely herself. Late in 1924, I became a chorus girl in *George White's Scandals*, and the next year a specialty dancer in the *Ziegfeld Follies*.

By 1925, I was living at the Marguery, an apartment hotel on Park Avenue at Forty-seventh Street, in a large room that looked down on three fine spruce trees crooning peacefully in the courtyard. That same John Lock who had given me the ermine coat had also given me a riding outfit and a course of riding lessons at Durland's Riding Academy, on Seventy-ninth Street. My riding master, Hugo, had been the groom of a German cavalry officer. He was small and compact, made for a commanding seat on a horse. My seat was so bad that he considered it a miracle every time the quiet little mare named Beauty carried me safely across Central Park West onto the bridle path in Central Park. On a mild morning in December, as we turned uptown on the bridle path, I presented to Hugo my weekly gift of a pint of brandy. Next to being separated from horses, his greatest fear was that of being separated from liquor in our land of Prohibition and thus finding himself hideously sober. For some horsy reason, Beauty, on that occasion, used our customary brandy ceremony as an excuse to run away. Instead of racing to save me, Hugo trotted behind, laughing his head off, and left my rescue to two mounted policemen, who galloped up on either side of me, snatched the reins from my hands, and brought Beauty to a halt.

Later that morning, while a woman named Mrs. Gard gave me my weekly massage, I laughed with her about my poor horsemanship and Hugo's unchivalrous conduct. She was one of the few people who loved me. And, oddly, I loved her, too. I loved her corpulent figure, in its tight black coat, and her kind, red Irish face under the old-fashioned hat decorated with a bird wing. I loved the tenderness with which she "cracked" my neck, almost snapping my head off, and her concern with my too-short shoes, which were "growing horns" on my heels. I could never get her to gossip about her famous clients – for instance, Mrs. William Randolph Hearst, whose husband was living openly with the movie star Marion Davies. But then neither did Mrs. Gard express her sorrow for my careless disposal of the body over which she sweated, contributing to its seductiveness. Nevertheless, I could hear it in her voice as she asked about a new beaver coat flung in a chair. "Oh, that," I said. "Walter Wanger sent it to me." A good Catholic, she knew that Walter was a married man. At that time, I was portraying a bathing beauty in *The American Venus*, a film that was being shot at Famous Players-Lasky's Long Island studio in Astoria, and Wanger was an executive in the Famous Players-Lasky (later to become Paramount) New York office, where I had recently signed a five-year contract.

One day, Mrs. Gard had just left me smelling of camphor oil and sitting in bed in a woolly bathrobe when the phone rang announcing the arrival of Ruth Waterbury, a staff writer on the

magazine *Photoplay*. The publicity department of the Paramount
New York office gave me no guidance in dealing with the press. I
got along well enough with the New York journalists I knew as a
chorus girl. But I could see I was in trouble the moment Ruth
Waterbury, from Hollywood, entered my room, because she
looked greatly surprised and greatly displeased to find me in
bed. She had obviously expected me to take her to lunch at the
chic Marguery Restaurant. I couldn't ask her to wait while I
bathed and dressed, so I asked whether she would like lunch
served in my room. She said something about not being hungry,
pulled a chair close to the bed, sat down, and removed a pad and
pencil from her hand-bag. Possessing that precious quality of
youth – indifference to the censure of those whom one did not
admire – I found my composure equal to an hour of Miss Waterbury's hostility. Her method of interviewing me was to recount
the publicity office's story of my "sudden success," expecting to
be able to write that I responded with rapture about going to
Hollywood. Her notetaking stopped when she discovered that I
was not overwhelmed by the magic of Hollywood, and that I
hadn't wanted to leave Ziegfeld but had let the screen-writer
Townsend Martin persuade me to play a part in his film *The
American Venus*. Whereas she looked upon me as a stupid
"chorus girl" who didn't appreciate her astonishing good luck,
I looked upon her as artistically retarded not to know that ten
years of professional dancing was the best possible preparation
for "moving" pictures. She told me how wonderful it was to go
from a small part in *The American Venus* to the lead opposite the
great star Adolphe Menjou in *A Social Celebrity*, directed by the
boy genius of high comedy Malcolm St. Clair. I asked her if she
had ever seen Ruth St. Denis and Ted Shawn dance, or if she had
heard of Martha Graham's sensational success in the *Greenwich
Village Follies*. She had not. I didn't realize then that this small
cultural conflict with Ruth Waterbury was merely the first
instance of the kind of contempt that was destined to drive
me out of Hollywood.

LIZ LOCHHEAD

On Midsummer Common

On midsummer common
it's too good to be true
backdrop of cricketers
punts on the river
the champ of horses
and mayflies in June
mere midsummer commonplace.

Not in midsummer,
but with the real rain of more normal weather
putting a different slant on things,
my hard edged steel town
seen through the blur of bus windows.
Saturday afternoon streets crammed
with shoppers under leaden skies.
Out of the constant comedown of the rain, old men
in the final comedown of old age
file into public libraries to turn no pages.
Saturday. My town
can't contain itself.
Roars rise and fall
stadiums spill
football crowds in columns
in the teeming rain.
Saturday buses are jampacked with football rowdies
all going over the score.
I am overlapped by all the fat and laughing losers
that pour from bingo parlours.
Outside cinemas, steadies
queue steadily to buy
their darkness by the square foot.
The palais and troc are choc-full

of gaudy girls dressed parrot fashion.
Saturday's all
social clubs, singers, swilled ale.
So much is spilt—
the steel clang, the clash of creeds,
the overflow of shouts and songs,
the sprawl of litter,
the seep of smells,
the sweat, the vinegar, the beer—
so much slops
into that night nothing goes gentle into,
not even rain.
such a town
I feel at home to be at odds with.

Here on midsummer common
on a midsummer Saturday
you, this day, this place and I
are just exchanging pleasantries.
Oh, it's nice here, but
slagheaps and steelworks
hem my horizons
and something compels
me forge my ironies from a steel town.

A. M. HOMES

Remedy

It is about wanting and need, wanting and need – a peculiar, desperate kind of need, needing to get what you never got, wanting it still, wanting it all the more, nonetheless. It is about a profound desire for connection. It is about how much we don't know, how much we can't say, what we don't understand. It is about how unfamiliar even the familiar can become.

It is about holding one's breath, holding the breath until you are blue in the face, holding the breath to threaten, to dare, to say if you do not give me what I want, I will stop breathing. It is about holding back, withholding. It is about being stuck. It is about panic. It is about realizing you are in over your head, something's got to give. It is about things falling apart. It is about fracture.

It is afternoon, just after lunch. She starts dialing. She dials, knowing no one is home. Her mother, retired, remains a worker, always out, doing, running. Her father is busy as well, taking classes, volunteering. She dials as a kind of nervous tic and then, when she can't get the call to go through, she dials more frantically as though in a nightmare; calling for help, screaming and no one hears, picking up to find the line is dead. She dials, forgetting the new area code.

"The area code for the number you're calling has changed. The new area code is 343. Please redial the number using the new area code."

She dials again, unsure of the last four digits of her calling card.

"The personal identification number you entered is incorrect. Please reenter the last four digits of your calling card."

She reenters.

"I'm sorry."

She is cut off.

She dials once more – if it doesn't work, she is going to dial 0 and have an operator place the call, she is going to dial 911 and tell them it is an emergency, somebody must do something. She dials 9 for an outside line and then she dials the number straight through, letting the office pay for the call – fuck it. The new area code feels odd on her fingers. She hates change, she absolutely hates change.

And then the phone is ringing, and on the second ring the answering machine picks up, and there is her mother's voice, distant, formal – the outgoing announcement of a generation that has never gotten used to the answering machine.

She hangs up without leaving a message.

She checks her schedule. There is a three o'clock meeting – the subject: pain relief.

She has not spoken to Steve today. That part of their relationship, calls during the day, is over. There used to be phone calls as soon as he walked out of the apartment, sometimes from the elevator going down, "I'm in the elevator, the neighbors are surrounding me, pick up the phone." A call when he got to the office, "Just checking in," after lunch, "I shouldn't have had the wine," in the late afternoon, "I'll be finished early," and then again before leaving, "What do you want to do about dinner?"

Now, they can't talk. Every conversation, every attempt turns into a fight. She can't say the right thing, he can't do the right thing, they hate each other – all the more for the disappointment. There is no negotiation, no interest in repair, only anger and inertia.

"It's not my fault," he says.

"If there's such a thing as fault – it's half your fault."

She hurries to prepare for the meeting, the launch of a combination acetaminophen/homeopathic preparation (Tylenol and Rescue Remedy) – Products for Modern Living, a pill for all your problems.

Wendy, the shared assistant, stops her as she's going down the hall. "I couldn't get you a conference room for a whole hour, so I got you two halves."

"Two halves of a conference room?"

"From three to three-thirty you're in two, and from three-thirty until four you're in six."

"Halfway through, we have to change rooms? That's crazy."

Wendy shrugs.

"It's not just about any headache," she says, sitting down with the client. "It's your headache. It's the sense that you're about to explode. Your head is pounding, the boss is droning on in the background, kids are screaming, you need relief and you need it fast."

The client nods.

"It's the classic headache ad – pumped up, there's throbbing and there's volume and pressure."

"Modern life is very stressful," the client says, happily counting the bucks.

"There's the emergency room doctor/trauma surgeon, the voice of authority. 'As a doctor at a leading trauma hospital, I know about pain, I know about stress, and I know how quickly I need to feel better.' The doctor moves through the emergency room – all kinds of horrible things are happening in the background. 'A combination of acetaminophen and a homeopathic supplement, Products for Modern Living offers safe, effective relief.' She picks up a patient's chart and makes a note. 'Sometimes what's old is what's new.'"

"I like it. It's fresh and familiar," the client says.

"Let's move from here into conference room six and we'll review the rest of our campaign," she says, seamlessly moving her team down the hall.

Later, she passes Wendy's desk; Wendy is obsessively dipping cookies into a container of orange juice.

"Are you okay?"

Wendy puts out her hands, they're shaking. "Low blood sugar. I spent from eight-thirty until three trying to get the damned computer to print. I called Information Services, they said they could come tomorrow, but the proposal had to go out today. Never mind. I did it. I got it done." She plunges a cookie into the juice.

She hands Wendy a sample of the remedy. "Try it," she says. "Call it market research and bill them for an extra twenty-five hundred bucks."

Again she dials. The phone rings and rings, maybe her mother is there, maybe she is on the other line. Maybe it is her father – her father always ignores the call-waiting, he doesn't know what call-waiting is.

"Didn't you hear me beeping? That was me trying to call you."

"Is that what that was? I was on the line, talking to a man about something."

She worries that one day she will call and no one will answer – one day she will call and they won't be there anymore.

She remembers dialing her grandmother's number just after her grandmother died. She called just as she had always done. The number rang and rang and somehow she didn't lose hope that her grandmother would find her way to the phone. She thought it might take longer, but she expected her grandmother would answer. And then one day there was a recorded voice, "The number you are trying to reach has been disconnected. If you need further assistance please hang up and dial the operator."

She hangs up. Six months after her grandmother died, she went to her grandmother's house and parked outside the front door. The plants that used to be on the sill of the kitchen window were gone. The light in the living room, always on, was off. She walked around back and peered through the sliding glass door. The house was filled with different furniture; different pictures of different grandchildren rested on the mantel.

"Can I help you?" Mr. Silver, the old man next door asked, as though he'd never seen her before.

"Just looking," she said and walked away.

It is getting dark: five-twenty-two. If she hurried she could take the six o'clock Metroliner, she could be in Washington by eight.

She wants to go home. It has been coming upon her for days. Almost like coming down with a cold, she has been coming down with the urgent need to go home, to sit at her place at the kitchen table, to look out her bedroom window at the trees she saw at one, at twelve, at twenty. She needs something, she can't say exactly what. She keeps brushing it off, hoping it will pass, and then it overwhelms her.

Again, she dials. A man answers. She hangs up and tries again, more carefully, looking at the numbers. Again, the unfamiliar man answers.

"Sorry," she says. "Wrong number."

Again, she tries again.

"May I help you?" he says.

"I keep thinking I'm calling home, I know this number, and yet you answer. Sorry. I'll check the number and try again."

She dials.

"Hello?" the man says. "Hello, hello?"

She says nothing.

He waits and then hangs up.

She puts on her coat and leaves the office. If she had reached her mother she might have felt good enough to go to the gym or to go shopping. But what started as a nervous tic has become something more, she is all the more uncomfortable, she goes directly to the apartment.

There is a message from Steve.

"Sorry we didn't talk. I meant to call earlier but things got crazy. Tonight's the game. I'll be home late."

The game. She forgot.

She takes off her coat and pours herself a glass of wine.

Steve is at the game with his best friend, Bill. Bill is forty-three, never married. Bill won't keep anything perishable in his apartment and has no plants because it's too much responsibility. When he's bored he drones "Next," demanding a change of subject. Inexplicably, it is Bill whom Steve turns to for advice.

Again, she dials.

"Who are you trying to reach?" the man asks. This time, no hello.

Without saying anything, she hangs up.

She orders Chinese. She calls her brother in California; she gets his machine. "When did you last talk to Mom and Dad? Were they okay? Did something happen to their phone? Call me."

By ten, she is beginning to imagine horrible things, accidents. She is dialing and dialing. Where are they? At seventy-six and eighty-three, how far can they have gotten?

She remembers New Year's Eves when she was young, when she was home eating Ruffles with Ridges and California Dip, watching New Year's Rockin' Eve and waiting.

Eleven-fifty-nine, the countdown, sixty seconds away from a new year; three, two, one. The ball drops. The crowd goes crazy.

"Happy New Year from Times Square in New York. Look and listen as America welcomes in 1973." She drinks her fizzy cider and waits. Ten minutes later the phone rings.

"Happy New Year, sweetie," her mother says. "We're having a wonderful time. Mrs. Griswald is just about to serve dessert and then we'll be home. It's going to be a good year."

She remembers checking the clock – twelve-twenty. At one, New Year's Rockin' Eve segued into the late, late movie and she began to wonder. At one-thirty wonder turned to worry. At quarter of two she was picturing her parents' car in a ditch by the side of the road. At two-twenty she wondered if it was too late to call the Griswalds and ask when they'd left. She was twelve years old and powerless. By two-forty when she heard their key in the door, she was livid. She slammed the door to her room and turned off the light.

"Honey, are you all right?"

"Leave me alone."

"I hope she didn't get into the liquor – should I check?"

"I hate you."

Happy New Year.

She gives it one last go – if they don't answer, she is going to call Mrs. Lasky, one of the neighbors, and ask if things are as odd as they seem.

Her mother answers on the first ring.

"Where were you?" she blurts.

"I was in the closet, looking for something."

"I've been trying to call you for hours, why do you sound so strange?"

"Strange?"

"Breathless."

"I was in the closet – foraging. What do you mean you've been calling for hours, we just got home. We had concert tickets."

"I didn't know where you were. I was worried."

"We're adults, Susan. We're allowed to go out." She pauses. "What day is it?"

"Wednesday."

"You usually call on Sunday."

"I was thinking of coming home."

"When?"

"This weekend."

"Well, I don't know what our schedule is like. I'll have to check. What's new?" her mother asks, changing the subject.

"Not much. I must have dialed your number a hundred times – first I couldn't get through then, then I got the machine, and the last few times some man answered. I was beginning to feel like I was losing my mind."

"That must have been Ray."

"Ray?"

"A friend of your father's."

"Daddy doesn't have any friends."

"This is someone he met at one of his classes – I think he's lonely, he brought his cat. It's good you're not here." She is allergic to cats.

"I thought it was me, I thought I dialed wrong. Why didn't he identify himself? Why didn't he say, Green residence? Why didn't he just say – I'm the one who's out of place?"

"I don't know," her mother says.

"Did Daddy go with you to the concert?"

"Of course – he drove."

"What was this Ray doing at the house when you weren't home?"

"Haven't I mentioned him?"

"No."

"Really? You would think I would have – he's staying with us."
There is a long pause.

"Mother – could you just check with your doctor, could you
just say, my daughter is concerned. She thinks I don't remember.
She thinks I forget. Could you do me the favor and ask the doctor
if everything is all right?"

"The truth is when I'm in there, I don't think of it."

"You forget."

"I'm in that paper gown. Who can think of anything when you
feel like at any second it might come undone?"

"How long has this Ray been around?"

"A couple of weeks. He's a lovely guy. You'd like him. He's
very tidy."

"Is he paying rent?"

"No," her mother says, horrified. "He's a friend of your
father's." She changes the subject. "Where's Steve?"

"At the game." As she says it, she hears Steve at the door. She
hurries to get off the phone. "I'll call you tomorrow, we'll figure
out the weekend." She snaps the bedroom light off.

She hears Steve in the living room, opening the mail. She hears
him in the kitchen, opening the fridge. She sees his shadow pass
down the hall. He is in the bathroom, peeing, then brushing his
teeth. He comes into the bedroom, half undressed. "It's only me,"
Steve says. "Don't get excited."

She doesn't respond.

"Are you in here?" He turns on the light.

"I just spoke to my mother."

"Yeah? It's Wednesday – don't you normally talk to them on
Sunday?"

"There is a strange man living at the house. He's been there for
two weeks – she forgot to tell me. A friend of my father's."

"Your father doesn't have any friends."

"Exactly."

"Maybe if you'd waited and called on Sunday, he wouldn't
have been there." Steve pulls his T-shirt off and drops it onto the
floor.

"Not funny." She gestures toward the hamper. "I was thinking I should go and see my parents this weekend – that's why I was calling. I haven't been in a long time. But I can't exactly go home if this guy is there."

"Stay in a hotel."

She sits up to set the alarm. "I'm not staying in a hotel. Am I going to have to do some sort of intervention, kidnap my parents and reprogram them?"

"It's deprogram."

"How's Bill?"

"Good."

"Did you ask him what you should do?"

"About what?" Steve punches at his pillow.

"Us."

Steve doesn't answer. She thinks of her parents, her parents' marriage. She thinks of her parents, of Steve, of having children, of when they stopped talking about it. She wishes they had children. He thinks it's good they didn't. She still wants to have one. "It's not going to fix it," he says. She doesn't want the child to fix it. She wants the child because she wants a child and she knows that without Steve she will not have children. She rolls away from him. There is an absence of feeling, a deadness, an opaque zone where there used to be more.

"Breathe," Steve says to her.

"What?"

"You weren't breathing. You were doing that holding-your-breath thing."

She takes a deep breath. Sighs.

"Do you want me to come with you to your parents?"

"No."

In the night, in the subtlety of sleep, they are drawn together, but when they wake it is as though they remember – they pull apart, they wake up en garde.

"I know it's been hard," he says in the morning as they're getting ready to go.

"What should we do?" she asks.

"I don't know," he says.

They don't say anything more. She is afraid to talk, afraid of what is happening, afraid of what she is feeling, afraid of what will happen next, afraid of just about everything.

The morning meeting is adult undergarments – Peer Pampers. There are boxes of the product on the conference room table. The client opens a box and starts passing them around – a cross between maxi-pads and diapers, there's something about them that's obscene.

"What we're selling here is a new gel insert – it's incredibly absorbent," the client says. He is the only one truly comfortable handling the product – he rips one of the diapers open, pulls apart the crotch area to expose the insert. "This is it," he says. "It sucks up water, up to ten ounces. Our research shows the average void is four to eight. The older you get, the more frequently you urinate and with slightly less volume, so we're estimating approximately six to seven ounces per use."

A junior creative executive picks up one of the garments and, as though giving a demonstration, pours his coffee in. "Afraid to have your morning cup because it runs right through you? Try these."

For a tenth of a second it's funny and then, as a liquidy brown stain spreads through the material, it becomes a problem. Blushing, he puts the dirty diaper in the trash.

"Not a good idea," someone says. "A very poopy diaper."

"That's all right," the client says. "Accidents happen."

"It's a control issue," she says, trying to pull the meeting back to order. "How to feel in control when you are out of control. Picture a man in his car stuck in traffic, a woman strapped into her seat on an airplane, she coughs. But she doesn't look stressed; in fact she's smiling. When everything around you feels out of control, help yourself feel in control. One less worry."

"Don't make it seem like we're encouraging people to piss their pants," the client says.

"The idea is to encourage people to lead healthy, normal lives, not to let bladder control issues stop them from activities that are part of everyday life. We'll spend some time with these," she says, gathering up the diapers. "Give us a call next week."

The client stands. There's a wet spot on his suit.

"I know what you're thinking," he says, "but it's not that. In the car on the way here – my muffin flipped. I got jam all over me. Imagine me," he says, "going through the day with a wet spot on my suit selling adult diapers."

"There's a one-hour cleaner down the block, maybe they can do something for you," she says.

"Now that's a good idea."

Steve calls. "I was wondering if we could have dinner?"

She thinks two thoughts – he wants them to work it out and he's leaving. Either way, whatever it is, she doesn't want to hear it. She isn't ready.

"I have plans," she says.

"Yeah, what?"

"I'm meeting Mindy for a drink. She's coming in for a matinee and then I'm meeting her."

"Well, I'll see you later then. What should I do about dinner?"

"Don't wait for me," she says.

She has no plans. She hasn't talked to Mindy in six months.

"Are you okay?" Steve asks.

"Fine," she says. "You?"

"Fine," he says. "Fucking fantastic."

After work she goes to Bloomingdale's. She wanders for two hours. She is tempted to take herself to a movie, to take herself to a bar and have a drink, to get home really late, really drunk, but she doesn't have the energy.

"Are you finding everything you need?" an overzealous sales associate wants to know.

What does she want? What does she need? She is thinking about Steve, trying to imagine a life apart. She's afraid that if they separate she will evaporate, she will cease to exist. He'll be fine, he'll hardly notice that she is gone. She hates him for that. Will she start dating? She can't picture it, can't imagine starting again with someone else.

When she gets home, Steve is on the bed, channel surfing. "I ate the Chinese – I hope you weren't saving it."

"I ate with Mindy," she says.

She goes into the kitchen. Dials.

Ray answers.

"Hello, is Mrs. Green there?"

"May I ask who's calling?"

She wants to say – you know damn well who's calling, but instead she pauses and then says, "Her daughter."

"One moment." There is a long pause and then Ray returns. "She's not available right now, may I take a message?"

"Yes, could you ask her to call me as soon as she is available. Thank you." She hangs up.

"Find anything?" Steve calls from the bedroom.

She doesn't respond. She stands in front of the open fridge, grazing.

The phone rings. "It's deeply disturbing to call home and have to ask to speak with your parents. What does that mean, you're not available?" she says.

"I was in the bathroom. I fell asleep in the tub."

"Why didn't he just say that?"

"He was being discreet."

"You're my mother. Does he know that?"

"Of course he knows."

"Why was he answering the phone? Why didn't Dad get it?"

"Maybe Dad was busy, maybe Dad didn't hear it, he doesn't hear as well as he used to. We're old, you know."

"You're not old. Who is this Ray character anyway? How much do you know about him?"

Her mother doesn't say anything.

"Mom, are you there? Is he right there? Can you not talk because the guy, the guest, the visitor, Ray, is right there?"

"Yes. Of course."

"Yes, of course, he's there? Can he hear you? Can you not talk because he can hear you?"

"No, not at all."

She stops for a minute, she takes a breath. "I feel like the SWAT team should be setting up next door with sharpshooters and a hostage negotiator. Are you all right? Are you safe?"

She overhears a mumbled conversation: "Oh thank you. Just milk, no sugar, thanks Ray." There is a slurping sound.

"Where does this Ray sleep?"

"Downstairs, in your brother's room. What train are you planning on taking?"

"I think I can get out early, two o'clock."

"We'll look forward to seeing you. Stay in touch."

She hangs up.

"When are you leaving?" Steve asks.

"Early afternoon – I'll go straight from the office."

"Should we talk?" he says.

"Are you seeing somebody?"

"No. Are you?"

"No. Then we don't have to talk."

She walks into the bedroom. "This is how we're having a conversation, yelling back and forth between rooms?"

"Apparently."

"Is this how Bill told you to do it?"

He doesn't say anything.

"There's some man living in my parents' house. Can't the rest of it wait?"

"Do you want to have a code word so you can tell me if something is really wrong?"

"I'll say, it's unbelievably hot. And that means call the police or something."

"Unbelievably hot," Steve says.

"And if I say my toes are cold, that means I'm confused and you should ask me some more questions."

"Hot house/cold toes, got it."

In the morning, Wendy's desk is too neat.

"Did she quit?" asks Tom, the executive who shares Wendy with Susan.

"She just needed a day off; the computer got to her."

By nine there's a temp in Wendy's place, a woman who arrives with her own name plate – MEMORABLE TEMPORARIES, MY NAME IS JUDY.

"Worst thing is not knowing someone's name, looking at her and wondering, Who is she? How can I ask her to do anything – I don't know her name. Now you know, it's Judy. And I'm here to help you."

"Thank you, Judy" she says, going into her office and closing the door.

"I have an appointment outside – I won't be back," she tells Judy at one-fifteen, when she emerges, wheeling her suitcase down the hall.

"Have a good weekend," Judy says with a wink.

The train pulls out – she has the sense of having left something behind, something smoldering, something worrisome – Steve.

The train pushes through the tunnel, rocking and rolling. It pops out over the swamps of New Jersey, and suddenly instead of skyscrapers and traffic there are swamps, leggy white egrets, big skies, chemical plants, abandoned factories, and the melancholy beauty of the afternoon light.

She takes a taxi from the train. Directing the driver toward home, she descends into a world that is half memory, half fantasy, a world so fundamentally at her core that it is hard to know what is real, what is not, what was then, what is now.

"Is there somebody home?" the driver asks, pulling up to the dark house.

"There's a key under the pot," she says, giving away the family secret.

It is twilight. She stands in the driveway, with her suitcase at her feet, watching light fade from the sky, wondering why she came home. On the telephone line above her, four crows sit waiting. The trees press in like dark shields, she listens to the breeze, to the birds still calling. Across the way she sees Mrs. Altman moving around in her kitchen. In the house that used to belong to the Walds, someone new is also doing the dinner dance.

She stands watching the sky, the branches of trees blackening against the dusk. There is a rustling in the woods beyond the house. She glances at the brush, expecting to see a dog or a child taking a shortcut home.

Her father pushes out, breaking twigs along the way. He is carrying a brown paper bag and a big stick.

"Dad?"

"Yeah?"

"Are you okay?"

"Yeah, I'm fine. I walked."

"Did you have car trouble?"

"Oh no," he says. "I didn't have any trouble. I took the scenic route." Her father peers into the carport. "Ray's not here? I must have beat him."

"Where's your car?"

"I left it with Ray. He had errands to run. I had a very nice walk. I went through the woods."

"You're eighty-three years old, you can't just go through the woods because it's more scenic."

"What would anyone want with me? I'm an old man."

"What if you fell or twisted your ankle?"

He waves his hand, dismissing her. "I could just as easily fall here at home and no one would notice." He bends to get the key. "You been here long?"

"Just a few minutes."

Her father opens the door, she steps inside, expecting the dog. She has forgotten that the dog is not there anymore, he died about a year ago.

"That's so strange – I was expecting the dog."

"Oh," her father says. "I do that all the time. I'm always thinking I shouldn't leave the door open, shouldn't let the dog out. We have him, for you, if you want," her father says. "His ashes are on the shelf over the washing machine. Do you want to take him with you?"

"If we could leave him for now, that would be good," she says.

"It's your dog," her father says. "So, how long are you here for?"

"I don't know."

"You don't usually stay long."

She takes her bag down the hall to her room. The house is still. It is orderly and neat. Everything is exactly the same and yet different. The house is smaller, her room is smaller, the twin bed is smaller. There is a moment of panic – a fear of being consumed by whatever it is that she came in search of. She feels worse, further from herself. She looks around, wondering what she is doing in this place, it is deeply familiar and yet she feels entirely out of place, out of sorts. She wants to run, to take the next train back. From her bedroom window she sees her mother's car glide into the driveway.

"Is she here?" She hears her mother's voice across the house.

"Hi Mom," she says and her mother does not hear her. She tries again. "Hi Mom." She walks down the hall saying, Hi Mom, Hi Mom, Hi Mom at different volumes, in different intonations, like a hearing test.

"Is that you?" her mother finally asks when she's two feet away.

"I'm home."

Her mother hugs her – her mother is smaller too. Everything is shrinking, compacting, intensifying. "Did you have a good flight?"

She has never flown home. "I took the train."

"Is Ray back?" her mother asks.

"Not yet," her father says as he puts two heaping tablespoons of green powder into a glass of water.

"Where did you meet this Ray?"

"Your father left his coat at the health food store and Ray found it and called him."

Her father nods. "I went to get the coat and we started talking."

"Your father and Ray go to vitamin class together."

"Vitamin class?"

"They go to the health store and a man speaks to them over a video screen."

"What does the man tell you?"

"He talks about nutrition and health. He tells us what to do."

"How many people go?"

"About thirty." Her father stirs, tapping the side of the glass with his spoon. "This is the green stuff, I have two glasses of this twice a day and then I have a couple of the red stuff. It's all natural." He drinks in big gulps.

It looks like a liquefied lawn.

"See my ankles," he says, pulling up the leg of his pants. "They're not swollen. Ever since I started taking the supplements, the swelling has gone down. I feel great. I joined a gym."

"Where was this Ray before he came to you?"

"He had a place over on Arlington Road, one of those apartments behind the A&P, with another fellow."

"Something happened to that man, he may have died or gone into a home. I don't really know," her mother says.

There is the sound of a key in the door.

"That's Ray."

The door opens. Ray comes in carrying groceries.

"In your honor, Ray is making vegetable chow mein for dinner," her mother says. And she is not sure why vegetable chow mein is in her honor.

"You must be Ray," she says, putting her hand out as Ray puts the bags down.

"You must be the daughter," Ray says, ignoring her hand.

"Did you get the crispy noodles?" her mother asks.

"I don't eat meat anymore," her father says. "I don't really eat much of anything. At my age, I don't have a big appetite."

"I got you some chocolate rice milk – I think you'll like it." Ray hands her father a box of milk.

"I like chocolate," her father says.

"I know you do." Ray is of indeterminate age, somewhere between fifty-five and sixty-five, sinewy with close-cropped hair, like a skullcap sprinkled with gray. Each of his features belongs to another place; he is a little bit Asian, a little bit Middle Eastern, a little bit Irish, and within all that he is incredibly plain and without affect, as though he has spent a lot of time trying not to be.

"And I got the noodles," Ray says.

"Oh good," her mother says. "I like things that are crunchy."

Her mother and father peer into the grocery bags. She wonders if Ray pays for these groceries – if that's why they're so interested – or if he makes them pay for it.

"Nuts," her father says, pulling out a bag of cashews. "And raisins."

"Organic," Ray says, winking.

Her father loves anything organic.

"Remember when we couldn't have lettuce because it wasn't picked by the right people, and then we couldn't have grapes. And after that it was something else," she says.

"Tuna," her mother says, "because of the dolphins."

"I have something to show you," her father says, leading Ray into the living room. There is a drawing on the dining table.

"Very nice," Ray says.

Her mother walks past them. She sits at the piano and begins to play. "I've started my lessons again."

"Let's hear the Schubert," Ray says.

Her father proudly shows her more drawings. "I'm taking classes, at the college. Free for seniors."

It is incredibly civilized and all she can think about is how bad things are with Steve and that she needs to come up with a slogan for adult diapers by Monday.

A little later, she is sitting in the den. As her mother knits, they watch the evening news. Her father is in the bedroom, blasting the radio. Ray is in the kitchen with the pots and pans. The smell of garlic and scallions fills the house.

"You let him just be in the kitchen? You don't worry what he does to the food – what he puts in it?"

"What's he going to do – poison us?" her mother says. "I'm tired of cooking. If I never cook again that's fine with me."

She looks at her mother – her mother is a good cook, she is what you'd call a food person.

"Does Ray have a crush on Dad?"

"Don't be ridiculous – what am I, chopped liver?" Her mother inhales. "Smells good doesn't it?"

A noise, an occasional small sound draws her out of the room and down the hall. She moves quietly thinking she will catch him, she will catch Ray doing something he shouldn't.

She finds him on the living room floor, sitting on a cushion. There are small shiny cymbals on his first and third fingers and every now and then he pinches his fingers together – *ping*.

She goes back into the den.

"He's meditating," her mother says, before she even asks. "Twice a day for forty minutes. He tried to get your father to do it and me too. We don't have the patience. Sometimes we sit with him, we cheat, I read, your father falls asleep."

Again there is the sound of the cymbals – *ping*.

"Isn't that the nicest sound?"

"Does he do it at specific intervals?"

"He does it whenever his mind begins to wander. He goes very deep. He's been at it for twenty years."

"Where is Ray from? Does he have a family? Does he have a job? Is he part of a cult?"

"Why are you so suspicious? Did you come all the way home to visit or to investigate us?"

"I came home to talk to you."

"I don't know that I have anything to say," her mother says.

"I need advice – I need you to tell me what to do."

"I can't. It's your life. You do what's right for you." She pauses. "You said you wanted to come home because you needed to get something, you wanted something – what was it, something you left in your room?"

"I don't know how to describe it," she catches herself. "It's something I never got. Something from you," she says.

"I don't really have much to give. Call some friends, make plans, live it up. Aren't any of your high school buddies around?"

She is thirty-five and suddenly needs her mother. She is thirty-five and doesn't remember who her high school buddies were.

"What does Ray want from you? What does he get?"

"I have no idea. He doesn't ask for anything. Maybe just being here is enough, maybe that's all he wants. Everyone doesn't need as much as you."

There is silence.

"Damn," her mother says. "I dropped a stitch."

She leaves the room. She goes downstairs. She wants to see exactly what he is up to.

The door to her brother's room is cracked open. She pushes it further. A brown cat is curled up on a pillow; it looks at her. She steps inside. The cat dives under the bed.

The room is clean and neat. Everything is put away. There is no sign of life, except for the dent in the pillow where the cat was, and a thin sweater folded over the back of a chair. By the side of the bed is a book of stories, an empty water glass, and an old alarm clock, ticking loudly.

"Can I help you?"

Ray is in the room. She doesn't know how he got there, how he got down the stairs without a sound.

"I was just looking for a book," she says.

"What book?"

She blushes as though this were a quiz. "Robinson Crusoe." She knows it is a book her brother had, a book they used to look at as children.

He takes the book from the shelf and hands it to her.

She sneezes. "Cat," she says.

"Bless you," he says. "You'll excuse me," he says, edging her out of the room. "I want to refresh myself before dinner."

In the downstairs bathroom, each of his personal effects is arranged in a tight row on top of a folded towel – tooth-brush, comb, nail clippers.

The cat's litter box is in the corner. There are four little lumps in it, shit rolled in litter, dirt balls dusted in ash.

Her mother sits at the table. "I haven't had chow mein since Aunt Lena used to make it with leftover soup chicken."

There is the scrape of a matchstick. Ray lights two tall tapers.

"Every night we have candles," her father says. "Ray makes the effort."

Ray has changed his clothes, he's wearing an orange silk shirt, he seems to radiate light. "From the Goodwill," he says, seeming to know what she is thinking. "It must have been a costume. In the back of the neck, in black marker, it's written – 'Lear.'"

"I'm tasting something delicious," her mother says, working the flavors in her mouth. "Ginger, soy, oh, and baby corn. Where did you find fresh baby corn?"

She has something to say about everything. "Such sharp greens. Olives, what an idea, so Greek. The color of this pepper is fabulous. Red food is very good for you, high in something." She gobbles. "Eating is such a pleasure when you don't have to cook."

"Did you take care of your errands?" her father asks Ray.

"Yes, thank you," Ray says. "Every now and then it helps to use a car. I filled it with gas."

"You didn't need to."

"And I put a quart of oil in. I also checked the tires; your right rear was down a little."

"Thanks, Ray."

She hates him. She absolutely hates him. He is too good. How does a person get to be so good? She wishes she could get behind it, she wishes she could think he was as wonderful as he seems. But she doesn't trust him for a minute.

"More," her mother says, holding her plate up for seconds. "What's the matter – you're not eating?"

She shakes her head. If Ray is poisoning them, putting a little bit of who knows what into the food, she wants none of it. "Not hungry."

"I thought you said you were starving."

She doesn't answer.

"White rice and brown," her mother says. "Ray is kinder than I could ever be. I would never make two rices."

"Two rices make two people happy – that's easy," Ray says.

Her mother eats and then gets up from the table, letting her napkin fall into her plate. "That was wonderful – divine." She walks out of the room.

It takes her father longer to finish. "Great, Ray, really great." He helps clear the table.

She is left alone with Ray.

"Marriage is a difficult thing," Ray says without warning. She wonders whom he is talking about and if he knows more. "I was married once." He hands her a pot to dry. "Attachment to broken things is not good for the self."

"Is that where you got to be such a good cook? You're really something, a regular Galloping Gourmet."

"To feed yourself well is a strong skill." He speaks as though talking in translation.

"Where are you from, Ray?"

"Philadelphia."

She is thinking Main Line, that would explain it. Maybe that's why he doesn't care about anything, maybe money means nothing to him, because he already has it, because if he needs it, there is always enough.

"And what did your family do in Philadelphia?"

"They were in business."

"What sort of business?" she asks.

"Dresses," he says.

Not Main Line. "Do you have many friends in the area?"

He shakes his head. "I am not so easy, I don't like everybody."

"Do you have a family?" she asks.

"I have myself," he says.

"And what do you want from us?"

"You and I have only just met."

"My parents are very generous, simple people," she says. It sounds as though she's making him a deal, an offer. She stops. "I noticed you on the floor with the cymbals. Are you a guru, a swami of some sort?"

"I have been sitting for many years; it does me good, just noticing what I feel."

She is noticing that she feels like hitting him, hauling off and slugging him. The unrelenting evenness of his tone, his lack of interest in her investigation, his detachment is arrogant, infuriating. She wants to say, I've got your number; you think you're something special, like you were sent here from some other place, with little cymbals on your fingers – *ping*. She wants to say, pretending you're so carefree, so absent of emotion, isn't going to get you anywhere – *ping*.

"Do not mistake me," he says, as though reading her mind. "My detachment is not arrogance, it is hard won."

If she hits him, he will not defend himself – she knows that. He will let her hit him; she will look like an idiot, it will look like proof of how crazy she is, it will look as though he did nothing to provoke her.

"This is just what you think of me," he says, nodding knowingly. "I am not anything. I am just here. I am not trying to go anywhere."

"I'm watching you," she says, walking out of the kitchen.

The door to her parents' room is closed. She knocks before entering. Her parents are sitting on the bed, reading.

"We're spending some time alone together," her mother says.

"Should I not bother you?"

"It's okay – you're not here very often," her mother says.

"What's Ray doing?" her father asks.

"Rearranging the shelves in the kitchen, throwing clay pots and firing them in the oven, and koshering chickens for tomorrow."

"What makes you always think everyone else is getting more than you?" her mother asks.

"You're hiding in your bedroom with the door closed and he's out there – loose in the house, doing God knows what. He's completely taken over, he's running the show, don't you see?"

"We're not hiding, we're spending time alone together."

She sneezes four times in quick succession. "Cat," she says.

"Did you bring anything to help yourself?"

"What the hell makes him so special that he gets to come and live here with his cat?"

"There's no reason not to share. In fact it's better, more economical, and he's very considerate," her father says. "If more people invited people in, it would solve the housing shortage, use less natural resources. We're just two people. What do we need a whole house for? It was my idea."

"Why don't you just open a shelter, take in homeless people and offer them free showers, et cetera?"

"Don't go completely crazy," her mother says. "There are no homeless people in Chevy Chase."

She looks around the room. "What happened to Grandma's table? It used to be in that corner."

"Mini-storage," her mother says. "We put a lot of things into storage."

"Boxes and boxes. We loaded a van and they took it all away."

"The house feels better now, doesn't it? Airier, almost like it's glad to be rid of all that crap," her mother says.

"Where is this mini-storage?" she asks.

"Somewhere in Rockville. Ray found it. Ray took care of the whole thing."

"Have you ever been there? How do you know your stuff is really there?" She is thinking she's figured it out, she finally has something on Ray.

"I have the key," her mother says. "And Ray made an inventory."

"Fine, first thing in the morning I'm going there. We'll see what's what."

"Why are you so suspicious? Your father doesn't have many friends, this is nice for him, don't ruin it."

"What do you even know about Ray – who is he really?"

"He writes," her father says.

"Yeah, he keeps a journal, I saw it downstairs."

"You shouldn't be poking around in his room," her mother says. "That's invasion of privacy."

"He's written five books, he's had stories in the *New Yorker*," her father says.

"If he's a world-famous writer, why is he living with you?"

"He likes us," her father says. "We're common travelers."

"We should all be so lucky to have someone willing to pay a little attention to us when we're old – it's not like you're going to move home and take care of us."

"I came home because I wanted you to take care of me. Steve and I are having a hard time. I think Steve may move out."

"You have to learn to leave people alone, you can't hound someone every minute. Maybe if you left him alone he'd come back." Her mother pauses. "Do you want Ray to go back with you?"

"And do what, help Steve pack?"

"He could keep you company. I'm not sure he's ever been to New York. He likes adventures."

"Mom, I don't need Ray. If I needed anyone, it would be you."

"No," her mother says. Simply no. She hears it and knows that all along the answer was no.

Her bedroom is simultaneously big and small. She is too big for the bed and yet feels like a child, intruding on her own life.

She pulls the shade and undresses. The night-light is on, it goes on automatically at dusk. She lies in the twin bed of her youth, looking at the bookcase, at the bear whose fur she tried to style, at her glass piggy bank still filled with change, at a *Jefferson Airplane – White Rabbit* poster clinging to the wall behind the dresser.

Stopped time. She is in both the past and present, wondering how she got from there to here. The mattress is hard as a rock. She rolls over and back. There is nowhere to go. She takes a couple of the new pills – Products for Modern Living.

She dreams.

Her mother and father are standing in the front hall with old-fashioned American Tourister suitcases.

"I'm taking your mother to Europe," her father says. "Ray is going to keep an eye on the house, he's going to take care of the dog."

"He's lonely," her mother says. "He came for coffee and brought us a cat."

She is hiding in the woods behind the house, watching the house with X-ray specs. Everything is black and white. She calls her brother from a walkie-talkie. "Are you out there? Can you hear me? Come in, come in?"

"Roger. I am here in sunny California."

"I'm watching Ray," she says.

"The mail just came," he says. "Ray sent me a birthday card and a hundred dollars in cash. That's more than Mom and Dad ever gave me."

"Do you know where Mom and Dad are?"

"I have no idea," he says. "They didn't even send a card."

And then Ray is chasing her around the yard with the cymbals on his fingers. Every time he punches his fingers together – *ping* – she feels a sharp electric shock. Her X-ray specs fall off. Everything changes from black-and-white to color.

Ray runs into the house and closes the door. The deadbolt slips into place.

She is on the other side of the glass. "Open the door, Ray."

She finds the key hidden under the pot. She tries it. The key doesn't work – Ray has changed the locks.

"Ray," she says, banging on the glass. "Ray, what have you done to my parents? Ray, I'm going to call the police."

"They're in Italy," Ray says, muffled through the glass.

She is on the walkie-talkie, trying to reach her mother in Italy.

"You're not understanding what I'm saying," she says. "Ray stole the house. He changed the locks. I can't get in."

"You don't have to yell, I'm not deaf," her mother says.

She wakes up. The house is silent except for two loud, sawing snores – her parents.

In the morning, she dresses in her room. With Ray in the house, she feels uncomfortable making the dash from the bedroom to the bathroom in her underwear. She gets dressed, goes to wash her face and pee, and then heads down the hall to the kitchen.

"Good morning," she says.

Ray is alone at the kitchen table.

"Where is everybody?"

"Your father had an art class and your mother went shopping with Mrs. Harris. She left you her car and the key for the mini-storage."

Ray holds up a string, dangling from it is a small key. He swings it back and forth hypnotically. "I'll give you directions," he says.

She nods.

"Would you like some herb tea? I just made a pot."

"No thanks." They sit in silence. "I'm not exactly a morning person," she says.

As she steps outside, Mrs. Lasky is across the way, getting into her car.

"How are you?" Mrs. Lasky calls out. "How is life in New York?"

"It's fine. It's fine." She repeats herself, having nothing more to say. "And how are you?"

"Very well," Mrs. Lasky says. "Isn't Ray wonderful? He keeps my bird feeder full. The most wonderful birds visit me. Just now, as I was having my breakfast, a female cardinal was having hers."

The mini-storage facility is called U-Store It. "U-store it. U-keep the key. U-are in charge." She locates the unit, unlocks the padlock, and pulls the door open.

There was something vaguely menacing about the way Ray was swinging the key through the air – yet he drew the map, he seemed not to know or care what she was thinking.

A clipboard hangs from a hook by the door. There is spare twine, tape, and a roll of bubble wrap. She recognizes the outlines of her grandmother's table, her father's old rocking chair. Each box is labeled, each piece of furniture well wrapped. On the clipboard is a typed list of boxes with appendices itemizing the contents of each box: Children's Toys, Mother's Dishes, World Book Encyclopedia A-Z (Plus YearBook 1960–1974), Assorted From Kitchen Closet, Beach Supplies, etc. She pries open a box just to be sure. She's thinking she might find wadded up newspaper, proof Ray is stealing, but instead, she finds her book reports from high school, a Valentine card her brother made for her mother, the hat her grandmother wore to her mother's wedding.

She seals the box up again. There is nothing to see. She pulls the door closed, locks it, and leaves.

Driving home, she passes her old high school – it's been gutted. BUILDING A BETTER FUTURE FOR TOMORROW'S LEADERS. READY FOR RE-OCCUPANCY FALL 2002. GO BARONS.

She drives up and down the streets, playing a nostalgic game of who lived where and what she can remember about them: the girl with the wonderful singing voice who ended up having to be extricated from a cult, the boy who in sixth grade had his own subscription to *Playboy*, the girl whose mother had Siamese twins. She remembers her paper route, she remembers selling Girl Scout cookies door to door, birthday parties, roller skating, Ice Capades.

She goes home.

Every time she comes to visit, it takes twenty-four hours to get used to things and then everything seems less strange, more familiar, everything seems as though it could be no other way – entirely natural.

She slides the car into the driveway. Her father is in the front yard, raking leaves. His back is toward her. She beeps, he waves. For a million years her father has been in the front yard, raking. He has his plaid cap on, his old red cardigan, and corduroys.

She gets out of the car.

"Remember when I was little," she calls down the hill. "And we used to rake together. You had the big one and I had the small bamboo . . ."

He turns. A terrifying sensation sweeps through her. It's Ray.

"I want you out," she says, shocked. "Now!" He intentionally misled her. He had to have known what she was thinking when she drove in, when she beeped and waved, when she said, remember when I was little. Why didn't he take off the hat, turn around, and say, I am not who you think I am?

"Where is my father? What have you done to my father? Those are not your clothes."

"Your father gave them to me."

She moves toward him.

Ray is standing there, her father's cap still on his head. She reaches out, she knocks it off. He bends to pick it up.

"It's not your hat," she says, grabbing it, throwing it like a Frisbee across the yard. "You can't just step inside someone's life and pretend you're them."

"I was invited."

"Get your stuff and get out."

"I'm not sure it's entirely up to you," Ray says. This is as close as he comes to protesting. "It's not your house."

"Oh, but it is," she says. "It's my house and it's my family and I have to have some influence on what happens here. They're old, Ray. Pick on someone else." She grabs the rake and uses it to shoo him inside. "It's over. Pack your bags."

Her mother comes home just as Ray is trying to put the cat into his travel case. The cat is screaming, howling. The cab is waiting outside.

"What's going on? Did something happen to the cat? Does he need me to take him to the vet?"

"He can't stay," she says. "He was in the yard acting like Daddy, he was wearing Daddy's clothes. He can't do that."

"He's your father's friend. We like having him here."

"He can't stay," she repeats.

"Maybe you shouldn't have come home," her mother says. "Maybe it's too hard. You know what they say."

"I'm just visiting," she says.

Ray comes up the stairs. He has a single suitcase, the cat carrier, and a brown paper bag filled with his supplements, his wheat germ, and the red and the green stuff.

"It doesn't have to be this way," her mother says.

"It does," she says.

"Good-bye," Ray says, shaking her mother's hand.

There's something about his shaking her mother's hand that's more upsetting than anything, it's heartbreaking and pathetic, it's more and less affecting than a clinging hug.

"Don't forget us, Ray," her mother says, walking him to the door, letting him out almost as easily as they let him in. "I'm so sorry, I apologize for the confusion."

And then he is gone. She goes down to his room. She checks the doors. He has left his key on the bed along with her father's clothes, neatly folded, his bedding all rolled up.

She comes back upstairs.

"Now what, Mrs. Big Shot?" her mother says. "Now who's going to take care of us?"

"I don't know."

"Your father didn't even have a chance to say good-bye."

"I'm not saying they can't be friends – I'm sure he'll see him at the next vitamin meeting – just that Ray can't live here. This isn't a commune."

She is sitting in the den. Her mother is knitting.

Her father comes home. "I made a nice drawing today," her father says.

"That's nice," her mother says.

"Were there any messages?"

"No," her mother says.

They sit in silence for a few minutes longer.

"Where's Ray?"

"She made him leave," her mother says, gesturing toward her with a knitting needle.

"He was in the yard, raking. He had your clothes on. I thought he was you – he scared me."

"He did a good job," her father says. "The yard looks good."

Again there is silence.

"Where'd he go?" her father asks.

"I have no idea, it all happened so quickly. Maybe back to the vitamin store," her mother says.

She feels as though she can't stay. She has shaken things up too much, she is really on the outside now.

"I guess I should go," she says.

Later that night she will take the train back to New York. The apartment will be empty. There will be a note from Steve. "I thought I should go. If you need me I'm at Bill's. Hope you had a good weekend."

"You come home, upset everything, and then you just leave?" her mother says. "What's the point of that?"

"I wanted to talk to you," she says.

"So talk," her mother says.

FRED D'AGUIAR

Bring Back, Bring Back

Bring back morning ice in enamel buckets
Fetched two at a time for balance from standpipes
Set at village squares, pipes shared by villages
Too numerous to name properly and too few to do
Anything but name for qualities shown by folk
Interviewed by administrators in hard hats on
Horseback way before Model-T and the Wrights'
First flight, when my grandparents, mere tadpoles,
Swished around in their parents as nothing more
Than wishes thought up in fields while minding
Indolent cows, sheep or goats or while poised
Over washing on a ribbed scrubbing board;
Bring them back as you would sprinters to a start line
After a false start where one bolts and the rest follow.

THE WORLD

THOMAS HARDY

The Darkling Thrush

I leant upon a coppice gate
  When Frost was spectre-gray,
And Winter's dregs made desolate
  The weakening eye of day.
The tangled bine-stems scored the sky
  Like strings of broken lyres,
And all mankind that haunted nigh
  Had sought their household fires.

The land's sharp features seemed to be
  The Century's corpse outleant,
His crypt the cloudy canopy,
  The wind his death-lament.
The ancient pulse of germ and birth
  Was shrunken hard and dry,
And every spirit upon earth
  Seemed fervourless as I.

At once a voice arose among
  The bleak twigs overhead
In a full-hearted evensong
  Of joy illimited;

An aged thrush, frail, gaunt, and small,
  In blast-beruffled plume,
Had chosen thus to fling his soul
  Upon the growing gloom.

So little cause for carolings
  Of such ecstatic sound
Was written on terrestrial things
  Afar or nigh around,
That I could think there trembled through
  His happy goodnight air
Some blessed Hope, whereof he knew
  And I was unaware.

ALICE OSWALD

Hymn to Iris

Quick-moving goddess of the rainbow
You whose being is only an afterglow of a passing-through

Put your hands
Put your heaven-taken shape down
On the ground. Now. Anywhere

Like a bent-down bough of nothing
A bridge built out of the linked cells of thin air

And let there be instantly in its underlight—
At street corners, on swings, out of car windows—
A three-moment blessing for all bridges

May impossible rifts be often delicately crossed
By bridges of two thrown ropes or one dropped plank

May the unfixed forms of water be warily leaned over
On flexible high bridges, huge iron sketches of the mathematics
    of strain
And bridges of see-through stone, the living-space of drips and
    echoes

May two fields be bridged by a stile
And two hearts by the tilting footbridge of a glance

And may I often wake on the broken bridge of a word,
Like in the wind the trace of a web. Tethered to nothing

TOVE JANSSON

Art in Nature

Translated by David McDuff

When the summer exhibition closed in the evenings and the last visitors went away, it became very quiet. A short time later boat after boat set off from the shore and sailed back to the village on the other side of the lake. The only member of staff who remained overnight was the caretaker; he slept in the sauna changing room at the bottom of the large lawn where the sculptures had been lined up among the trees. He was very old and had a bad back, but it had been hard to get hold of someone who didn't mind the long, lonely evenings. And there had to be a night caretaker because of the insurance.

It was a large exhibition; it was called "Art in nature". Every day the caretaker unlocked the gates and people streamed into the beautiful grounds, they came in cars and buses from every part of the country, and even from the capital, they brought their children with them and made great excursions, they swam among the water-lilies and drank coffee and strolled under the birch trees, the children played on the swings and had their photographs taken on the big bronze horse, and more and more people wanted to look at "Art in nature".

The caretaker was very proud of the exhibition. All day he sat in the enormous glass box that held paintings and graphics, and saw hundreds of feet go by. Because of his back he was unable to see much of their faces, but he began to observe the feet and made a game of guessing what they were a part of, what the rest of the person looked like. Sometimes he craned his neck to see if he was right, and often he was. Most of them were women in sandals, and from their toes you could see that they were not particularly young. Nearly all the feet moved respectfully. If they had a guide with them they stood still for a while and were turned the same way, then they changed direction, at precisely

the same time, in order to look at something else. The solitary
feet were undecided at first, then slowly they began to walk on,
diagonally, stopped, stood with their legs crossed, twisted round;
sometimes they raised one leg and scratched themselves because
there were a lot of midges. Then they went on again, along the
last wall quite quickly. The caretaker saw a lot of feet with
sturdy shoes, they often stood quite still, went past without
concern and stood still again, for quite a long time. He always
checked to see what the old shoes looked like on top. The old
people walked with their toes turned out, the young people with
their toes turned slightly in, and the children ran parallel. That
amused the caretaker. One day two old shoes and a stick stopped
in front of him. He could see that she was very tired.

"Do you know," she asked, "do you know what No. 34 is meant
to be? It looks like a parcel with string round it. Is one supposed
to open it?"

"I don't think so," replied the caretaker. The guide said that
some foreigner had started making works of art like that. Then
they went on with it, wrapping up sculptures and finally whole
mountains, it might have been in Arizona.

"Are there any chairs here?" asked the old lady. "It's such a
big exhibition."

He made room for her beside him on the bench, and they sat
next to each other for a while.

"What I admire," she said, "is that they think of so many
things and that they manage to make them and manage to
believe in what they make. I'll come back another day and look
at the sculptures. With an exhibition like this you can't take it
all in right away, you have to go very slowly."

The caretaker said that he liked the sculptures best.

They grew up out of the lawn, enormous dark monuments of
smooth, incomprehensible shapelessness, or broken, prickly
things, challenging and disturbing. They stood everywhere
among the birch trees as though they had sprouted from the
earth, and when the summer night came and the mist drifted in
from the lake they were as beautiful as rocks or dead trees.

He went and locked the gates and continued along the shore
and extinguished the sausage grill and saw that everything was

as it ought to be. He picked up the moss that the children had brought down from the large stones and gathered the coins in the wishing well and put them on a newspaper to dry. He made sure there was nothing burning in the ashtrays and emptied them carefully in the open sculptural incinerator. The June night was quiet and the lake lay motionless with a reflection under each small island. The caretaker loved his customary evening walk, to lock up for the night. By the gates there was a scent of hay and manure from the surrounding farms, along the shore there was the smell of mud and grass, then the wet soot of the sauna, and as he walked past the sculptures that were made of plaster he detected the smell of tar, they had all been impregnated with tar to withstand the rain. He himself had helped to paint them. In the daytime one could not smell it, one heard only voices and feet. The caretaker liked the evenings and the night, he did not need much sleep and often sat down by the edge of the shore for many hours in peace and quiet with himself. He did not remember, he did not worry, he simply was. The only thing that troubled him was the knowledge that the exhibition would close in the autumn, but he had got used to it and could not imagine any other way of life.

One evening he took his usual walk along the whole of the grounds, he had locked the gates and everything was supposed to be in order. Then the caretaker smelled smoke, smoke from a burning fire. He grew quite beside himself, there was a fire, a fire somewhere! Half stumbling, he tried to run, a little bit this way, a little bit that, and finally realised it was only that someone had lit the sausage grill. Marauders had hidden in the grounds, and now they were cooking sausages down on the shore. His relief made him furious. He crossed the lawn down to the edge of the shore as quickly as he could, but kept quiet. Very soon he heard voices, it was a man and a woman, and they were quarrelling. The caretaker sneaked up on them and peered to see what they looked like. They were middle-aged people who ought to have had enough sense not to break the exhibition rules. The man seemed awfully pale and had an American shirt and a salmon fly in his hat, she was rather fat and was dressed in something that had little flowers on it. They were cooking sausages and drinking beer, and they were quarrelling. The caretaker listened for a while, it was a perfectly ordinary marital quarrel, and then he came out and banged his stick on the ground and shouted: "This won't do at all! You can't have a fire here after the exhibition is closed, it's absolutely prohibited! When the exhibition's closed it's closed, and what are you doing here?"

"Oh my God!" cried the woman. "Albert, I told you we shouldn't have!"

The man jumped to his feet and was about to pour sea-water over the sausage grill, but the caretaker shouted: "Don't do that, you'll crack the grill, it has to burn out by itself!" He suddenly felt very tired, and sat down on a stone. The man and the woman were silent.

"Responsibility," said the caretaker. "Does that mean anything to you? What do you know about it all? Every night I'm responsible for the whole of this big art exhibition and also for the forest. There are works of art here by some of the greatest artists in the land, and it all rests on me."

"Svea," said the man, "ask him if he'd like some sausage and a glass of beer." But the caretaker said no thank you, he did not want to be conciliated. The evening had faded into summer night, and a light mist came gliding in across the lake, hiding the islands. The trunks of the birch trees became whiter.

"Perhaps we ought to introduce ourselves," said the man.

"Fagerlund."

"Räsänen," said the caretaker.

The woman began to pack her baskets, it was clear that they did not dare to eat or drink any more.

"And what's that there?" asked Räsänen, pointing his stick at a brown parcel they had placed on a stone. The woman at once explained that it was a work of art they had chosen and paid for, it was the first picture they had ever bought, and they had to celebrate, and the picture was a silk screen print.

"You don't need to apologise," said Räsänen. "Actually, the real name is serigraphy. They make lots of copies of them, but it's considered art anyway. Well, what's it a picture of?"

"It's an abstract," replied Fagerlund. "But we think it represents two chairs that are slightly turned away from each other."

Räsänen said he couldn't remember any chairs like that, and then the woman said it was right at the back on the right, two perfectly ordinary kitchen chairs against some wallpaper, she talked eagerly and it was clear that she was trying to ingratiate herself.

"You're wrong," said her husband, "they're folding chairs, the kind you can put away in a moment, and anyway they're not important, it's the background that matters." He turned to Räsänen and said: "You know, it opens outwards. You can see the life outside. It could be a big city, it has nothing to do with kitchen wallpaper."

His wife laughed, and said, "You and your ideas, it's wallpaper, anyone can see that. Don't be so self-important. They've been sitting in their chairs and have got up and left and pushed the chairs away when they left. Perhaps they'd quarrelled, what do you think, had they quarrelled?"

"They probably just got tired," said Fagerlund. "They got damned tired and went out."

"You bet they did," she said. "One of them went to the bar on the corner."

Räsänen waited for a while and then he said it was a funny thing about art. Everyone saw what he was able to, and that was the intention. But why had they not purchased something lighter and more attractive, a landscape, for example?

They did not reply. The woman had turned away from them towards the lake, and she was wiping her eyes and blowing her nose.

The caretaker said: "You could also take it this way, for example. Since a work of art can be just about anything, and you just see what you want to see, you could just not bother to unwrap it, and hang the parcel on the wall. Then you wouldn't need to quarrel." He raked the embers with his stick, the grill had almost burnt out.

After a while, she said: "How do you mean, the parcel?"

"I mean the parcel, with paper and string and all. You saw those parcels at the exhibition, didn't you, that's the kind of thing they produce nowadays. Maybe you're best just to imagine what's inside and see something different every time you look."

She turned round and asked: "Are you serious?"

Fagerlund said: "Svea, Mr Räsänen is making fun of you. Let's be off."

She got up and began violently gathering together baskets and sweaters and all the things they had brought with them.

"Wait a minute," said the caretaker. "I'm serious. It only dawned on me just now. All you need to do is wrap the picture up a bit more nicely and use more string – fishing line or cobblers' thread, for example. Lots of string. I've seen what it ought to look like." He drew with his stick in the sand. "Like this, and like this, very neatly. And glass on top of it all."

"But it was expensive!" she burst out. "Anyone can make an art parcel like that at home and hang it up!"

"No," replied the caretaker. "I don't think they can. Then there's nothing mysterious about it all." He was glad, almost cheerful, at having finally understood the idea behind the wrapped-up works of art. "You can go home now," he said. "You'll have to climb over the gate, for I can't be bothered going all that way to unlock it."

"Albert," she said, "you'll have to carry the parcel." She looked at it as though it were on fire, and dangerous.

Fagerlund picked up the parcel and set it down again. "No," he said. "We'll unwrap it right here and now. We'll let Mr Räsänen decide what it represents."

Then she shouted: "Stop it!" and began to cry in earnest, and said she didn't want to know, just wanted to see it in her own way and not be cheated, she said.

The caretaker was silent for a while. Then he said: "It's too dark. You can't see anything." He stood up and said goodbye to his guests. When they had gone, he sat for a while and tended to the grill, and then walked slowly back between the sculptures which now, when the summer night was at its darkest, looked like nothing but enormous, strongly-shaped shadows. He thought: "But what I said was perfectly true. It's the element of mystery that's important, very important in some way." He went and lay down in the sauna room, which had four empty walls. It was pleasant to look at them and fall asleep without those old recurring thoughts he was used to.

WALLACE STEVENS

Earthy Anecdote

Every time the bucks went clattering
Over Oklahoma
A firecat bristled in the way.

Wherever they went,
They went clattering,
Until they swerved
In a swift, circular line
To the right,
Because of the firecat.

Or until they swerved
In a swift, circular line
To the left,
Because of the firecat.

The bucks clattered.
The firecat went leaping,
To the right, to the left,
And
Bristled in the way.

Later, the firecat closed his bright eyes
And slept.

SYLVIA PLATH

Black Rook in Rainy Weather

On the stiff twig up there
Hunches a wet black rook
Arranging and rearranging its feathers in the rain.
I do not expect miracle
Or an accident

To set the sight on fire
In my eye, nor seek
Any more in the desultory weather some design,
But let spotted leaves fall as they fall,
Without ceremony, or portent.

Although, I admit, I desire,
Occasionally, some backtalk
From the mute sky, I can't honestly complain:
A certain minor light may still
Leap incandescent

Out of kitchen table or chair
As if a celestial burning took
Possession of the most obtuse objects now and then—
Thus hallowing an interval
Otherwise inconsequent

By bestowing largesse, honour,
One might say love. At any rate, I now walk
Wary (for it could happen
Even in this dull, ruinous landscape); sceptical,
Yet politic; ignorant

Of whatever angel may choose to flare
Suddenly at my elbow. I only know that a rook

Ordering its black feathers can so shine
As to seize my senses, haul
My eyelids up, and grant

A brief respite from fear
Of total neutrality. With luck,
Trekking stubborn through this season
Of fatigue, I shall
Patch together a content

Of sorts. Miracles occur,
If you care to call those spasmodic
Tricks of radiance miracles. The wait's begun again,
The long wait for the angel,
For that rare, random descent.

XANDRA BINGLEY

Bertie, May & Mrs Fish

Mrs Fish

I put my fingers in my ears and run up the yard to the woodsaw that is screaming in the cart shed. Mr Munday pushes apple branches at circular whirling teeth spinning in and out of a slit in an iron table. A running tractor engine powers a long wide-webbed belt looped on the saw arm. As each slit log opens sawdust flies and a sawn log tumbles off the table. The saw whines until Munday feeds the branches to the spinning teeth again. I run back down the yard and unblock my ears going indoors.

In the kitchen jodhpur sweat is boiling out in a black cauldron before Mrs Fish scrubs the legs. My mother says . . . Shall we make a cake or meringues . . . I've got eggs to use up and enough sugar. I twiddle the wireless knob and see Mr Munday's knuckles knock at glass in the kitchen door. My mother says . . . Open it for him . . . there must be something he wants.

Mr Munday comes in and one hand holds the other and his brown hand-knitted vest has wet patches and he says . . . The saw had my fingers off.

My mother pushes a black saucepan off a hot Esse plate and closes the chrome mushroom lid. She picks up a tumbler off the drainer and turns a tap and fills the glass and pushes the rim at Munday's mouth and says . . . Drink some water . . . I can hold it for you . . . water will help . . . well done . . . that is enough . . . lift your hands up higher . . . up near your shoulder . . . keep as still as you can.

She tears a roller towel down the seam and tips two silver
safety pins out of a jam jar by the wireless and says to me . . . Get
cotton wool out of the dresser drawer. She wraps a sling round
Munday's chest and sticks in a pin at the back of his collarless
shirt and a pin at the back of his elbow and looks in the sling and
says . . . Give me the roll . . . and stuffs in all the cotton wool. She
rinses blood off her hand under the tap and says . . . Come on . . .
hurry . . . in the van . . . quickly . . . I'll get the saddle room
cotton wool . . . you jump in . . . Mr Munday in the front.

I run ahead and open the van door and clamber between the
front seats onto the corrugated tin floor and pull a blue-and-
yellow-checked horse rug flat. Mr Munday sits down sideways in
the passenger seat and faces the house and I say . . . Put your feet
in Mr Munday . . . I'll do your door.

I clamber out of the van and run round the bonnet past the
silver fox galloping in a horseshoe and slam his door and run
back round and climb in again over the driver's seat and my
mother races down the yard in her blue dungarees and blue
canvas lace-ups with hard jelly soles and says . . . Good girl.

She leans over the gearstick and unrolls the white cotton wool
pad in royal-blue paper and stuffs a handful inside the blue-and-
white-striped towel sling. Her hands get wet and she wipes
cotton wool up her fingers and drops the red-and-white sticky
lump by her feet. She starts the van. She backs past pigsties and
swerves by the barn. The van roars up through the gateway past
granary steps and the tractor shed's dark-green corrugated door
in bottom gear and stops at the cart shed by the tractor.

The saw whines and whirls and my mother leans over the
spinning belt to the tractor and the blade slows down. She looks
at the sawdust and kneels on one knee and reaches under the
table and picks up – once and twice – and runs to the van and
says . . . Don't look . . . look away . . . both of you . . . and I see a
fingernail black round the rim and cuticle and cut skin end and a
second finger.

She puts Mr Munday's cut-off fingers in cotton wool and wraps
them in dirty green velvet she keeps for cleaning the windscreen
and pushes the bundle onto the glove ledge in front of her knees
beside a torch and a spanner and says . . . All right in the back

. . . well done . . . sit on the rug . . . you made a good start on the wood, Munday . . . it is bad luck . . . they will take you in right away at the hospital . . . I will make sure you are seen to . . . then I can drive home and find Mrs Munday and bring her down . . . does she do up at Foxcote today . . . am I right? . . . until Jimmy comes home from school.

Mr Munday doesn't speak. The van hits potholes by Sheep Dip hump and uphill by Five Acre and Triangle Field. My mother steers zigzags to miss the bumps and at the red gate on the main road she corners and changes gear up to top on the level past Wistley Common. At Chatcombe Hill brow she goes down into second and accelerates through the double bend along the rim of the steep drop to Chatcombe Wood edge and at Seven Springs she says . . . Look left Mr Munday . . . if you are well enough . . . anything coming on the Cirencester road . . . and he stares ahead.

She brakes and looks left to Cirencester and straight across towards Gloucester and right to Cheltenham. She takes her chance and accelerates right and free-wheels down Leckhampton Hill and says . . . Now we are moving . . . it is good luck the road is clear for us . . . the dry wood left from last winter is enough for you Munday . . . and for us . . . plus two loads for Joe . . . and for Mrs Fish . . . we can use any old there is and add the new when you are well enough to carry on . . . there is plenty to creosote for now . . . that will be easier for you . . . larch posts for Grindstone fencing . . . and stable doors . . . the creosoting will keep you going . . . I will make sure there is work for you . . . Joe can take on things that need shifting . . . how are you holding up . . . not far now.

In Charlton Kings suburbs she says . . . Shall I risk it . . . thirty miles an hour will not get us there in a hurry . . . I am going to hope for the best. She cuts the red lights at the Prestbury Gymkhana field crossroads and says . . . Needs must . . . and she and I chant . . . When the devil drives . . . and the van corners right hard and right again onto gravel and stops and she looks back at me and says . . . You stay there . . . I won't be long . . . I promise . . . if I have to be I will come to get you . . . out you get Munday . . . we will have those fingers stitched on again in no time . . . if that is at all possible.

She walks up the hospital steps and opens the door for Mr Munday and holds the velvet bundle in her other hand.

Mr Munday's bloody vest comes home in brown paper and my mother hands it to Mrs Fish and says . . . Mr Munday had a bad time . . . two fingers lost on the circular saw . . . will you soak his vest . . . if it dries he will have it when he comes back from hospital . . . which hopefully will be before tonight.

She says to me . . . You stay here with Mrs Fish . . . I don't know what time I will be back . . . have a hunt for eggs in the top barns . . . I see one hen going in and out . . . she may be thinking of sitting . . . if you count six or more in a nest we will move her into a coop . . . thank you Mrs Fish . . . the wireless says afternoon weather is uncertain . . . good luck with the drying.

Mrs Fish drops Mr Munday's vest in a white enamel bucket of cold water and colours thicken from pale pink swirls to crimson. She turns back to the white china sink and her Woodbine ash falls and powders my mother's pink brassieres and silk peach camiknickers and linen blouses and blue dungarees piled on the flagstone floor. Her orange ringlets bounce under a bright-green crocheted beret she keeps on indoors and she leans forward in hot water steam. Her splashed crossover cotton apron has flower faces and the black plimsoles she keeps in the coal shed and changes into from white rubber boots have no laces.

I go in the larder and scoop up food in my fingers. Pastry crust on rabbit pie and rice pudding from under brown skin and pale-pink rhubarb fool. I watch Mrs Fish through larder door hinges. She dangles jodhpurs on a thick wooden spoon. Dirty water trickles in the sink and she dumps the sopping wet lump on the drainer and spreads the legs and scrubs at buckskin thighs with yellow Sunlight soap.

I tip up a glass bottle of Kia-Ora orange squash and the bottle mouth knocks my front teeth and I lick hurt nerves. Three chrome thermoses for harvest teas stand in a row and under the slate shelf cider and ginger beer and Guinness brown glass bottles fill a cardboard box and a note says . . . Brown bottles – keep out of light.

I stand beside Mrs Fish at the sink and run cold water in a glass of orange squash. She hisses . . . Get me a gin then . . . go on

. . . you heard. She grins and the Woodbine sticks to a lip and her teeth close on the little cigarette.

I can hear my father saying when he was home on leave . . . Here's to mother's ruin . . . and see him lift a cut-glass tumbler of gin and fizzy tonic . . . Shall we celebrate our beloved home by getting nicely foxed . . . what say you . . . how's that for the best idea the Colonel has had all day . . . and he sips from the glass and says . . . That washerwoman has been at the gin again . . . she damned well has . . . taste this . . . it's simply awful . . . watered down to cat's piss . . . she will simply have to go . . . I will not tolerate petty thieving in my house . . . I most certainly will not.

Mrs Fish puts her face close to mine . . . If I don't get my gin I'll tie these sodding jodhpurs round your neck . . . I am telling you.

Her wet red fingers open and the soap bar slips underwater. She pulls a blue-and-white stained tea towel off the Esse chrome rail and twists the linen in her hands and shoves the tea towel back and walks down the long white dining room her black plimsoles squeaking.

The dining room has a rosewood sideboard spinette. The keyboard has been sawed out and there it stands ruined and pretty at the end of the dining room and along the polished top stands Dutch and Irish and English silver. A rosebowl engraved with my mother's maiden name – "May Lenox-Conyngham – 1936 Pytchley Hunt Ladies' Race". Two silver cock pheasants . . . one pecking and one peering sideways. Two filigree jam pots with silver coolie hat lids and blue glass jars and a silver filigree pattern of tigers climbing flowers. Four glass decanters line up in grooved oak coasters with circular silver miniature picket fences. An Irish Waterford crystal decanter pair hold dark-crimson port and brown sherry. Two square Dutch ship's decanters hold transparent gin and tawny whisky.

Mrs Fish pours three fingers of gin and carries the tumbler and decanter to the kitchen and runs cold water in the decanter and holds the glass neck out to me and says . . . You put it back . . . go on . . . I'm telling you. Her soapy fingers slip and I catch and hug the cut-glass and tiptoe to the sideboard and say under my breath . . . Don't drop . . . don't drop . . . and think I can hear my father's

voice shout . . . What the bloody hell is going on in here . . . I
damned well want to know . . . speak up.

Mrs Fish drinks half a glass of gin and leans on the kitchen
table and coughs. Her coughs are rough and brittle. I go out of
the kitchen door and run up the yard slopping orange squash on
dandelions and stones.

Outside the harness room the mounting block is a two-step
concrete throne in sunshine. Behind a creosoted stable door
horses' shoes scratch cement and straw shifts under a pony's
feet. A crow flies over to Fishpond Wood. My father's horse kicks
a pine partition plank and splinters break. A horsefly comes at my
face and swerves. My black pony hangs his head over a half-door
and sighs and pricks his ears. I see creosote blister on stable doors
facing south. Mrs Fish carries a clothes basket out of the kitchen
door and weaves up coal shed cinder path and drops the basket. A
forked ash pole props the washing line and Mrs Fish gives the
pole a slap so the fork slides down the wire and the line sinks. She
flings wet clothes up over the wire and clips stripped bark hazel
pegs on overlaps of jodhpurs . . . knickers . . . blouses . . . brassieres . . . nightdresses . . . vests . . . dungarees. She stands on two
sawn-off logs and throws white sheets up and over and steps down
and tugs the sheets flat along the wire. Under the oak branches
she does a dance with the forked ash pole to hoist the line and the
wet clothes rise up and flap between the tree and coal shed roof.

I go in the stable and dandy-
brush dust out of the black
pony's silky summer coat and
finger yellow wavy dandy bristles and hold up my hand in
sunlight strips of dust. I hear
Mrs Fish's gumboots flap up
the stable path and she looks
in over the half-door . . . You
can take me back home now
. . . get him out . . .

I say . . . No thanks . . .

And she says . . . Get him
out here . . . I'm telling you.

She slams back the barrel bolt and the pony's head jerks up and I push his face in a webbing halter and lead the pony. Mrs Fish steps up on the mounting block under swallows playing in the blue sky. She lifts one white gumboot and hops a circle on her other foot and says . . . Come on then . . . bring him close . . .

And I say . . . I've got to get on first.

I vault on off the ground and ride past the mounting block and she steps behind me across the pony's broad back. We turn out of the yard and start down Rickyard Lane. White elder flowers big as saucers lean over stone walls on either side. Mrs Fish begins to sing . . . If you were the only boy in the world, and I was the only girl . . . in a sweet, husky treble and I groan.

At Fiveacre gate the stream parts clumps of gold kingcups and goes under the lane and oak and ash and larch grow along steep slopes either side and the path gets darker. Low branches stretch across and meet. The pony walks in hardly any light. Mrs Fish finishes singing "God Save the King" and begins . . . If you walk through a storm hold your head up high and don't be afraid of the dark . . . and we come to the wide-open Valley gate. The pony trots across baked mud ruts and starts to canter on the grass and I yell . . . I can't stop him . . . and Mrs Fish shouts close to my ear . . . Let him go then.

Her bony arms are tight round my waist and her fingers hold a butcher's grip. The galloping pony rocks. I pull up my knees and crouch and grip mane hair in both hands and hold the halter rope. Mrs Fish leans her chest on my back.

The pony gallops flat out over Valley cowslips and thistles. Rabbits run past bluebells and disappear down warrens in trees. Hoofbeats rumble and jays scream. A pigeon swerves above us as we race down the long bright-green strip. Where the woods end a chaotic plan of anthills circles Alexandra's Gorse hillside. Green tumps bulge high as the pony's knees and at a tall one the pony swerves downhill. Gravity pulls Mrs Fish sideways and she hugs me tightly. Her thighs slip. Our bodies cling and wobble and our legs stick out sideways and wave.

Mrs Fish and I fall . . . rolling over gorse twigs . . . stuck by green gorse needles . . . squashing yellow gorse flowers . . . red ants scurry . . . lucky for us ancient grass is spongy. We sit up side by side between anthills puffing hard. Downhill the pony pulls couch grass and mows small brilliant blue speedwell flowers and Mrs Fish says . . . Go on then . . . fetch him up here.

A rabbit skims a gorse bush and scuds uphill to the wicket gate and the flowering horse-chestnut tree and the pony's head comes up and his ears prick.

I say to Mrs Fish . . . Stand on an anthill . . . and I tug the pony up close and say . . . Bend your knee . . . one two three . . . and I lift her foot and she lands astride. I jump off the bouncy anthill behind her.

The pony walks to the Valley end and I see smoke from Mrs Fish's cottage and above Windmill blackthorn spinney grey windmill blades spin on a frame of legs and bars. Mrs Fish sings hymns – "For Those in Peril on the Sea" and "All Things Bright and Beautiful" and "And Did Those Feet in Ancient Times" – up to Needlehole Cottages. In the paddock the scent of dead lilac and cow-parsley and wood and stone blow past and I slide off and Mrs Fish swings her gumboot across the pony's neck. She sits side-saddle and slips down and I pull the pony round the way we came. Mrs Fish says . . . I'll have a ride back after Betty comes in for tea.

She hauls a split elm rail across the paddock track and pokes it in a horseshoe nailed on the gatepost and says . . . I'll fetch water . . . you let him go.

Dog roses grow up broken walls and stick through empty pigsty windows. Orange marigolds flower against a dark-green waterbutt. Mrs Fish drops in a wooden bucket for water. The pony pulls at roses. Mrs Fish shouts . . . Get him off the flowers.

She throws a stone so the wall rings. The pony backs away. She lugs the bucket up the garden path and water slips inside her white rubber boot. The pony drinks and huffs. His breathing starts a whirlpool in the bucket. He sucks and gulps and his long top hairstar lip wipes inside the rim and the bucket falls over and rolls and rattles. His front legs rear up towards Halfmoon Spinney and he prances along the trees with his nostrils flared and his tail crooked high. He halts and his knees and hocks fold and he sinks on the grass and rolls and chucks his body side to side and gallops his legs upside down. He sits front legs straight and stands and shakes his skin and starts to graze.

Mrs Fish says . . . You come along indoors.

I cross my legs and stand still. She opens the blue front door and looks round and shouts . . . The privy's round the back.

I hear water pour and wood fall inside the cottage. I can't see past geranium flowers and green leaves clambering up smeared window-panes. I go along a grass strip between carrot rows and peas twined in hazel sticks to a corrugated-iron hut. I shove my finger in an opening and lift a wire hook. Inside the hut torn newspaper hangs on mouldy green string and a circle is cut in board on a box and down the hole is black water and floating brown lumps and the smell's sweet rotted muck. I hunch off dungaree straps with my thumbs and shove down white cotton knickers and sit on the damp wood ring and shut my eyes tight. I can hear piss splash and see pink garden worms and shiny grey slugs crawl on my skin.

I don't touch the paper flaps. I hoist up knicker elastic and trouser bib and one strap and lift the hook and run along the grass path strip.

Mrs Fish's lovely daughter Betty comes in the garden gate. She is taller than Mrs Fish. Her auburn hair shines in the sun. She wears a white cotton puff-sleeve blouse and daffodil-yellow full gathered skirt and white ankle socks and slip-on black elastic plimsoles. Her blue eyes look my way. She smiles my father's smile and says . . . You coming in?

I don't follow her. In the paddock the backs of my legs press the drystone wall. I pick off yellow lichen cushions and hear chair legs scratch brick floor. The sun goes in. Swallows fly low over the two cottage chimneys. The cold breeze raises goose bumps on my skin. I lean on the pony's withers and fold my arms and put my cheek on my hands and when he steps I step.

Rain begins. I turn over the water bucket and step up and spring off onto the pony and whack his neck with the halter rope knot.

He stops grazing and I pull his head away from the cottage and whack his shoulder again and again and we jump the paddock sliprail and gallop down the stony lane. His ears lie back and he catsprings from green verge to centre strip. I sit tight. Soaking wet we gallop flat out beside a field of blue lucerne and he slides to a stop at top valley gate.

I leave the valley at Hilcot Lane by the stream. The rain gets less. Birds flicker in trees. A dog rose pricks my ankle bone. The pony's hooves slap stone. His tail whisks and slips off his backside. His head pulls down to graze and the rope knot jerks my fingers loose. He swipes at grasses and I hear him munch the tangled stalks.

At Hilcot Ford he walks in the water and drinks and cold fills my shoes. I slither off and my dungaree legs soak darker blue. In my pockets sugar lumps are syrup. Two green dragonflies dive and cling head to head. Four white ducks quack. I pick the halter rope out of the water and pull towards the elm plank bridge and stand and jump and land lying across the pony's back and wriggle and twist and sit up.

Churchbells ring the other side of Hilcot Hill and from the top

I see cars outside the churchyard wall. I ride down and knot the pony's rope to the churchyard gate and tiptoe over dandelions and gravel. I twist the iron ring and push the door and hear words from prayers . . . Beloved . . . born again . . . for ever . . . amen . . . and singing . . . the Lord is my shepherd, I shall not want . . .

A thick red velvet curtain is behind the oak door. I breathe in dust behind. People wear black in the three front pews and flowers are laid on a purple cloth. The singing stops. A parson speaks muffled words. I can't breathe. I press my thumb hard on a nail head in the oak door. I think I hear a voice say . . . Out you come, monkey face . . . no time like the present.

At the churchyard gate the pony dozes. I hug an arm round his face and my other arm across his neck and pull his head close to my chest. Men I don't recognise carry a coffin out on their shoulders and through the churchyard. On the church roof drainpipe a gargoyle grins. I jump on the pony and kick his sides and trot and bump bareback down the road and turn in the Abells' Hundred Acre grass field.

Skylarks sing and the pony gallops high above Foxcote village. I crouch forward and pull my knees up racing. I canter on

Roughill Lane and trot past Keeper's Cottages and Valley gate and the vegetable garden and up Rickyard Lane slope. In the stable I pull off the halter and wriggle the bolt shut and sit on the mounting block and hear milk buckets clang. My mother looks up the yard from top cowshed doors and calls . . . Come and give a hand . . . Mrs Fish has gone home . . . no one seems to be about.

HUGH MACDIARMID

Bairns Arena Frightened

Bairns arena frightened when they first
See the haill world transformed by snow
But accept the change and shout delightedly
As out to play in it they go.

This means, I think, that if our hearts are pure
We are prepared for any change at all
Owing no allegiance to the world we know
And always eager to renounce its thrall.

Bairns arena frightened when they first
See the haill world transformed by snow
Tho' they canna foresee it will not last forever
And the status quo ante come buldering through.

JACKIE KAY

Old Aberdeen

You'll never see what I'll give you
Out in the open country; the light coming in from the North Sea.
You'll never see what I'll give you
Up in the north, growing old under the lights of old Aberdeen.
You'll never see what I'll give you
A stone door opening to sunshine, the corn rigs the barley oh,
You'll never see, you'll never know
A song for every single day my love – Maxwellton braes are bonny.
You'll never see what I'd give you
Not now my lovely lassie oh.

JEANETTE WINTERSON

The 24-Hour Dog

He was soft as rainwater. On that first night I took him across a field mined with pheasants that flew up in our faces when we fused them out. The vertical explosion of a trod pheasant is shock enough when you know it. I knew it and it still skitters me. What could he know at two months old, head like a question mark?

I made him walk on a lead and he jumped for joy, the way creatures do, and children do, and adults don't do, and spend their lives wondering where the leap went.

He had the kind of legs that go round in circles. He orbited me. He was a universe of play. Why did I walk so purposefully in a straight line? Where would it take me? He went round and round and we got there all the same.

I had wanted to swim. I had wanted to wash off the hot tyre marks of the day. I wanted to let my body into the obliging water and kick the stars off the surface. I looped my dog-lead through a trough-hoop and undressed. Oh this was fun, a new pair of socks to chew and an old pair of boots to lie on. His questioning head sank to a full stop and he didn't notice me disappear under the water. The night smelled of rosemary and hay.

Oh, this was not fun, his sun drowned and him lost in a dark world without his own name. He started to yap with the wobbly bark he had just discovered and then he discovered he could use his long nose as a Howitzer and fire misery into the fearful place where there had been no fear.

I used my arms as jack levers and raised myself out of the pool. I spoke to him, and he caught the word as deftly as if I had thrown it. This was the edge of time, between chaos and shape. This was the little bit of evolution that endlessly repeats itself in the young and new-born thing. In this moment there are no cars or aeroplanes. The Sistine Chapel is unpainted, no book has been written. There is the moon, the water, the night, one creature's need and another's response. The moment between chaos and shape and I say his name and he hears me.

I had to carry him home, legs folded, nose in my jacket, he was twice as big as a grown cat even now, but small as my arms would allow.

I had collected him that morning from his brothers and sister, his mother, his friends on the farm. He was to be my dog, shot out of a spring litter, a coil of happiness. Bit by bit he would unfold.

He liked my sports car until it moved. Movement to him was four legs or maybe two. He had not yet invented the wheel. He lay behind my neck in stone-age despair, not rigid, but heavy, as his bladder emptied his enterprise, and the blue leather seats were puddled under puppy rain.

We were home in less than five minutes and he staggered from the car as though it were the hold of a slave ship and him left aboard for six months or more. His oversize paws were hesitant on the gravel because he half believed the ground would drive off with him.

I motioned him to the threshold; a little door in a pair of great gates. He looked at me: What should he do? I had to show him that two paws first, two paws after, would jump him across the wooden sill. He fell over but wagged his tail.

I had spent the early morning pretending to be a dog. I had crawled around my kitchen and scullery on all fours at dog height looking for toxic substances (bleach), noxious hazards (boot polish), forbidden delights (rubber boots), death traps (electric wires), swallowables, crunchables, munchables and saw-the-dog-in-half shears and tools.

I had spent the day before putting up new shelving and re-arranging the cupboards. A friend from London asked me if I was doing Feng Shui. I had to explain that this was not about energy alignments but somewhere to put the dog biscuits.

I re-routed the washing machine hoses. I had read in my manual that Lurchers like to chew washing machine hoses but only when the machine is on; thus, if they fail to electrocute themselves, they at least succeed in flooding the kitchen.

The week before I had forced my partner to go into Mothercare to purchase a baby gate. The experience nearly killed her. It was not the pastel colours, piped music and cartoon screen, or the assistants, specially graded into mental ages 2–4 and 4–6, or the special offers, 100 bibs for the price of 50, it was that she was run down by a fork lift truck moving a consignment of potties.

I fitted the gate. I tried to patch up my relationship. I spent a sleepless night on our new bean bag. I was pretending to be a dog.

The farmer telephoned me the following day.

"Will you come and get him now?"

Now. This now. Not later. Not sooner. Here now. Quick now.

Yes I will come for you. Roll my strength into a ball for you. Throw myself across chance for you. I will be the bridge or the pulley because you are the dream.

He's only a dog. Yes but he will find me out.

Dog and I did the gardening that virgin morning of budding summer. That is, I trimmed the escallonia and he fetched the entire contents of the garage, apart from the car. It began with a pruning gauntlet which he could see I needed. There followed a hanging basket, a Diana Ross cassette, a small fire extinguisher, a handbrush that made him look like Hitler, and one by one a hoarded collection of Victorian tiles. Being a circular kind of dog he ran in one door to seek the booty and sped out of another to bring it to me. He had not learned the art of braking. When he wanted to stop he just fell over.

I looked at the hoard spread before me. Perhaps this was an exercise in Feng Shui after all. Why did I need a Diana Ross tape? Why was I storing six feet of carpet underlay? I don't have any carpets.

The questions we ask of the universe begin and end with questions like these. He was a cosmic dog.

The light had the quality of water. I was moving through a conscious element. Time is a player. Time is part of today, not simply a measure of its passing.

The dimensionality of time is not usually apparent. I felt it today in the light like water. I knew I was moving through something that had substance. Something serious. Here was the dog, me, the sun, the sky, in a pattern, in a dance, and time was dancing with us, in the motes of light. The day was in the form of us and we were in the form of the day. Time would return it, as memory and as futurity; part of the pattern, the dance that I had refused.

He lay under the table fast asleep while I shelled broad beans. My cats, of which there are four, had taken up sentinel positions on the window ledges. The dog was bottom dog, no doubt, but twice as big as they were. They had not yet understood their psychic advantage. This dog did not know what size he was; he felt tiny to himself. He was still a pocket dog.

I looked at him, trusting, vulnerable, love without caution. He was a new beginning and every new beginning returns the world. In him, the rain forests were pristine and the sea had not been blunted. He was a map of clear outlines and unnamed hope. He was time before or time after. Time now had not spoilt him. In the space between chaos and shape there was another chance.

Night came. We made our journey to the pool. We swam back through the ripples of night. The light wind blew his ears inside out. He whimpered and fell asleep. When I finally staggered him home he was upside down.

I had bought him a bean bag with a purple cover tattooed with bones and chops. Who designs these items and why? What person, living in a town in England, sits down to doodle bones and chops? What kind of a private life does this design suggest? Is it a male or a female?

All these questions had presented themselves but there had been no alternative. A friend had once told me that as soon as she had become a parent, the discriminating good taste of her adult life had been ambushed by a garish crowd of design-bandits. She was finally at the mercy of the retail mob. You want a romper suit? Well, they've all got bunnies on them. You want a doggy bean bag? Well, we cover them in an orgy of chops.

Chops away! Over he went in a somersault of yelping pleasure. Was this really for him? He hurled himself at it and cocked an eye at me from under his paw. Would I shout at him? No! He was a new dog. The world was his bean bag.

I shut the cats in the kitchen with their cat flap. I shut the dog in the scullery with his ball and his bed. I shut myself away in the room that is sleep.

I had read in my manual that a dog must be dominated. He must not sleep upstairs. He must sleep alone.

An hour later I woke up. I understood that my dog had not read the manual. He told this to the night in long wails. I did not know what I should do and so I did nothing. He had been used to sleeping in a heap with his brothers and sister. Now he was alone. He called and kept calling and this time I did not answer. Chaos was complete.

About nine o'clock I went downstairs into the kitchen. The cats were on their perches, glaring at me with bags under their eyes like a set of Louis Vuitton luggage.

"We're leaving home" they said. "Just give us our breakfast and we're off."

I fed them and they queued up at the cat flap like a column of ants.

I glanced in the mirror. The bags under my eyes needed a porter's trolley.

Next question. The dog?

I opened the door into the scullery. The dog was lying on his bean bag, nose in his paws, a sight of infinite dejection. I stood for a moment, then he unsteadily got up and crawled across the floor to me on his belly. As anticipated by the manual, I had become the master.

I let him out into the sunlight. I gave him his gigantic bowl of cereal and milk. I have always loved the way dogs eat their food; the splashy, noisy, hog pleasure of head in trough. I am a great supporter of table manners but it is worthwhile to be reminded of what we are.

And that was the problem; the dog would pour through me and every pin hole would be exposed. I know I am a leaky vessel but do I want to know it every day?

He's only a dog. Yes but he has found me out.

I clipped on his lead and walked him round the fields in my dressing gown and boots. If this seems eccentric, remember that my soul had been exposed and whatever I wore was of no use to cover it. Why dress when I could not be clothed?

He circled along in his warm skin, happy again because he was free and because he belonged. All of one's life is a struggle towards that; the narrow path between freedom and belonging. I have sometimes sacrificed freedom in order to belong, but more often I have given up all hope of belonging.

It is no use trying to assume again the state of innocence and acceptance of the animal or the child. This time it has to be conscious. To circle about in such gladness as his, is the effort of a whole lifetime.

The day was misty and settled on his coat like a warning. I was looking into the future, thinking about what I would have to be to the dog in return for what he would be to me. It would have been much easier if he had been an easier dog. I mean, less intelligent, less sensitive, less brimful of that jouissance which should not be harmed.

It would have been much easier if I had been an easier person. We were so many edges, dog and me, and of the same recklessness. And of the same love. I have learned what love costs. I never count it but I know what it costs.

I telephoned the farmer. "You will have to take him back" I said. "I can't do this."

It had been the arrangement between us from the start; when there were six puppies in a squealing heap and one by one sensible country people had come to claim them. There is no reason why I should not keep a dog. I have enough land, enough house, enough time, and patience with whatever needs to grow.

I had thought about everything carefully before I had agreed to him. I had made every preparation, every calculation, except for those two essentials that could not be calculated; his heart and mine.

My girlfriend carried the bean bag. I walked the dog, gaiety in the bounce of him, his body spinning as the planet spins, this little round of life.

We were escorted off the premises by my venerable cat, an ancient, one-eyed bugger of a beast, of whom the dog was afraid. At the boundary of our field, the cat sat, as he always does, waiting for us to come back, this time by ourselves.

As we reached the farm, the dog hesitated and hung his head. I spoke to him softly. I tried to explain. I don't know what he understood but I knew he understood that he would not be my dog any more. We were crossing an invisible line high as a fence.

For the last time I picked him up and carried him.

Then of course there was his mother and his brothers and sister and I gave them biscuits and bones and the bean bag was a badge of pride for him. Look what he had been and got.

We put him in the run and he began to play again, over and tumble in a simple doggy way, and already the night, the pool, the wind, his sleeping body, the misty morning that had lain on us both, were beginning to fade.

I don't know what the farmer thought. I mumbled the suitable excuses, and it was true that my partner had just heard she would be working away for some weeks, and that it is tough to manage one's own work, the land, the house, the animals, even without a brand-new dog.

What I couldn't say was that the real reason was so much deeper and harder and that we spend our lives deceiving ourselves of those real reasons, perhaps because when they are clear they are too painful.

I used to hear him barking in the weeks that followed. His bark aimed at my heart. Then another person claimed him and called him Harry, and took him to live on a farm where there were children and ducks and company and things to do and the kind of doggy life he never would have had with me. What would I have done? Taught him to read?

I know he won't be the dog he could have been if I had met him edge to edge, his intensity and mine. Maybe it's better that way. Maybe it's better for me. I live in the space between chaos and shape. I walk the line that continually threatens to lose its tautness under me, dropping me into the dark pit where there is no meaning. At other times the line is so wired that it lights up the soles of my feet, gradually my whole body, until I am my own beacon, and I see then the beauty of newly created worlds, a form that is not random. A new beginning.

I saw all this in him and it frightened me.

I gave him a name. It was Nimrod, the mighty hunter of Genesis, who sought out his quarry and brought it home. He found me out. I knew he would. The strange thing is that although I have given him away, I can't lose him, and he can't die. There he is, forever, part of the pattern, the dance, and running beside me, joyful.

WILLIAM CARLOS WILLIAMS

Pastoral

When I was younger
it was plain to me
I must make something of myself.
Older now
I walk back streets
admiring the houses
of the very poor:
roof out of line with sides
the yards cluttered
with old chicken wire, ashes,
furniture gone wrong;
the fences and outhouses
built of barrel-staves
and parts of boxes, all,
if I am fortunate,
smeared a bluish green
that properly weathered
pleases me best
of all colors.

No one
will believe this
of vast import to the nation.

PHILIP LARKIN

The Trees

The trees are coming into leaf
Like something almost being said;
The recent buds relax and spread,
Their greenness is a kind of grief.

Is it that they are born again
And we grow old? No, they die too.
Their yearly trick of looking new
Is written down in rings of grain.

Yet still the unresting castles thresh
In fullgrown thickness every May.
Last year is dead, they seem to say,
Begin afresh, afresh, afresh.

NAN SHEPHERD

The Living Mountain: A Celebration of the Cairngorm Mountains of Scotland

Frost and Snow

The freezing of running water is another mystery. The strong white stuff, whose power I have felt in swollen streams, which I have watched pour over ledges in endless ease, is itself held and punished. But the struggle between frost and the force in running water is not quickly over. The battle fluctuates, and at the point of fluctuation between the motion in water and the immobility of frost, strange and beautiful forms are evolved. Until I spent a whole midwinter day wandering from one burn to another watching them, I had no idea how many fantastic shapes the freezing of running water took. In each whorl and spike one catches the moment of equilibrium between two elemental forces.

The first time I really looked at this shaping process was in the Slugain valley on a January day. The temperature in Braemar village had fallen the previous night to –2°F. We had climbed Morrone in the afternoon, and seen sunset and the rise of a full moon together over a world that was completely white except for some clumps of firewood that looked completely black. (In Glen Quoich next day the ancient fir trees far up the valley had the same dead black look – no green in them at all.) The intense frost, the cloudless sky, the white world, the setting sun and the rising moon, as we gazed on them from the slope of Morrone, melted into a prismatic radiation of blue, helio, mauve, and rose. The full moon floated up into green light; and as the rose and violet hues spread over snow and sky, the colour seemed to live its own life, to have body and resilience, as though we were not looking at it, but were inside its substance.

Next day a brilliant sun spangled the snow and the precipices of Ben a' Bhuird hung bright rose-red above us. How crisp, how bright a world! but, except for the crunch of our own boots on the snow, how silent. Once some grouse fled noiselessly away and we lifted our heads quickly to look for a hunting eagle. And down valley he came, sailing so low above our heads that we could see the separate feathers of the pinions against the sky, and the lovely lift of the wings when he steadied them to soar. Near the top of the glen there were coal-tits in a tree, and once a dipper plunged outright into the icy stream. But it was not an empty world. For everywhere in the snow were the tracks of birds and animals.

The animals had fared as we did: sometimes we stepped buoyantly over the surface of drifts, sometimes sank in well above the knees. Sometimes the tracks were deep holes in the snow, impossible to read except by the pattern in which they were placed; sometimes the mark of the pad was clear, just sunk into the snow surface, and at other times only four, or five, spaced pricks showed where the claws had pierced.

These tracks give to winter hill walking a distinctive pleasure. One is companioned, though not in time. A hare bounding, a hare trotting, a fox dragging his brush, grouse thick-footed, plover thin, red deer and roes have passed this way. In paw depressions may be a delicate tracery of frost. Or a hare's tracks may stand up in ice-relief above the softer snow that has been blown from around them. In soft dry snow the pad of a hare makes a leaflike pattern. A tiny track, like twin beads on a slender thread, appears suddenly in the middle of virgin snow. An exploring finger finds a tunnel in the snow, from which the small mouse must have emerged.

But while birds and tracks (we saw nothing four-footed that morning) amused us as we went up the Slugain, our most exquisite entertainment came from the water. Since then I have watched many burns in the process of freezing, but I do not know if description can describe these delicate manifestations. Each is an interplay between two movements in simultaneous action, the freezing of frost and the running of water. Sometimes a third force, the blowing of wind, complicates the forms still further. The ice may be crystal clear, but more probably is translucent; crimpled, crackled or bubbled; green throughout or at the edges.

Where the water comes wreathing over stones the ice is opaque, in broken circular structure. Where the water runs thinly over a line of stones right across the bed and freezes in crinkled green cascades of ice, then a dam forms further up of half frozen slush, green, though colourless if lifted out, solid at its margins, foliated, with the edges all separate, like untrimmed hand-made paper, and each edge a vivid green. Where water drips steadily from an overhang, undeflected by wind, almost perfect spheres of clear transparent ice result. They look unreal, in this world of wayward undulations, too regular, as though man had made them. Spray splashing off a stone cuts into the slowly freezing snow on the bank and flutes it with crystal, or drenches a sprig of heather that hardens to a tree of purest glass, like an ingenious toy. Water running over a rock face freezes in ropes, with the ply visible. Where the water fell clear of the rock icicles hang, thick as a thigh, many feet in length, and sometimes when the wind blows the falling water askew as it freezes, the icicles are squint. I have seen icicles like a scimitar blade in shape, firm and solid in their place. For once, even the wind has been fixed. Sometimes a smooth portion of stream is covered with a thin coat of ice that, not quite meeting in the middle, shows the level of the water several inches below; since the freezing began, the water up-stream has frozen and less water is flowing. When a level surface has frozen hard from bank to bank, one may hear at times a loud knocking, as the stream, rushing below the ice, flings a stone up against its roof. In boggy parts by the burnside one treads on what seems solid frozen snow, to find only a thin crisp crust that gives way to reveal massed thousands of needle crystals of ice, fluted columns four or five inches deep. And if one can look below the covering ice on a frozen burn, a lovely pattern of fluted indentations is found, arched and chiselled, the obverse of the water's surface, with the subtle shift of emphasis and super-imposed design that occurs between a painting and the land-scape it represents. In short, there is no end to the lovely things that frost and the running of water can create between them.

When the ice-paws crisped round the stones in the burns, and the ice-carrots that hang from the ledges, are loosened, and the freed ice floats down the river, it looks like masses of floating water lilies, or bunching cauliflower heads. Sunset plays through this greenish-white mass in iridescent gleams. At one point (I have heard of it nowhere else) near the exit of a loch, the peculiar motion of the current among ice-floes has woven the thousands of floating pine-needles into compacted balls, so intricately intertwined that their symmetrical shape is permanently retained. They can be lifted out of the water and kept for years, a botanical puzzle to those who have not been told the secret of their formation.

Snow too can be played with by frost and wind. Loose snow blown in the sun looks like the ripples running through corn. Small snow on a furious gale freezes on the sheltered side of stones on a hilltop in long crystals; I have seen these converge slightly as the wind blows round both sides of the stones. Another fixation of the wind. Or the wind lifts the surface of loose snow but before it has detached it from the rest of the snow, frost has petrified the delicate shavings in flounces of transparent muslin. "Prince of Wales Feathers", one of my friends has called a similar materialisation of wind and frost. Snow can blow past in a cloud, visible as it approaches, but formed of minute ice particles, so fine that the eye cannot distinguish them individually as they pass. Set the hand against them and it is covered by infinitesimal droplets of water whose impact has hardly been felt, though if the face is turned towards them, the spicules sting the eyeball. Such snow lies in a ghostly thin powdering on the hillside, like the "glaister o' sifted snaw" that fell on the head of the old Scots minister in his ill-roofed kirk.

The coming of snow is often from a sky of glittering blue, with serried battalions of solid white cumuli low on the horizon. One of them bellies out from the ranks, and from its edge thin shreds of snow, so fine one is hardly aware of their presence, eddy lightly in the blue sky. And in a few minutes the air is thick with flakes. Once the snow has fallen, and the gullies are choked and ice is in the burns, green is the most characteristic colour in sky and water. Burns and river alike have a green glint when seen between snowy banks, and the smoke from a woodman's fire looks greenish against the snow. The shadows on snow are of course blue, but where snow is blown into ripples, the shadowed undercut portion can look quite green. A snowy sky is often pure green, not only at sunrise or sunset, but all day; and a snow-green sky looks greener in reflection, either in water or from windows, than it seems in reality. Against such a sky, a snow-covered hill may look purplish, as though washed in blaeberry. On the other hand, before a fresh snowfall, whole lengths of snowy hill may appear a golden green. One small hill stands out from this greenness: it is veiled by a wide-spaced fringe of fir trees, and behind them the whole snowy surface of the hill is burning with a vivid electric blue.

The appearance of the whole group, seen from without, while snow is taking possession, changes with every air. A thin covering of snow, through which the rock structure breaks, can look more insubstantial than the most diaphanous blue – a phantom created from reality. When the snow is melting, and the plateau is still white but the lower slopes are streaked and patched, against a grey-white sky only the dark portions show; the plateau isn't there, the ridges that run up to the corries stand out like pinnacles and aiguilles. Later, at evening, the sky has turned a deep slate blue, identical with the blue that now washes the bare lower stretches of the mountains, and the long high level summit of snow, with its downward-reaching tentacles, hangs unsupported.

When the mountains are at last completely covered in with snow (and it doesn't happen every winter, so unpredictable is this Cairngorm weather – the skiers may wait far into the spring in vain for the right depth and surface of snow), then on a sunny day the scintillation is bright but does not wound. The winter light has not the strength to harm. I have never myself found it distressing to the eyes, though sometimes I have walked all day through millions of sparkling sun spangles on the frosty snow. The only time I have suffered from snow-blindness was at the very end of April, by which time, five or six weeks after the equinox, this northern light has become strong. I have heard of a strange delusion that the sun does not shine up here. It does; and because of the clarity of the air its light has power: it has more power, I suppose, in light than in heat. On that late April day, after some halcyon weather, a sudden snow storm blew up. It snowed all night – thick heavy snow that lay even under the next day's sunshine. We were going to the Dubh Loch of Ben a' Bhuird, with no intention of a summit, and I had taken no precautions against exposure; I had expected neither frosty wind nor hot sun to play havoc with my skin, nor had I had till then any experience of strong light upon snow. After a while I found the glare intolerable; I saw scarlet patches on the snow; I felt sick and weak. My companion refused to leave me sitting in the snow and I refused to defeat the object of his walk, which was to photograph the loch in its still wintry condition; so I struggled on, with his dark handkerchief veiling my eyes – a miserable blinkered imprisonment – and in time we were shadowed by the dark sides of the corrie. I was badly burned that day too; for some days my face was as purple as a boozer's; all of which discomfort I might have avoided had I remembered that snow can blow out of a warm sky.

It is not, however, such freak storms that are of moment, but the January blizzards, thick, close and wild – the *blin' drift* that shuts a man into deadly isolation. To go into such conditions on the mountain is folly; the gamekeeper's dictum is: if you can't see your own footsteps behind you in the snow, don't go on. But a blizzard may blow up so rapidly that one is caught. The great storms, when the snow beats down thick and solid for days on end, piling into the bowls of the corries, pressing itself down by its own weight, may be seen gathering over the mountains before they spread and cover the rest of the earth. I watched the preparation of the storm that was called, when it broke upon the country, the worst for over fifty years. I watched, from the shoulder of Morrone, the Cairngorm mass eddy and sink and rise (as it seemed) like a tossed wreck on a yellow sea. Sky and the wrack of precipice and overhang were confounded together. Now a spar, now a mast, just recognisable as buttress or cornice, tossed for a moment in the boiling sea of cloud. Then the sea closed on it, to open again with another glimpse of mounting spars – a shape drove its way for a moment through the smother, and was drawn under by the vicious swirl. Ashen and yellow, the sky kicked convulsively.

All this while the earth around me was bare. Throughout

December the ground had been continuously white, but in the first week of the year there came a day like April, the snow sunned itself away and the land basked mildly in the soft airs. But now the commotion among the mountains lashed out in whips of wind that reached me where I stood watching. Soon I could hardly stand erect against their force. And on the wind sailed minute thistledowns of snow, mere gossamers. Their fragility, insubstantial almost as air, presaged a weight and solidity of snow that was to lie on the land for many weeks.

In the corries the tight-packed snow stands for many months. Indeed, until a succession of unusually hot summers from 1932 to 1934, even in July there were solid walls of snow, many feet thick and as high as the corrie precipices, leaning outwards from the rock and following its contours. There was snow worth seeing in those old summers. I used to believe it was eternal snow, and touched it with a feeling of awe. But by August 1934, there was no snow left at all in the Cairngorms except a small patch in the innermost recess of the Garbh Choire of Braeriach. Antiquity has gone from our snow.

It was in the storm whose beginnings I have described, during a blizzard, that a plane containing five Czech airmen crashed into Ben a' Bhuird. That its impact was made in deep snow was clear from the condition of the engines, which were only a little damaged.

Blizzard is the most deadly condition of these hills. It is wind that is to be feared, even more than snow itself. Of the lives that have been lost in the Cairngorms while I have been frequenting them (there have been about a dozen, excepting those who have perished in plane crashes) four were lost in blizzard. Three fell from the rock – one of these a girl. One was betrayed by the ice-hard condition of a patch of snow in May, and slipped. All these were young. Two older men have gone out, and disappeared. The body of one of these was discovered two years later.

Of the four who were caught in blizzard, two died on 2 January 1928, and two on the same date in 1933. The former two spent their last night in the then disused cottage where I have since passed some of the happiest times of my life. Old Sandy Mackenzie the stalker, still alive then, in the other small house on the croft, warned the boys against the blizzard. As I sit with Mrs Mackenzie, now, by the open fireplace, with a gale howling in the chimney and rattling the iron roof ("this tin-can of a place", she calls it), and watch her wrinkled hands build the fir-roots for a blaze, she tells me of the wind that was in it. I listen to the smashing of this later gale, which has blown all night. "If you had been getting up and going away the house would have been following you," she says, knowing my habit of sleeping by the door and prowling at all sorts of hours. And remembering how I crept down into my bag last night, I picture those two boys lying on the floor in the empty house, with the roof rattling and the icy wind finding every chink. Not that they had cared. They asked for nothing but a roof. "And salt – they asked for salt." Strange symbolic need of a couple of boys who were to find no hospitality again on earth. Her old bleared eyes look into the distance. She says, "the snow would be freezing before it would be on your cheek." John, the son, found the second body in March, in a snow drift that he and his West Highland terrier had passed many times. "But that morning," he told me, "she was scraping." "You will not be finding a thing but in the place where it will be", says the old woman. She had fetched the bellows and blown the logs into a flame. "Sandy used to say, *The fire is the finest flower of them all*, when he would be coming in from the hill." She makes the tea. But she has brought the storm in to our fireside, and it stays there through the night.

The other two boys went over Cairn Gorm in the kind of miraculous midwinter weather that sometimes occurs, and slept the night at the Shelter Stone beside Loch Avon. They were local boys. In the July of that year, on a very fine Sunday when we had gone out at dawn and had an empty hill all morning to ourselves, we saw with amazement a stream of people come up the hill the easy way from Glenmore and pass over and down to the Shelter Stone. We counted a hundred persons on the hill. They had come to see the place where the two boys slept and to read their high-spirited and happy report in the book that lies in its waterproof cover beneath the huge balanced boulder that has sheltered so many sleepers. That they would not reach home when they set out that morning after writing it, they could not dream. One of them was an experienced hill walker. But they reckoned without the wind. The schoolmistress of the tiny school at Dorback, which lies under Cairn Gorm on the Abernethy side, told me, of that wind, that her crippled sister, crossing the open space of the playground, was blown from her feet. And five miles from Glenmore and safety, crawling down Coire Cas on hands and knees, the boys could fight the wind no further. It was days later till they found them; and one of the men who was at the finding described to me their abraded knees and knuckles. The elder of the two was still crawling, on hands and knees, when they found him fast in the drift. *So quick bright things come to confusion.* They committed, I suppose, an error of judgment, but I cannot judge them. For it is the risk we must all take when we accept individual responsibility for ourselves on the mountain, and until we have done that, we do not begin to know it.

ALAN SPENCE

into the sea I launch
a piece of driftwood – with
great ceremony!

J. M. SYNGE

Prelude

Still south I went and west and south again,
Through Wicklow from the morning till the night,
And far from cities, and the sites of men,
Lived with the sunshine and the moon's delight.

I knew the stars, the flowers, and the birds,
The grey and wintry sides of many glens,
And did but half remember human words,
In converse with the mountains, moors, and fens.

In May

In a nook
That opened south,
You and I
Lay mouth to mouth.

A snowy gull
And sooty daw
Came and looked
With many a caw;

"Such," I said,
"Are I and you,
When you've kissed me
Black and blue!"

GERTRUDE STEIN

On the Meaning of "rose is a rose is a rose"

Now listen. Can't you see that when the language was new – as it was with Chaucer and Homer – the poet could use the name of a thing and the thing was really there. He could say "O moon", "O sea", "O love", and the moon and the sea and love were really there. And can't you see that after hundreds of years had gone by and thousands of poems had been written, he could call on those words and find that they were just wornout literary words. The excitingness of pure being had withdrawn from them; they were just rather stale literary words. Now the poet has to work in the excitingness of pure being; he has to get back that intensity into the language. We all know that it's hard to write poetry in a late age; and we know that you have to put some strangeness, as something unexpected, into the structure of the sentence in order to bring back vitality to the noun. Now it's not enough to be bizarre; the strangeness in the sentence structure has to come from the poetic gift, too. That's why it's doubly hard to be a poet in a late age. Now you all have seen hundreds of poems about roses and you know in your bones that the rose is not there. All those songs that sopranos sing as encores about "I have a garden! oh, what a garden!" Now I don't want to put too much emphasis on that line, because it's just one line in a longer poem. But I notice that you all know it; you make fun of it, but you know it. Now listen! I'm no fool. I know that in daily life we don't go around saying ". . . is a . . . is a . . . is a . . .". Yes, I'm no fool; but I think that in that line the rose is red for the first time in English poetry for a hundred years.

HISTORIES

WILLIAM BLAKE

Infant Joy

I have no name
I am but two days old.—
What shall I call thee?
I happy am
Joy is my name,—
Sweet joy befall thee!

Pretty joy!
Sweet joy but two days old.
Sweet joy I call thee:
Thou dost smile.
I sing the while
Sweet joy befall thee.

A Poison Tree

I was angry with my friend:
I told my wrath, my wrath did end.
I was angry with my foe:
I told it not, my wrath did grow.

And I waterd it in fears,
Night & morning with my tears:
And I sunned it with smiles,
And with soft deceitful wiles.

And it grew both day and night,
Till it bore an apple bright.
And my foe beheld it shine,
And he knew that it was mine.

And into my garden stole,
When the night had veild the pole;
In the morning glad I see,
My foe outstretchd beneath the tree.

LEWIS GRASSIC GIBBON

Sunset Song

from Prelude

Kinraddie lands had been won by a Norman childe, Cospatric de Gondeshil, in the days of William the Lyon, when gryphons and suchlike beasts still roamed the Scots countryside and folk would waken in their beds to hear the children screaming, with a great wolf-beast, come through the hide window, tearing at their throats. In the Den of Kinraddie one such beast had its lair and by day it lay about the woods and the stench of it was awful to smell all over the countryside, and at gloaming a shepherd would see it, with its great wings half-folded across the great belly of it and its head, like the head of a meikle cock, but with the ears of a lion, poked over a fir tree, watching. And it ate up sheep and men and women and was a fair terror, and the King had his heralds cry a reward to whatever knight would ride and end the mischieving of the beast.

So the Norman childe, Cospetric, that was young and landless and fell brave and well-armoured, mounted his horse in Edinburgh Town and came North, out of the foreign south parts, up through the Forest of Fife and into the pastures of Forfar and past Aberlemno's Meikle Stane that was raised when the Picts beat the Danes; and by it he stopped and looked at the figures, bright then and hardly faded even now, of the horses and the charging and the rout of those coarse foreign folk. And maybe he said a bit prayer by that Stone and then he rode into the Mearns, and the story tells no more of his riding but that at last come he did to Kinraddie, a tormented place, and they told him where the gryphon slept, down there in the Den of Kinraddie.

But in the daytime it hid in the woods and only at night, by a path through the hornbeams, might he come at it, squatting in bones, in its lair. And Cospatric waited for the night to come and rode to the edge of Kinraddie Den and commended his soul to God and came off his horse and took his boar-spear in his hand, and went down into the Den and killed the gryphon. And he sent the news to William the Lyon, sitting drinking the wine and fondling his bonny lemans in Edinburgh Town, and William made him the Knight of Kinraddie, and gave to him all the wide parish as his demesne and grant to build him a castle there, and wear the sign of a gryphon's head for a crest and keep down all beasts and coarse and wayward folk, him and the issue of his body for ever after.

So Cospatric got him the Pict folk to build a strong castle there in the lithe of the hills, with the Grampians bleak and dark behind it, and he had the Den drained and he married a Pict lady and got on her bairns and he lived there till he died. And his son took the name Kinraddie, and looked out one day from the castle wall and saw the Earl Marischal come marching up from the south to join the Highlandmen in the battle that was fought at Mondynes, where now the meal-mill stands; and he took out his men and fought there, but on which side they do not say, but maybe it was the winning one, they were aye gey and canny folk, the Kinraddies.

And the great-grandson of Cospatric, he joined the English against the cateran Wallace, and when Wallace next came marching up from the southlands Kinraddie and other noble folk of that time they got them into Dunnottar Castle that stands out in the sea beyond Kinneff, well-builded and strong, and the sea splashes about it in the high tides and there the din of the gulls is a yammer night and day. Much of meal and meat and gear they took with them, and they laid themselves up there right strongly, they and their carles, and wasted all the Mearns that the Cateran who dared rebel against the fine English king might find no provision for his army of coarse and landless men. But Wallace came through the Howe right swiftly and he heard of Dunnottar and laid siege to it and it was a right strong place and he had but small patience with strong places. So, in the dead of one night, when the thunder of the sea drowned the noise of his feint, he climbed the Dunnottar rocks and was over the wall, he and the vagabond Scots, and they took Dunnottar and put to the slaughter the noble folk gathered there, and all the English, and spoiled them of their meat and gear, and marched away.

Kinraddie Castle that year, they tell, had but a young bride new home and she had no issue of her body, and the months went by and she rode to the Abbey of Aberbrothock where the good Abbot, John, was her cousin, and told him of her trouble and how the line of Kinraddie was like to die. So he lay with her that was September, and next year a boy was born to the young bride, and after that the Kinraddies paid no heed to wars and bickerings but sat them fast in their Castle lithe in the hills, with their gear and bonny leman queans and villeins libbed for service.

And when the First Reformation came and others came after it and some folk cried *Whiggam!* and some cried *Rome!* and some cried *The King!* the Kinraddies sat them quiet and decent and peaceable in their castle, and heeded never a fig the arguings of folk, for wars were unchancy things. But then Dutch William came, fair plain a fixture that none would move, and the Kinraddies were all for the Covenant then, they had aye had God's Covenant at heart, they said. So they builded a new kirk down where the chapel had stood, and builded a manse by it, there in the middle of the yews where the cateran Wallace had hid when the English put him to rout at last. And one Kinraddie, John Kinraddie, went south and became a great man in the London court, and was crony of the creatures Johnson and James Boswell and once the two of them, John Kinraddie and James Boswell, came up to the Mearns on an idle ploy and sat drinking wine and making coarse talk far into the small hours night after night till the old laird wearied of them and then they would steal away and as James Boswell set in his diary, *Did get to the loft where the maids were, and one* Πεγγι Δυνδας ωας φατ ιν τηε βυττοςχς ανδ ι διδ λιε ωιτη ηερ.

But in the early days of the nineteenth century it was an ill time for the Scots gentry, for the poison of the French Revolution came over the seas and crofters and common folk like that stood up and cried *Away to hell!* when the Auld Kirk preached submission from its pulpits. Up as far as Kinraddie came the poison and the young laird of that time, and he was Kenneth, he called himself a Jacobin and joined the Jacobin Club of Aberdeen and there at Aberdeen was nearly killed in the rioting, for liberty and equality and fraternity, he called it. And they carried him back to Kinraddie a cripple, but he would still have it that all men were free and equal and he set to selling the estate and sending the money to France, for he had a real good heart. And the crofters marched on Kinraddie Castle in a body and bashed in the windows of it, they thought equality should begin at home.

More than half the estate had gone in this driblet and that while the cripple sat and read his coarse French books; but nobody guessed that till he died and then his widow, poor woman, found herself own no more than the land that lay between the coarse hills, the Grampians, and the farms that stood out by the Bridge End above the Denburn, straddling the outward road. Maybe there were some twenty to thirty holdings in all, the crofters dour folk of the old Pict stock, they had no history, common folk, and ill-reared their biggins clustered and chaved amid the long, sloping fields. The leases were one-year, two-year, you worked from the blink of the day you were breeked to the flicker of the night they shrouded you, and the dirt of gentry sat and ate up your rents but you were as good as they were.

So that was Kenneth's leaving to his lady body, she wept right sore over the pass that things had come to, but they kittled up before her own jaw was tied in a clout and they put her down in Kinraddie vault to lie by the side of her man. Three of her bairns were drowned at sea, fishing off the Bevie braes they had been, but the fourth, the boy Cospatric, him that died the same day as the Old Queen, he was douce and saving and sensible, and set putting the estate to rights. He threw out half the little tenants, they flitted off to Canada and Dundee and parts like those, the others he couldn't move but slowly.

But on the cleared land he had bigger steadings built and he let them at bigger rents and longer leases, he said the day of the fine big farm had come. And he had woods of fir and larch and pine planted to shield the long, bleak slopes, and might well have retrieved the Kinraddie fortunes but that he married a Morton quean with black blood in her, she smitted him and drove him to drink and death, that was the best way out. For his son was clean

daft, they locked him up at last in an asylum, and that was the
end of Kinraddie family, the Meikle House that stood where the
Picts had builded Cospatric's castle crumbled to bits like a
cheese, all but two-three rooms the trustees held as their offices,
the estate was mortgaged to the hilt by then.

So by the winter of nineteen eleven there were no more than nine
bit places left the Kinraddie estate, the Mains the biggest of
them, it had been the Castle home farm in the long past times. An
Irish creature, Erbert Ellison was the name, ran the place for the
trustees, he said, but if you might believe all the stories you
heard he ran a hantle more silver into his own pouch than he ran
into theirs. Well might you expect it, for once he'd been no more
than a Dublin waiter, they said. That had been in the time before
Lord Kinraddie, the daft one, had gone clean skite. He had been
in Dublin, Lord Kinraddie, on some drunken ploy, and Ellison
had brought his whisky for him and some said he had halved his
bed with him. But folk would say anything.

So the daftie took Ellison back with him to Kinraddie and
made him his servant, and sometimes, when he was real drunk
and the fairlies came sniffering out of the whisky bottles at him,
he would throw a bottle at Ellison and shout *Get out, you bloody
dish-clout!* so loud it was heard across at the Manse and fair
affronted the minister's wife. And old Greig, him that had been
the last minister there, he would glower across at Kinraddie
House like John Knox at Holyrood, and say that God's hour
would come. And sure as death it did, off to the asylum they
hurled the daftie, he went with a nurse's mutch on his head and
he put his head out of the back of the waggon and said *Cock-
adoodledoo!* to some school bairns the waggon passed on the road
and they all ran home and were fell frightened.

But Ellison had made himself well acquainted with farming
and selling stock and most with buying horses, so the trustees
they made him manager of the Mains, and he moved into the
Mains farmhouse and looked him round for a wife. Some would
have nothing to do with him, a poor creature of an Irishman who
couldn't speak right and didn't belong to the Kirk, but Ella

White she was not so particular and was fell long in the tooth herself. So when Ellison came to her at the harvest ball in Auchinblae and cried *Can I see you home to-night, me dear?* she said *Och, Ay*. And on the road home they lay among the stooks and maybe Ellison did this and that to make sure of getting her, he was fair desperate for any woman by then.

They were married next New Year's Day, and Ellison had begun to think himself a gey man in Kinraddie, and maybe one of the gentry. But the bothy billies, the ploughmen and the orra men of the Mains, they'd never a care for gentry except to mock at them and on the eve of Ellison's wedding they took him as he was going into his house and took off his breeks and tarred his dowp and the soles of his feet and stuck feathers on them and then they threw him into the water-trough, as was the custom. And he called them *Bloody Scotch savages*, and was in an awful rage and at the term-time he had them sacked, the whole jingbang of them, so sore affronted he had been.

But after that he got on well enough, him and his mistress, Ella White, and they had a daughter, a scrawny bit quean they thought over good to go to the Auchinblae School, so off she went to Stonehaven Academy and was taught to be right brave and swing about in the gymnasium there with wee black breeks on under her skirt. Ellison himself began to get well-stomached, and he had a red face, big and sappy, and eyes like a cat, green eyes, and his mouser hung down each side of a fair bit mouth that was chokeful up of false teeth, awful expensive and bonny, lined with bits of gold. And he aye wore leggings and riding breeks, for he was fair gentry by then; and when he would meet a crony at a mart he would cry *Sure, bot it's you, thin, ould chep!* and the billy would redden up, real ashamed, but wouldn't dare say anything, for he wasn't a man you'd offend. In politics he said he was a Conservative but everybody in Kinraddie knew that meant he was a Tory and the bairns of Strachan, him that farmed the Peesie's Knapp, they would scraich out

> *Inky poo, your nose is blue,*
> *You're awful like the Turra Coo*

whenever they saw Ellison go by. For he'd sent a subscription to the creature up Turriff way whose cow had been sold to pay his Insurance, and folk said it was no more than a show off, the Cow creature and Ellison both; and they laughed at him behind his back.

So that was the Mains, below the Meikle House, and Ellison farmed it in his Irish way and right opposite, hidden away among their yews, were kirk and manse, the kirk an old, draughty place and in the winter-time, right in the middle of the Lord's Prayer, maybe, you'd hear an outbreak of hoasts fit to lift off the roof, and Miss Sarah Sinclair, her that came from Netherhill and played the organ, she'd sneeze into her hymnbook and miss her bit notes and the minister, him that was the old one, he'd glower down at her more like John Knox than ever.

Next door the kirk was an olden tower, built in the time of the Roman Catholics, the coarse creatures, and it was fell old and wasn't used any more except by the cushat-doves and they flew in and out the narrow slips in the upper storey and nested there all the year round and the place was fair white with their dung. In the lower half of the tower was an effigy-thing of Cospatric de Gondeshil, him that killed the gryphon, lying on his back with his arms crossed and a daft-like simper on his face; and the spear he killed the gryphon with was locked in a kist there, or so some said, but others said it was no more than an old bit heuch from the times of Bonny Prince Charlie. So that was the tower, but it wasn't fairly a part of the kirk, the real kirk was split in two bits, the main hall and the wee hall, and some called them the byre and the turnip-shed, and the pulpit stood midway.

Once the wee hall had been for the folk from the Meikle House and their guests and suchlike gentry but nearly anybody that had the face went ben and sat there now, and the elders sat with the collection bags, and young Murray, him that blew the organ for Sarah Sinclair. It had fine glass windows, awful old, the wee hall with three bit creatures of queans, not very decent-like in a kirk, as window-pictures. One of the queans was Faith, and faith she looked a daft-like keek for she was lifting up her hands and her eyes like a heifer choked on a turnip and the bit blanket round her shoulders was falling off her but she didn't seem to heed, and there was a swither of scrolls and fiddley-faddles all about her.

And the second quean was Hope and she was near as unco as Faith, but had right bonny hair, red hair, though maybe you'd call it auburn, and in the winter-time the light in the morning service would come splashing through the yews in the kirkyard and into the wee hall through the red hair of Hope. And the third quean was Charity, with a lot of naked bairns at her feet and she looked a fine and decent-like woman, for all that she was tied about with such daft-like clouts.

But the windows of the main hall, though they were coloured, they had never a picture in them and there were no pictures in there at all, who wanted them? Only coarse-creatures like Catholics wanted a kirk to look like a grocer's calendar. So it was decent and bare-like, with its carved old seats, some were cushioned and some were not, if you weren't padded by nature and had the silver to spend you might put in cushions to suit your fancy. Right up in the lithe of the pulpit, at angles-like to the rest of the kirk, were the three seats where the choir sat and led the hymn-singing; and some called it the calfies' stall.

The back door, that behind the pulpit, led out across the kirkyard to the Manse and its biggings, set up in the time of the Old Queen, and fair bonny to look at, but awful damp said all the ministers' wives. But ministers' wives were aye folk to complain and don't know when they're well off, them and the silver they get for their bit creatures of men preaching once or twice a Sunday and so proud they hardly know you when they meet you on the road. The minister's study was high up in the house, it looked out over all Kinraddie, at night he'd see from there the lights of the farmhouses like a sprinkling of bright sands below his window and the flagstaff light high among the stars on the roof of the Meikle House. But that nineteen eleven December the Manse was empty and had been empty for many a month, the old minister was dead and the new one not yet voted on; and the ministers from Drumlithie and Arbuthnott and Laurencekirk they came time about in the Sunday forenoons and took the service there at Kinraddie; and God knows for all they had to say they might well have bidden at home.

But if you went out of the kirk by the main door and took the road east a bit, and that was the road that served kirk and Manse and Mains, you were on to the turnpike then. It ran north and south but opposite to the road you'd just come down was another, that went through Kinraddie by the Bridge End farm. So there was a cross-roads there and if you held to the left along the turnpike you came to Peesie's Knapp, one of the olden places, no more than a croft of thirty-forty acres with some rough ground for pasture, but God knows there was little pasture on it, it was just a fair schlorich of whins and broom and dirt, full up of rabbits and hares it was, they came out at night and ate up your crops and sent a body fair mad. But it wasn't bad land the most of the Knapp, there was the sweat of two thousand years in it, and the meikle park behind the biggings was black loam, not the red clay that sub-soiled half Kinraddie.

Now Peesie's Knapp's biggings were not more than twenty years old, but gey ill-favoured for all that, for though the house faced on the road – and that was fair handy if it didn't scunner you that you couldn't so much as change your sark without some ill-fashioned brute gowking in at you – right between the byre and the stable and the barn on one side and the house on the other was the cattle-court and right in the middle of that the midden, high and yellow with dung and straw and sharn, and Mistress Strachan could never forgive Peesie's Knapp because of that awful smell it had.

But Chae Strachan, him that farmed the place, he just said *Hoots, what's a bit guff?* and would start to tell of the terrible smells he'd smelt when he was abroad. For he'd been a fell wandering billy, Chae, in the days before he came back to Scotland and was fee'd his last fee at Netherhill. He'd been in Alaska, looking for gold there, but damn the bit of gold he'd seen, so he'd farmed in California till he was so scunnered of fruit he'd never look an orange or a pear in the face again, not even in a tin. And then he'd gone on to South Africa and had had great times there, growing real chieflike with the head one of a tribe of blacks, but an awful decent man for all that. Him and Chae had

fought against Boers and British both, and beaten them, or so
Chae said, but folk that didn't like Chae said all the fighting he'd
ever done had been with his mouth and that as for beaten, he'd be
sore made to beat the skin off a bowl of sour milk.

For he wasn't well liked by them that set themselves up for
gentry, Chae, being a socialist creature and believing we should
all have the same amount of silver and that there shouldn't be
rich and poor and that one man was as good as another. And the
silver bit of that was clean daft, of course, for if you'd all the
same money one day what would it be the next? – Rich and Poor
again! But Chae said the four ministers of Kinraddie and Auchinblae and Laurencekirk and Drumlithie were all paid much
the same money last year and what had they this year? – Much
the same money still! *You'll have to get out of bed slippy in the
morning before you find a socialist tripping and if you gave me any
of your lip I'll clout you in the lug, my mannie.*

So Chae was fell good in argy-bargying and he wasn't the
quarrelsome kind except when roused, so he was well-liked,
though folk laughed at him. But God knows, who is it they don't
laugh at? He was a pretty man, well upstanding, with great
shoulders on him and his hair was fair and fine and he had a
broad brow and a gey bit coulter of a nose, and he twisted his
mouser ends up with wax like that creature the German Kaiser,
and he could stop a running stirk by the horns, so strong he was
in the wrist-bones. And he was one of the handiest billies in
Kinraddie, he would libb a calf or break in a horse or kill a pig,
all in a jiffy, or tile your dairy or cut the bairns' hair or dig a well,
and all the time he'd be telling you that socialism was coming or
if it wasn't then an awful crash would come and we'd all go back
to savagery, *Dam't ay, man!*

But folk said he'd more need to start socializing Mistress
Strachan, her that had been Kirsty Sinclair of Netherhill,
before he began on anybody else. She had a fell tongue, they
said, that would clip clouts and yammer a tink from a door, and
if Chae wasn't fair sick now and then for his hut and a fine
black quean in South Africa damn the hut or the quean had he
ever had. He'd feed'd at Netherhill when he came back from
foreign parts, had Chae, and there had been but two daughters

there, Kirsty and Sarah, her that played the kirk organ. Both were wearing on a bit, sore in the need of a man, and Kirsty with a fair let-down as it was, for it had seemed that a doctor billy from Aberdeen was out to take up with her. So he had done and left her in a gey way and her mother, old Mistress Sinclair, near went out of her mind with the shame of it when Kirsty began to cry and tell her the news.

Now that was about the term-time and home to Netherhill from the feeing market who should old Sinclair of Netherhill bring but Chae Strachan, with his blood warmed up from living in those foreign parts and an eye for less than a wink of invitation? But even so he was gey slow to get on with the courting and just hung around Kirsty like a futret round a trap with a bit meat in it, not sure if the meat was worth the risk; and the time was getting on and faith! Something drastic would have to be done.

So one night after they had all had supper in the kitchen and old Sinclair had gone pleitering out to the byres, old Mistress Sinclair had up and nodded to Kirsty and said *Ah well, I'll away to my bed. You'll not be long in making for yours, Kirsty?* And Kirsty said *No,* and gave her mother a sly bit look, and off the old mistress went up to her room and then Kirsty began fleering and flirting with Chae and he was a man warm enough and they were alone together and maybe in a minute he'd have had her couched down right well there in the kitchen but she whispered it wasn't safe. So he off with his boots and she with hers and up the stairs they crept together into Kirsty's room and were having their bit pleasure together when *ouf!* went the door and in burst old Mistress Sinclair with the candle held up in one hand and the other held up in horror. *No, no,* she'd said, *this won't do at all, Chakie, my man, you'll have to marry her.* And there had been no escape for Chae, poor man, with Kirsty and her mother both glowering at him.

So married they were and old Sinclair had saved up some silver and he rented Peesie's Knapp for Chae and Kirsty, and stocked the place for them, and down they sat there, and Kirsty's bairn, a bit quean, was born before seven months were past, well-grown and finished-like it seemed, the creature, in spite of its mother swearing it had come fair premature.

They'd had two more bairns since then, both laddies, and both the living spit of Chae, these were the bairns that would sing about the Turra Coo whenever they met the brave gig of Ellison bowling along the Kinraddie Road, and faith, they made you laugh.

Right opposite Peesie's Knapp, across the turnpike, the land climbed red and clay and a rough stone road went wandering up to the biggings of Blawearie. *Out of the World and into Blawearie* they said in Kinraddie, and faith! it was coarse land and lonely up there on the brae, fifty-sixty acres of it, forbye the moor that went on with the brae high above Blawearie, up to a great flat hill-top where lay a bit loch that nested snipe by the hundred; and some said there was no bottom to it, the loch, and Long Rob of the Mill said that made it like the depths of a parson's depravity.

That was an ill thing to say about any minister, though Rob said it was an ill thing to say about any loch, but there the spleiter of water was, a woesome dark stretch fringed rank with rushes and knife-grass; and the screeching of the snipe fair deafened you if you stood there of an evening. And few enough did that for nearby the bit loch was a circle of stones from olden times, some were upright and some were flat and some leaned this way and that, and right in the middle three big ones clambered up out of the earth and stood askew with flat sonsy faces, they seemed to listen and wait. They were Druid stones and folk told that the Druids had been coarse devils of men in the times long syne, they'd climb up there and sing their foul heathen songs around the stones; and if they met a bit Christian missionary they'd gut him as soon as look at him. And Long Rob of the Mill would say what Scotland wanted was a return of the Druids, but that was just a speak of his, for they must have been awful ignorant folk, not canny.

Blawearie hadn't had a tenant for nearly a year, but now there was one on the way, they said, a creature John Guthrie from up in the North. The biggings of it stood fine and compact one side of the close, the midden was back of them, and across the close was the house, a fell brave house for a little place, it had three storeys and a good kitchen and a fair stretch of garden between it and Blawearie road. There were beech trees there, three of them, one was close over against the house, and the garden hedges grew as bonny with honeysuckle of a summer as ever you saw;

and if you could have lived on the smell of honeysuckle you might have farmed the bit place with profit.

Well, Peesie's Knapp and Blawearie were the steadings that lay Stonehavenway. But if you turned east that winter along the Auchinblae road first on your right was Cuddiestoun, a small bit holding the size of Peesie's Knapp and old as it, a croft from the far-off times. It lay a quarter-mile or so from the main road and its own road was fair clamjamfried with glaur from late in the harvest till the coming of Spring. Some said maybe that accounted for Munro's neck, he could never get the glaur washed out of it. But others said he never tried. He was on a thirteen years' lease there, Munro, a creature from down south, Dundee way, and he was a good six feet in height but awful coarse among the legs, like a lamb with water on the brain, and he had meikle feet that aye seemed in his way. He was maybe forty years or so in age, and bald already, and his skin was red and creased in cheeks and chin and God! you never saw an uglier brute, poor stock.

For there were worse folk than Munro, though maybe they were all in the jail, and though he could blow and bombast till he fair scunnered you. He farmed his bit land in a then and now way, and it was land good enough, the most of it, with the same black streak of loam that went through the Peesie parks, but ill-drained, the old stone drains were still down and devil the move would the factor at Meikle House make to have them replaced, or mend the roof of the byre that leaked like a sieve on the head of Mistress Munro when she milked the kye on a stormy night.

But if anybody, chief-like, were to say, *God, that's an awful byre you have, mistress*, she would flare up in a minute *It's fine and good enough for the like of us*. And if that body, not knowing better, poor billy, were to agree that the place was well enough for poor folk, she'd up again *Who's poor? Let me tell you we've never needed anybody come to our help, though we don't boast and blow about it all over the countryside, like some I could mention*. So the body would think there was no pleasing of the creature, and she was right well laughed at in all Kinraddie, though not to her face. And that was a thin one and she had black hair and snapping black eyes like a futret, and a voice that fair set your hackles on edge when she girned. But she was the best midwife for miles around, right often in the middle of the night some poor distracted billy would come chapping at her window *Mistress Munro, Mistress Munro, will you get up and come to the wife?* And out she'd get, and into her clothes before you could whistle, and out into the cold of Kinraddie night and go whipping through it like a futret, and soon be snapping her orders round the kitchen of the house she'd been summoned to, telling the woman in childbed she might easily be worse, and being right brisk and sharp and clever.

And the funny thing about the creature was that she believed none spoke ill of her, for if she heard a bit hint of such, dropped slylike, she'd redden up like a stalk of rhubarb in a dung patch and look as though she might start to cry, and the body would feel real sorry for her till next minute she'd be screeching at Andy or Tony, and fleering them out of the little wits they had, poor devils.

Now, Andy and Tony were two dafties that Mistress Munro had had boarded out on her from an Asylum in Dundee, they weren't supposed to be dangerous. Andy was a meikle slummock of a creature, and his mouth was aye open, and he dribbled like a teething foal, and his nose wabbled all over his face and when he tried to speak it was just a fair jumble of foolishness. He was the daftest one, but fell sly, he'd sometimes run away to the hills and stand there with his finger at his nose, making faces at Mistress Munro, and she'd scraich at him and he'd yammer back at her and then over the moor he'd get to the bothy at Upperhill where the ploughmen would give him cigarettes and then torment him till he fair raged; and once tried to kill one with an axe he caught up from a hackstock. And at night he'd creep back to Cuddiestoun, outside he'd make a noise like a dog that had been kicked, and he'd snuffle round the door till the few remaining hairs on the bald pow of Munro would fair rise on end. But Mistress Munro would up and be at the door and in she'd yank Andy by the lug, and some said she'd take down his breeks and skelp him, but maybe that was a lie. She wasn't feared at him and he wasn't feared at her, so they were a gey well-matched pair.

And that was the stir at Cuddiestoun, all except Tony, for the Munros had never a bairn of their own. And Tony, though he wasn't the daftest, he was the queer one, too, right enough. He was small-bulked and had a little red beard and sad eyes, and he walked with his head down and you would feel right sorry for him for sometimes some whimsy would come on the creature right in the middle of the turnpike it might be or half-way down a rig of swedes, and there he would stand staring like a gowk for minutes on end till somebody would shake him back to his senses. He had fine soft hands, for he was no working body; folk said he had once been a scholar and written books and learned and learned till his brain fair softened and right off his head he'd gone and into the poorhouse asylum.

Now Mistress Munro she'd send Tony errands to the wee shop out beyond the Bridge End, and tell him what she wanted, plain and simple-like, and maybe giving him a bit clout in the lug now and then, as you would a bairn or a daftie. And he'd listen to her and make out he minded the messages and off to the shop he'd go, and come back without a single mistake. But one day, after she'd told him the things she wanted, Mistress Munro saw the wee creature writing on a bit of paper with a pencil he'd picked up somewhere. And she took the paper from him and looked at it and turned it this way and that, but feint the thing could she made of it. So she gave him a bit clout in the lug and asked him what the writing was. But he just shook his head, real gowked-like and reached out his hand for the bit of paper, but Mistress Munro would have none of that and when it was time for the Strachan bairns to pass the end of the Cuddiestoun road on their way to school down there she was waiting and gave the paper to the eldest the quean Marget; and told her to show it to the Dominie and ask him what it might mean.

And at night she was waiting for the Strachan bairns to come back and they had an envelope for her from the Dominie; and she opened it and found a note saying the writing was shorthand and that this was what it read when put in the ordinary way of writing: *Two pounds of sugar The People's Journal half an ounce of mustard a tin of rat poison a pound of candles and I don't suppose I can swindle her out of tuppence change for the sake of a smoke, she's certainly the meanest bitch unhung this side of Tweed.* So maybe Tony wasn't so daft, but he got no supper that night; and she never asked to see his notes again.

ALASDAIR GRAY

Houses and Small Labour Parties

Eight men dug a trench beside a muddy crossroads, and the mud made two remember Italy where they had fought in a recent war. These two had not known each other in Italy, but both had seen a dead German who lay at a crossroads near Naples, though one thought it was perhaps nearer Pisa. They discussed the matter when the gang paused for a smoke.

"Not Pisa, no, Pisa was miles away," said one, "Naples was the place. He was a handsome big fella. We called him Siegfried."

"Our lot called him Adolf, because of the fuckin moustache," said the other, "He wasnae handsome for fuckin long."

"I don't remember a moustache, but you're right, he wasnae handsome for long. He went all white and puffy and swole up like a balloon – I think only his uniform stopped him bursting. The heavy traffic must have kept the rats away. Every time we went that road I hoped to God someone had shifted him but no, there he always was, more horrible than ever. Because eventually a truck ran over him and burst him up properly. Do you mind that?"

"I mind it fuckin fine."

"Every time we went that road we would say, 'I wonder how old Siegfried's doing,' and look out for him, and there was always something to see, though at last it was only the bones of a foot or a bit of rag with a button on it."

There was a silence. The older navvies thought about death and the youngest about a motorcycle he wanted to buy. He was known for being the youngest of them and fond of motorcycles. Everybody in the gang was known for something. Mick the ganger was known for being Irish and saying queer things in a solemn voice. One navvy was known for being a Highlander, one for having a hangover every morning, one for being newly married. One of the ex-army men was known for his war stories, the other for his fucking adjectives. One of them was a communist who thought *The Ragged Trousered Philanthropists* a better book than the Bible and kept trying to lend it; but schooling had given most of them a disgust of books. Only Old Joe borrowed it and he said it was a bit out of date. The communist wanted to argue the point but Old Joe was known for being silent as well as old. The youngest navvy liked working with these folk though he hardly ever listened to what they said. Too many of them wanted his attention. They remembered, or thought they remembered, when they too had been just out of school, sixteen and good-looking, happy because their developing muscles could still enjoy the strain of working overtime, happy because it was great to earn a wage as big as their fathers earned. The worst paid workers reach the peak of their earning power early in life.

"The Signoras!" announced the story teller suddenly, "The Signorinas! They were something else. Am I right? Am I wrong?"

"Aye, the fuckin Signoras were somethin fuckin else," said the other ex-army man. With both hands he shaped a huge bosom on the air before his chest.

"I'll give you a bit of advice Ian," the story-teller told the youngest navvy, "If you ever go to Italy take a few tins of bully beef in your suitcase. There is nothing, I'm telling you nothing you won't get from the Italian Signorinas in return for a can of bully beef."

"That advice may be slightly out of date," said Mick the ganger.

"You're sticking up for the Tally women because they're Papes and so are you, ye fuckin Fenian Irish Papal prick ye," said one of the ex-army men pleasantly.

"He's right, of course," the ganger told the youngest navvy, "I am a Papal Fenian. But if these warriors ever return to Italy they may find the ladies less welcoming now the babies have stopped starving."

He nipped his cigarette, stuck it under his cap brim above the right ear and lifted his pick. The gang began digging again.

Though their work was defined as unskilled by the Department of Labour they worked skilfully in couples, one breaking the ground with a pick, the other shovelling loose earth and stones from under his partner's feet and flinging it clear. At the front end Mick the ganger set a steady pace for all of them. The youngest navvy was inclined to go too fast, so Mick had paired him with Old Joe who was nearly sixty, but still worked well by pacing himself carefully. The two ex-army men were liable to slow down if paired together, so Mick always paired one of them with himself. The gang belonged to a workforce of labourers, brickies, joiners, plumbers, slaters, electricians, painters, drivers, foremen and site clerks who were enlarging a city by turning a hillside into a housing estate. During the recent war (which had ended seven years before but still seemed recent to all who remembered it) the government had promised there would be no return to unemployment afterward, and every family would eventually have a house with a lavatory and bath inside. The nation's taxes were now being spent on houses as well as armed forces, motorways, public health et cetera, so public housing was now profitable. Bankers and brokers put money into firms making homes for the class of folk who laboured to build them. To make these fast and cheaply standards of spaciousness and craftsmanship were lowered, makeshifts were used which had been developed during the war. Concrete replaced stonework. Doors were light wooden frames with a hardboard sheet nailed to each side. Inner walls were frames surfaced with plasterboard that dented if a door-knob swung hard against it. A tall man could press his fingers to the ceilings without standing on tiptoe. But every house had a hot water system, a bath and flush lavatory, and nearly everyone was employed. There was so much work that firms advertised for workers overseas and natives of the kingdom were paid extra to work at week-ends and during public holidays. In the building industry the lowest paid were proudest of what they earned by overtime work so most of this gang worked a six-day week. A labourer who refused overtime was not exactly scorned as a weakling, but thought a poor specimen of his calling. Recently married men were notoriously poor specimens, but seldom for more than a fortnight.

A heavily built man called McIvor approached the trench and stood for a while watching the gang with a dour, slightly menacing stare which was a tool of his trade. When his presence was noticed by the ganger, McIvor beckoned him by jerking his head a fraction to the side. Mick laid his pick carefully down, dried his sweating face with a handkerchief, muttered, "No slacking, men, while I confabulate with our commanding officer," and climbed out of the trench. He did not confabulate. He listened to McIvor, stroked his chin then shouted, "Ian! Over here a minute!"

The youngest navvy, surprised, dropped his spade, leapt from the trench and hurried to them. McIvor said to him, "Do you want some overtime? Sunday afternoons, one to five."

"Sure."

"It's gardening work but not skilled weeding, cutting grass, that sort of thing. It's at the house of Mr Stoddart, the boss. He'll give the orders. The rate is the usual double time. You get the money in your weekly pay packet."

"I thought Old Joe did that job."

"He does, but the boss says Joe needs help now. What do you say? Yes or no?"

"Aye. Sure," said the youngest navvy.

"Then I'll give you a word of advice. Mick here has pointed you out as a good worker so you'd better be, because the boss has a sharp eye for slackers – comes down on them like a ton of bricks. He also has a long memory, and a long arm. If you don't do right by Mr Stoddart you won't just get yourself in the shit, you'll make trouble for Mick here who recommended you. Right, Mick?"

"Don't put the fear of death into the boy," said the ganger, "Ian will do fine."

In the bothy where the navvies had their lunch an ex-army man said loudly and cheerfully, "I see the fuckin Catholics are stickin to-fuckin-gether as per fuckin usual."

"Could that be a hostile remark?" the ganger asked Ian, "Do you think the foul-mouthed warrior is talking about us?"

"Fuckin right I'm talking about yous! You could have gave the fuckin job to a fuckin family man like me with fuckin weans to feed but no, you give it to a fuckin co-religionist who's a fuckin wean himself."

"I'm not a Catholic!" said the youngest navvy, astonished.

"Well how do you come to be so fuckin thick with Mick the Papal prick here?"

"I recommended the infant of the gang for three reasons," said the ganger, "One, he is a bloody hard worker who gets on well with Old Joe. Two, some family men enjoy Sunday at home. Three, if one of us starts working around the boss's house he'll get the name of being a boss's man, which is good for nobody's social life, but Ian is too young to be thought that, just as Joe is too old."

"Blethers!" said the communist, "You are the boss's man here, like every ganger. You're no as bad as bastarding McIvor, but he comes to you for advice."

"Jesus Mary and Joseph!" cried Mick to the youngest navvy, "For the love of God get out of this and apprentice yourself to a decent trade! Go up to the joiners' bothy and talk to Cameron – they're wanting apprentice joiners."

"I'm not a Catholic, I've never been a Catholic," said the youngest navvy, looking around the others in the bothy with a hurt, alarmed and pleading expression. The Highlander (who was also suspected of being Catholic because he came from Barra, and someone had said everyone from that island were Catholics) said, "You are absolved – go in peace," which caused general amusement.

"Did you hear me Ian?" said the ganger sharply, "I told you to get out of this into a decent trade."

"I might, when I've bought my Honda," said the youngest navvy thoughtfully. He saw the sense in the ganger's advice. A time-served tradesman was better paid and had more choices of work than a labourer, but during the apprentice years the wage would be a lot less.

"Why did a clever fella like you never serve your time as a tradesman, Mick?" asked the communist. "Because at sixteen I was a fool, like every one of us here, especially that silly infant. I never wanted a motorbike, I wanted a woman. So here I am, ten years later, at the peak of my profession. I've a wife and five children and a job paying me a bit more than the rest of you in return for taking a lot of lip from a foul-mouthed warrior and from a worshipper of Holy Joe Stalin."

"You havenae reached the peak yet Mick," said the communist, "In a year or three they'll give you McIvor's job."

"No, I'll never be a foreman," said the ganger sombrely, "The wages would be welcome, but not the loneliness. Our dirty tongued Orange friend will get that job – he enjoys being socially obnoxious."

The foreman had given the youngest navvy a slip of paper on which was written *89 Balmoral Road, Pollokshields*, and the route of a bus that would take him past there, and the heavily underlined words *1 a.m. on the dot*. The boy's ignorance of the district got him to the boss's house seven minutes late and gasping for breath. He lived with his parents on a busy thoroughfare between tenements whose numbers ran into thousands. When the bus entered Balmoral Road he saw number 3 on a pillar by a gate and leapt off at the next stop, sure that 89 must be nearby. He was wrong. After walking fast for what seemed ten minutes he passed another bus stop opposite a gate pillar numbered 43, and broke into a jog-trot. The sidewalk was a gravel path with stone kerb instead of a pavement, the road was as wide and straight as the one where he lived, but seemed wider because of the great gardens on each side. Some had lawns with flowerbeds behind hedges, some shrubberies and trees behind high walls, both sorts had driveways leading up to houses which seemed as big as castles. All of well-cut stone, several imitated castles by having turrets, towers and oriel windows crowned with battlements. Signboards at two or three entrances indicated nursing homes, but names carved on gate pillars (Beech Grove, Trafalgar, Victoria Lodge) suggested most houses were private, and so did curtains and ornaments in the windows. Yet all had several rooms big enough to hold the complete two-room flat where he lived with his parents, or one of the three-room-and-kitchen flats being built on the site where he laboured. But the queerest thing about this district was the absence of people. After the back of the bus dwindled to an orange speck in the distance, then vanished, the only moving things he saw were a few birds in the sky and what must have been a cat crossing the road a quarter mile ahead. His brain was baffled by no sight or sign of buildings he thought always went with houses: shops, a post-office, school or church. Down the long length of the road he could not even see a parked car or telephone box. The place was a desert. How could people live here? Where did they buy their food and meet each other? Seeing number 75 on another gate pillar he broke into an almost panic-stricken run.

Number 89 was not the biggest house he had seen but still impressive. On rising ground at a corner, it was called The Gables and had a lot of them. The front garden was terraced with bright beds of rose bushes which must have been recently tended by a professional gardener. A low, new brick wall in front hid none of this. The young navvy hurried up a drive of clean granite chips which scrunched so loudly underfoot that he wanted to walk on the trim grass verge, but feared his boots would dent it. Fearful of the wide white steps up to the large front door he went crunching round the side to find a more inviting entrance, and discovered Old Joe building a rockery in the angle of two gables.

"Hullo Joe. Am I late? Is he angry?"

"I'm your gaffer today so don't worry. Fetch ower yon barrow and follow me."

Behind the house was a kitchen garden, a rhododendron shrubbery and a muddy entry from a back lane. Near the entry lay a pile of small boulders and a mound of earth with a spade in it. Joe said, "Bring me a load of the rocks then a load of the earth and keep going till I tell ye different. And while we're away from the house I don't mind telling you ye're on probation."

"What's that supposed to mean?"

"He watches us. He's seen you already."

"How? Why do ye think that?"

"You'll know why when he talks to ye later."

As they worked on the rockery the young navvy looked cautiously about and gradually grew sure they were the only folk in the garden. The walls of the house where they worked were blank, apart from a wee high-up window that probably ventilated a lavatory. When he wheeled the barrow to the back entry he was in view of larger windows. He kept bringing boulders and earth to Joe who worked kneeling and sometimes said, "Put that there, son," or "Give a shovelful here." Nearly an hour passed then Joe sighed, stood slowly up, straightened his shoulders and said, "Five minutes."

"I'll just get another load," said the young navvy, lifting the shafts of the barrow. He was uneasily aware of the black little lavatory window above and behind him.

"We're entitled to five minute spells," said Old Joe quietly, "We need them."

"I don't need them. And I was late, you werenae." He went off with the barrow, loaded it and found Joe working when he returned. An hour later a gaunt, smartly dressed lady looked round a corner, called, "Your tea is in the tool-shed," then vanished behind the corner.

"Was that his wife?" asked the young navvy.

"His housekeeper. Are you working through the tea-break too?"

The young navvy blushed.

The tool-shed, like the garage, was part of a big newly built outhouse, and windowless, and had a roller shutter door facing the back entry. It smelt of cement, timber and petrol; had shelves and racks of every modern gardening and construction tool, all shiningly new; also a workbench with two mugs of tea and a plate of chocolate biscuits on it; also a motorcycle leaning negligently against a wall, though there were blocks for standing it upright.

"A Honda!" whispered the young navvy, going straight to it and hunkering down so that his eyes were less than a foot from the surface of the thing he worshipped, "Whose is this?"

"The boss's son's."

"But he hasnae been using it," said the young navvy indignantly, noting flat tyres, dust on seat and metal, dust on a footpump and kit of keys and spanners strewn near the front wheel. What should be shining chromium was dull, with rust spots. "He's got better things to think of," said Joe after swallowing a mouthful of tea, "He's a student at the Uni."

"Why does he no sell it?"

"Sentimental reasons. His da gave it him as a present, and he doesnae need the money."

The young navvy puffed out his cheeks and blew to convey astonishment, then went over to the bench. Since they were not in sight or earshot of anyone he said, "What's the boss like?"

"Bossy."

"Come on Joe! There's good and bad bosses. What sort is he?"

"Middling to average. You'll soon see."

Ten minutes later they returned to the garden and worked for over an hour before Joe said, "Five minutes," and straightened his back, and surveyed his work with a critical eye. The young navvy paused and looked too. He could see the rocks were well-balanced and not likely to sink under heavy rains, but the impending presence of the unseen Stoddart (maybe the biggest and bossiest boss he would ever meet) made him restless. After a minute he said, "I'll just get us another load," and went off with the barrow.

Half an hour later the rockery was complete. As they stood looking at it the young navvy suddenly noticed there were three

of them and for a moment felt he had met the third man before.
He was a massive man with a watchful, impassive face, clean
white open-necked shirt, finely creased flannel slacks and white
canvas sports shoes. At last the stranger, still looking at the
rockery, said, "Seven minutes late. Why?"

"I got off at the wrong stop – I didnae know the street was so
long."

"Makes sense. What's your name youngster?"

"Ian Maxwell."

"Apart from the lateness (which will not be docked from your
wages) you've done well today, Ian. You too Joe. A very decent
rockery. The gardener can start planting tomorrow. But the
day's work is not yet done as Joe knows, but perhaps as you
do not know, Ian. Because now the barrow, spade, fork, trowel go
back to the tool-shed and are cleaned – cleaned thoroughly.
There's a drain in the floor and a wall-tap with a hose attached.
Use them! I don't want to find any wee crumbs of dirt between the
tyre and the hub of that barrow. A neglected tool is a wasted tool.
What you'd better know from the start Ian (if you and me are
going to get on together) is that I am not gentry. I'm from the
same folk you are from, so I know what you are liable to do and
not do. But do right by me and I'll do right by you. Understood?"

The young navvy stared, hypnotized by the dour impassive
face now turned to him. Suddenly it changed. The eyes stayed
watchful but the mouth widened into what the young navvy
supposed was a smile, so he nodded. The big man patted him on
the shoulder and walked away.

The navvies went to the tool-shed and cleaned the tools in
silence. The youngest was depressed, though he did not know
why. When they had returned the tools to their places (which
were easy to see, because there were three of everything so a gap
in the ranks was as obvious as a missing tooth) the young navvy
said, "Do we just leave now?"

"No. We wait for the inspection."

They did not wait long. There was a rattling of at least two
locks then an inner door opened and Stoddart came through

carrying a tray with two glasses, a whisky bottle and a jug of water. His inspection was a quick sideways glance toward the tool-racks before he said, "How old are you, Ian?"

"Nearly seventeen."

"Too young for whisky. I'm not going to teach you bad habits. But Joe and me haven't had our ne'erday yet. A bad thing, me forgetting old customs. A large one, Joe? Macallan's Glenlivet Malt?"

"Thanks, aye"

"Water?"

"No thanks."

"Quite right, better without . . . Good stuff Joe?"

"Aye."

"How's the old back, the old lumbago, Joe?"

"No bad, considering."

"Aye, but age gets us all in the end – even me. I'm not as young as I was. We have to learn to take things easy, Joe."

"Aye," said Joe, and emptied the glass straight down his throat.

"God, that went fast!" said Stoddart, "Another one, Joe?"

"Goodnight," said Joe, and walked out. "Goodnight Joe, and goodnight to you Ian. See you next week on the dot of one youngster. Joe will be taking a bit of a rest. Right?"

"Thanks," said the young navvy, and hurried after Joe wondering why he had said thanks instead of goodnight when he had been given nothing, had not even been paid yet for his labour.

The young navvy overtook Joe walking into the back lane and said, "Are you no going for a bus, Joe?"

"No. This is a shortcut."

"Can I come with you?" asked the young navvy, wondering why he was asking. Joe said nothing. They walked beside each other in a lane with a brick wall on one side, a railway embankment on the other. It could have been in the depths of the country. Grass, daisies and clover grew between two parallel paths made by car wheels and the verges were thick with dandelions, dockens, thistles, burdock. Branches from trees in

the gardens behind the wall hung overhead. From the embankment hawthorns and brambles stuck thorny, leafy shoots between the sagging wires of a fence. The old and young navvy
walked side by side in silence, each on one of the parallel tracks.
The young one felt Joe was angry, feared it had to do with him,
tried to think of something to say.

And at last said, "When the boss turned up beside us there I
thought he was McIvor at first."

Joe said nothing.

"Don't you think he's a bit like McIvor, Joe?"

"Of course he's like McIvor. McIvor is a foreman. Stoddart is
the foreman's foreman – the gaffer's gaffer. Of course he's like
McIvor."

"But he's cheerier than McIvor – he calls ye by your first name.
Have you had drinks with him before, Joe?"

"That was the first and last."

"The last? Why the last?"

"Because you've done for me."

"What do you mean?" asked the young navvy, suddenly seeing
exactly what the old one meant but confused by two amazements:
amazement that the boss preferred him to Joe, amazement at the
unfairness and speed of the result. Together these amazements
stopped him feeling very happy or very angry. But he liked Joe so
the unfairness puzzled him.

"Are you sure he doesnae ever want ye back Joe? I never heard
him say so."

"Then you need your ears washed."

"But that cannae be right, Joe! I've got more muscle than you
but I havenae the head yet – the skill. That's why Mick keeps
pairing us. If I'm working just by myself I won't do so much
because I'll need to keep stopping to think."

"Too true!" said Joe, "Stoddart is stupider than he knows, but
he's a boss so nobody can put him right. In a week or two when he
sees you arenae doing as well as you did today he'll think you've
started slacking so give you the heave and get in someone else.
Or maybe no! If ye arrive ten minutes early every day, and work

your guts out till he tells ye to stop, and if you take a five minutes tea-break or none at all when the housekeeper forgets ye – well, if ye sweat enough at showing you're a boss's man he'll maybe keep ye."

Joe climbed over the fence and went up the embankment by a path slanting through willow herb and the young navvy followed, his confused feelings tinged by distress. Joe led him across three sets of railway lines to a gap in a fence of upright railway sleepers. They were now in a broad, unpeopled street between old warehouses. "What should I do Joe?" asked the youngest navvy. He was not answered, so said it again. After a long silence Joe suddenly said, "Get out of this into civil engineering, son. No bastard can own you in civil engineering because ye travel all over. Highland power stations, motorways in the Midlands, reservoirs in Wales – if ye tire of one job ye just collect your jotters and wages, clear out the same day and go to another. Naebody minds. No questions asked. And the money, the overtime is phenomenal. Once at Loch Sloy I worked a forty-eight hour stint – forty-eight hours with the usual breaks of course, but I was on the job the whole time without one wink of sleep. Someone bet me I couldnae but I could and I did. Civil engineering is the life, son, for folk like you and me. Of course most of the money goes on booze and betting, there's nothing much else to do with it. Some keep a wife and weans on the money but why bother? Ye only get to see them one week in six maybe. Family life is a con, a bloody imposition. Not that I'm advocating prostitutes! Keep clear of all women, son, is my advice to you: if they don't give you weans they'll give you some other disease. Chuck Stoddart and go into civil engineering. It's the only life for a man while he has his strength. That's what I did and I've never regretted it."

Joe seldom said more than one sentence at a time so the young navvy brooded over this speech. Booze, betting and prostitutes did not attract him. He wanted to hurl himself through the air toward any target he chose, going faster than a mile a minute with maybe a girl clinging on a pillion behind. But a good bike cost nearly £400. After paying his people two thirds of his weekly earnings in return for the home and services he had enjoyed since infancy, about £4 remained which (despite his intentions of saving £3 a week) seemed always to get eaten up by tram, café, cinema, dancehall, football, haircut and clothes expenses – he had begun to like dressing well on his few nights out. But if he worked on a big civil engineering job in the Highlands, and did all the twelve or sixteen hour shifts his strength allowed, and slept and ate cheaply in a workers' hostel, and paid his people a few shillings a week till he felt like returning, he might earn enough to buy a good bike in less than a year. Then the neglected Honda in the boss's tool-shed came to mind, and Stoddart's words *A neglected tool is a wasted tool.* He decided that next Sunday, perhaps during the tea-break, he would set the Honda in its blocks, clean it and tidy away the tools. Stoddart would certainly notice this and say something during the five o'clock inspection, and the young navvy had a feeling this might lead to something useful. He did not know what, but found the prospect oddly exciting, though he still felt sorry for Joe.

While he pondered these things they crossed a bridge over a railway cutting and came to Kilmarnock Road. It was a busy road with the railway on one side and on the other wee shops and pubs on the ground floors of ordinary tenements. The young navvy knew this road well. He travelled it by tramcar six days a week from his home to the building site and back. He was perplexed to find it so near the foreign, almost secret city of huge rich houses. A few blocks away he noticed a sign of a station where a subway train would take him home in time for the usual family tea. His distress vanished. He said, "I don't think my ma or da would like me going off to civil engineering just yet, Joe, but I'll take a crack at it one day. Thanks for the tip. See you the morrow."

Joe nodded and they separated.

HELEN OYEYEMI

Independence

Bisi and I are in a strange situation. But yesterday I watched a film in which a white woman was in a strange situation, and she decided that she didn't need to think about it that same day. This white woman decided that she would think about the situation the next day instead, since tomorrow is a new day. It is true. Bisi can rest in her bed for the moment. Never believe anyone who tells you that black people are the same as white people; that is most certainly a dirty lie. There are only straightforward white people (who are alright) and white people who are smoked black inside by evil or too much tar. If you want to know who is black inside, or if you think you might be black inside, you must consider other people's behaviour, or your own behaviour. Some people do evil after long consideration; they do evil so that good might come. Those are white people. Some people do bad things automatically and without much interest, blinding alley cats at close range with stones, for example. Or those people who insult and frighten tiny elders with blue-ish hair and absolutely no desire for *wahala*, *wahala* meaning trouble. Those are the black people. If you are one such, I am telling you now that it is better to stay inside, as a strong gust turns a white person inside out. If the person is white inside, or pink, then of course the person dies after being turned inside out. The blacks are the survivors. I am one such, so I speak with authority. Now listen: once you are arranged this way, arranged so that your whiteness is inside and your blackness is outside, people punish you for your evil in many, many ways. In fact the punishments for outer blackness are really just so incredible and insidious that I will say no more on the matter since you are very sly and will certainly pretend that you don't know what I'm talking about. I wish I didn't notice all of this blackness and whiteness. But I read too much as a child, mostly magazines and newspapers. Everyone told me I was reading too much. At first I didn't listen to Them, and then later when I tried to stop, it was too late. Of course I got ideas. I grew up wanting to murder everyone who had ever gained pleasure from playing with a golliwog toy. Which is, I suppose, more proof that my outside showed my bad insides. You take the African outside of Africa, or you put the African inside a new language, and they learn to say, "I am black, see my food, it is black." When before you just were you, and your food was just your food. In Cuba, when they cook black beans they call the beans "moors" because they are dark, and they cook them with white rice so that the textures don't fight but the colours do. In Nigeria black beans are slowly barbecued with palm oil and atarado and onion and then they are set atop rice like a soft, smoking crown. It is just beans still. I was born in a godforsaken African shantytown, and by "shantytown" I mean that our family was the only family on our street that had a television, and that very bastard television didn't work. By "godforsaken" I mean that everyone listened to the BBC World Service on battered radios. Elizabeth Street was just a row of cups, by cups I mean ears, filling with those flat news beeps every morning and evening, and outside was Africa and mosquitoes and markets and basically just everything. Because I was born in May 1960, hardly anyone except my mother noticed that I was born. There was a lot going on in 1960. Nigeria and many other African countries were either newly independent or getting ready to be independent. You will have to look up the names of the other countries if you are interested, as I am not sure of the rest of Africa. As an infant I was not endearing; I seemed melted. I congealed in the bottom of my cot and just looked at people. I think the English word closest to describing my gaze as an infant is "baleful", people thought my gaze was "baleful", but they didn't say it, and that was unfortunate. You see my mother is a lie detector, she detects lies all the time without understanding what is happening – it is miraculous and it really shows the power of prayer. When my mother's people saw that she had been born a girl and that there was nothing to be done about that, they did some hard praying for three days and nights without pausing to eat, and they insisted on some gift for her. The gift is that when somebody is not telling the truth, my mother begins grinning like an idiot. Her lips stretch out over her teeth and keep going until it seems that maybe they will run off her face, and her eyes, pure confusion. The worse a person lies the more my mother keeps smiling like that until she has to hide her face because it is embarrassing for everybody. So when people finally fell to celebrating my birth and praising my childish good looks and my health, my mother's face almost cracked in half with her smiling smiling. I am not ugly. But my face says that I am angry all the time. This is wrong; I have never meant anyone much harm. I just want to understand things and that really is all. I am no judge. Anyway I left Nigeria because I was sick of everything. Elders, men, kept smacking my head because they said I thought I was too high and how dare I look at them the way that I was looking? My mother despaired of my expression and she took to wrapping me in bandages and saying that I couldn't walk by myself. She started hinting that I was retarded and a dunce and that there was no meaning in my staring. Then she would fall into such long fits of grinning at her own lies, her own nonsense. One day the entire family, some ninety five of us, were sitting in the parlour listening to the next-door-neighbour's radio, as it was time for the BBC World Service news and our own radio was broken. Something buzzed; a fly. It could not have been a mosquito, as it was daylight and the mosquitoes were not yet so bold in 1990. And my father, he looked past my cousin Sola's plump torso and my sister Tolu's bony backside and he suddenly looked at me. And I looked back, wondering, who is this man after all? After that my father gasped and called everyone to watch me. Through my bandages I mumbled, "What? What is it?" Finally my father said, "Look at this girl, see that darkness in her eyes. How can I have her in my house? Tell me how can I have this one in my house when she wants to kill me?" My mother tried to tell him that I was like this because everyone was busy when I was born. And when my father wouldn't listen and came at me with a broom to make me leave the house, my mother put her body between mine and his and cried out, "What darkness, where is the darkness, her eyes match her skin like yours and mine!" But my father flung my mother aside. He broke the broom on my back and cursed me. Being thirty, I said, "My God, Baba *mi*, what do you mean by this?" I picked up one end of the broom to hand it back to him but when he saw me holding the broom, he became extremely afraid and dragged my mother into the house and he slammed the door. Then everybody inside that parlour praised God so loudly that the radio news could not be heard for a minute or so. I can't remember where my friend Bisi was born, though she has told me maybe three times. When it comes to friends you remember things like the way she never gets tired of stealing the snacks that I put aside for watching films with, or the way her thighs come together to make a strange, tense "k" when she wears a short skirt. With Bisi it is a strange situation. I would like to blame Mrs Marshall's grandson and his blackness for the trouble with Bisi. But I really think it could have been anything. Jack Marshall blew Bisi kisses and I saw him do it, and I understood why he did it. He blew embarrassed kisses to Bisi because she is young and because she straightens her hair so that it falls shiny black, hair from elsewhere, not tough, clumpy backstreet hair. Hair from elsewhere around a face as sweet as sugar. Bisi is a thief and she is not supposed to be in England of course of course but somehow none of this shows in her eyes. I wish I were a wind so that I could turn Jack inside out and then everyone would see that there is no light in him. After I left my father's house I went from Nigeria to England, since England is the place that Services the World through the BBC. I thought you would need a headband and a deep rabbit hole to get to England but it is not true. My mother came to me secretly and she gave me so much cash money in one go that we both wept. All you need to get to England are plane tickets, a purchased letter of invitation from an English professor and a lot of grinning and soft-talking at the British Embassy in Lagos. After that, only one more thing is needed: a good hiding place in the outskirts of London for when the month long visa runs out. "What charming eyes," the man behind the British Embassy counter in Lagos said to me. That was when I knew that England was going to be interesting. I wonder how many lies would I detect if I was a Miracle of Prayer like my mother. Actually, better not to know. England is fine after all. I don't want to talk about Africa anymore as there is no use hiding behind Africa if and when things are not going well in

England. I have got to be careful about talking memories anyway. Because I want to become English even though I am told
that the English don't want me to be English. I have been told
that the best way to handle this is not to talk too much about
coming from Africa in case people think that I am angry about
something or in case they think that I haven't realised where I
am. In the Nigerian newspapers that I read growing up, the ones
that ruined me, I remember one poem very well: "There once was
a Scramble/for Africa/now everyone Scrambles/Away – ha! ha!"
England is better because people like my eyes here. People like
my eyes here because they don't look at me properly; they only
look at my hair, which is not straight like Bisi's. Also, through a
friend, a National Insurance card has come into my possession,
so I can work, as long as I remember that my name is Judith Hill.
I work at an All Hours Cash and Carry run by a Pakistani couple
who laughed and laughed when I told them my name is Judith
Hill. They are a very jolly pair. And they didn't run a check on
the N I card. When it gets to 4 am and there are only two other
people on the tills and no customers, I knock tins off the shelves
and dent them under my heel so that the next day's stocktaking
will bring us deep discounts on mushy peas. The other two
workers don't speak English but they are very good at pretending that they do. They don't help me with the cans, but they nod
and give me thumbs ups. They are not Nigerian. It is easy to
make friends with other Nigerians in London; while you're
waiting for a bus or a train other Nigerians examine you out
of the corners of their eyes and then they suddenly start telling
you nightmare stories about friends of friends who suddenly got
deported. That is how I ended up sharing a flat near the river
Thames with Bisi. I do not mother Bisi because she is an old soul
and because I am not a mother. Bisi makes money with a group of
Cameroonians that steal from travellers' pockets and bags at
Heathrow airport. When Bisi manages to take a passport she
sells it, buys five kilos of rice and maybe ten chickens and the
two of us cook all day and throw an *owambe* party all night. I
understand that the smell of the egusi soup, the simmering
peppers and the aduki beans makes the neighbours cough and
fling open their windows and say *"Fucking hell what is that*

weird smell". There are very many people living in this place, on
this estate, different people, some from India and a few from
China and some Turks and so on. But we do not like the smell of
each others' food, it is offensive and it is not manners. I understand that. I cannot have curry smells filling our flat because our
flat is a flat that Nigerians live in, not Indians or whoever makes
curry. Our flat belongs to the council first and to us second and
after that nobody else, nobody else. I also understand that the
music that Bisi and I play must make the neighbours think of the
Devil because our drumbeat are ones that an English heart
cannot catch up with. When the neighbours come to talk about
the music I answer the door in sunglasses and say "Okay" and
turn it down, and I don't talk about the music from the people
above, the loud American rap with people spitting chunky words
that fall and die on my forehead. The flat is very small, but Bisi
and I keep it very clean except for birdseed on the windowsills so
that birds can come and make their noise there. Neither of us can
find any music in birdsong, but it seems very English to care
about birds and try to attract them. Feed the birds, tuppence a
bag. Bisi often tests me on types of bird, she has some flashcards,
but I still cannot differentiate between a pigeon and a sparrow,
especially when both are thin. The thing that makes England so
good is the fact that we so often have someone new-and-not-new,
a Nigerian stranger, sleeping on our sofa. And the ones that are
hiding because their Visa stay is finished, they are so delighted
by everything: Frosties with plain cow's milk, hamburgers, the
Tube. The only thing that I am sorry for is that I don't see my
mother anymore. But I'm not worried about her. In my mother's
mind the world is the same as it was when the gods were first
conceived of, she lives in a time when people were only newly
aware that they were people and they had not yet decided what
the rules of being people were. The earliest of my people were not
certain that they could commit to walking on the ground when
they might feel like flying – one king even hung himself without
first deciding whether or not he would consent to staying dead,
and he ended up becoming the god of Iron. So you see, though my
mother has said that 120 years is probably enough for a life, my
mother may well forget that she has said that and continue on for

240 years. My mother was not present at the Great Council that met to decide the rules of being people, and being born far later, she also missed the manner in which the people who missed that meeting were forced to walk always on the ground, first with guiding hands pressed on shoulders, and later with chains and manacles, until they could be trusted not to rise. So my mother cannot be trusted to walk on the ground, and unfortunately I am the same. I see now that I will not marry. I would like to be the spinster, in love with some hill, my body packed solid with English soil. The little old white lady in the flat below, Mrs Marshall, her husband is a long time dead. Mrs Marshall does not need her husband, because she is a secret queen. Mrs Marshall is so powerful that she appears exactly the opposite, frail and old. And she works her will through her grandson without ever giving a sign that any of his actions are her doing. Mrs Marshall's grandson is nineteen like Bisi is and he covers his head doubly; a baseball cap over a bandana, I think he is afraid of the space above his eyes. I also know that Jack Marshall is black inside; we look at each other and we recognize each other. He is not really angry, he just wants to understand things. Sometimes to understand things you break them open and have a look. Mrs Marshall, powerful queen. Her grandson breaks things open and sneers, but for her he does food shopping and garden weeding. Jack and his friends put on black balaclavas and break into cars around the estate with no regard for the car alarm. And if the owner dares to come down and defend his car Jack and his friends laugh and chase the owner with a length of pipe. I see all this from behind the curtain, the same way I saw Bisi stop and smile at the ground one day last week when Jack took her hand. But Bisi saw me looking and she made Jack Marshall let her go. When Bisi came in to me I said: "Bisi. Bisi. Why do you like him?" She said, "I don't like him. He is a stupid yeye boy. He is not a serious person." Of course I am not my mother but I smiled at that lie. Then: Bisi, out so late, so late each night. But she is an old soul and I am not a mother. Then comes the strange situation, and I am sitting with the smell of it at my back now. Bisi came back two nights ago with her hand to her side and blood under her hand, she did not talk but she wept

and her other hand made a shaky wall around her ear as if there was too loud a sound beside her. Her coat was ripped and her hair was roughened, I saw the black boy's hand on her. Dark must run to dark and then nobody can safely leave, nobody can see the way out. Bisi lay down in her bed and we knew the rule, no ambulance. An ambulance would bring help but a lot of questions. Anyway, Bisi said finally, it's not serious. I used hot water and Robb ointment and bandages for her. Robb is effective for all ailments. But Robb is just so much yellow wax when it comes to replacing flesh and blood that has fled from a knife. Bisi is dead and so far she has not been troubling me. But you know the body smells. There is three months' rent in Bisi's purse. I have not looked but she told me so. Bisi is dead and she is silent and she is at peace. But whenever I try to move her body, she giggles and says, "Please don't, it tickles." I had not noticed how good her English accent has become. Mrs Marshall comes and knocks; she comes to complain about the smell. Usually she sends Jack to complain. I look down at Mrs Marshall the power-ful queen and I want to make *wahala* for this tiny elder. I cannot tell if she is black or white. Behind me the smell of the strange situation reaches over my shoulders and pinches Mrs Marshall's nostrils. "I know you like your traditional cooking," Mrs Mar-shall murmurs, "But please can you ask the Council for better ventilation or something? I can smell this stuff everywhere in my flat, it's taking over." She says that the smell is interfering with the taste of her food.

RAMONA HERDMAN

He died on Friday

He died on Friday.
I've seen the photos, grey and convulsed
and thin as origami.
His bones a burst ribcage
femurs and spine spilt and clotted
piled to start a fire.
Jaw fixed like a biting horse.
Splinters, paper rubbed off at the elbows
dry tendon biting wire.

It took till Thursday
for them to blanch him in the mausoleum
for them to bloat him into cherubim,
face a puffball, reposed, strokable.
I wondered, in the plush stillness,
if the spores would cyclone out
at the push of his cheek;
what they had stuffed him with,
my emaciate infant brother,
to make him wisefaced as sixty
in that hiatus week.

He lived, despite prayer and prediction,
spastic, to thirteen.
He never dried his newborn stuck-down feathers,
or lost his fledgling shivering fits,
his saturated scrawn,
every finger a conflicting cripple.
He ticked like a water-clock
every breath a suck of spittle
loud as straw-bubbles,
the broken wing-beat of his lungs.

It took a week to drain him like a pharaoh.
Set his lips prim as a compact
powder his skin irresistible as a sugar mouse.
Maybe they broke his neck.
I don't know how else they wrenched it back
from its lifelong shudder over his shoulder.
He'd watched his back with shunted eyes
waiting for its twisted pucker
to burst out into wings and spines.
Taste the ache of each bone with your finger
wisdom teeth breaking ranks.

It was like the hiatus before crying,
the lacuna after an unwanted kiss,
the week they took to perfect his head and neck.
They drew satin up to his tied-up chin.
They cut and discarded the rest of him,
a muddled carcass too tangled to lay straight.
Doubly incontinent, vomiting, nose-bleeding
he had never been neat.
His casket is perfectly dovetailed,
heavy wood from the old trees on a residential street.

I don't think of him straight.
I think of him in the hiatus of a spasm,
outflung, white,
floating naked as a knotted hollow crab
in a midnight mausoleum vat,
pummelled in the last physiotherapy
the convulsions' retreat.
Salting down into softness the mouth that did not speak.

The family gentle, amputated
normal, in that hiatus week.

EDWIN MUIR

The Child Dying

Unfriendly friendly universe,
I pack your stars into my purse,
And bid you, bid you so farewell.
That I can leave you, quite go out,
Go out, go out beyond all doubt,
My father says, is the miracle.

You are so great, and I so small:
I am nothing, you are all:
Being nothing, I can take this way.
Oh I need neither rise nor fall,
For when I do not move at all
I shall be out of all your day.

It's said some memory will remain
In the other place, grass in the rain,
Light on the land, sun on the sea,
A flitting grace, a phantom face,
But the world is out. There is no place
Where it and its ghost can ever be.

Father, father, I dread this air
Blown from the far side of despair,
The cold cold corner. What house, what hold,
What hand is there? I look and see
Nothing-filled eternity,
And the great round world grows weak and old.

Hold my hand, oh hold it fast—
I am changing! – until at last
My hand in yours no more will change,
Though yours change on. You here, I there,
So hand in hand, twin-leafed despair—
I did not know death was so strange.

MAGGIE O'FARRELL

The House I Live In

is tall and narrow, with many rooms, all stacked on top of each other. The staircase winds back and back on itself like a hank of wool held on a pair of hands. The floorboards lean towards the street; if you dropped a marble from your pocket, it would roll, slowly at first, then picking up speed and direction, towards the windows. The walls refuse to meet together at a perfect angle. People who move in here try to shove furniture into the corners, and when they see the ungeometricness of the place, that nothing will ever fit, they curse and swear.

The windows at the front look out on to the matching faces of the houses opposite, and at the back, these days, patches of gardens, with sheds, paths, flowers and large iron arches with a wooden seat at the end of two chains. Children come and sit on the seats and swoop up then swoop back, their cries left behind, imprinted on the air.

Before, there were slatted-doored privies and an alleyway, running like a feud between the two terraces – rank-smelling, filled with rotten food and rats with tails like whips and a creature with the head of a dog and the thick, bristling body of a pig. It once snip-snapped at my ankle as I hurried past, a parcel of dripping held in my hands. But that was before.

These streets were built on a marsh, a damp well of land that belonged to a rich man who lived in a large house over the hill and beyond the trees. He built them quickly, draining the soil and covering it in a lattice of branches to buoy up his buildings like ships on the sea. In wet weather, the houses remember. They creak downwards, into the earth: wainscots strain and split, walls fracture, windowframes and chimney stacks loosen and rupture. Some people nowadays dig up the foundations and buffet them with concrete. But it won't work, I want to tell them. Houses don't forget.

Neither does the soil. When people lift up the tiled paths that were laid then, by the rich man's men, seeds that have lain dormant in the soil for a hundred years spring upwards into the light, triumphant and gleeful. Everyone wonders why marsh-plants are suddenly filling their dry-soil gardens.

The rich man put in as many rooms as he could, then filled every room with a family, then asked for rent. All day, people were running up and down the stairs in their wooden-soled shoes, babies cried, men shouted, women cooked and cleaned and tried to feed their children. We all queued up for the privy out the back.

I know all this because my mother told me. Before. Money follows money, she would say, from the poor to the rich. That's the way of things. And she would look at me across our room and shrug.

The houses were the same design. Streets and streets of them, all identical. My mother said when we first came here she used to lose her way, especially in the dark, in this maze of blueprinted streets. Except for this one. My one. It was always slightly different. It stands at the junction where two streets meet, at the end of a row, like the final book on a shelf, and is slightly askew, slightly foreshortened, as if a piece of it has been bitten off and swallowed.

My mother had hair so black it was almost blue. Her hands were marbled with frozen rivers that stood up underneath the skin. Her face is indistinct to me now, but I know it was pale and angular. I see it as if through steam – a white oval with wide brown eyes.

There was no father. Or none that I remember. My mother told me I was born in East London, a place where the air was crammed with different languages, the smells of strange foods, dyes and the throat-catching stench of tanneries.

She said she walked all the way here, me strapped to her back with some old sacking, through Shoreditch, then Islington. She lost her way around Kings Cross, she said, the great, panting, fire-breathing engines frightened and distracted her, she said. But she walked on, further north, through markets and shops and factories and then on again into rows of houses being built. It took her all day. She needed rests and I was heavy. When she got to the house, the sun was setting.

Our room was the smallest, right at the top, right at the back, at the end of a long, long row. Looking down to the ground was so vertiginous it sometimes felt as if we were in mid-air, like the crow's nest of a galleon, above the street that wound its way towards the heath.

The people in all the rooms of all four floors of the house came and went: babies arrived, husbands left. At one time my mother and I, lying side by side in the narrow bed, fitting into each other like pieces of a jigsaw, counted thirty-eight of us, including the new twins on the first floor – scrawny, bawling creatures with identical rodenty faces.

Knowing your numbers, she said, was very important, would distinguish me from all the rest. So when she returned from work late at night she would push her feet up close to the fire until they steamed and, taking a piece of chalk, would write on the floorboards: 1 2 3 4 5 6 7 8 9. These I remember. Her in the act of writing my name, I can picture: I see her bending forwards over the floor, the grey-white chalk gripped in her fingers, damp hair scribbled on her neck, I can see her arm moving up and down, forming the loops, lines and curves of my name. But the name itself, the mark in chalk, is gone.

My mother worked for a glove maker in Camden, her needle puncturing and pursing together the finest leather, flayed from the backs of young goats, to make new, extra, close-fitting skins for the hands of the rich. From the window, she could see barges with coal, lime, iron ore and lead gliding through the brown, brackish water of the canal.

Sometimes she would bring back tiny triangular scraps of leather. Off cuts, she called them. I would rub them over my face when she left me alone during the day. They were the softest things imaginable.

She told me not to leave the room while she was out. She warned me. But I did. Of course I did.

I liked the staircase, the way it wound around and around, how you could stare at the wall until your eyes blurred and then you could make yourself forget which floor you were on. I liked the solid smoothness of the banister handle. I liked sliding down it. I liked the struts, white and evenly spaced as ribs. I liked to wander past the doors, listening in to other people's lives. Those rooms seemed much fuller than ours, more exciting, more interesting. From behind the bevelled doorplates came the sound of shrieking, laughing, shouting, gasping. I hated being alone.

There was a stove on every landing, a coughing, belching, crouched black monster, and in cold weather I could curl myself around it.

Somehow, though, she always knew.

"You went out of the room, didn't you?" she would hold me at arm's length, searching my face.

I would always shake my head.

"You did. I know you did. We'll get thrown out. We will. And then where will we be?"

One day I was down by the door which led out on to the street, where the light came in red, blue, green and yellow, through the writhing patterns of coloured glass. If you pressed your face to it, the street beyond was a fabulous, one-colour world, like the lantern show my mother had taken me to see one year on the heath. One of the twins, walking about now in a grime-smeared vest, appeared next to me. Together, we stared out at a blue street, where people were moving through aquamarine air, where a blue horse toiled up the street, dragging a cart of blue coal. Next to me the twin was gripping a thick slice of bread, clotted with red jam. He wasn't eating it, not at all, just letting bits of it ooze through his fingers. And I was so hungry. So very hungry.

It was easy to take it from him. I was twice his size, and his hand was small and pliable. I pushed it between my teeth in one go. He stared at me, astonished, for a few seconds, then he opened his mouth in a wide, wet square of misery and yelled. And yelled and yelled.

When my mother came back later that day, she sat right in the middle of the sag in the bed and cried, her face clamped into her hands.

That night she told me something she'd never told me before. That in the middle of the city was a big, grey building, built on four sides around a big, grey courtyard. It was a foundation, she said, which looked after the babies of unmarried women.

She'd gone there, she told me, just before I came. She filled in forms, signed her name at the bottom of documents and, from the huge, cross-barred windows, saw lines and lines of children in grey uniforms crossing the courtyard like ants.

After I was born, she wrapped me up and carried me there through the city. She said it was a cold, cold day. The Thames, someone told her, was frozen in parts, great blocks of ice riding the filthy tides. I picture her, breath steaming from her mouth, walking up the big, grey steps.

There were twelve steps, she said, count to twelve. I did. She only got to number nine before she turned round and went back. Count to nine and back again. I did.

The next day, she stood over me with a long piece of dark red material. A scarf or a shawl I'd never seen before. She snagged one end of it around the end of the cast iron bed and tied it firm. I realised too late what was happening. I made a dash for the door, still only half-dressed, but she was too quick for me. She grabbed my arm and lifted me, kicking and squealing, over the boards where letters and numbers had got rubbed to unreadable runes.

We tussled and fought each other for the first time in our lives together, my mother and I, me twisting and turning in her grip, her with silent tears coursing down her cheeks. Some of them fell on to me in dark circles, I remember.

"I have to do this," she cried as I thrashed around, "I don't want to but I have to. I'm not supposed to have you here. They," she pointed down to the floors below, "know that. I'm sorry," she whispered, kissing my hair, my face, my hands, "I'm sorry."

After she'd gone I lay for a while on the floor, exhausted and spent. Then I examined her work: a stretch of material tethered me to the bed, an intricate knot bound my ankles together, heavy and dark as a human heart.

Every day this happened. And everyday we fought and wept.

Then one day she never came back.

I waited and waited, my feet held out before me, ready for her to unravel her undecipherable knot, as she always did, even before taking off her coat.

The room got darker and darker until the window was pitchy with gloom and the room sunk into invisibility. I sat awake on the floor and watched a weak grey light waver back into the room.

I knew I shouldn't cry. Boys mustn't. But I wanted to. On the second day, the water in the kettle ran out. I tried again to untie the knot, but it was complex, tangled, dense. I couldn't free myself. And any second now she would appear through the door and she'd be angry if I'd untied myself. The skin on my ankles split and bled as I kicked against my bindings. I licked out the inside of the kettle, and then its lid.

On the third day a strange, high keening sound filled the room like smoke. I cocked my head from side to side to listen to it, curious, awe-struck.

There was a sudden drumming from the floor below me, as if horses were galloping over the landing to save me. But it was only Mrs Bunt from the room below, banging on the ceiling with her broom-end.

I slept and woke, slept and woke. Light rose and faded in the room. I lay crooked on the floor, watching a crack in the wall spread, widen and fragment as Mrs Bunt drummed and drummed on her ceiling. I dreamt strange, hectic dreams: blue horses dragging blue carts laden with my mother's inert blue body; my mother climbing up and down and up and down a flight of stone stairs; the twin downstairs gripping a tiny mannequin of my mother in his fist and squeezing, squeezing.

Sometimes the knot seemed very far away, as far as the trees shielding the rich man from us and sometimes it was so big it was all I could see.

Then I had a very long, heavy sleep, as opaque and thick as the night dark. It was dreamless and compressed and close. When I woke, something solid and heavy was crashing at the door. I stared at it, relief washing over me.

She had come back.

I wanted to cry but knew I mustn't. The latch was straining on its screws. I was just moving towards it, to ask her where have you been, why did you leave me like that, when the door burst open and three men stepped inside.

I knew them – they lived downstairs. They didn't look at me at all. I spoke to them. I said, where is my mother, can you tell me, where is she, but none of them were listening.

Their expressions frightened me: odd, stretched, fearful.

One of them leant down and picked up something that looked like a bundle of clothes. He picked it up carefully and gently as if it was a very precious, very rare thing. Don't, I said, that's my mother's. Then I saw that the bundle had feet and a long red swathe of material was falling from it, like a tail, like a wound, and I was speechless.

I was speechless for a long time after that. I think I forgot how to speak.

Some people moved into our room, mine and my mother's – two men. They strung a curtain between their beds. One was very tidy, hung up his clothes, combed his hair every morning; the other scattered things around him like snow. I hated them being there. They ignored me. And I had nowhere to go.

The Bunts moved out. I was on the first-floor landing as they left. The twins saw me as they passed by, I'm sure of it. They gaped and stared then clung to their father's leg, screaming my name, over and over. That was the last time I ever heard it.

I hung around our room. I drifted up and down the stairs. I waited by the front door. She might come back, she might. At any moment. I slipped out of the door, once, when one of the brothers was off to his job in the morning, ready to find my way to Camden to look for her. But outside the house, I felt my strength and substantiality ebbing away from me, as if there was different air out there, air I couldn't breathe. I slumped on the doorstep, gasping, suffocating, and just managed to crawl back in when someone else, a woman now living in the room next to mine with her squalling crowd of children, opened the door to come in.

The alley out the back was flattened and low walls put up. Flowers stretched themselves up the brickwork. A man with luxuriant side whiskers moved into the whole of the lower two floors, along with his wife who never seemed to blink. Imagine, all those rooms between just two people.

She carried a handkerchief constantly in her right hand, into which she sneezed, meekly and quietly, like a cat. The man called her Pussy. He spent hours grooming his side whiskers, combing and oiling and waxing them. I stared into the mirror with him, fascinated. The smell of hair oil. The long fingers teasing and primping. The intent, absorbed look on his face. There was no reflection for me.

Pussy had a tiny bird in a cage, as yellow as her hair. All morning, she would bend and peer at it, pushing bits of food through the golden bars, trying to entice a melodious warble from its soft yellow throat. That bird hated me. Whenever I came near to look it would roll its ochre bead of an eye, screech and flap about, crashing its feathers into the bars. This made Pussy weep.

They never saw me. Or at least I don't think so. He would shiver in my presence occasionally, as if he felt a draft threading in from a gap around a window or from under a door. She would stare glassily in my direction at times. But then she looked at him in this way, too, so it didn't really mean anything.

Upstairs, at this time, were a brother and his two sisters. He read aloud to them every night, at great length, from a book with a leather casing and gilt-edged pages, fragile as onion skins. They were as bored as me, I could tell, although they smiled whenever he looked up, their eyes swimming with suppressed yawns.

This is where I discovered that if I concentrated really hard, shut my eyes, held my breath, and thought about the ball of displeasure in my chest, I could move things. I really could. Almost as if I were still a real, flesh boy.

His pen, his pipe, his shoes, his snuffbox. His glasses were my favourite. They were loops of wire, the size of small coins, surrounding glass. He barely needed them, I was convinced, but I think he liked the way they looked, the way they felt, the embracing press of them on either side of his nose.

I would uplift them and put them under papers, inside drawers, behind cushions, down chair arms. I couldn't carry them far, somehow, but it was enough. It made his face puce with rage and he would storm about, whirling papers, antimacassars, books around him like the great north wind. It made me laugh for the first time in years.

But one day I made the mistake of hiding them in the elder sister's sewing basket. He struck her twice, once on the arm, and once on the shoulder, two glancing, sharp blows. Crick crack. She fell back against the fireplace and even before she had stood upright again she was apologising, over and over, I'm sorry I'm sorry I'm sorry. I never touched his glasses again.

He would never have struck the younger sister. I saw the way he looked at her, like a cat looks at a bird, his tongue licking around his teeth.

She saw me once, the younger sister. It was in the big front room on the second floor, their drawing room they called it, though I never saw them doing any drawing, ever, in their whole time here. I was leaning on the arm of her chair. The brother was reading from his accursed book again. I was feeling that dense hatred in my chest, that hard knot of badness within me, its contours, its dips, the way it has sat there ever since –

And my mind was running over ways I could get to him without him taking it out on his sister, when I saw her, the younger one. She had turned her head to look at me, only six inches from her. I saw it in her eyes, that sentience, that knowingness, that sudden realisation.

I was so shocked I was motionless. I watched her face fade to a greenish white, saw the tiny, golden hairs on her wrists raise themselves, her skin shrink into bumps.

She shut her eyes and turned away, back to her brother. Deliberately. Determinedly. She knew I knew she knew I was there. I could see the violet pulse in her temple, the rapid rise and fall of her chest. I touched her sleeve and she shuddered as if feeling the clammy, webbed tread of a goose across her gravestone.

She died soon after, in the back room at the top. My room. Coughing up blood into a basin. I have to admit I was quite pleased. I thought I might finally have some company, that that might be how it worked. I liked the younger sister, you see, there was a restlessness in her face that appealed to me.

I was there the moment she died – we all were. Her sister sat beside the bed, holding her hand; me crosslegged on the bed, holding the other. The brother was over by the window making obscene, spiralling noises.

And I saw it, her spirit, her soul, whatever you want to call it, lift up out of her body, stretch into the air, and then vanish like steam.

Just like that.

I was furious. Why hadn't that happened to me?

They all left – the brother and sister, something wordless solidified between them like ice, and Pussy, her husband, and the yellow bird from downstairs, all muttering about damp air and disease.

The rooms were empty for a while after that. I slid down the banisters, climbed up the stairs, slid down again. I walked through the big rooms, criss-crossed by draughts. I pressed my skin to the cold of the windows to see out. People passed below me and no matter how hard I banged on the glass, they did not look up.

Three dishevelled men arrived with lots of implements: wooden frames with blank cloth stretched over them, fistfuls of hair-tipped brushes, and tubes of pungent-smelling colour that made my eyes water. They set up their paintings, leaning their imperfect backs against the walls and soon the floorboards were smattered with bright shoeprints.

I liked them. Creamy-skinned women would come and shed their clothes, one by one, into a small, neat pile, then lie back on cushions, the pink-brown eyes of their breasts tipped up towards the ceiling. The men stared at them, frowns pleating their faces.

Four more painters arrived: three men and a woman who dressed like a man, her trousers tied around her waist with a length of haired string. She saw me sometimes. But only after she'd swallowed down a black-smelling liquid from a green bottle. She never believed herself the day after, so I stopped bothering with her after a while.

They had big parties, clearing the sofas and the paintings from the big room on the ground floor, which reached right from the front of the house to the windows at the back, draping the walls with cloth and winding a small box until music etched itself into the air. The room would heat up then. Sometimes I would stay with them, watching the men holding the women to them as they danced, the flat of their hand pressed into the small, low curve at the base of their backs, their feet moving together as if they shared a secret no one else had. And sometimes I would go up to the room above, feel the heat rising to my face and gaze down through the lighted fissures to the movement in the room below.

You can miss great gouts of time, like this. You can sit or lie down for a rest, close your eyes, and all of a sudden a decade or more has gone by. The artists were thrown out. One day a man in a coat cut from smooth, soft cloth stepped in through the front door and told them all to leave. I wondered for a moment if he was the rich man whose house it was, come back to reclaim it. I was going to ask him if he knew where my mother was. But then I remembered he had probably been dead for years.

Two couples lived here for a while. On evenings when their spouses were out somewhere in the mist-veiled, street-lamped city evening, the man from the lower floors would climb the stairs to see the woman from the upper floors. Together they groaned and struggled and clutched each other beneath the tight clinch of bedsheets.

I didn't like them. Didn't like the first husband's grease-sheened skin. Or the downturn in the mouth of his wife. I made it my business to walk about at night, moving things around. They didn't stay long.

Next came people with children. They were the first children I'd seen since the Bunts. A boy and a girl. She had wide, watery blue eyes and hair pulled into two stiff plaits, a white line drawn through her scalp. When the parents weren't looking, the boy would give the plaits a sharp tug.

"Please," the mother would say when the girl cried out in pain, without looking up from her sewing, "Don't be wearing. At least try and behave."

They had the whole house. The whole house. For only four of them. The father, Arthur, had many tools, like the artists a long time ago, except he painted the walls with his brushes, and hammered nails and shelves into the asymmetric walls. He liked doing this, I could tell. It made him happy. If he could have pulled the whole place apart and rebuilt it, he would have done it.

Caroline was given the high room at the back. My room. I took this as a sign.

One night I crept in, slowly, slowly. Her bed was in the exact position as my mother's, pushed up against the outer edge of the house. I curled my fingers around the brass bed end and stared down at her. She looked as if she'd been dropped from a height, her arms flung wide, her yellow hair fanned out behind her. She breathed heavily, as if with difficulty, through her mouth.

I looked at the floor, at the seam of light coming in from around the curtain edges, at the door where there were still holes made by the latch being ripped off by the men from downstairs.

"What's your name?"

I turned. Caroline was looking straight at me, her face softened, blurred by sleep. One of her knuckles was burrowing into her cheek. She yawned, her eyes rolling back in her skull, then focussed on me again.

I don't know, I tried to say.

"Mmm," she said. Then she turned over and went back to sleep, dipping below the surface of consciousness and sinking away from me.

She introduced me to all her dolls, one by one: "This is Rosie this is Isabel this is Imogen this is Claire and this is Jenny. She lost an arm. Richard pulled it off and threw it into the pond. That was in our old house, before we came here. Daddy said he'd get it back, but he couldn't. He spent hours and hours and hours with a net, but all that came up was weeds and plants and things like that."

The dolls were odd creatures. Rigid, unyielding limbs and glassy eyes that rattled inside their head. But I listened to all their names, determined to remember them.

She showed me her books, dense packages of pages with columns of letter marching across them like ants, and pictures of children playing.

Downstairs, her father was taking a chisel and a mallet to the fireplaces, wrenching them away from the walls, then covering the scars with boards and plaster. Richard was hurling stones at birds in the garden.

"This is where I keep my dresses." She pulled at the closet door that had always stuck in damp weather. "This is the one for best," she pointed at something white and blue and thin, "This is one my cousin gave me. My cousin Cecile. She's horrible. When she comes round she –"

Suddenly her mother was in the room, the door slamming behind her. "Who are you talking to, Caroline?"

Caroline bit her lip, uncertain. She glanced at me, cross-legged on the floor beside the bed. "I wasn't talking," she muttered.

"I heard you, Caroline, coming up the stairs. There's no one here." The mother spun round, her eyes circling the room. "There's no one there," she repeated. She marched to the window, her hand flying up to the lock. "It's freezing in here. Have you opened this window?" She seized her daughter by the hand. "Come downstairs with me."

I tiptoed up behind the mother one day when they were all out. Amy, she was called. She was sitting in the big room downstairs, where the artists used to have their parties, a cardigan on her shoulders, her legs crossed. She was leafing through a book stuffed with scribbled bits of paper and newspaper cuttings.

I came up behind her chair, softly, softly. I breathed on the tiny, short hairs at the nap of her neck, I rubbed my fingertips over the woollen nap of her cardigan, I sniffed at the soap smell of her hair, I inhaled as much air as I could into my lungs, and then I yelled

BOO!

Amy leapt several inches in the air, letting out a small shrieking squawk as if she'd been burnt. The book flew up into the air like a bird, pages, notes, cuttings falling from it and fluttering to the ground. She sprang from the chair, her shoesoles slipping and skidding on the loose pages all over the floor, putting up her hands to cover the back of her neck.

"Who's there?" she screamed at the room.

I laughed and laughed and laughed, rolling around on the carpet her husband had laid, tiny nails held painstakingly in his mouth as he tacked it down at the edges.

"Who's there?" She scurried out into the hallway. The light through the front door made her skin a kaleidoscope of wild colour. She bolted through it and out into the street.

Who's there? Who's there? It's me, of course.

Two days later, she let a priest in at the door. He was being choked by a white band around his neck and the bones of his face pushed up through the flesh. His eyes were pale and darting.

They stood in the hallway for a while, him saying words like exorcism, soul, damned, over and over again.

"We're going to cleanse this restless spirit away," he said to her, his hand on her sleeve, "don't you worry."

I thought of soap bubbles, whirling around and around before being swallowed down into the black gullet of a drain. I didn't like the sound of this. Not one bit.

The priest sparked a match against the sandpaper rasp of a matchbox, and lit a tall, thick candle. He walked up and down the stairs, along each landing, and into every room, intoning long, melodious words which merged into each other: *in nomini patris et filis et spiritus sanctus amen.*

From his left hand he scattered drops of liquid which sat as raised silver beams on the hem of his cassock, as if the nap of the cloth refused them entry.

In the third-floor front room, where the brother had struck his sister twice, crick crack, the priest stopped. The fireplace she fell against was still there – Arthur hadn't managed to prise it away from the wall, but he'd covered it with a thin screen of wood and plastered over it. You'd never have known it was there at all. Out of sight, out of mind. Or something like that.

"I sense . . ." The priest trailed off.

Amy leant forward, her ringed hands clasped together. "Yes?"

"I sense," he began again, ". . . an . . . old presence."

The end of his sentence rose, as if he wasn't quite sure, as if he was waiting for her to speak. Which she didn't. I circled their ankles like a cat.

"Possibly . . . female?" he scanned her face.

She frowned. "My daughter did say it was a child," she said. "A boy."

"A boy a boy a boy a boy," he gabbled. "That's what I meant. A male presence. An old spirit, is what I mean. I sense an old spirit." He passed the back of his hand over his brow and stared down at the black book in his hand as if he might find the answers there. Clearing his throat, he began again: *in nomini patris et –*

AMEN! I bawled. AMEN!

Amy flinched as if slapped across the face. "There!" she hissed at the priest. "There! Did you hear that? Did you?"

The priest gazed at the ceiling. Was he hoping I'd be swinging from the frilled lampshade?

She was moving round the room in tight, nervous circuits,

dodging the furniture. "And it gets so cold." She stretched her cardigan around her. "Do you feel it? It's freezing in here, all of a sudden. Freezing. Do you feel it?"

The priest held out his hand as if checking for rain. "Um. Yes. I think . . ." he began, clearing his throat again, "I think what we have is a very unhappy child spirit. It's interesting, don't you think, that it chose your daughter as the person with whom he would communicate because maybe it's trying to tell us something, to get through somehow. Often, in cases like this, the spirit wants to speak and once it has spoken, it will be at rest."

She nodded, desperation distorting her face.

"Maybe," the priest struggled on, "we should ask it what it wants."

"Do you think so?" Amy was doubtful.

The priest squared his feet a few inches apart on the rug and, still clutching the lit candle, addressed a point midway up the wall. "What do you want?" he said in a clear, slow voice. "Why have you come?"

He waited. The words hung like gas on the air. He closed his eyes, straining for sound. Amy glanced down at his shoes, pursed her lips, then back at his face. I clamped my hands over my mouth to silence my laughter.

"Can you tell us?" He was using the same slow, silly voice. "What is it you want from these people?"

I had to stuff my sleeve into my mouth. But a kind of suppressed snort escaped. I couldn't help it. He looked so ridiculous there in the middle of the rug, in his black dress with his eyes closed and his candle held up like a weapon. Amy glared suspiciously in my direction.

He sighed. "Let us pray," he said to Amy. She arranged her features into a pious sneer and placed her palms together. "Dear Lord," and he launched himself into a long, monotone slew of words.

My laughter ebbed away. I waited for them to finish, to see what would happen next. But he talked on and on. Amy fidgeted slightly, tweaking at the material of her skirt, opening one of her eyes a crack, then closing it again.

I crept forward. I trod on the polished, reflective toes of his shoes, tugged the hem of his cassock, tickled Amy's ankle bones, blew up her skirt. And there was a great furore of stampeding feet, shrieks from Amy, muttered exclamations to God from him and they ran right down the stairs. I was laughing too much to follow them. I hadn't had so much fun in years.

I was hoping the priest would come back. But he didn't. There were others, though. Exorcists, spiritualists, diviners – the lot. A man with a curling blond beard and wide, flat hands told Amy to put mirrors opposite every doorway, "to drive back bad spirits". A woman with trailing, reddish hair claimed that I was hungry and that they should put out plates of food for me. She was right. I was hungry. But how could I eat their food?

The mirrors gathered thin films of dust on their surfaces and opaque holes appeared in their silver. The plates of food became fringed with green mould. Arthur threw them out eventually, going round the house with a rubbish bag, muttering about mumbo-jumbo.

Caroline knew not to talk to me again. She avoided meeting my gaze, wouldn't answer me when I spoke to her. Sometimes I still used to watch beside her bed at night. She asked to move to another room. They kept that room, my room, stuffed full of boxes, old furniture, toys they had outgrown – and locked. After a while, I really believe she stopped seeing me altogether.

One day I caught her reflection looking in one of the mirrors they still had around the house, and I realised she was no longer a child at all. She had grown up without me.

Richard left, then Caroline. Amy left one morning, too, on a stretcher. She'd been ill for a while, spluttering and complaining into a handkerchief. She never came back. Arthur sawed wood for shelves, replastered the stairs, built a greenhouse, filled in the cracks that filligreed the walls in wet weather, laid lino on top of other lino and laid carpets on top of that. He fed crumbs and slivers of suet to the birds, on a bird table he'd made himself. He walked around the perimeters of the garden wall, his back bent. When winter came around, he would sit at the window, looking out at the sky. I sat with him.

He stopped going into the top floors of the house. They became cold; the wallpaper he'd put up curled at the edges and eventually flopped forward to the floor. He slept in a bed on the ground floor and every day a woman would arrive at the door with a meal for him on a plastic tray.

He ate it alone, standing up in the kitchen.

I was upstairs when he fell – somewhere, hovering about, drifting. I heard a series of regular thuds, like a stick held against railings. I came down.

Arthur was lying at the bottom of the stairs, beside the front door, right where the Bunt twin and I had been standing before I took his crust of bread. His body looked splayed, uncomfortable. His face was pressed up close to the cold tiles as if he loved them, as if he worshipped them.

Arthur, I said, Arthur.

He'd already gone. I hadn't been quick enough to see the rise and disappearance of his soul, or to try and catch it. I sat down on the bottom step.

Days and nights turned into each other, then back. I zoomed up and down the stairs, rattling the windowpanes at passersby. Nobody came. Arthur's skin turned a silvery blue. When the sun shone, he was dappled with the colour of jewels from the front door glass. I'd always been afraid he'd take his chisel to it one day. But he hadn't.

The phone rang a couple of times, then cut dead. The plants drooped and yellowed. The milkman came up the path once a day and I tried to speak to him through the letterbox but he just turned away.

One evening I was sitting on the bottom step again with Arthur when the thundering thuds of the people going up and down the stairs in the adjoining house gave me an idea. I walked up and down, pressing my ear to the wall like a doctor in search of a heartbeat. It was thinnest on the second-floor landing. I'd never tried this before. I breathed in and just as the cold grain of the bricks bit into my skin, I breathed out, dissolving myself, mingling myself with the mortar of the house, and pushed and pushed and pushed.

When I breathed in again, I was standing on a landing. It looked just like my landing. I blinked. It was like the reflection of my landing in a mirror: there was the looping staircase with the exact same fluted banisters, the door to the room that had been Pussy's sitting-room, the four steps down to the lower landing, the window to the garden. But all the wrong way round.

Then I saw something that nearly made me faint. A big, mottled, white-pink animal, on the landing above, looking straight at me, lips drawn back to reveal a row of long, serrated teeth. It stretched out its neck and shouted

WOOF

then that rumbling, strangled noise from its throat.

I knew it, of course. It was the creature that had chased me down the alleyway a long time ago. I'd always wondered where it lived. I took a deep breath and pushed my way back through the bricks, quick as I could, terrified I might leave a limb, an ankle, a wrist behind around which it could clamp its fangs.

Caroline appeared, just when I had given up, when I had taken to sleeping in the doorway near Arthur, to keep him company. She fitted a key into the teeth of a lock and let the door swing open. She stood over her father's body for a few seconds then moved towards the phone. And when I looked into her face, I saw that she was old, older than my mother had been.

She had Arthur's body taken away. A few days later, a large, red van emblazoned with letters I couldn't read pulled up outside and men in overalls started taking everything from the house and loading into the waiting mouth of the van, until everywhere was empty, empty, empty.

This was the hardest time. I slept a great deal. And when I wasn't sleeping I would drift from empty room to empty room, wailing. They looked the same, all of a sudden. I could no longer tell them apart. Sometimes I forgot where I was in the house and that would make me cry more. I hated being alone. The floorboards creaked up and down, depending on the rain, the cracks Arthur had filled in widened and spread. The wind whistled down chimneys to fireplaces no longer there.

Occasionally, people would come and walk round the house, peering up at the ceilings, tutting at the fallen wallpaper, rapping their knuckles against Arthur's plastering. A man in a suit the colour of wet earth and a smile that came and went too fast always came with them. An "agent" he called himself. I didn't like them. I didn't like any of them. I didn't want them to live here. So I cried louder and louder until the backs of their necks prickled and they left as quickly as they could.

It was raining the day the young couple came, water rushing down the guttering to form rivers in the street. I was feeling the house shifting, remembering, the timbers creaking. He came in first, shaking the rain from his coat. When I saw her, something slipped and coiled inside me. Her hair was so black it was almost blue and she had big, dark eyes that skittered around the hallway, taking in the glass, the tiles on the floor, the staircase leading up to the rest of the house.

They held on to each other by the hand, as if they were afraid the other might vanish if they let go. The agent with the smile was with them but they ignored him, mostly. They didn't like him either, I could tell. On the landing, behind the agent's back, the man kissed the white of her neck, rubbed his palm over her cropped hair.

In the third-floor front room she looked at the wall where Arthur had hammered a board and said: "I bet there's a fireplace behind that."

The man turned to the smiling agent, "So how come it's been on the market for so long?"

The agent stopped smiling. Then he recovered himself and bared his teeth. "You know . . ." he circled his hand in the air, ". . . market forces." He turned up the collar of his coat as if he was suddenly cold.

"They've dropped the price a lot, haven't they?" The man persisted.

"A little," the agent conceded. "They're eager for a quick sale, I believe."

"But why hasn't it sold? I mean, round here houses go overnight. What is it about this one that . . ."

The girl slipped out of the room and up the stairs. I followed her, tiptoeing so that she wouldn't hear me, so that she wouldn't know I was there. In the back, top room she stopped. She sat on the windowsill, just as my mother used to when she brushed her hair, letting the tangle from her brush fall from her fingers to be lifted away by the breeze. The man stuck his head round the door.

"What do you think?" he whispered. "Do you want it?"

She just smiled.

He went downstairs, to measure something, he said. She stood and wandered to the edge of the room. I stayed close to her. I wanted to look into her face for a long time; I had this feeling it would have all the answers to everything I had ever wanted to know.

She nudged the edge of the lino with her toe, then bent down and tugged at it. It peeled back easily, like damp paper. There were two more layers (Arthur had liked lino). She knelt on the bare boards.

"Hey!" she shouted to the man, "there are great floorboards under all this stinky lino."

I saw her look down. She reached out her hand. Across the boards where she was kneeling were scratches. Deep, frantic scratches in the wood where I had kicked and kicked against my bindings, the nails in the soles of my boots scoring the wood. An incomprehensible intersection of lines, like Chinese characters.

She touched them once, twice, rubbing her fingertips along their grooves. Then she looked up. Straight at me.

I waited, holding my breath, for her to scream, run away, shut her eyes. But she didn't. Her hand on the floorboards stilled. The black centres of her eyes swelled and stretched. In the street below, someone shouted.

She stood up slowly and went downstairs, wending her way through the house. I flitted behind her, trying to stop myself from grabbing hold of her loose material of her trousers or touching her hand with my icy fingers or pressing my cheek to the warmth of her neck.

In the garden, the man was pacing up and down the width of the house, counting his steps, muttering about how it was going to need underpinning. I stood in the doorway. She squinted up at the house. She was standing where Mrs Bunt used to hang her carpets and beat them with a wicker bat, near where privy used to be. She sniffed the air. I knew she was smelling the ghost of that foul alley. I knew she'd be back.

When they moved in, they filled the house's foundations with concrete, pulled down all of Arthur and Amy's curtains and ripped up all the lino so that the windows were bare and sunlight spilled in over the wooden floorboards. The man scuffed with his toe at the coloured-paint shoeprints left by the artists, shrugged to himself and left them there.

The girl grew her hair. The man liked it, I could tell. He liked to push his fingers into it and draw them out again slowly and when she leant over him at night, he pushed his face into it, so that it covered him on all sides, like a tent.

They were always touching each other. When one of them left the house, the other would wait, eyes straying to the door.

But I was sick of women. They pretend, they forget, they leave and they don't come back. I wanted the man to see me, just once, just so I knew a man could. I tried everything – loud noises, stamping, crying, shrieking, wafting, hovering, shouting, touching, tugging, moving things around. My complete repertoire. Nothing. He looked through me as if I wasn't there.

It made her jump, though.

At first, I thought the girl was ill. She started dozing on the sofa during the day, her face soft and confused in sleep. I could stand just above her then, my face warmed by her breath. She would no longer run up the stairs, but plod, yanking herself up each step, gripping the banister.

Her stomach puffed and swelled out and one day while she was dozing, her cheek creased red by the cushion, I pressed my palm to it. There was a quick, sudden twist of movement, like something shedding a skin, and then I understood.

The man painted the top back room a deep red, tutting as the paint pooled and dripped into the crack in the wall made by Mrs Bunt's banging. I watched from a corner, my teeth set into each other. No child would live in this house but me.

I was right there when the first pain came. She and I were climbing the stairs. I was waiting for her to catch up, standing on the landing where the stove used to be, where my mother would get live coals to light our fire. As she neared me, she snapped in two like a tree hit by lightning, and a long, low sound escaped her lips.

She lowered herself down to the top step, her legs stretched out, breathing in and out like a pair of bellows. She clenched her hands together, then released them. She pushed her hair back from her eyes. She counted to nine and back again. Then she did it again.

The phone rang twice then cut dead. She didn't move, sweat dampening her face and hair, her hands gripping the rounded bones of her knees. I was anxious suddenly. What if something went wrong? What if the man didn't come back? What if –

A scream razored the air. I moved past her to come and crouch in front of her. Her face was pallid, marble grey, her eyes screwed shut. I reached out and put a small, cold hand on the dome of her belly.

Her eyes sprang open. She studied my face. Then I watched as she was clenched again by pain. Her mouth stretched open and she gasped and as she did so I felt the air around me stir, rush past, as if I was moving.

I panicked, tried to still myself, tried to grip on to the solid, worn wood of stair-tread. But I was being pulled, dragged by something bigger than me, stronger than me. As she breathed in to the bottom of her lungs I felt myself yanked inside her. And swallowed.

Everything is very hot and close and airless. I am being pressed and I cannot breathe and I cannot make any sound even though my mouth is open and I am screaming. I am screaming for the feel of the familiar wooden boards under my feet, for the touch of coloured glass under my fingers, for my mother. But she never came back.

I am being pushed now, towards something, or through something and I have not felt anything like this before. Or maybe I have but I can't remember. I don't like it. I want to get out. I batter my fists against this thing that is restraining me, squeezing me, and I am still battering them when I realised I am out in the open and that terrible noise drilling into my head is me.

I open my eyes.

I am back, it seems. Almost as if I never went away. I inhale again, ready for another outraged yell. She is not going to get away with this.

Then I realise they are bending over me. Both of them. Right over me. I stare back, thrown, still furious. They look as if they have something they want to tell me.

She is looking straight at me. He is looking straight at me. They smile.

JOYCE CAROL OATES

Small Avalanches

I kept bothering my mother for a dime, so she gave me a dime, and I went down our lane and took the shortcut to the highway, and down to the gas station. My uncle Winfield ran the gas station. There were two machines in the garage and I had to decide between them: the pop machine and the candy bar machine. No, there were three machines, but the other one sold cigarettes and I didn't care about that.

It took me a few minutes to make up my mind, then I bought a bottle of Pepsi-Cola.

Sometimes a man came to unlock the machines and take out the coins, and if I happened to be there it was interesting – the way the machines could be changed so fast if you just had the right key to open them. This man drove up in a white truck with a license plate from Kansas, a different color from our license plates, and he unlocked the machines and took out the money and loaded the machines back up again. When we were younger we liked to hang around and watch. There was something strange about it, how the look of the machines could be changed so fast, the fronts swinging open, the insides showing, just because a man with the right keys drove up.

I went out front where my uncle was working on a car. He was under the car, lying on a thing made out of wood that had rollers on it so that he could roll himself under the car; I could just see his feet. He had on big heavy shoes that were all greasy. I asked him if my cousin Georgia was home – they lived about two miles away and I could walk – and he said no, she was babysitting in Stratton for three days. I already knew this but I hoped the people might have changed their minds.

"Is that man coming today to take out the money?"

My uncle didn't hear me. I was sucking at the Pepsi-Cola and running my tongue around the rim of the bottle. I always loved the taste of pop, the first two or three swallows. Then I would feel a little filled up and would have to drink it slowly. Sometimes I even poured the last of it out, but not so that anyone saw me.

"That man who takes care of the machines, is he coming today?"

"Who? No. Sometime next week."

My uncle pushed himself out from under the car. He was my mother's brother, a few years older than my mother. He had bushy brown hair and his face was dirty. "Did you call Georgia last night?"

"No. Ma wouldn't let me."

"Well, somebody was on the line because Betty wanted to check on her and the goddam line was busy all night. So Betty wanted to drive in, all the way to Stratton, drive six miles when probably nothing's wrong. You didn't call her, huh?"

"No."

"This morning Betty called her and gave her hell and she tried to say she hadn't been talking all night, that the telephone lines must have gotten mixed up. Georgia is a goddam little liar and if I catch her fooling around . . ."

He was walking away, into the garage. In the back pocket of his overalls was a dirty rag, stuffed there. He always yanked it out and wiped his face with it, not looking at it, even if it was dirty. I watched to see if he would do this and he did.

I almost laughed at this, and at how Georgia got away with murder. I had a good idea who was talking to her on the telephone.

The pop made my tongue tingle, a strong acid-sweet taste that almost hurt. I sat down and looked out at the road. This was in the middle of Colorado, on the road that goes through, east and west. It was a hot day. I drank one, two, three, four small swallows of pop. I pressed the bottle against my knees because I was hot. I tried to balance the bottle on one knee and it fell right over; I watched the pop trickle out onto the concrete.

I was too lazy to move my feet, so my bare toes got wet.

Somebody came along the road in a pickup truck, Mr. Watkins, and he tapped on the horn to say hello to me and my uncle. He was on his way to Stratton. I thought, *Damn it, I could have hitched a ride with him.* I don't know why I bothered to think this because I had to get home pretty soon, anyway, my mother would kill me if I went to town without telling her. Georgia and I did that once, back just after school let out in June, we went down the road a ways and hitched a ride with some guy in a beat-up car we thought looked familiar, but when he stopped to let us in we didn't know him and it was too late. But nothing happened, he was all right. We walked all the way back home again because we were scared to hitch another ride. My parents didn't find out, or Georgia's, but we didn't try it again.

I followed my uncle into the gas station. The building was made of ordinary wood, painted white a few years ago but starting to peel. It was just one room. The floor was concrete, all stained with grease and cracked. I knew the whole place by heart: the ceiling planks, the black rubber things hanging on the wall, looped over big rusty spikes, the Cat's Paw ad that I liked, and the other ads for beer and cigarettes on shiny pieces of carboard that stood up. To see those things you wouldn't guess how they came flat, and you could unfold them and fix them yourself, like fancy things for under the Christmas tree. Inside the candy machine, behind the little windows, the candy bars stood up on display: *Milky Way, O Henry, Junior Mints, Mallow Cup, Three Musketeers, Hershey*. I liked them all. Sometimes *Milky Way* was my favorite, other times I only bought *Mallow Cup* for weeks in a row, trying to get enough of the cardboard letters to spell out *Mallow Cup*. One letter came with each candy bar, and if you spelled out the whole name you could send away for a prize. But the letter "w" was hard to find. There were lots of "I's," it was rotten luck to open the wrapper up and see another "I" when you already had ten of them.

"Could I borrow a nickel?" I asked my uncle.

"I don't have any change."

Like hell, I thought. My uncle was always stingy.

I pressed the "return coin" knob but nothing came out. I pulled the knob out under *Mallow Cup* but nothing came out.

"Nancy, don't fool around with that thing, okay?"

"I don't have anything to do."

"Yeah, well, your mother can find something for you to do."

"She can do it herself."

"You want me to tell her that?"

"Go right ahead."

"Hey, did your father find out any more about the guy in Polo?"

"What guy?"

"Oh, I don't know, some guy who got into a fight and was arrested – he was in the Navy with your father, I don't remember his name."

"I don't know."

My uncle yawned. I followed him back outside and he stretched his arms and yawned. It was very hot. You could see the fake water puddles on the highway that were so mysterious and always moved back when you approached them. They could hypnotize you. Across from the garage was the mailbox on a post and then just scrub land, nothing to look at, pasture land and big rocky hills.

I thought about going to check to see if my uncle had any mail, but I knew there wouldn't be anything inside. We only got a booklet in the mail that morning, some information about how to make money selling jewelry door-to-door that I had written away for, but now I didn't care about. "Georgia has all the luck," I said. "I could use a few dollars myself."

"Yeah," my uncle said. He wasn't listening.

I looked at myself in the outside mirror of the car he was fixing. I don't know what kind of car it was, I never memorized the makes like the boys did. It was a dark maroon color with big heavy fenders and a bumper that had little bits of rust in it, like sparks. The running board had old, dried mud packed down inside its ruts. It was covered with black rubber, a mat. My hair was blown-looking. It was a big heavy mane of hair the color everybody called dishwater blond. My baby pictures showed that it used to be light blond.

"I wish I could get a job like Georgia," I said.

"Georgia's a year older than you."

"Oh hell. . . ."

I was thirteen but I was Georgia's size, all over, and I was smarter. We looked alike. We both had long bushy flyaway hair that frizzed up when the air was wet, but kept curls in very well when we set it, like for church. I forgot about my hair and leaned closer to the mirror to look at my face. I made my lips shape a little circle, noticing how wrinkled they got. They could wrinkle up into a small space. I poked the tip of my tongue out.

There was the noise of something on gravel, and I looked around to see a man driving in. Out by the highway my uncle just had gravel, then around the gas pumps he had concrete. This man's car was white, a color you don't see much, and his license plate was from Kansas.

He told my uncle to fill up the gas tank and he got out of the car, stretching his arms.

He looked at me and smiled. "Hi," he said.

"Hi."

He said something to my uncle about how hot it was, and my uncle said it wasn't too bad. Because that's the way he is – always contradicting you. My mother hates him for this. But then he said, "You read about the dry spell coming up? – right into September?" My uncle meant the ranch bureau thing but the man didn't know what he was talking about. He meant the *Bureau News & Forecast*. This made me mad, that my uncle was so stupid, thinking that a man from out of state and probably from a city would know about that, or give a damn. It made me mad. I saw my pop bottle where it fell and I decided to go home, not to bother putting it in the case where you were supposed to.

I walked along on the edge of the road, on the pavement, because there were stones and prickles and weeds with bugs in them off the side that I didn't like to walk in barefoot. I felt hot and mad about something. A yawn started in me, and I felt it coming up like a little bubble of gas from the pop. There was my cousin Georgia in town, and all she had to do was watch a little girl who wore thick glasses and was sort of strange, but very nice and quiet and no trouble, and she'd get two dollars. I thought angrily that if anybody came along I'd put out my thumb and hitch a ride to Stratton, and the hell with my mother.

Then I did hear a car coming but I just got over to the side and waited for him to pass. I felt stubborn and wouldn't look around to see who it was, but then the car didn't pass and I looked over my shoulder – it was the man in the white car, who had stopped for gas. He was driving very slow. I got farther off the road and waited for him to pass. But he leaned over to this side and said out the open window, "You want a ride home? Get in."

"No, that's okay," I said.

"Come on, I'll drive you home. No trouble."

"No, it's okay. I'm almost home," I said.

I was embarrassed and didn't want to look at him. People didn't do this, a grown-up man in a car wouldn't bother to do this. Either you hitched for a ride or you didn't, and if you didn't, people would never slow down to ask you. This guy is crazy, I thought. I felt very strange. I tried to look over into the field but there wasn't anything to look at, not even any cattle, just land and scrubby trees and a barbed-wire fence half falling down.

"Your feet will get all sore, walking like that," the man said.

"I'm okay."

"Hey, watch out for the snake!"

There wasn't any snake and I made a noise like a laugh to show that I knew it was a joke but didn't think it was very funny.

"Aren't there rattlesnakes around here? Rattlers?"

"Oh I don't know," I said.

He was still driving right alongside me, very slow. You are not used to seeing a car slowed down like that, it seems very strange. I tried not to look at the man. But there was nothing else to look at, just the country and the road and the mountains in the distance and some clouds.

"That man at the gas station was mad, he picked up the bottle you left."

I tried to keep my lips pursed shut, but they were dry and came open again. I wondered if my teeth were too big in front.

"How come you walked away so fast? That wasn't friendly," the man said. "You forgot your pop bottle and the man back there said somebody could drive over it and get a flat tire, he was a little mad."

"He's my uncle," I said.

"What?"

He couldn't hear or was pretending he couldn't hear, so I had to turn toward him. He was all-right-looking, he was smiling. "He's my uncle," I said.

"Oh, is he? You don't look anything like *him*. Is your home nearby?"

"Up ahead." I was embarrassed and started to laugh, I don't know why.

"I don't see any house there."

"You can't see it from here," I said, laughing.

"What's so funny? My face? You know, when you smile you're a very pretty girl. You should smile all the time. . . ." He was paying so much attention to me it made me laugh. "Yes, that's a fact. Why are you blushing?"

I blushed fast, like my mother; we both hated to blush and hated people to tease us. But I couldn't get mad.

"I'm worried about your feet and the rattlers around here. Aren't there rattlers around here?"

"Oh I don't know."

"Where I come from there are streets and sidewalks and no snakes, of course, but it isn't interesting. It isn't dangerous. I think I'd like to live here, even with the snakes – this is very beautiful, hard country, isn't it? Do you like the mountains way over there? Or don't you notice them?"

I didn't pay any attention to where he was pointing, I looked at him and saw that he was smiling. He was my father's age but he wasn't stern like my father, who had a line between his eyebrows like a knife-cut, from frowning. This man was wearing a shirt, a regular white shirt, out in the country. His hair was dampened and combed back from his forehead; it was damp right now, as if he had just combed it.

"Yes, I'd like to take a walk out here and get some exercise," he said. His voice sounded very cheerful. "Snakes or no snakes! You turned me down for a free ride so maybe I'll join you in a walk."

That really made me laugh: *join you in a walk.*

"Hey, what's so funny?" he said, laughing himself.

People didn't talk like that, but I didn't say anything. He parked the car on the shoulder of the road and got out and I heard him drop the car keys in his pocket. He was scratching at his jaw. "Well, excellent! This is excellent, healthy, divine country air! Do you like living out here?"

I shook my head, no.

"You wouldn't want to give all this up for a city, would you?"

"Sure. Any day."

I was walking fast to keep ahead of him, I couldn't help but giggle, I was so embarrassed – this man in a white shirt was really walking out on the highway, he was really going to leave his car parked like that! You never saw a car parked on the road around here, unless it was by the creek, fishermen's cars, or unless it was a wreck. All this made my face get hotter.

He walked fast to catch up with me. I could hear coins and things jingling in his pockets.

"You never told me your name," he said. "That isn't friendly."

"It's Nancy."

"Nancy what?"

"Oh I don't know," I laughed.

"Nancy I-Don't-Know?" he said.

I didn't get this. He was smiling hard. He was shorter than my father and now that he was out in the bright sun I could see he was older. His face wasn't tanned, and his mouth kept going into a soft smile. Men like my father and my uncles and other men never bothered to smile like that at me, they never bothered to look at me at all. Some men did, once in a while, in Stratton, strangers waiting for Greyhound buses to Denver or Kansas City, but they weren't friendly like this, they didn't keep on smiling for so long.

When I came to the path I said, "Well, good-by, I'm going to cut over this way. This is a shortcut."

"A shortcut where?"

"Oh I don't know," I said, embarrassed.

"To your house, Nancy?"

"Yeah. No, it's to our lane, our lane is half a mile long."

"Is it? That's very long . . ."

He came closer. "Well, good-by," I said.

"That's a long lane, isn't it? – it must get blocked up with snow in the winter, doesn't it? You people get a lot of snow out here – "

"Yeah."

"So your house must be way back there . . . ?" he said, point-ing. He was smiling. When he stood straight like this, looking over my head, he was more like the other men. But then he looked down at me and smiled again, so friendly. I waved good-by and jumped over the ditch and climbed the fence, clumsy as hell just when somebody was watching me, wouldn't you know it. Some barbed wire caught at my shorts and the man said, "Let me get that loose – " but I jerked away and jumped down again. I waved good-by again and started up the path. But the man said something and when I looked back he was climbing over the fence himself. I was so surprised that I just stood there.

"I like shortcuts and secret paths," he said. "I'll walk a little way with you."

"What do you – " I started to say. I stopped smiling because something was wrong. I looked around and there was just the path behind me that the kids always took, and some boulders and old dried-up manure from cattle, and some scrubby bushes. At the top of the hill was the big tree that had been struck by lightning so many times. I was looking at all this and couldn't figure out why I was looking at it.

"You're a brave little girl to go around barefoot," the man said, right next to me. "Or are your feet tough on the bottom?"

I didn't know what he was talking about because I was worried; then I heard his question and said vaguely, "I'm all right," and started to walk faster. I felt a tingling all through me like the tingling from the Pepsi-Cola in my mouth.

"Do you always walk so fast?" the man laughed.

"Oh I don't know."

"Is that all you can say? Nancy I-Don't-Know! That's a funny name – is it foreign?"

This made me start to laugh again. I was walking fast, then I began to run a few steps. Right away I was out of breath. That was strange – I was out of breath right away.

"Hey, Nancy, where are you going?" the man cried.

But I kept running, not fast. I ran a few steps and looked back and there he was, smiling and panting, and I happened to see his foot come down on a loose rock. I knew what would happen – the rock rolled off sideways and he almost fell, and I laughed. He glanced up at me with a surprised grin. "This path is a booby trap, huh? Nancy has all sorts of little traps and tricks for me, huh?"

I didn't know what he was talking about. I ran up the side of the hill, careful not to step on the manure or anything sharp, and I was still out of breath but my legs felt good. They felt as if they wanted to run a long distance. "You're going off the path," he said, pretending to be mad. "Hey. That's against the rules. Is that another trick?"

I giggled but couldn't think of any answer.

"Did you make this path up by yourself?" the man asked. But he was breathing hard from the hill. He stared at me, climbing up, with his hands pushing on his knees as if to help him climb. "Little Nancy, you're like a wild colt or a deer, you're so graceful – is this your own private secret path? Or do other people use it?"

"Oh, my brother and some other kids, when they're around," I said vaguely. I was walking backward up the hill now, so that I could look down at him. The top of his hair was thin, you could see the scalp. The very top of his forehead seemed to have two bumps, not big ones, but as if the bone went out a little, and this part was a bright pink, sunburned, but the rest of his face and his scalp were white.

He stepped on another loose rock, and the rock and some stones and mud came loose. He fell hard onto his knee. "Jesus!" he said. The way he stayed down like that looked funny. I had to press my hand over my mouth. When he looked up at me his smile was different. He got up, pushing himself up with his hands, grunting, and then he wiped his hands on his trousers. The dust showed on them. He looked funny.

"Is my face amusing? Is it a good joke?"

I didn't mean to laugh, but now I couldn't stop. I pressed my hand over my mouth hard.

He stared at me. "What do you see in my face, Nancy? What do you see – anything? Do you see my soul, do you see *me*, is that what you're laughing at?" He took a fast step toward me, but I jumped back. It was like a game. "Come on, Nancy, slow down, just slow down," he said. "Come on, Nancy . . ."

I didn't know what he was talking about, I just had to laugh at his face. It was so tense and strange; it was so *important*.

I noticed a big rock higher up, and I went around behind it and pushed it loose – it rolled right down toward him and he had to scramble to get out of the way. "Hey! Jesus!" he yelled. The rock came loose with some other things and a mud chunk got him in the leg.

I laughed so hard my stomach started to ache.

He laughed too, but a little different from before.

"This is a little trial for me, isn't it?" he said. "A little preliminary contest. Is that how the game goes? Is that your game, Nancy?"

I ran higher up the hill, off to the side where it was steeper. Little rocks and things came loose and rolled back down. My breath was coming so fast it made me wonder if something was wrong. Down behind me the man was following, stooped over, looking at me, and his hand was pressed against the front of his shirt. I could see his hand moving up and down because he was breathing so hard. I could even see his tongue moving around the edge of his dried-out lips. . . . I started to get afraid, and then the tingling came back into me, beginning in my tongue and going out through my whole body, and I couldn't help giggling.

He said something that sounded like "– won't be laughing –" but I couldn't hear the rest of it. My hair was all wet in back where it would be a job for me to unsnarl it with the hairbrush. The man came closer, stumbling, and just for a joke I kicked out at him, to scare him – and he jerked backward and tried to grab onto a branch of a bush, but it slipped through his fingers and he lost his balance and fell. He grunted. He fell so hard that he just lay there for a minute. I wanted to say I was sorry, or ask him if he was all right, but I just stood there grinning.

He got up again; the fleshy part of his hand was bleeding. But he didn't seem to notice it and I turned and ran up the rest of the hill, going almost straight up the last part, my legs were so strong and felt so good. Right at the top I paused, just balanced there, and a gust of wind would have pushed me over – but I was all right. I laughed aloud, my legs felt so springy and strong.

I looked down over the side where he was crawling, down on his hands and knees again. "You better go back to Kansas! Back home to Kansas!" I laughed. He stared up at me and I waited for him to smile again but he didn't. His face was very pale. He was staring at me but he seemed to be seeing something else, his eyes were very serious and strange. I could see his belt creasing his stomach, the bulge of his white shirt. He pressed his hand against his chest again. "Better go home, go home, get in your damn old car and go home," I sang, making a song of it. He looked so serious, staring up at me. I pretended to kick at him again and he flinched, his eyes going small.

"Don't leave me –" he whimpered.

"Oh go on," I said.

"Don't leave – I'm sick – I think I—"

His face seemed to shrivel. He was drawing in his breath very slowly, carefully, as if checking to see how much it hurt, and I waited for this to turn into another joke. Then I got tired of waiting and just rested back on my heels. My smile got smaller and smaller, like his.

"Good-by, I'm going," I said, waving. I turned and he said something – it was like a cry – but I didn't want to bother going back. The tingling in me was almost noisy.

I walked over to the other side, and slid back down to the path and went along the path to our lane. I was very hot. I knew my face was flushed and red. "Damn old nut," I said. But I had to laugh at the way he had looked, the way he kept scrambling up the hill and was just crouched there at the end, on his hands and knees. He looked so funny, bent over and clutching at his chest, pretending to have a heart attack or maybe having one, a little one, for all I knew. This will teach you a lesson, I thought.

By the time I got home my face had dried off a little, but my hair was like a haystack. I stopped by the old car parked in the lane, just a junker on blocks, and looked in the outside rearview mirror – the mirror was all twisted around because people looked in it all the time. I tried to fix my hair by rubbing my hands down hard against it, but no luck. "Oh damn," I said aloud, and went up the steps to the back, and remembered not to let the screen door slam so my mother wouldn't holler at me.

She was in the kitchen ironing, just sprinkling some clothes on the ironing board. She used a pop bottle painted blue and fitted out with a sprinkler top made of rubber, that I fixed for her at grade school a long time ago for a Christmas present; she shook the bottle over the clothes and stared at me. "Where have you been? I told you to come right back."

"I did come right back."

"You're all dirty, you look like hell. What happened to you?"

"Oh I don't know," I said. "Nothing."

She threw something at me – it was my brother's shirt – and I caught it and pressed it against my hot face.

"You get busy and finish these," my mother said. "It must be ninety-five in here and I'm fed up. And you do a good job, I'm really fed up. Are you listening, Nancy? Where the hell is your mind?"

I liked the way the damp shirt felt on my face. "Oh I don't know," I said.

ANNE FRANK

The Diary of A Young Girl

Saturday, 8 July 1944

Dearest Kitty,

Mr Broks was in Beverwijk and managed to get hold of straw-berries at the produce auction. They arrived here dusty and full of sand, but in large quantities. No fewer than twenty-four crates for the office and us. That very same evening we bottled the first six jars and made eight jars of jam. The next morning Miep started making jam for the office.

At twelve-thirty the outside door was locked, crates were lugged into the kitchen, with Peter, Father and Mr van Daan stumbling up the stairs. Anne got hot water from the water-heater, Margot went for a bucket, all hands on deck! With a funny feeling in my stomach, I entered the overcrowded office kitchen. Miep, Bep, Mr Kleiman, Jan, Father, Peter: the Annexe contingent and the Supply Corps all mixed up together, and that in the middle of the day! Curtains and windows open, loud voices, banging doors – I was trembling with excitement. I kept think-ing, "Are we really in hiding?" This must be how it feels when you can finally go out into the world again. The pan was full, so I dashed upstairs, where the rest of the family was hulling straw-berries around the kitchen table. At least that's what they were supposed to be doing, but more was going into their mouths than into the buckets. They were bound to need another bucket soon. Peter went back downstairs, but then the doorbell rang twice. Leaving the bucket where it was, Peter raced upstairs and shut the bookcase behind him. We sat kicking our heels impatiently; the strawberries were waiting to be rinsed, but we stuck to the house rule: "No running water when strangers are downstairs – they might hear the drains."

Jan came up at one to tell us it had been the postman. Peter hurried downstairs again. Ding-dong . . . the door-bell, about-turn. I listened to hear if anyone was coming, standing first at the bookcase, then at the top of the stairs. Finally Peter and I leaned over the banister, straining our ears like a couple of burglars to hear the sounds from downstairs. No unfamiliar voices. Peter tiptoed halfway down the stairs and called out, "Bep!" Once more: "Bep!" His voice was drowned out by the racket in the kitchen. So he ran down to the kitchen while I nervously kept watch from above.

"Go upstairs at once, Peter, the accountant's here, you've got to leave!" It was Mr Kugler's voice. Sighing, Peter came upstairs and closed the bookcase.

Mr Kugler finally came up at one-thirty. "Gosh, the whole world's turned to strawberries. I had strawberries for breakfast, Jan's having them for lunch, Kleiman's eating them as a snack, Miep's boiling them, Bep's hulling them, and I can smell them everywhere I go. I come upstairs to get away from all that red and what do I see? People washing strawberries!"

The rest of the strawberries were bottled. That evening: two jars came unsealed. Father quickly turned them into jam. The next morning: two more lids popped up; and that afternoon: four lids. Mr van Daan hadn't got the jars hot enough when he was sterilizing them, so Father ended up making jam every evening. We ate porridge with strawberries, buttermilk with strawberries, bread with strawberries, strawberries for dessert, strawberries with sugar, strawberries with sand. For two days there was nothing but strawberries, strawberries, strawberries, and then our supply was either exhausted or in jars, safely under lock and key.

"Hey, Anne," Margot called out one day, "Mrs van Hoeven has let us have some peas, twenty pounds!"

"That's nice of her," I replied. And it certainly was, but it's so much work . . . ugh!

"On Saturday, you've all got to shell peas," Mother announced at the table.

And sure enough, this morning after breakfast our biggest enamel pan appeared on the table, filled to the brim with peas. If you think shelling peas is boring work, you ought to try removing the inner linings. I don't think many people realize that once you've pulled out the linings, the pods are soft, delicious and rich in vitamins. But an even greater advantage is that you get nearly three times as much as when you eat just the peas.

Stripping pods is a precise and meticulous job that might be suited to pedantic dentists or finicky spice experts, but it's a horror for an impatient teenager like me. We started work at nine-thirty; I sat down at ten-thirty, got up again at eleven, sat down again at eleven-thirty. My ears were humming with the following refrain: snap the end, strip the pod, pull the string, pod in the pan, snap the end, strip the pod, pull the string, pod in the pan, etc., etc. My eyes were swimming: green, green, worm, string, rotten pod, green, green. To fight the boredom and have something to do, I chattered all morning, saying whatever came into my head and making everyone laugh. The monotony was killing me. Every string I pulled made me more certain that I never, ever, want to be just a housewife!

At twelve we finally ate breakfast, but from twelve-thirty to one-fifteen we had to strip pods again. When I stopped, I felt a bit seasick, and so did the others. I had a nap until four, still in a daze because of those wretched peas.

Yours, Anne M. Frank

DILYS POWELL

An Affair of the Heart

Reconciliation

Under a deep soft drift of forgetfulness I slept until half-past five next morning, when I was brought three brick-like rusks and a cup of tea stiff with sugar. It was dark, and as the bus climbed out of Amphissa two or three lights winked in the town. But work was beginning; men and women drove their mules up the hill with urgent cries, and shy-eyed donkeys minced home with loads of fodder. On our left cloud piled so solidly that I took it for a mountain with spires and long flanks, until the dawn wind frayed and shredded it, and behind us the sun came up, a pink neon light glistering through grey scarves. We drove through desolate hills to a plain where the dried stalks of the gathered maize stood in the fields, and sheep grazed by a waterless stream-bed. Drinks and Cold Water, said the notice at a wayside café; goatskins, stiff and dead, were stacked in the dust by the road, and outside a solitary shanty a peasant was pressing his grapes; his harvest waiting in two tall baskets, his trousers rolled to his thighs and his legs stained purple, he stood in his one-man vat, trampling, trampling.

Lidhoriki stands under mountains at the head of the valley. At half-past seven, when we arrived, it was still in shadow, and the witnesses of war were veiled. When day lightened, ruin edged forward: blackened walls, disembowelled houses, houses with their eyes put out; ruin more deliberate than the wreckage of an air raid, and more malignant. But the village on this Sunday morning was full of life: homes being rebuilt, masons and carpenters at work. I went into the confectioner's, which was also the dairy, and ordered coffee and a saucer of crema, a sweet which is served everywhere in Greece.

Why, I asked the proprietor, was the destruction in Lidhoriki so terrible? The Germans burned the village in reprisal, he told me, half in Greek, half with a courteous but mistaken hope of making himself clearer to me, in Italian. There was a battle in the district; the andartes fell upon the Germans and killed three hundred of them, only one escaped; so the village was burned, and those who were too old to move were burned in their houses. There was an Englishman with the andartes, he added: an Englishman whom they called Geoff.

As I walked along the stony paths between the dead and the living houses a group of women working in a doorway greeted me, and I stopped to talk.

"Where were you," I asked, "when they burned your village?"

"Here," said one in the total black of the old, "they drove us out."

"What happened, where did you go?"

A handsome, deep-breasted girl with shining red cheeks and brown hair streaking from under her scarf answered me. "To the mountains!" she cried, laughing, "we went to the mountains!"

"But when you came back?"

"We had nothing, no clothes, nothing!" For a moment her voice hardened, then, seeing the question in my face, she laughed again. "If you have no animals you cannot carry anything with you. Nothing we had, no houses, nothing!"

"Where did you live, then?"

"Here!" She pointed to the doorway. It led into a mud-floored shed where in the darkness hens were picking at the ground. In many Greek villages it is the practice to stall the animals underneath the living quarters, and I realized that this had once been the stable of a house. "Here we lived!" And she roared with laughter.

By half-past eight the village was full of sun, and two buses were making ready to leave, one towards Amphissa, one onwards in the direction I should presently take. But I wanted to walk at any rate a little way through the country between Lidhoriki and Naupaktos. It was a region strange to me, for Humfry and I never achieved the plan we had made to cross it on foot; a region haunted once, I knew from the reports I had read in the war, by guerillas; a secret region too, walled in on the north by the bastions of the Pindus, hidden from the Gulf of Corinth on the south by the vertical mountains of the coast. Instead of taking the morning bus, then, I sat watching the movement in the plateia; the donkey swaying off with suitcases and bags brought in on the early morning trip, the piles of sacks, packages, boxes collecting for departure, the men in Sunday suits with a bundle of hens strung together by their feet, the women screaming to the driver as he hoisted a netful of vegetables to the roof.

Presently a middle-aged man wearing a suit more sophisti-cated in stuff and cut than the rest came across to the café outside which I was sitting and addressed me in my own lan-guage. He introduced himself: Timbelis, he said, was his name. Was I not English? Would I allow him to sit down and offer me a cup of coffee? I congratulated him on his English. Ah, he said, he had lived in America; he had a married daughter in Missouri; but in 1927 he came back because he loved his own country.

Lidhoriki, I said, has suffered much; in England we heard of what you had been through. Lidhoriki, he rejoined, has had a long, famous history: "When I came back from America, an old man, a hundred and four years old, told me that Dhiakos – you know Dhiakos, whom the Turks roasted alive at Lamia? – used to come to Lidhoriki."

We sat drinking our coffee, and my new friend, with the gift for story-telling which heaven has bestowed on the Greeks, held me with tales of the hero of the War of Independence: Dhiakos firing his gun at a wedding and accidently killing a man; Dhiakos imprisoned in a house, now destroyed, near the bridge I could see from where I sat; Dhiakos in his prison refusing an invitation from the Pasha, who had heard of the young man's good looks ("I am ashamed to tell you this, but the Pasha was how you say anomalous"); Dhiakos, as water-carrier for a band of patriots, seeing one of them fall, dropping the water-skins and rushing into the fight. Lidhoriki, it seemed, was among the hero's fa-vourite villages; the used to sit under a tree in the plateia – "you see the plane tree? There he would sit and talk, not under that tree but under another one which used to stand near it". Indeed he wanted to open the struggle for independence by freeing the Lidhoriki district and making it the headquarters for a general rising; like the guerillas of the 1940s, he understood its natural

advantages, its command of the defiles to Amphissa and Naupaktos.

"But the others refused, so he took his gun and went off. Under
the same tree he said goodbye to his friends. "Well, boys," he
said, "I am going now . . ."

The voice wavered and stopped, and I saw that the narrator
was affected by the story he was telling. His face flushed, tears
stood in his eyes, and he struck himself lightly on the throat with
the back of his hand to recover.

"Pardon me," he said presently, "I have always been how you
say tender-hearted. If I listen to music, Beethoven or Schubert, it
makes me cry. And to think of Dhiakos here in Lidhoriki . . ."

"You are from Lidhoriki yourself?"

"No, I am from another village, but I have property in the
valley. My daughter, who studied law, is in Larissa."

"But you were here during the war?"

Yes indeed, he was working for the Allies, he was imprisoned
for five months by the Italians. One day a guard came to him
secretly: "There is something terrible, I cannot tell thee." "But
what is it? Tell me, whatever it is I can bear it." "Then I must tell
thee that in the morning thou art to be shot, and eight others as
well."

"But," Timbelis went on, "I had fifteen gold sovereigns, I had
them hidden, I gave them to the guard and I escaped."

"You were working with the British?"

Yes, he said, and with the Americans too; he had found clothes
for them, he had helped them to hide and get away. And from his
wallet he took out with fond fingers two letters, photographi-
cally reproduced with type in white on a black background,
thanking him for his services to the Allied cause; one was signed
by an American general, one by Field-Marshal Alexander.

The buses had driven off with their loads, the square was quiet
in the sun; the story of death and conspiracy murmured like a
fairy-tale in my ear. There was a memorial by the bus-stop, and
before setting off on the next stage of my journey I went to look.
It was a war memorial, a cenotaph with dates and names. Fallen
in war, said the front face; the dates were of the wars Greece has
fought in this century: 1912–13, the Balkan wars; 1920–22, war in

Asia Minor; 1940–41, against Mussolini and Hitler; 1944, the liberation; 1946–49, against the guerillas – for to the Greeks, as I have said, the internal struggle with Communism was a full-scale war. On the right-hand face, nine names: Fallen in Lidhoriki, 1947–49. On the left face: Executed by the Germans and Italians, eleven names, nine of them civilians; Executed by the Symmorites, eleven names, all civilians. Death on foreign soil, death at an enemy's hand and now death at the hand of a brother; war, resistance, reprisals and the division of a whole people, village against village, family against family. The history of Greece for half a century is written in Lidhoriki.

ARMANDO

From Berlin

Fragments

MAN: Just imagine, I was lying there on the Russian front, in the mud, with another lad. We were barely eighteen years old. We lay flat on our stomachs for hours and hours in the silence. Our own men were a long way behind us, and we lay there in that huge lonely landscape all by ourselves. Still, we knew there was a sniper in the woods. Snipers lie in wait for you for hours until they get a chance to blow your brains out. It's a kind of game. Suddenly the bloke next to me says: Here, mate, got a cigarette? Yes, I'd saved one, my last one. We split it and we talked a little, and half an hour later he gets a bullet right in the head. Dead. I go through his pockets so I can take his personal effects back with me to the rear, and what do I find but a whole packet of cigarettes. And he'd asked me for my last cigarette. I've never been able to work that one out.

WOMAN: I was twenty when the war broke out. Whenever I think back to that period, I see myself waving goodbye at some station or another. Time and time again, standing by a train and waving goodbye.

MAN: I was seventeen when I volunteered for the army. Or maybe I should say for Hitler. I went through the entire offensive in the Ardennes. We were all dead keen. Propaganda was all we'd ever heard at school and at Hitler Youth meetings. We'd been in-doctrinated with that nonsense for years. Yes, I really did believe in Hitler. I thought he was a kind of god. Until after the war, when I found out who and what I'd been fighting for. I was confused for a long, long time. Other blokes my age were able to shake it off, from one day to the next, but I never managed to. I never really got my bearings. So now I lead the antisocial life of a taxi driver who only drives at night. I've been at it for 25 years. I never go on holiday, since I have trouble switching from night to day. My body just can't take it anymore. I like the night. I'm a real night owl. I like the lights at night, and the sounds. For example, the sound of the rain pattering on the windows. I'm crazy about the night. You may not believe it, but as I drive I think about the past, about the time when I still had ideals. I was even married for a year, but my wife left me. She couldn't put up with my working hours, and I wasn't willing to give up the night for my wife. Nope. So I'm on my own, and I'm going to stay that way. It's how I'm happiest.

WOMAN: I'm half-Jewish, so you can understand why my family longed for the Russians to come liberate us here in Berlin. Well, I tell you, it was awful. As far as the Russians were concerned, there was no such thing as a good German. The only words they knew were *Frau* (woman) and *Uhr* (watch). Sometimes I thought, haven't you got enough watches? I can imagine not having enough women, but what can you do with all those watches. Sometimes their entire arms were lined with watches. I have a Jewish patient now who went into hiding when she was young, and of course she was happy when the Russians came. A truck full of soldiers drove past and she waved to them. They stopped. One of them yelled *Du Frau Hier* (You woman here) and grabbed her. Oh, you could say you were Jewish and had been in hiding, but a fat lot they cared. She was carted off to Russia along with other young women who'd been snatched off the streets, and she spent ten years (ten years!) in Russian camps. To this day she doesn't know why. She was suddenly released, and now she's moved back to Berlin. As you can imagine, she has a huge number of physical problems, but mentally she's in tiptop shape. People can be amazingly tough.

WOMAN: You must often have heard people say that the Russians really went berserk when they entered Berlin. It's true, it was a very bad time. Except that they were quite nice to us children. But don't forget: the Russians had nothing and the Americans had everything, so the Americans didn't need our possessions. The Russians hadn't been on leave in I don't know how long, and everything we had (and after the bombings, that wasn't much) was a luxury to them. Light from the roof and water from the wall, they said. By which they meant: a lamp on the ceiling and water from the tap. I'm not kidding. What did peasants from Kirghizia know about life in the city. They'd never been to Moscow or any other big city. They washed their clothes in the toilet bowl and did their business in the garden or even in the corner of the living-room. Later on another type of Russian arrived, and they were much more civilized. There were officers who spoke fluent German and had read German literature. But it was very bad in the beginning. My oldest sister's girlfriend was raped, and they beat her up so badly that she died a month later. What makes it even sadder is that she'd done a lot to help Jews in hiding. But let's drop the subject, it's pointless to think about it at this late date, absolutely pointless.

WOMAN: I was very much in favour of Hitler, because he got people working again. You can't imagine what a hard time we'd had, but then Hitler became Chancellor and things got better. You had the feeling you belonged again, you no longer felt like an outcast. Then he started the war, and I'll never forgive him for that. And to think he was the one who promised us peace. As for what happened to the Jews, well, that still bothers me. To ordinary people like us, the Jews were perfect examples of capitalist exploiters. And Hitler was opposed to capitalism, or at any rate, we thought he was. But then he should have made sure the guilty ones – and believe me, there were plenty of non-Jewish capitalists – were taken to court, instead of rounding up all the Jews, including the women and children, and having them killed. He should never have done that. It was a terrible crime. A lot of Jews aren't capitalists at all. For example, they're good musicians. Did you know that?

WOMAN: My grandmother had seven children, and after the fourth one the Nazis gave you a *Mutterkreuz*, a kind of Iron Cross for mothers. They sent you a notice, and then presented the *Mutterkreuz* with a certain amount of ceremony. My grandmother didn't even bother to go get hers, and when they posted it to her she sent it back with a letter saying that she and her husband had wanted a large family, and had had the children for themselves and not for the Führer. I bet you think my grandmother was an anti-Nazi, but she wasn't. She didn't support the Nazis, but she didn't oppose them either. And it wouldn't have occurred to her to protest. I knew another woman like that. She had a Dachshund, and she hung her *Mutterkreuz* around its neck. The dog walked down the street wearing a *Mutterkreuz*. And that wasn't an act of protest either, though it could be interpreted as one. It just so happens that neither of the women got into any trouble over this. Oh yes, people like that did exist. But protest, no.

RACHEL SEIFFERT

Field Study

Summer and the third day of Martin's field study. Morning, and he is parked at the side of the track, looking out over the rye he will walk through shortly to reach the river. For two days he has been alone, gathering his mud and water samples, but not today.

A boy shouts and sings in the field. His young mother carries him piggyback through the rye. Martin hears their voices, thin through the open window of his car. He keeps still. Watching, waiting for them to pass.

The woman's legs are hidden in the tall stalks of the crop and the boy's legs are skinny. He is too big to be carried comfortably, and mother and son giggle as she struggles on through the rye. The boy wears too-large trainers, huge and white, and they hang heavy at his mother's sides. Brushing the ears of rye as she walks, bumping at her thighs as she jogs an unsteady step or two. Then swinging out wide as she spins on the spot: whirling, stumbling around and around. Twice, three times, four times, laughing, lurching as the boy screams delight on her back.

They fall to the ground and Martin can't see them any more. Just the rye and the tops of the trees beyond: where the field slopes down and the river starts its wide arc around the town. Three days Martin has been here. Only another four days to cover the area, pull enough data together for his semester paper, already overdue. The young woman and her child have gone. Martin climbs out of the car, gathers his bags and locks the doors.

This river begins in the high mountains Martin cannot see but knows lie due south of where he stands. Once it passes the coal and industry of the foothills, it runs almost due west into these flat, farming lands, cutting a course through the shallow valley on which his PhD studies are centred. Past the town where he is staying and on through the provincial capital, until it finally mouths in the wide flows which mark the border between Martin's country and the one he is now in. Not a significant stretch of water historically, commercially, not even especially pretty. But a cause for concern nonetheless: here, and even more so in Martin's country, linking as it does a chemical plant on the eastern side of the border with a major population centre to the west.

Martin has a camera, notebooks and vials. Some for river water, others for river mud. Back in the town, in his room at the guesthouse, he has chemicals and a microscope. More vials and dishes. The first two days' samples, still to be analysed, a laptop on which to record his results.

The dark, uneven arc of the trees is visible for miles, marking the course of the river through the yellow-dry countryside. The harvest this year will be early and poor. Drought, and so the water level of the river is low, but the trees along its banks are still full of new growth, thick with leaves, the air beneath them moist.

Martin drinks the first coffee of the day from his flask by the water's edge. The river has steep banks, and roots grow in twisted detours down its rocky sides. He has moved steadily west along the river since the beginning of the week, covering about a kilometre each day, with a two-kilometre gap in between. Up until now, the water has been clear, but here it is thick with long fronds of weed. Martin spreads a waterproof liner on the flat rock, lays out vials and spoons in rows. He writes up the labels while he drinks his second coffee, then pulls on his long water-proof gloves. Beyond the branches, the field shimmers yellow-white and the sun is strong; under the trees, Martin is cool. Counting, measuring, writing, photographing. Long sample spoon scratching river grit against the glass of the vials.

Late morning and hot now, even under the trees. The water at this point in the river is almost deep enough to swim. Martin lays out his vials, spoons and labels for the third time that morning. Wonders a moment or two what it would be like to lie down in the lazy current, the soft weed. Touches his gloved fingertips to the surface and counts up all the toxic substances he will test his samples for later. He rolls up his trouser legs as high as they will go before he pulls on the waders, enjoys the cool pressure of the water against the rubber against his skin as he moves carefully out to about mid-stream. The weed here is at its thickest, and Martin decides to take a sample of that, too. The protective gauntlets make it difficult to get a grip, but Martin manages to pull one plant from the river bed with its root system still reasonably intact. He stands a while, feeling the current tug its way around his legs, watching the fingers of weed slowly folding over the gap he has made. Ahead is a sudden dip, a small waterfall that Martin had noted yesterday evening on the map. The noise of the cascade is loud, held in close by the dense green avenue of trees. Martin wades forward and when he stops again, he hears voices, a laugh-scream.

The bushes grow dense across the top of the drop, but Martin can just see through the leaves: young mother and son, swimming in the pool hollowed out by the waterfall. They are close. He can see the boy take a mouthful of water and spray it at his mother as she swims around the small pool. Can see the mud between her toes when she climbs out and stands on the rock at the water's edge. The long black-green weed stuck to her thigh. She is not naked, but her underwear is pale, pink-white like her skin, and Martin can also see the darker wet of nipples and pubic hair. He turns quickly and wades back to the bank, weed sample held carefully in gauntleted hands.

He stands for a moment by his bags, then pulls off the waders, pulls on his shoes again. He will walk round them, take a detour across the fields and they will have no cause to see him. He has gathered enough here already, after all. The pool and waterfall need not fall within his every 100 metres remit. No problem.

Martin sleeps an hour when he gets back to the guest-house. Open window providing an occasional breeze from the small back court and a smell of bread from the kitchen. When he wakes the sun has passed over the top of the building and his room is pleasantly cool and dim.

He works for an hour or two on the first day's mud and water vials, and what he finds confirms his hypothesis. Everything within normal boundaries, except one particular metal, present in far higher concentrations than one should expect.

His fingers start to itch as he parcels up a selection of samples to send back to the university lab for confirmation. He knows this is psychosomatic, that he has always been careful to wear protection: doesn't even think that poisoning with this metal is likely to produce such a reaction. He includes the weed sample in his parcel, with instructions that a section be sent on to botany, and a photocopy of the map, with the collection sites clearly marked. In the post office, his lips and the skin around his nostrils burn, and so, despite his reasoning, he allows himself another shower before he goes down to eat an early dinner in the guesthouse café.

The boy from the stream is sitting on one of the high stools at the bar doing his homework, and the waitress who brings Martin his soup is his mother. She wishes him a good appetite in one of the few phrases he understands in this country, and when Martin thanks her using a couple of words picked up on his last visit, he thinks she looks pleased.

Martin watches her son while he eats. Remembers the fountain of river-water the boy aimed at his mother, wonders how much he swallowed, if they swim there regularly, how many years they might have done this for. Martin thinks he looks healthy enough, perhaps a little underweight.

His mother brings Martin a glass of wine with his main course, and when he tries to explain that he didn't order it, she just puts her finger to her lips and winks. She is thin, too, but she looks strong; broad shoulders and palms, long fingers, wide nails. She pulls her hands behind her back, and Martin is aware now that he has been staring. He lowers his eyes to his plate, watches her through his lashes as she moves on to the next table. Notes: *good posture, thick hair*. But Martin reasons while he eats that such poisons can take years to make their presence felt; nothing for a decade or two, then suddenly tumours and shortness of breath in middle age.

The woman is sitting at the bar with her son when Martin finishes his meal. She is smoking a cigarette and checking through his maths. The boy watches as Martin walks towards them, kicking his trainers against the high legs of his barstool.

– I'm sorry. I don't really speak enough of your language. But I wanted to tell you something.

The woman looks up from her son's exercise book and blinks as Martin speaks. He stops a moment, waits to see if she understands, if she will say something, but after a small smile and a small frown, she just nods and turns away from him, back to her son. At first Martin thinks they are talking about him, and that they might still respond, but the seconds pass and the boy and his mother keep talking, and then Martin can't remember how long he has been standing there looking at the back of her head, so he looks away. Sees his tall reflection in the mirror behind the bar. One hand, *left, no right*, moving up to cover his large forehead, *sunburnt*, and red hair.

– What do you want to say to my mother?

The boy speaks Martin's language. He shrugs when Martin looks at him. Martin lets his hand drop back down to his side.

– Oh, okay. Okay, good. Can you translate for me then?

The boy shrugs again, which Martin takes to be assent, and so he starts to explain. About the river, how he saw them swimming in the morning and he didn't want to disturb them, but that he has been thinking about it again this evening. And then Martin stops talking because he sees that the boy is frowning.

– Should I start again?

– You were watching my mother swimming.

– No.

The boy whispers to his mother, who flushes and then puts her hand over her mouth and laughs.

– No. No, that's not right.

Martin shakes his head again, holds both hands up, but it is loud, the woman's laughter in the quiet café, and the other two customers look up from their meals.

– I was not watching. Tell her I was not watching. I was taking samples from the river, that's all. I'm a scientist. And I think you should know that it is polluted. The river is dirty and you really shouldn't swim there. That's all. Now please tell your mother.

The young woman keeps laughing while Martin speaks, and though he avoids looking in the mirror again, he can feel the blush making his sunburn itch, the pulse in his throat. The boy watches him a second or two, lips moving, not speaking. Martin thinks the boy doesn't believe him.

– *You could get sick. The river will make you sick. I just thought you should know. Okay?*

Martin is angry now. With the suspicious boy, his laughing mother. He counts out enough to pay for his meal, including the wine. Leaves it on the table without a tip and goes to his room.

In the morning, a man serves Martin his breakfast, but before he leaves for the river again the young mother comes into the café, pushing her son in front of her. She speaks in a low whisper to the boy, who translates for Martin in a monotone.

– My mother says she is sorry. We are both sorry. That she is Ewa, I am Jacek. She says you should tell me about the river so I can tell her.

Martin is still annoyed when he gets back from the river in the afternoon. Doesn't expect the woman and her boy to stick to their appointment, still hasn't analysed day two and three's samples, half hopes they won't turn up. But when he comes downstairs after his shower, he finds them waiting for him in the café as arranged.

The boy helps Martin spread out his maps, asks if he can boot up the laptop. His mother murmurs something, and her son sighs.

– She says I should say please. Please.

– *It's okay.*

Martin shows them the path of the river from the mountains to the border and where the chemical plant lies, almost a hundred kilometres upstream from the town. Amongst his papers, he finds images of what the metal he has found in the river looks like, its chemical structure and symbol, and he tells them its common name. He says that as far as they know, the body cannot break it down, so it stores it, usually in the liver. He speaks a sentence at a time and lets the boy translate. Shows them the graphs he has plotted on his computer. Waits while the boy stumbles over his grammar, watches his mother listening, thinks: *Jacek and Ewa.*

– Where do you come from?

Ewa speaks in Martin's language, points at the map. Martin looks at her, and Jacek clears his throat.

– I am teaching her.

Martin smiles. He shows them where he is studying and then, a little further to the west, the city where he was born. And then Jacek starts to calculate how many kilometres it is from Martin's university to the border and from the border to the town. Martin asks Ewa:

– *How old is he?*

– Nearly eleven.

He nods. Thinks she must have been very young when she got pregnant.

– *He's just about bilingual already.*

An exaggeration, a silly thing to say, and Martin can see in Ewa's eyes that she knows it, but she doesn't contradict him.

– School. He is a good student. Also a good teacher.

She smiles and Martin is glad that they came today, Ewa and her son. Pushes last night's laughter to the back of his mind. Sees that Ewa's smile is wide and warm and that her tongue shows pink behind her teeth.

Day five and Martin works his way along the river again. The hot fields are empty, the road quiet. The water here is wider, deeper; flies dance above the surface.

Mid-morning and Jacek crashes through the undergrowth.

– Martin! There you are. I am here.

Martin looks up from the water, startled. He nods, then he doesn't know what to say to the boy, so he carries on working. Jacek watches him a while, and then pulls off his trainers, rolls up his trousers, picks up a vial.

– *No! You shouldn't come in.*

– I can help you. You work faster when I can pass them to you.

– *Shouldn't you be at school?*

Jacek frowns.

– *Does your mother know you are here?*

– She don't mind.

Martin thinks a moment.

– *We don't know enough yet about this metal, you see. It's too much of a risk.*

Jacek avoids eye contact, rubs his bare ankles.

– *You really can't help me without boots and gloves, Jacek. I only have one pair of each. I'm sorry.*

An hour later the boy is back with pink washing-up gloves and a pair of outsize rubber boots, soles caked in mud. He holds up a bag of apples.

– For you. From my mother.

In the evening the café is crowded and Ewa is busy; another waitress brings Martin his dinner. His table is near the bar, where Jacek is doing his homework again. New vocabulary, and he asks Martin to correct his spelling. Ewa makes a detour past his table on her way to the kitchen.

– Thank-you.

– *No problem.*

He scratches his sunburn, stops. Feels huge at the small table after she has gone.

Jacek brings his mother with him on day six. Ewa stands at the water's edge while her son changes into his boots and washing-up gloves. Midday already, and the sky is clear, the sun high. Martin has sweat patches under his arms, on his back. He watches Ewa hold the front of her T-shirt away from her chest, and then flap it back and forth to get cool air at the hot skin beneath. He sees yellow pollen on her shoes, the hem of her skirt, damp hair at her temples.

They work for a while, and Jacek asks questions which Martin answers. Ewa says very little. She crouches on the bank and looks at the water. Lids down, lips drawn together, arms wrapped around her shins. When Martin says it's time to move downstream 100 metres, Jacek says he wants come with him and Ewa says she will go home.

Jacek watches Martin watching his mother as she wades through the long grass back to the road.

– She used to swim here with my Tata, I think.

– *Your father?*

Martin tries to remember a wedding ring. Sees Ewa's strong palms, her long fingers.

– He is in your country.

– *Oh?*

– He is illegal. Too much problems at the border, so he don't come home.

Martin watches Jacek as they unpack the bags again. Fair with freckles. Narrow lips, pale eyes, broad nose. A good looking boy, but not at all like his mother.

Day seven and Martin doesn't go to the river. After breakfast he sets up his computer, a new graph template, and plots the data from days two and three. Both agree with day one's graph, with Martin's predictions, and he starts sketching out a structure for his argument, writes a first draft conclusion. The sample results should have come back from the university yesterday, including the mud and weed from day four, which would speed up Martin's analysis. He goes downstairs to the small office mid-morning to check for faxes again, but the guesthouse is quiet, café closed, reception deserted. Sunday. So there won't be anybody at the labs, either, but Martin walks out to the phone boxes in the town square anyway.

Jacek hammers on the glass.

– Where were you?

– *Wait.*

Martin holds up one finger, but the phone just keeps ringing out at the other end. Jacek peels his pink gloves off while Martin leaves a message on the lab answerphone. The boy cups his hands around his eyes, presses them up to the glass, watching him. It is stifling inside the phone box and Jacek's hands leave a sweaty streak on the pane outside.

When Martin opens the door, Jacek has his fists on his hips. Rubber boots on the paving stones beside him.

– Why didn't you come?

– *I've finished. I only need to do a couple more tests.*

– Oh.

Jacek picks up his boots and falls into step with Martin. The sun is strong and they walk together on the shady side of the narrow street which leads back up to the guesthouse.

– *I'm going home tomorrow.*

– Tomorrow?

He looks up at Martin for a second or two, then turns heel and runs.

Martin sleeps in the afternoon and is woken by the landlady's husband with a message.

– *Is it from the university?*

– No. From my wife's sister.

Martin stares at the man. Eyes unfocused, face damp with heat and sleep.

– From Ewa. Jacek's mother. She works here. My wife's sister.

– *Oh, yes. Yes, sorry.*

– She says you should come to her house. She will cook you something to eat this evening. To say thank-you.

Martin showers and sits down at his computer again but finds he can't work. Looks out at the birds instead, washing in a puddle on the flat roof of the building opposite. The concrete is mossy and Martin wonders where the water came from. He has been here a week and it's been 30 degrees straight through and hasn't rained once. The skin on his back is damp again, and under his arms, and he thinks he hasn't anything clean to wear this evening, so he takes a T-shirt down the hall with him and washes it in the bathroom, lays it out on his windowsill to dry.

It is still slightly damp when he goes out to find Ewa's. Bottle of wine bought from the guesthouse bar under one arm, map and address on a scrap of paper from the landlady's husband. There is a slight breeze and the T-shirt is cool against his skin. He catches sight of himself in the bakery window as he passes, pushes his hair down over his forehead a little as he turns the corner. An involuntary gesture he hopes nobody saw.

Jacek opens the door.

– You're early!

– *Sorry.*

He leads Martin up the stairs, two at a time, cartons of cigarettes and cake mix piled high along one wall. The narrow entrance hall of Ewa's flat is similarly crowded: disposable nappies, tuna fish, toothbrushes in different shades, pink and green and yellow. Jacek sees Martin looking at the boxes.

– The man we rent from. He keeps things here, we pay him not so much. Every week is something new coming for him to sell.

A table stands in the middle of the room, a wardrobe in the corner. Mattress leant up against the wall and draped with a sheet. The window is open and the radio on. Martin recognises the song, a current hit, but can't understand what the announcer says afterwards. He goes into the kitchen, where Ewa is chopping and Jacek stirring.

– *Can I help?*

– No!

Ewa pours him a glass of wine and pushes him out into the bedroom-dining room again.

– Five minutes.

The wind is blowing into town from the river, and Martin can hear church bells ringing out the evening service.

They eat, Martin and Ewa smiling and nodding, Jacek concentrating on his food, not worried by the silence.

– *Jacek, can you ask your mother to tell me a little about the town, please?*

The boy looks up with his mouth full, Martin swallows.

– *I know very little. I would like to know.*

It is not true. He knows what she tells him already, what the boy translates for her about the nine churches, the resistance during the war and occupation, the failed collectivisation of the fruit growers during the communist era.

– There was a jam factory here when she was my age. Everybody was working there, or they were farmers. Apricots, pears, apples, and I don't know how you say those small ones. Berries?

Martin asks about the communist years.

– You want to hear about no food and unhappiness, yes?

Martin rubs his sunburn, and Ewa slaps her son's hands.

– Jacek! Sorry. I don't understand him, but I see he was bad. You translate only, yes? Yes?

Ewa points at her son and then pours them all more wine, offers to make Martin some tea.

– The way we drink it here.

Jacek's translation is sulky, sleepy. Black, in a glass so you can see the leaves floating. Boiling water, hot glass with no handles so your fingerprints get smooth and hard from the holding. Martin looks at the tips of his fingers, Ewa smiles.

– *I didn't know your sister owns the guesthouse.*

– Yes.

Ewa smiles, Jacek yawns.

– She gives my mother work.

– *And her husband?*

– Tadeusz?

– Uncle Tadeusz does no work.

– Sh! Not true.

Ewa speaks more herself now, interrupts her son's translations. She tells him her brother-in-law is a plumber. That he put his faith in the church. Her explanations are ungrammatical, sometimes nonsensical, but Martin enjoys listening to her. She says that they built new houses a year or two after the elections, a whole row, right in the centre. New times, new buildings. Flats above, shop spaces below. Brick, solid, good windows. And Tadeusz put in all the pipes, toilets, baths, taps, sinks. He got a loan to pay for all the materials. Copper piping and ceramics, imported from the west. He had the houses blessed when they were finished, but not yet painted. The priest came and threw his holy water around the empty rooms and Tadeusz was so proud. She remembers the wet, dark spots on the pink-red plasterwork, that it was a hot day, and that the dark spots left white marks behind when they dried.

– He never got paid, Tadeusz, and he cries often now.

Each time he defaults on his loan, and the houses are still empty. A while ago there was new graffiti on the wall of the last one in the row: send the nuns abroad and the priests to the moon.

Ewa looks at Jacek, who isn't listening any more, eyes half closed, head propped in his hands. She whispers to Martin:

– I think Tadeusz wrote that.

Martin feels her breath on his neck as she speaks, can smell wine and soap mixed.

– My sister, she wanted that Jacek and me should live with her. After Piotr left.

– *Your husband?*

Ewa doesn't answer, her eyes are unfocused.

– I couldn't. Not live with Tadeusz. He's not a bad man, but so much bitterness.

Martin is drunk and so is Ewa.

– I don't want my son be bitter, you see. I want him to like his life, this town, his country.

Martin nods.

– There is not so much here now, but I show him places, take him to the river.

Ewa sighs. They sit with the breeze from the open window on their bright cheeks and Jacek has his head on the tablecloth, asleep.

– I don't make him be at school this week. I think he can't swim in the river now, but it is good that he speaks with you. Has some nice time, learns someone new. More than in a classroom.

Ewa smiles into the middle distance and Martin looks at her. Only half a metre between them, the corner of the table, knees almost touching underneath.

He leans towards her. But Ewa catches him.

– No.

One hand on each of his shoulders, she holds him at arms' length. Martin blinks.

An empty wine glass rolls on the table. Ewa shakes her head.

– Sorry, no.

She smiles and then Martin sits back in his chair again, sunburn itching, sweat prickling in his scalp.

He doesn't look at her and for a minute or so they sit in silence.

Jacek's even breathing in the room and the church bells sounding again outside. When Martin looks up, Ewa is blinking, smiling at him.

– I am sorry. She rights the glass on the table, then covers her mouth with her hand and laughs.

In the morning there is a fax from the department lab. Martin has a hangover, asks for coffee and water to be sent up to his room. His eyes skim the figures, cannot settle. He boots up the laptop, plots the lab's figures onto his graph, though he already sees the disparity between the last set of results and his predictions. Days one and two show serious levels of contamination in mud and water, and correspond with Martin's own data. Day three's samples, however, are almost low enough to be considered clear.

Martin sits on the narrow bed a while, trying to decide if he is relieved or disappointed. The weedy water, the pool under the waterfall: *Clean. As good as.* But the premise of his paper: *Void.* His headache is bad, the day hot already, the shame of yesterday evening still fresh. Martin presses the heels of his palms against his eyes.

He wants to go home, he needs to get dressed. He goes to the bathroom where the window is open, the air much cooler than in his room. He stands under the shower a long time, warm flow on face and shoulders taking the edge off his headache, filling his ears, closing his eyes, replacing Ewa and her laughter with water falling on tile.

The room he returns to is strewn with papers and clothes. Martin works his way round it methodically, folding and sorting into piles. Before he packs, he checks through the lab technician's tidy columns once more, notes the memo at the end of the fax: the weed sample has been sent on to botany.

On the way downstairs, he reasons with himself: if the weed results are interesting, he can propose to further investigate the river fauna in the conclusion to his paper. Over breakfast, he thinks he could propose a joint venture with botany, perhaps. Something to please the department. Zoology might even be interested: the weed may be thriving, but crowding other species out. At the very least, it is good news for Ewa. She is not working this morning, but Martin thinks he will leave a note for her, tell her it's okay to take Jacek swimming again. He finishes his roll. Thinks he made a mess of the field study, the week in general, but there are still ways to make amends.

Martin stands in the narrow reception hall with his bags, sees Ewa happy by the waterfall while her sister calculates his bill. Then he remembers how sad she looked the day she came with Jacek to the river, and he is shocked at the satisfaction the memory gives him.

There is paper on the counter in front of him. He has a pencil in his back pocket, but he doesn't get it out. He pays and picks up his bags. While he loads up the car he tells himself it is too soon to know for certain. He has yet to test all his samples, examine all the possibilities; swimming at the waterfall could still be dangerous.

On the road out of town, he sees Ewa's hand over her mouth, her eyes pressed shut, Jacek woken by her laughter and staring at him.

At the border, the road runs parallel with the river for a kilometre or so, and the traffic moves slowly. To his right, trees grow tall along the riverbanks and in his rear-view mirror Martin can see the rest of the country spread out behind him, dry and flat. His chest is tight with shame, but the border guard is waving him through now, and he is driving on again.

NICOLA BARKER

The Butcher's Apprentice

If he had come from a family of butchers maybe his perspective
would have been different. He would have been more experienced, hardened, less naïve. His mum had wanted him to work
for Marks and Spencers or for British Rail. She said, "Why do
you want to work in all that blood and mess? There's something
almost obscene about butchery."

His dad was more phlegmatic. "It's not like cutting the Sunday
roast, Owen, it's guts and gore and entrails. Just the same, it's a
real trade, a proper trade."

Owen had thought it all through. At school one of his teachers
had called him "deep." She had said to his mother on Parents'
Evening, "Owen seems deep, but it's hard to get any sort of real
response from him. Maybe it's just cosmetic."

His mum had listened to the first statement but had then
become preoccupied with a blister on the heel of her right foot.
Consequently her grasp of the teacher's wisdom had been somewhat undermined. When she finally got home that evening, her
stomach brimming with sloshy coffee from the school canteen,
she had said to Owen, "Everyone says that you're too quiet at
school, but your maths teacher thinks that you're deep. She has
modern ideas, that one." Owen had appreciated this compliment.
It made him try harder at maths that final term before his exams,
and leaving. At sixteen he had pass marks in mathematics, home
economics and the whole world before him.

In the Careers Office his advisor had given him a leaflet about
prospective employment opportunities to fill out. He ticked
various boxes. He ticked a yes for "Do you like working with
your hands?" He ticked a yes for "Do you like working with
animals?" He ticked a yes for "Do you like using your imagination?"

When his careers guidance officer had analysed his prefer-
ences she declared that his options were quite limited. He seemed

such a quiet boy to her, rather dour. She said, "Maybe you could be a postman. Postmen see a lot of animals during their rounds and use their hands to deliver letters." Owen appeared unimpressed. He stared down at his hands as though they had suddenly become a cause for embarrassment. So she continued, "Maybe you could think about working with food. How about training to be a chef or a butcher? Butchers work with animals. You have to use your imagination to make the right cut into a carcass." Because he had been in the careers office for well over half an hour, Owen began to feel obliged to make some sort of positive response. A contribution. So he looked up at her and said, "Yeah, I suppose I could give it a try." He didn't want to appear stroppy or ungrateful. She smiled at him and gave him an address. The address was for J. Reilly and Sons, Quality Butchers, 103 Oldham Road.

Later that afternoon he phoned J. Reilly's and spoke to someone called Ralph. Ralph explained how he had bought the business two years before, but that he hadn't bothered changing the name. Owen said, "Well, if it doesn't bother you then it doesn't bother me."

Ralph asked him a few questions about school and then enquired whether he had worked with meat before. Owen said that he hadn't but that he really liked the sweet smell of a butcher's shop and the scuffling sawdust on the floor, the false plastic parsley in the window displays and the bright, blue-tinged strip-lights. He said, "I think that I could be very happy in a butcher's as a working environment."

He remembered how as a child he had so much enjoyed seeing the arrays of different coloured rabbits hung up by their ankles in butcher shop windows, and the bright and golden-speckled pheasants. Ralph offered him a month's probationary employment with a view to a full-time apprenticeship. Owen accepted readily.

His mum remained uncertain. Over dinner that night she said, "It'll be nice to get cheap meat and good cuts from your new job, Owen, though I still don't like the idea of a butcher in the family. I've nothing against them in principle, but it's different when it's so close to home."

Owen thought carefully for a moment, then put aside his knife and fork and said, "I suppose so, but that's only on the surface. I'm sure that there's a lot of bloodletting and gore involved in most occupations. I like the idea of being honest and straightforward about things. A butcher is a butcher. There's no falseness or pretence."

His dad nodded his approval and then said, "Eat up now, don't let your dinner get cold."

Owen arrived at the shop at seven sharp the following morning. The window displays were whitely clean and empty. Above the windows the J. Reilly and Sons sign was painted in red with white lettering. The graphics were surprisingly clear and ornate. On the door was hung a sign which said "closed". He knocked anyway. A man with arms like thin twigs opened the door. He looked tiny and consumptive with shrewd grey eyes and rusty hair. Owen noticed his hands, which were reddened with the cold, calloused and porkish. The man nodded briskly, introduced himself as Ralph then took Owen through to the back of the shop and introduced him to his work-mate, Marty. Marty was older than Ralph – about fifty or so – with silvery hair and yellow skin. He smiled at Owen kindly and offered him a clean apron and a bag of sawdust. Owen took the apron and placed it over his head. Ralph helped him to tie at the back. Both Marty and Ralph wore overalls slightly more masculine in design. Owen took the bag of sawdust and said, "Is this a woman's apron, or is it what the apprentice always wears?"

As Ralph walked back into the main part of the shop he answered, "It belongs to our Saturday girl, so don't get it too messy. We'll buy you a proper overall at the end of the week when we're sure that you're right for the job."

As he finished speaking a large van drew up outside the shop. Ralph moved to the door, pulled it wide and stuck a chip of wood under it to keep it open. He turned to Owen and by way of explanation pointed and said, "Delivery. The meat's brought twice a week. Scatter the sawdust, but not too thick."

Owen put his hand into the bag of dust and drew out a full, dry, scratchy handful which he scattered like a benevolent farmer throwing corn to his geese. The delivery man humped in half of an enormous sow. She had a single greenish eye and a severed snout. He took it to the back of the shop through a door and into what Owen presumed to be the refrigerated store-room. Before he had returned Ralph had come in clutching a large armful of plucked chickens. As Owen moved out of his way he nodded towards the van and said, "I tell you what, why not go and grab some stuff yourself but don't overestimate your strength and try not to drop anything."

Owen balanced his packet of shavings against the bottom of the counter and walked out to the van. Inside were a multitude of skins, feathers, meats and flesh. He grabbed four white rabbits and a large piece of what he presumed to be pork, but later found out was lamb. The meat was fresh and raw to the touch. Raw and soft like risen dough. He lifted his selections out of the van and carried them into the shop, careful of the condition of his apron, and repeated this process back and forth for the next fifteen or so minutes. While everyone else moved the meat, Marty busied himself with cutting steaks from a large chunk of beef. When finally all of the meat had been moved Ralph went and had a cigarette outside with the delivery man and Owen picked up his bag of shavings and finished scattering them over the shop floor. On completing this he called over to Marty, "Do I have to spread this on the other side of the counter as well?"

Marty smiled at him. "I think that's the idea. It should only take you a minute, so when you've finished come over here and see what I'm doing. You never know, you might even learn something."

Owen quickly tipped out the rest of his bag over the floor at the back of the counter and scuffed the dust around with his foot. It covered the front of his trainer like a light, newgrown beard. Then he walked over to Marty and stood at his shoulder watching him complete his various insertions into the beef. Marty made his final cut and then half turned and showed Owen the blade he was using. He moved the tip of the blade adjacent to the tip of Owen's nose. "A blade has to be sharp. That's the first rule of butchery. Rule two, your hands must be clean." He moved the knife from side to side and Owen's eyes followed its sharp edge. It was so close to his face that he could see his hot breath steaming up and evaporating on its steely surface. Marty said thickly, "This blade could slice your nose in half in the time it takes you to sneeze. Aaah-tish-yooouh!"

Then he whipped the knife away and placed it carefully on the cutting surface next to a small pool of congealing blood. He said, "Rule three, treat your tools with respect."

Owen cleared his throat self-consciously. "Will I be allowed to cut up some meat myself today, or will I just be helping out around the shop?" Marty frowned. "It takes a long time and a lot of skill to be able to prepare meat properly. You'll have to learn everything from scratch. That's what it means to be the new boy, the apprentice."

Ralph came back into the shop and set Owen to work cleaning the insides of the windows and underneath the display trays. Old blood turned the water brown. Soon the first customers of the day started to straggle into the shop and he learned the art of pricing and weighing. The day moved on. At twelve he had half-an-hour for lunch.

After two o'clock the shop quietened down again and Owen was sent into the store-room to acquaint himself with the lay-out, refrigeration techniques and temperatures. As he looked around and smelt the heavy, heady smell of ripe meat, he overheard Ralph and Marty laughing at something in the shop. Ralph was saying, "Leave him be. You're wicked Mart." Marty replied, "He won't mind. Go on, it'll be a laugh."

A few seconds later Ralph called through to him. Owen walked into the shop from the cool darkness of the storeroom. The light made his eyes squint. The shop was empty apart from Ralph and Marty who were standing together in front of the large cutting board as though hiding something. Ralph said, "Have you ever seen flesh, dead flesh, return to life, Owen?" Owen shook his head. Marty smiled at him. "Some meat is possessed, you know. If a live animal is used as part of a satanic ritual at any point during its life, when it dies its flesh lives on to do the devil's work. After all, the devil's work is never done."

As he finished speaking he stepped sideways to reveal a large chunk of fleshy meat on the chopping board. It was about the size of a cabbage. Everyone stared at it. They were all silent. Slowly, gradually, almost imperceptibly, the meat shuddered. Owen blinked to make sure that his eyes were clear and not deceiving him. After a couple of seconds it shuddered again, but this time more noticeably. It shivered as though it were too cold, and then slowly, painfully, began to crawl across the table. It moved like a heart that pumped under great duress, a struggling, battling, palpitating heart.

Owen's face blanched. His throat tightened. Ralph and Marty watched his initial reactions and then returned their gazes to the flesh. By now it had moved approximately five or six inches across the cutting board. Its motions were those of a creature in agony, repulsive and yet full of an agonizing pathos. Owen felt his eyes fill, he felt like howling.

Ralph turned back to look at Owen and saw, with concern, the intensity of his reactions. He said, "Don't get all upset, it's only a joke. It's got nothing to do with the devil, honest."

He smiled. Owen frowned and swallowed hard before attempting to reply. "Why is it moving? What have you done to it?"

Marty reached towards the piece of convulsing flesh with his big butcher's hand and picked it up. As he lifted it the flesh seemed to cling to the table. It made a noise like wet clay being ripped into two pieces, like a limpet being pulled from its rock. He turned it over. Underneath, inside, permeating the piece of meat, was a huge round cancer the size of Marty's fist. A miracle tumour, complete, alive. The tumour was contracting and then relaxing, contracting and relaxing. Maybe it was dying. Owen stared at the tumour in open-mouthed amazement, at its orangy, yellowy completeness, its outside and its core. Marty said, "Sometimes the abattoir send us a carcass that shouldn't really be for human consumption. They know that an animal is ill but they slaughter it just before it dies. They have to make a living too, I suppose."

With that he threw the meat and its cancerous centre into a large half-full refuse bag and began to wipe over the work surface as though nothing had happened. Owen could still make out the movements of the cancer from inside the bag. A customer came into the shop and Ralph walked over to serve her. Owen felt overwhelmed by a great sense of injustice, a feeling of enormous intensity, unlike anything he had ever experienced before. He felt as though his insides were tearing. He felt appalled. Then instinctively he grabbed at the back of his apron and yanked open its bow. He pulled it over his head and slammed it on to the counter. He said, "I'm going home now. I'm going home and I'm taking this with me."

Before anyone could respond Owen had grabbed the heavy refuse bag full of bones and gristle and off-cuts and had struggled his way out of the shop. When he had gone, Ralph turned to Marty and said, "He was a nice enough kid."

Marty shrugged.

Owen got out of the shop and walked a short distance down the road before placing the bag on the pavement and opening it. He reached inside and felt for the cancer. When he finally touched it, it sucked on his finger like a fish or a baby. He took it out of the bag, pulled off his sweater and bundled the cancer up inside it. He carried it on the bus as though it were a sick puppy. It moved very slightly. When he got home he crept upstairs and locked himself in his room. He closed the curtains and then sat on his bed and unbundled the tumour. He placed it gently on his bedside table under the warm glow of his lamp. It was growing weaker and now moved only slowly.

Owen wondered what he could do for it. He debated whether to pour water on it or whether to try and keep it warm. He wondered whether it might be kinder to kill it quickly, but he couldn't work out how. He wondered if you could drown a tumour (that would be painless enough), or whether you could chop it in half. But he couldn't be sure that tumours weren't like the amoebas that he'd studied in biology at school that could divide and yet still survive. He couldn't really face destroying it. Instead he decided to simply stay with it and to offer it moral support. He whispered quietly, "Come on, it'll be all right. It'll soon be over."

After a few hours the tumour was only moving intermittently. Its movements had grown sluggish and irregular. Owen stayed with it. He kept it company. He chatted. Eventually the tumour stopped moving altogether. Its meaty exterior was completely still. He knew that it was dead. He picked it up tenderly and cradled it in his arms as he carried it downstairs, out of the house and into the garden. Placing it gently on the grass, he dragged at the soft soil in the flower-beds with both his hands until he had dug a hole of significant proportions. Then he placed the still tumour into the hole and covered it over. In a matter of minutes the soil was perfectly compacted and the flowerbed looked as normal.

He went inside and lay on his bed awhile. At six he went downstairs to the kitchen where his mother was beginning to prepare dinner. As he poured himself a glass of water she said, "I didn't know that you were home. How did your first day go?"

Owen gulped down the water and then placed his glass upside down on the draining board. He said, "I think I'm going to be a postman."

Then he dried his hands on a kitchen towel and asked what was for dinner.

BELIEFS

WILLIAM SHAKESPEARE

Cymbeline

Act IV Scene II: Song

Gui. Fear no more the heat o' th' sun
    Nor the furious winter's rages;
Thou thy worldly task hast done,
    Home art gone, and ta'en thy wages.
Golden lads and girls all must,
As chimney-sweepers, come to dust.

Arv. Fear no more the frown o' th' great;
    Thou art past the tyrant's stroke.
Care no more to clothe and eat;
    To thee the reed is as the oak.
The sceptre, learning, physic, must
All follow this and come to dust.

Gui. Fear no more the lightning flash,
Arv.   Nor th' all-dreaded thunder-stone;
Gui. Fear not slander, censure rash;
Arv.   Thou hast finish'd joy and moan.
Both. All lovers young, all lovers must
Consign to thee and come to dust.

Gui. No exorciser harm thee!
Arv. Nor no witchcraft charm thee!
Gui. Ghost unlaid forbear thee!
Arv. Nothing ill come near thee!
Both. Quiet consummation have,
And renowned be thy grave!

LEONORA CARRINGTON

The Happy Corpse Story

White girl dappled mare
the stags and the ferns in the wood.
Tuft of black hair caught on a thorn
She went by so fast
Now she is gone.

The young man, dressed in purple and gold with a blond wig and carrying a jukebox, threw a tantrum and fell on the mossy knoll in a passionate fit of weeping.

"She never returned," he cried.

"Sentimentality is a form of fatigue," said the Happy Corpse, greyish, swinging to and fro on the gnarled elm, like a wasps' nest.

"Nevertheless," shrieked the youth, "I must seek her, because I am in love."

The Happy Corpse laughed. "You mean your secret thread got wound around a galloping damsel. The thinness of it being pulled is a sinful waste and woeful want."

The young man's wig fell off, showing a skull covered with black bristles.

"However," continued the Happy Corpse, "if you catch hold of me and ride on my back, I may help you to find this woman."

"Whoop!" yelped the youth and grabbed at the corpse, which fell into ashes and appeared on the other side of a brandleberry bush.

"Not so fast."

Around and around the brandleberry bush they ran, and as the young man got nearer and nearer the corpse got thicker and thicker, till the youth leapt on its back; whereupon the Happy Corpse stamped its foot and away they ran.

Thorns grabbed at the pair as they hurried through the wood. Great Scot, a nasty black-and-white terrier, ran constantly at the corpse's heels, snapping. This mangy creature lurked the haunts where Happy Corpses abide, since one can hardly say live in this case. The dog smelled as bad as the corpse; it was practically impossible to tell one from the other. They just looked different.

Being full of holes and dents, the corpse could talk out of any part of its body. "Now," said the corpse through the back of its head, "I shall tell you a story." The youth heaved a groan like a death rattle. He felt too preoccupied to listen. Nevertheless the story began. Think of listening to a story told straight into your face out of a hole in the back of the head with bad breath: surely this must have troubled the delicate sensibility of the young man. However, what can't be cured must be endured.

"The story," said the Happy Corpse, "is all about my father." As they unravelled themselves from the tendrils of some poison ivy, the story continued: "My father was a man so utterly and exactly like everybody else that he was forced to wear a large badge on his coat in case he was mistaken for anybody. Any body, if you see what I mean. He was obliged to make constant efforts to make himself present to the attention of others. This was very tiring, and he never slept, because of the constant banquets, bazaars, meetings, symposiums, discussions, board meetings, race meetings, and simple meatings where meat was eaten. He could never stay in one place for more than a minute at a time because if he did not appear to be constantly busy he was afraid somebody might think he was not urgently needed elsewhere. So he never got to know anybody. It is quite impossible to be truly busy and actually ever be with anybody because business means that wherever you are you are leaving immediately for some other place. Relatively young, the poor man turned himself into a human wreckage."

A thing like a great black rag flew past heavily, saying, "Hands up, Infidel."

"What was that?" asked the youth, alarmed. The Happy Corpse smiled through the hole in its head. "That was Dick Turpin, once a Highwayman, always a ghost. He is going to the Fantomat."

"The Fantomat?"

"Yes, the Fantomat is an automatic Fantomator. There are a lot of them, chainwise, as we get nearer and nearer to Hell."

Terrified by now, the youth became blue around the lips and was too alarmed to reply.

"As I was saying about my father," continued the Corpse, "he eventually became an executive for a firm. This meant that he actually executed persons with showers of legal documents proving that they owed him quantities of money which they did not have. 'Firm' actually means the manufacture of useless objects which people are foolish enough to buy. The firmer the firm the more senseless talk is needed to prevent anyone noticing the unsafe structure of the business. Sometimes these Firms actually sell nothing at all for a lot of money, like 'Life Insurance,' a pretense that it is a soothing and useful event to have a violent and painful death."

"What happened to your father?" asked the youth, mostly to listen to his own voice for comfort during the increasing horror of the journey. Now the woods kept fluctuating with apparitions: beasts, garbage cans overflowing with decomposed entities, leaves chasing each other chaotically, so that no shape was ever constant; grass behaving like animated spaghetti, and a number of nameless vacuums, causing events that were always unhappy or catastrophic.

"My father died of a heart attack during a telephone conversation, and then of course he went to Hell. Now he is in Telephone Hell, where everyone has these apparatuses constantly glued to their lips or ears. This causes great anguish. My father will be with his Telephone for nine hundred and ninety-nine billion aeons before he gets rid of it. Afterwards he might even become a saint. Before actually maturing into a real Entity, everybody goes to Hell first, and if they are not too careful, afterwards they must begin all over again."

"You mean that your father is actually in Hell?" asked the youth. "And why do you never mention your mother?"

Here the Corpse almost paused. The trees were scarcer, so that a stretch of desert was visible in the distance.

"My mother committed suicide from boredom. My father was so busy that she had nobody to talk to. So she ate and ate and then shut herself into the refrigerator and half froze and half suffocated to death. She also went to Hell, but in the refrigerator, eating constantly. I composed a poem to her memory. It goes like this:

> *When Father's Face was hard to bear*
> *Mother got into the Frigidaire,*
> *Father, said I, I'm so unhappé*
> *Mother is completely frappé.*

Tears were now streaming down the face of the young man. "The whole story is quite dreadful. And really much worse, because my own poor mother also committed suicide. She shot herself with a machine gun."

The Happy Corpse stopped suddenly, throwing the youth to the ground, saying: "You silly boy, do you suppose I don't know that? I am your mother. How would I ever have carried you so near to Hell had I been another, a stranger?"

"Mummy?" said the youth, trembling violently. "Forgive me."

"You always used to eat strawberry-jam sandwiches for tea."

They were both lost for a moment in memories of the strawberry-jam sandwiches. After a while the Happy Corpse said: "Now you had better return, since you forgot the white girl on the dappled horse, as those on their way to Hell forget.

"Now you must remember, and in order to remember you must return again, alone."

So that the boy should find his way back, she tied his leg to Great Scot the terrier with a long black hair. Off they went, and one can only hope they found their way back. The Happy Corpse dissolved into ashes and, laughing heartily, returned to the tree.

AMOS TUTUOLA

from *The Palm-Wine Drinkard*

When it was the fifth month since I had left that town, then I reached another town which was not so big, although there was a large and famous market. At the same time that I entered the town, I went to the house of the head of the town who received me with kindness into his house; after a little while he told one of his wives to give me food and after I had eaten the food, he told his wife to give me palm-wine too; I drank the palm-wine to excess as when I was in my town or as when my tapster was alive. But when I tasted the palm-wine given to me there, I said that I got what I wanted here. After I had eaten the food and drunk the palm-wine to my satisfaction, the head of the town who received me as his guest asked for my name, I told him that my name was called "Father of gods who could do anything in this world." As he heard this from me, he was soon faint with fear. After that he asked me what I came to him for. I replied that I was looking for my palm-wine tapster who had died in my town some time ago. Then he told me that he knew where the tapster was.

After that he told me that if I could help him to find out his daughter who was captured by a curious creature from the market which was in that town, and bring her to him, then he would tell me whereabouts my tapster was.

He said furthermore that as I called myself "Father of gods who could do anything in this world," this would be very easy for me to do; he said so.

I did not know that his daughter was taken away by a curious creature from the market.

I was about to refuse to go and find out his daughter who was taken away from the market by a curious creature, but when I remembered my name I was ashamed to refuse. So I agreed to find out his daughter. There was a big market in this town from where the daughter was captured, and the market-day was fixed for every 5th day and the whole people of that town and from all the villages around the town and also spirits and curious creatures from various bushes and forests were coming to this market every 5th day to sell or buy articles. By 4 o'clock in the evening, the market would close for that day and then everybody would be returning to his or her destination or to where he or she came from. But the daughter of the head of that town was a petty trader and she was due to be married before she was taken away from the market. Before that time, her father was telling her to marry a man but she did not listen to her father; when her father saw that she did not care to marry anybody, he gave her to a man for himself, but this lady refused totally to marry that man who was introduced to her by her father. So that her father left her to herself.

This lady was very beautiful as an angel but no man could convince her for marriage. So, one day she went to the market on a market-day as she was doing before, or to sell her articles as usual; on that market-day, she saw a curious creature in the market, but she did not know where the man came from and never knew him before.

THE DESCRIPTION OF
THE CURIOUS CREATURE:—

He was a beautiful "complete" gentleman, he dressed with the finest and most costly clothes, all the parts of his body were completed, he was a tall man but stout. As this gentleman came to the market on that day, if he had been an article or animal for sale, he would be sold at least for £2000 (two thousand pounds). As this complete gentleman came to the market on that day, and at the same time that this lady saw him in the market, she did nothing more than to ask him where he was living, but this fine gentleman did not answer her or approach her at all. But when she noticed that the fine or complete gentleman did not listen to her, she left her articles and began to watch the movements of the complete gentleman about in the market and left her articles unsold.

By and by the market closed for that day then the whole people in the market were returning to their destinations etc., and the complete gentleman was returning to his own too, but as this lady was following him about in the market all the while, she saw him when he was returning to his destination as others did, then she was following him (complete gentleman) to an unknown place. But as she was following the complete gentleman along the road, he was telling her to go back or not to follow him, but the lady did not listen to what he was telling her, and when the complete gentleman had tired of telling her not to follow him or to go back to her town, he left her to follow him.

DO NOT FOLLOW UNKNOWN MAN'S BEAUTY

But when they had travelled about twelve miles away from that market, they left the road on which they were travelling and started to travel inside an endless forest in which only all the terrible creatures were living.

RETURN THE PARTS OF BODY TO THE OWNERS; OR HIRED PARTS OF THE COMPLETE GENTLEMAN'S BODY TO BE RETURNED

As they were travelling along in this endless forest then the complete gentleman in the market that the lady was following, began to return the hired parts of his body to the owners and he was paying them the rentage money. When he reached where he hired the left foot, he pulled it out, he gave it to the owner and paid him, and they kept going; when they reached the place where he hired the right foot, he pulled it out and gave it to the owner and paid for the rentage. Now both feet had returned to the owners, so he began to crawl along on the ground, by that time, that lady wanted to go back to her town or her father, but the terrible and curious creature or the complete gentleman did not allow her to return or go back to her town or her father again and the complete gentleman said thus: – "I had told you not to follow me before we branched into this endless forest which belongs to only terrible and curious creatures, but when I became a half-bodied incomplete gentleman you wanted to go back, now that cannot be done, you have failed. Even you have never seen anything yet, just follow me."

When they went furthermore, then they reached where he hired the belly, ribs, chest etc., then he pulled them out and gave them to the owner and paid for the rentage.

Now to this gentleman or terrible creature remained only the head and both arms with neck, by that time he could not crawl as before but only went jumping on as a bull-frog and now this lady was soon faint for this fearful creature whom she was following. But when the lady saw every part of this complete gentleman in the market was spared or hired and he was returning them to the owners, then she began to try all her efforts to return to her father's town, but she was not allowed by this fearful creature at all.

When they reached where he hired both arms, he pulled them out and gave them to the owner, he paid for them; and they were still going on in this endless forest, they reached the place where he hired the neck, he pulled it out and gave it to the owner and paid for it as well.

A FULL-BODIED GENTLEMAN REDUCED TO HEAD

Now this complete gentleman was reduced to head and when they reached where he hired the skin and flesh which covered the head, he returned them, and paid to the owner, now the complete gentleman in the market reduced to a "SKULL" and this lady remained with only "Skull". When the lady saw that she remained with only Skull, she began to say that her father had been telling her to marry a man, but she did not listen to or believe him.

When the lady saw that the gentleman became a Skull, she began to faint, but the Skull told her if she would die she would die and she would follow him to his house. But by the time that he was saying so, he was humming with a terrible voice and also grew very wild and even if there was a person two miles away he would not have to listen before hearing him, so this lady began to run away in that forest for her life, but the Skull chased her and within a few yards, he caught her, because he was very clever and smart as he was only Skull and he could jump a mile to the second before coming down. He caught the lady in this way: so when the lady was running away for her life, he hastily ran to her front and stopped her as a log of wood.

By and by, this lady followed the Skull to his house, and the house was a hole which was under the ground. When they reached there both of them entered the hole. But there were only Skulls living in that hole. At the same time that they entered the hole, he tied a single cowrie on the neck of this lady with a kind of rope, after that, he gave her a large frog on which she sat as a stool, then he gave a whistle to a Skull of this kind to keep watch on this lady whenever she wanted to run away. Because the Skull knew already that the lady would attempt to run away from the hole. Then he went to the back-yard to where his family were staying in the day time till night.

But one day, the lady attempted to escape from the hole, and at the same time that the Skull who was watching her whistle to the rest of the Skulls that were in the back-yard, the whole of them rushed out to the place where the lady sat on the bull-frog, so they caught her, but as all of them were rushing out, they were rolling on the ground as if a thousand petrol drums were pushing along a hard road. After she was caught, then they brought her back to sit on the same frog as usual. If the Skull who was watching her fell asleep, and if the lady wanted to escape, the cowrie that was tied on her neck would raise up the alarm with a terrible noise, so that the Skull who was watching her would wake up at once and then the rest of the Skull's family would rush out from the back in thousands to the lady and ask her what she wanted to do with a curious and terrible voice.

But the lady could not talk at all, because as the cowrie had been tied on her neck, she became dumb at the same moment.

THE FATHER OF GODS SHOULD FIND OUT
WHEREABOUTS THE DAUGHTER OF THE HEAD
OF THE TOWN WAS

Now as the father of the lady first asked for my name and I told him that my name was "Father of gods who could do anything in this world," then he told me that if I could find out where his daughter was and bring her to him, then he would tell me where my palm-wine tapster was. But when he said so, I was jumping up with gladness that he should promise me that he would tell me where my tapster was. I agreed to what he said; the father and parent of this lady never knew whereabouts their daughter was, but they had information that the lady followed a complete gentleman in the market. As I was the "Father of gods who could do anything in this world," when it was at night I sacrificed to my juju with a goat.

And when it was early in the morning, I sent for forty kegs of palm-wine, after I had drunk it all, I started to investigate whereabouts was the lady. As it was the market-day, I started the investigation from the market. But as I was a juju-man, I knew all the kinds of people in that market. When it was exactly 9 o'clock A.M., the very complete gentleman whom the lady followed came to the market again, and at the same time that I saw him, I knew that he was a curious and terrible creature.

THE LADY WAS NOT TO BE BLAMED FOR
FOLLOWING THE SKULL AS A COMPLETE
GENTLEMAN

I could not blame the lady for following the Skull as a complete gentleman to his house at all. Because if I were a lady, no doubt I would follow him to wherever he would go, and still as I was a man I would jealous him more than that, because if this gentleman went to the battle field, surely, enemy would not kill him or capture him and if bombers saw him in a town which was to be bombed, they would not throw bombs on his presence, and if they did throw it, the bomb itself would not explode until this gentleman would leave that town, because of his beauty. At the same time that I saw this gentleman in the market on that day, what I was doing was only to follow him about in the market. After I looked at him for so many hours, then I ran to a corner of the market and I cried for a few minutes because I thought within myself why was I not created with beauty as this gentleman, but when I remembered that he was only a Skull, then I thanked God that He had created me without beauty, so I went back to him in the market, but I was still attracted by his beauty. So when the market closed for that day, and when everybody was returning to his or her destination, this gentleman was returning to his own too and I followed him to know where he was living.

INVESTIGATION TO THE SKULL'S FAMILY'S HOUSE

When I travelled with him a distance of about twelve miles away to that market, the gentleman left the really road on which we were travelling and branched into an endless forest and I was following him, but as I did not want him to see that I was following him, then I used one of my juju which changed me into a lizard and followed him. But after I had travelled with him a distance of about twenty-five miles away in this endless forest, he began to pull out all the parts of his body and return them to the owners, and paid them.

After I had travelled with him for another fifty miles in this forest, then he reached his house and entered it, but I entered it also with him, as I was a lizard. The first thing that he did when he entered the hole (house) he went straight to the place where the lady was, and I saw the lady sat on a bull-frog with a single cowrie tied on her neck and a Skull who was watching her stood behind her. After he (gentleman) had seen that the lady was there, he went to the back-yard where all his family were working.

THE INVESTIGATOR'S WONDERFUL WORK IN THE SKULL'S FAMILY'S HOUSE

When I saw this lady and when the Skull who brought her to that hole or whom I followed from the market to that hole went to the back-yard, then I changed myself to a man as before, then I talked to the lady but she could not answer me at all, she only showed that she was in a serious condition. The Skull who was guarding her with a whistle fell asleep at that time.

To my surprise, when I helped the lady to stand up from the frog on which she sat, the cowrie that was tied on her neck made a curious noise at once, and when the Skull who was watching her heard the noise, he woke up and blew the whistle to the rest, then the whole of them rushed to the place and surrounded the lady and me, but at the same time that they saw me there, one of them ran to a pit which was not so far from that spot, the pit was filled with cowries. He picked one cowrie out of the pit, after that he was running towards me, and the whole crowd wanted to tie the cowrie on my neck too. But before they could do that, I had changed myself into air, they could not trace me out again, but I was looking at them. I believed that the cowries in that pit were their power and to reduce the power of any human being whenever tied on his or her neck and also to make a person dumb.

Over one hour after I had dissolved into air, these Skulls went back to the back-yard, but there remained the Skull who was watching her.

After they had returned to the back-yard, I changed to a man as usual, then I took the lady from the frog, but at the same time that I touched her, the cowrie which was tied on her neck began to shout; even if a person was four miles away he would not have to listen before hearing, but immediately the Skull who was watching her heard the noise and saw me when I took her from that frog, he blew the whistle to the rest of them who were in the back-yard.

Immediately the whole Skull family heard the whistle when blew to them, they were rushing out to the place and before they could reach there, I had left their hole for the forest, but before I could travel about one hundred yards in the forest, they had rushed out from their hole to inside the forest and I was still running away with the lady. As these Skulls were chasing me about in the forest, they were rolling on the ground like large stones and also humming with terrible noise, but when I saw that they had nearly caught me or if I continued to run away like that, no doubt, they would catch me sooner, then I changed the lady to a kitten and put her inside my pocket and changed myself to a very small bird which I could describe as a "sparrow" in English language.

After that I flew away, but as I was flying in the sky, the cowrie which was tied on that lady's neck was still making a noise and I tried all my best to stop the noise, but all were in vain. When I reached home with the lady, I changed her to a lady as she was before and also myself changed to man as well. When her father saw that I brought his daughter back home, he was exceedingly glad and said thus: – "You are the 'Father of gods' as you had told me before."

But as the lady was now at home, the cowrie on her neck did not stop making a terrible noise once, and she could not talk to anybody; she showed only that she was very glad she was at home. Now I had brought the lady but she could not talk, eat or loose away the cowrie on her neck, because the terrible noise of the cowrie did not allow anybody to rest or sleep at all.

THERE REMAIN GREATER TASKS AHEAD

Now I began to cut the rope of the cowrie from her neck and to make her talk and eat, but all my efforts were in vain. At last I tried my best to cut off the rope of the cowrie; it only stopped the noise, but I was unable to loose it away from her neck.

When her father saw all my trouble, he thanked me greatly and repeated again that as I called myself "Father of gods who could do anything in this world" I ought to do the rest of the work. But when he said so, I was very ashamed and thought within myself that if I return to the Skulls' hole or house, they might kill me and the forest was very dangerous travel always, again I could not go directly to the Skulls in their hole and ask them how to loose away the cowrie which was tied on the lady's neck and to make her talk and eat.

BACK TO THE SKULL'S FAMILY'S HOUSE

On the third day after I had brought the lady to her father's house, I returned to the endless forest for further investigation. When there remained about one mile to reach the hole of these Skulls, there I saw the very Skull who the lady had followed from the market as a complete gentleman to the hole of Skull's family's house, and at the same time that I saw him like that, I changed into a lizard and climbed a tree which was near him.

He stood before two plants, then he cut a single opposite leaf from the opposite plants; he held the leaf with his right hand and he was saying thus: – "As this lady was taken from me, if this opposite leaf is not given her to eat, she will not talk for ever," after that he threw the leaf down on the ground. Then he cut another single compound leaf from the compound plant which was in the same place with the opposite plant, he held the compound leaf with his left hand and said that if this single compound is not given to this lady, to eat, the cowrie on her neck could not be loosened away for ever and it would be making a terrible noise for ever.

After he said so, he threw the leaf down at the same spot, then he jumped away. So after he had jumped very far away (luckily, I was there when he was doing all these things, and I saw the place that he threw both leaves separately), then I changed myself to a man as before, I went to the place that he threw both leaves, then I picked them up and I went home at once.

But at the same time that I reached home, I cooked both leaves separately and gave her to eat; to my surprise the lady began to talk at once. After that, I gave her the compound leaf to eat for the second time and immediately she ate that too, the cowrie which was tied on her neck by the Skull, loosened away by itself, but it disappeared at the same time. So when the father and mother saw the wonderful work which I had done for them, they brought fifty kegs of palm-wine for me, they gave me the lady as wife and two rooms in that house in which to live with them. So, I saved the lady from the complete gentleman in the market who afterwards reduced to a "Skull" and the lady became my wife since that day. This was how I got a wife.

Now as I took the lady as my wife and after I had spent the period of six months with the parents of my wife, then I remembered my palm-wine tapster who had died in my town long ago, then I asked the father of my wife to fulfil his promise or to tell me where my tapster was, but he told me to wait for some time. Because he knew that if he told me the place by that time, I would leave his town and take his daughter away from him and he did not like to part with his daughter.

SIMONE DE BEAUVOIR

Memoirs of a Dutiful Daughter

from Book 1

I was very pious; I made my confession twice a month to Abbé Martin, received Holy Communion three times a week and every morning read a chapter of *The Imitation of Christ*; between classes, I would slip into the school chapel and, with my head in my hands, I would offer up lengthy prayers; often in the course of the day I would lift up my soul to my Maker. I was no longer very interested in the Infant Jesus, but I adored Christ to distraction. As supplements to the Gospels, I had read disturbing novels of which He was the hero, and it was now with the eyes of a lover that I gazed upon His grave, tender, handsome face; I would follow, across hills covered with olive groves, the shining hem of His snow-white robe, bathe His naked feet with my tears; and He would smile down upon me as He had smiled upon the Magdalen. When I had had my fill of clasping His knees and sobbing on His blood-stained corpse, I would allow Him to ascend into heaven. There He became one with that more mysterious Being to whom I owed my existence on earth, and whose throne of glory would one day, and for ever, fill my eyes with a celestial radiance.

How comforting to know that He was there! I had been told that He cherished every single one of His creatures as if each were the one and only; His eye was upon me every instant, and all others were excluded from our divine conversations; I would forget them all, there would be only He and I in the world, and I felt I was a necessary part of His glory: my existence, through Him, was of infinite price. There was nothing He did not know: even more definitely than in my teachers' registers my acts, my thoughts, and my excellences were inscribed in Him for eternity; my faults and errors too, of course, but these were washed so clean in the waters of repentance that they shone just as brightly as my virtues. I never tired of admiring myself in that pure mirror that was without beginning or end. My reflection, all radiant with the joy I inspired in God's heart, consoled me for all my earthly shortcomings and failures; it saved me from the indifference, from the injustice and the misunderstandings of human nature. For God was always on *my* side; if I had done wrong in any way, at the very instant that I dropped upon my knees to ask His forgiveness He breathed upon my tarnished soul and restored to it all its lustre. But usually, bathed as I was in His eternal radiance, the faults I was accused of simply melted away; His judgement was my justification. He was the supreme arbiter who found that I was always right. I loved Him with all the passion I brought to life itself.

Each year I went into retreat for several days; all day long, I would listen to my priest's instructions, attend services, tell my beads and meditate; I would remain at school for a frugal repast, and during the meal someone would read to us from the life of a saint. In the evenings, at home, my mother would respect my silent meditations. I wrote down in a special notebook the outpourings of my immortal soul and my saintly resolutions. I ardently desired to grow closer to God, but I didn't know how to go about it. My conduct left so little to be desired that I could hardly be any better than I already was; besides, I wondered if God was really concerned about my general behaviour. The majority of faults that Mama reprimanded my sister and me for were just awkward blunders or careless mistakes. Poupette was severely scolded and punished for having lost a civet-fur collar. When, fishing for shrimps in "the English river", I fell into the water, I was overcome with panic at the thought of the telling-off I felt was in store for me; fortunately I was let off that time. But these misdemeanours had nothing to do with Sin, and I didn't feel that by steering clear of them I was making myself any more perfect. The embarrassing thing was that God forbade so many things, but never asked for anything positive apart from a few prayers or religious practices which did not change my daily course in any way. I even found it most peculiar to see people who had just received Holy Communion plunging straight away into the ordinary routine of their lives again; I did the same, but it embarrassed me. Taken all in all, it seemed to me that believers and non-believers led just the same kind of life; I became more and more convinced that there was no room for the supernatural in everyday life. And yet it was that other-wordly life that really counted: it was the only kind that mattered. It suddenly became obvious to me one morning that a Christian who was convinced of his eternal salvation ought not to attach any importance to the ephemeral things of this world. How could the majority of people go on living in the world as it was? The more I thought about it, the more I wondered at it. I decided that I, at any rate, would not follow their example: my choice was made between the finite and the infinite. "I shall become a nun," I told myself. The activities of sisters of charity seemed to me quite useless; the only reasonable occupation was to contemplate the glory of God to the end of my days. I would become a Carmelite. But I did not make my decision public: it would not have been taken seriously. I contented myself with the announcement that I did not intend to marry. My father smiled: 'We'll have plenty of time to think about that when you're fifteen years old." In my heart of hearts I resented his smile. I knew that an implacable logic led me to the convent: how could you prefer having nothing to having everything?

This imaginary future provided me with a convenient alibi. For many years it allowed me to enjoy without scruple all the good things of this world.

My happiness used to reach its height during the two and a half months which I spent every summer in the country. My mother was always more relaxed there than in Paris; my father devoted more time to me then; and I enjoyed a vast leisure for reading and playing with my sister. I did not miss the Cours Désir: that feeling of necessity which study gave my life spilled over into the holidays. My time was no longer strictly measured by the exigencies of a timetable; but its absence was largely compensated for by the immensity of the horizons which opened themselves before my curious eyes. I explored them all unaided: the mediation of grown-ups no longer interposed a barrier between the world and myself. The solitude and freedom which were only rarely mine during the course of the year were now almost boundless, and I had my fill of them. In the country all my aspirations seemed to be brought together and realized; my fidelity to the past and my taste for novelty, my love for my parents and my growing desire for independence.

At first we usually spent a few weeks at La Grillière. The castle seemed to me to be vast and very old; it had been built barely fifty years ago, but none of the objects – furniture or ornaments – that had been brought there half a century ago were ever changed or taken away. No hand ventured to sweep away the relics of the past: you could smell the odour of vanished lives. A collection of hunting horns hanging in the tiled hall, all of them made of shining copper, evoked – erroneously, I believe – the magnificence of bygone stag-hunts. In what was called the "billiard room", which was where we usually foregathered, stuffed foxes, buzzards, and kites perpetuated this bloodthirsty tradition. There was no billiard table in the room, but it contained a monumental chimney-piece, a bookcase, always carefully locked, and a large table strewn with copies of hunting magazines; there were pedestal tables laden with yellowing photographs, sheaves of peacock feathers, pebbles, terracotta ornaments, barometers, clocks that would never go and lamps that were never lit. Apart from the dining-room, the other rooms were rarely used: there was a drawing-room, embalmed in the stink of moth balls, a smaller drawing-room, a study and a kind of office whose shutters were always closed and that served as a kind of lumber room or glory-hole. In a small box-room filled with a pungent smell of old leather lay generations of riding boots and ladies' shoes. Two staircases led to the upper storeys where there were corridors leading to well over a dozen rooms, most of them disused and filled with dusty bric-à-brac. I shared one of them with my sister. We slept in fourposter beds. Pictures cut out of illustrated magazines and amateurishly framed decorated the walls.

The liveliest place in the house was the kitchen, which occupied half the basement. I had my breakfast there in the mornings: *café au lait* and wholemeal bread. Through the window high in the wall you could see hens parading; guinea-fowl, dogs, and

sometimes human feet passed by. I liked the massive wood of the
table, the benches and the chests and cupboards. The cast-iron
cooking range threw out sparks and flames. The brasses shone:
there were copper pots of all sizes, cauldrons, skimming ladles,
preserving pans, and warming pans; I used to love the gaiety of
the glazed dishes with their paint-box colours, the variety of
bowls, cups, glasses, basins, porringers, hors d'œuvre dishes,
pots, jugs, and pitchers. What quantities of cooking pots, frying
pans, stock pots, stewpans, *bains-marie*, cassolettes, soup tu-
reens, meat dishes, saucepans, enamel mugs, colanders, graters,
choppers, mills, mincers, moulds, and mortars – in cast-iron,
earthenware, stoneware, porcelain, aluminium, and tin! Across
the corridor, where turtle doves used to moan, was the dairy.
Here stood great vats and pans of varnished wood and glazed
earthenware, barrel-churns made of polished elm, great blocks of
pattern-patted butter, piles of smooth-skinned cheeses under
sheets of white muslin: all that hygienic bareness and the aroma
of breast-fed babies made me take to my heels. But I liked to visit
the fruit loft, where apples and pears would be ripening on
wicker trays, and the cellar, with its barrels, bottles, hams, huge
sausages, ropes of onions, and swags of dried mushrooms. Whatever luxury there was at La Grillière was to be found down there
in the nether regions. The grounds were as dull as the upper
parts of the house: not a single bed of flowers, not one garden
seat, not even a sunny corner to sit and read in. Opposite the
great central flight of stone steps there was a fishing stream
where servants often did the household wash with a great
whacking of wooden beaters; a lawn fell steeply away to an
edifice even older than the château itself: the "back place", as it
was called, full of old harness and thick with spiders' webs. Three
or four horses could be heard whinnying in the adjacent stables.

My uncle, my aunt, and my cousins led an existence which
fitted this setting very well. Starting at six o'clock in the morning, Aunt Hélène would make a thorough inspection of all the
cupboards. With so many servants at her disposal, she didn't
have to do any housework; she rarely did any cooking, never
sewed, and never read a book, and yet she always complained of
never having a minute to herself: she never stopped poking

about, from the cellars to the attic. My uncle would come downstairs about nine o'clock; he would polish his leggings in the harness-room, and then go off to saddle his horse. Madeleine would look after her pets. Robert stayed in bed. Lunch was always late. Before sitting down to table, Uncle Maurice would season the salad with meticulous care and toss it with wooden spatulas. At the beginning of the meal there would be a passionate discussion about the quality of the cantaloups; at its end, the flavours of different kinds of pears would be thoroughly compared. In between, much would be eaten and but few words spoken. Then my aunt would go back to her cupboard inspection, and my uncle would stump off to the stables, laying about him with his hunting-crop. Madeleine would join Poupette and me in a game. Robert usually did nothing at all; sometimes he would go trout-fishing; in September he would hunt a little. A few elderly, cut-rate tutors had tried to din into him the rudiments of arithmetic and spelling. Then an oldish lady with yellowed skin devoted herself to Madeleine, who was less of a handful and the only one in the family ever to read a book. She used to gorge herself on novels, and had dreams of being very beautiful and having lots of loving admirers. In the evenings, everyone would gather in the billiard room; Papa would ask for the lamps to be lit. My aunt would cry out that it was still quite light, but in the end would give way and have a small oil lamp placed on the centre table. After dinner, we would still hear her trotting about in the dark corridors. Robert and my uncle, with glazed eyes, would sit rigidly in their armchairs waiting silently for bed-time. Very occasionally one of them would pick up a sporting magazine and flick desultorily through it for a few minutes. The next morning, the same kind of day would begin all over again, except on Sundays, when, after all the doors had been locked and barred, we would all climb into the dog-cart and go to hear Mass at Saint-Germain-les-Belles. My aunt never had visitors, and she never paid visits herself.

This way of life suited me very well. I used to spend the best part of my days on the croquet lawn with my sister and cousin, and the rest of the time I would read. Sometimes we would all three of us set off to look for mushrooms in the chestnut plantations. We ignored the insipid meadow varieties, the tawny *grisettes* and the tough, crinkled *chanterelles* as well as the clumps of wild chicory: we studiously avoided the lurid Devil's Boletus with its red-veined stem and the sham flap-mushroom which we recognized by their dull colour and their rigid look. We despised mature *ceps* whose flesh was beginning to go soft and produce greenish whiskers. We only gathered young ones with nicely curved stalks and caps covered with a fine nigger-brown or blueish nap. Rummaging in the moss and parting fans of bracken and ferns, we would kick to pieces the puff-balls, which when they burst gave off clouds of filthy dust. Sometimes we would go with Robert to fish for fresh-water crayfish; or in order to get food for Madeleine's peacocks we would dig up ant-hills and wheel away barrow-loads of whiteish eggs.

The big waggonette was no longer allowed to leave the coach-house. In order to get to Meyrignac we had to spend an hour sitting in a little train that stopped every ten minutes, pile our luggage on a donkey cart and then walk over the fields to the house: I couldn't imagine any more agreeable place on earth to live. In one sense, our life there was an austere one. Poupette and I had no croquet or any other kind of outdoor amusement; my mother had refused, I don't know why, to let my father buy us bicycles. We couldn't swim, and besides the River Vézère was some distance away. If occasionally we heard the sound of a motor-car coming up the drive, Mama and Aunt Marguerite would hurriedly leave the garden to go and tidy themselves up; there were never any children among the visitors. But I could do without frivolous distractions. Reading, walking, and the games I made up with my sister were all I wanted.

The chief of my pleasures was to rise early in the morning and observe the awakening of nature; with a book in my hand, I would steal out of the sleeping house and quietly unlatch the garden gate: it was impossible to sit down on the grass, which would be all white with hoar-frost; I would walk along the drive, beside the meadow planted with specially chosen trees that my grandpapa called "the landscape garden"; I would read a little from time to time, enjoying the feeling of the sharp air softening against my cheeks; the thin crust of rime would be melting on the ground; the purple beech, the blue cedars, and the silvery poplars would be sparkling with the primal freshness of the first morning in Eden: and I was the only one awake to the beauty of the earth and the glory of God, which mingled agreeably deep inside me with a dream of a bowl of hot chocolate and warm buttered toast. When the bees began to hum and the green shutters were opened on the sunny fragrance of wistaria, I felt I was already sharing a secret past with the day that for the others was only just beginning. After the round of family greetings and breakfast, I would sit at a metal table under the catalpa tree and get on with my "holiday tasks". I liked those moments when, pretending to be busied with some easy exercise, I let my ear be beguiled by the sounds of summer: the fizzing of wasps, the chattering of guinea-fowls, the peacocks' strangulated cry, the whisperings of leaves; the scent of phlox mingled with the aromas of caramel and coffee and chocolate that came wafting over to me from the kitchen; rings of sunlight would be dancing over my exercise book. I felt I was one with everything: we all had our place just here, now, and for ever.

Grandpapa would come down about noon, his chin freshly shaven between his white side-whiskers. He would read the *Écho de Paris* until lunch-time. He liked good solid food: partridge with crisply steamed cabbage, chicken vol-au-vent, duck stuffed with olives, saddle of hare, pâtés, flans, tarts, marzipans, shapes, and trifles. While the ancient horned gramophone played a selection from *Les Cloches de Corneville*, he would be joking with Papa. They would chaff each other all through the meal, laughing, declaiming, singing even; again and again they would trot out the memories, anecdotes, quotations, witticisms, and nonsense-talk of the family folk-lore. After that, I usually went walking with my sister; scratching our legs on gorse and our arms on brambles, we would explore for miles around the chest-nut groves, the fields, the moors. We made great discoveries: ponds; a waterfall; at the centre of a lonely heath, blocks of grey granite which we climbed to get a glimpse of the blue line of the Monédières. As we rambled along, we would sample the hazel-nuts and brambleberries in the hedges, arbutus berries, cornel berries, and the acid berries of the berberis; we had bites out of apples from every orchard; but we were careful not to suck the milk of the wild-spurge or to touch those handsome bright-red spikes which are the proud bearers of the enigmatic name "Solomon's Seal." Drowsy with the scent of freshly mown hay, with the fragrance of honeysuckle and the smell of buckwheat in flower, we would lie down on the warm moss or the grass and read. I also sometimes used to spend the afternoons on my own in the landscape garden, when I would read and read to my heart's content as I watched the trees' shadows lengthening and the butterflies tumbling over and over on another.

On rainy days, we stayed in the house. But while I chafed at restraints imposed by other people's wills, I felt no resentment at those inflicted on me by things like the weather. I liked being in the drawing-room with its armchairs upholstered in green plush, its french windows draped with yellowed muslin; on the marble chimneypiece, on the occasional tables and sideboards, quantities of dead things were slowly mouldering away; the stuffed birds were moulting, the everlasting dried flowers were crumbling to dust and the sea-shells were turning a dull, lifeless grey. I would climb on a stool and ransack the library shelves; there I could always find some novel by Fennimore Cooper or some *Pictorial Magazine*, its pages badly foxed, which I had not seen before. There was a piano, several of whose notes did not play or were completely out of tune; Mama would prop up on the music-stand the vocal score of the *Grand Mogul* or the *Noces de Jeannette* and warble grandfather's favourite airs: he would join in all the choruses with us.

When the weather was fine, I would go for a walk in the gardens after dinner; with the Milky Way overhead, I would smell the heart-stirring fragrance of the magnolias and keep an eye open for shooting stars. Then, a lighted candle in my hand, I would go up to bed. I had a room to myself; it gave on to the yard, overlooking the wood-shed, the laundry, and the coach-house which sheltered a victoria and a berlin, as out-of-date to me as the carriages of olden times. I was charmed by the smallness of the room: there was a bed, a chest of drawers, and, standing on a sort of locker, the wash bowl and water jug. It was a cell, made to my own measure, like the little niche under Papa's desk where I once used to hide myself away. Although my sister's company did not weigh upon me in any way, solitude exalted me. When I was going through one of my saintly periods, a room to myself allowed me to enjoy the mortifying bliss of sleeping on the bare floor. But above all, before going to bed I would stand a long time at my casement, and often I would rise in the middle of the night to look out upon the night breathing softly in its sleep. I would lean out and plunge my hands in the fresh leaves of a clump of cherry laurels; the water from the spring would be gurgling over a mossy stone; from time to time a cow would kick her hoof against the door of the byre: I could almost smell the odour of straw and hay. Monotonous and dogged as the beat of the heart would sound the stridulations of a grasshopper; against the infinite silence and the sky's infinities I used to feel that the earth itself was echoing that voice within me which kept on whispering: "Here I am." My heart oscillated between its living warmth and the frigid blazing of the stars. There was God up there, and He was watching me; under the breeze's soft caress I was intoxicated by the heady perfumes of the night, by this celebration in my blood that brought eternity within my reach.

TOM LEONARD

baa baa black sheep

baa baa black sheep
have you any wool
yes sir yes sir
three bags full

one for thi master
n anuthir wan fur thi master
n wan fur thi fuckin church

LORNA SAGE

Our Lady of the Accident

Silver hearts, discarded leg irons, crutches, dented helmets, exploded shotguns, bent steering wheels, shreds of shirt – the Madonna of Montenero specialises in accidents, and her sanctuary on the hill above Livorno is hung with the macabre but theoretically cheery debris of lives almost lost, dusty votive offerings that commemorate moments when the routine horrors of life were suspended by the grace of Our Lady. Inarticulate offerings, too – it seems impossible to imagine the donors. Or it would, except that at Montenero there developed a tradition of offering not just objects but paintings. They line the sanctuary's corridors, often six deep, and insist on the graphic reality of what happened, when, and exactly whom it happened to. They were done, almost all, by local craftsmen from 1800 on, and they provide an extraordinary sub-history (life-through-accidents) of Livorno and environs, a bit of Tuscany pictured without glamour for once, miles mentally, if not physically, off the tourist track.

It all started with a painting of a rather different kind. On 15 May, 1345 – when Livorno was a wretched village surrounded by malarial fen – the altar painting of the Madonna from the island of Eubea appeared miraculously at a cross-roads at the foot of Montenero. It was found by a shepherd who, prompted by inspiration, carried it up the hill, until it suddenly became too heavy for him. There, under the brow, on the spot she had chosen for herself, a shrine was set up to the Madonna of Montenero.

She was a very local Madonna from the start, and perhaps partly for that reason her cult was often in danger of decay or suppression. The curious lay order of the Jesuats took it on until they were suppressed in 1668, then the Teatines until they were expelled from Tuscany in 1783. Then from 1792 the Benedictine monks of Vallombrosa, who warded off Napoleon (1810) and the Italian State (1866), expanded the sanctuary, encouraged evidences of their Lady's special favour – hence the paintings – and finally achieved full recognition in 1947, when Pius XII proclaimed the Madonna of Montenero to be the patron Madonna of the whole of Tuscany.

She's a slightly sulky Byzantine lady holding a serious, tired-looking baby Jesus, but on her feast days, on the lucky medals, postcards and gilt-framed miniatures that the nuns sell, she's crowned and festooned with jewellery. Her image hovers in this exotic guise, sometimes enthroned, in the corner of each votive painting – more the kind of thing, people say, you'd expect to find in the south (with all the dark, dubious stress northern Italians put on that word).

And she must indeed owe something of her anomalous character to the weirdly cosmopolitan nature of Livorno itself: a thriving "free" port from the late 16th century, crowded with Jews, Muslims, Protestants (it had the first and, for a long time, the only Protestant cemetery in Italy); a seamy emporium (coral, cloth, slaves and, in the early days, "Leghorn" hats, hides, soap, rags). It can't have been a pious town, and it certainly wasn't beautiful – "colourful" perhaps, violent too, but lacking a culture of its own. Except for a semi-pagan devotion to its own Madonna on the hill. To her, observed Her Britannic Majesty's Consul in Livorno in 1900, "the least principled have some attachment".

Sailors, for instance. The shipwreck from which one escaped with one's life is probably the most insistent single theme among Montenero's 9,000 or so *ex voto* paintings, naturally enough. Many of the 19th century examples are gloomily obscure: a particularly splendid one – evidence of the range of the Madonna's prestige – is an oil-on-glass virtuoso piece contributed by a thankful Polish captain called Luca Mergovitch.

The stylised rents in the sails of his ship conspire threateningly with the curly waves, and the legend underneath in pidgin Italian leaves no doubt of his peril. At five in the morning on 28 December 1859 "latitude 46:48, longitude 5:10 . . . hit by a hurricane of wind", but through the intervention of the Blessed Virgin arrived safe at the port of Falmouth on 4 January.

The monks' own favourite among the blue and black seascapes, however, is the wreck of the steamer "Montegrappa" in the Atlantic in 1922, given by Giacomo Sassano "For Grace Received". It's unmistakably more home-produced – Captain Mergovitch's painter missed out the hovering Madonna – and in many ways typical of the Montenero vision of the sea: the smart ship on its side still belching smoke, huge swathes of water, lifeboats so small you hardly see them at first glance.

The shipwrecks bring the human scale up against God's in time-honoured fashion. They also exactly occupy the dividing-line between those awful but inevitable events that have to be accepted, and those lesser assaults of circumstance – perhaps equally awful, equally common – which you can survive if you're lucky, if the Madonna intercedes for you, if you're wearing her medal, if . . .

There are very few paintings at Montenero that deal with the perils of childbirth or sickness or war. These things, it seems, you greet with resignation, unless you can feel there's some special ingredient in your particular case – a miraculously successful operation, a shell-burst in North Africa that only failed to kill you by some fluke.

Thus, though Livorno was half flattened in 1943, there are no paintings giving thanks for escaping from bombed houses, but there are – in surprising numbers, throughout the last century and this – pictures of people falling through the floors of jerry-built tenements, or crushed under collapsing ceilings. (Whole families sitting down to supper descend to the next storey in stiff postures of surprise. A housewife who looks at first as though she's leaning on a kitchen counter turns out to be clinging for dear life to a beam, above a void in which a seagull hovers.) You thanked the Madonna of Montenero for your escape from the essentially avoidable calamities that befell you at work, at home, in the street. She wasn't too grand to tinker with the arbitrary details of existence.

Dry land isn't a great deal more stable than the sea. The painters' primitive techniques and the absence of perspective emphasise the queasy sense of vertigo. Even if your apartment building stays up, it's full of dangers. In picture after picture tiny doll-like figures plummet from high windows: "Laira Angiolini, 12 years old . . . on the day of 12 November 1871 from the third floor, escaped unharmed, catching herself on a clothes-line on the second floor, from which she fell to the ground." The lucky clothes-line itself is coiled inside the frame.

The ground floor too has pitfalls: "Giuseppe Puccini, 22 months, fell into a sewer. After about four minutes of desperate struggle he was pulled to safety with the help of the Most Sacred Virgin of Montenero, whose miraculous medal he wore on his breast . . . Pieve S. Paolo (Lucca) 13.9.53". The painter here has made Giuseppe far too big for once. His rescuers look rather as if they're trying to fit a giant boy into a small black hole, but a photograph in the corner sets things right.

Recent donors, though, do seem specially anxious about authenticity. Alvaro Ceccarini, gored by the bull while he was cleaning out its pen ("perforating his stomach so that his intestines came out . . . saved from certain death by the grace of the Most Sacred Madonna . . . 8.10.50"), offers his bloody vest and a passport-style photograph as well as proof of his good faith. Whereas Angiola Chionzini, who was attacked by a cow on the last day of December 1837, was content to let the painting speak for her. Which it does: the cow is very definitely a cow, it's happening in an empty street, and the odd-sized houses stacked on each side seem at once claustrophobically close and – if you're looking for a refuge – unhelpfully distant.

Traffic accidents account for some of Montenero's most memorably horrid offerings. You see small humans lying under the hooves/wheels of every form of conveyance since 1800: carriages, traps, trucks, bicycles, trams, cars, buses – plus the odd train. Not all of them are harrowing – the party of eight ("counting the driver") who squeezed into a cart on the blue, blue evening of 4 July 1851, to go hunting in the Maremma, and who overturned at speed on a pile of stones somebody left in the road, seem to have had rather a jolly spill.

Not so Giuseppe, 4, and Fortunata, 16, who ran to save him, "both children of Rosa Polesi": they lie pathetically scrambled under a smart cab, outside the butcher's shop, in June of that same year. Nor "Santi Martelli of Livorno, 53, carter by profession, who fell off his wagon when he was unloading at the Finochielle Steps on 26 April 1893, and gave no sign of life . . ." He recovered "in a month, by the Grace of the Madonna", but you can see he was at that moment – and felt himself to be – a dead man.

There are other street dangers that might strike one as less accidental. Antonio Navi thanks the Madonna for his recovery from "having been mortally wounded by treachery" on 15 January 1863, between 10 and 11 at night. He's seen being stabbed in the back, quite literally, by a brisk enemy on a black street with dark doorways straight out of nightmare.

Violence erupts in broad daylight too. Cesare di Michele Tocchini's narrow escape took place under the eyes of the butcher, the baker, the cooked-meat man. His story is appropriately breathless: "Chased by his brother with a knife", it begins, "his sister-in-law appeared, grabbed the poor boy by the hair, took the bread knife from the counter, and began stabbing him pitilessly, as if he was a barbarous foreigner. He fell to the ground, and the neighbours disarmed the cruel woman . . ."

"This all happened," he ends, "in Via del Giglio on August 1st of the year 1840." It's not a bad phrase – "this all happened" – to sum up the feeling the paintings express, including the less sensational ones: a mixture of acceptance and outrage, faith, fear and resentment. Life was bloody murder, is murder, you reflect, peering at illustrations of other people's bad luck.

Montenero is a "human document", and like many things cushioned and sanitised by that label its fascination is rather grubby. It's not about the dignity of suffering at all, but about the craven and utterly natural desire to escape it.

If you join the visitors and pilgrims doing the rounds and adding their own pious or pointless graffiti to the walls, you're caught up in a murmur of nasty curiosity, vicarious shudders, sympathetic clucks. It's hard to believe that many people still feel that "there but for the grace of the Madonna of Montenero . . ." The sanctuary flourishes (they're blasting new holy grottoes out of the rock, building extra wings), but the new *ex voto* offerings seem to be merely bland or expensive or occasionally gruesome. The tradition of painting petered out during the late 1950s, and with it a whole local way of seeing, a whole region of feeling, recedes into the past, or at least into invisibility.

Perhaps when the Madonna of Montenero became the patron of Tuscany in 1947, it was already a sign that she was losing her potency as a local deity who could counteract the malice of events. And perhaps the visual world has changed too much – everyone with a camera; newspaper and television close-ups of world-wide random violence – for local craftsman to get calamities down the street or round the corner into focus any more. Perspective has, in a sense, intervened at last. Certainly what happens to a Giacomo Sassano or an Angiola Chionzini doesn't appear in the same flat, revealing light.

CLARICE LISPECTOR

from *State of Grace*

Anyone who has experienced a state of grace will know what I
am talking about. I am not referring to inspiration, which is a
special grace that comes to those who struggle with art.

The state of grace to which I refer cannot be used for anything.
It would appear to come just to let us know it really exists. When
in this state, the tranquil happiness which radiates from people
and things is enhanced by a lucidity which can only be described
as light because in a state of grace everything is so very, very
bright. It is the lucidity of those who are no longer surmising:
they simply know. Just that: they know. Do not ask me what they
know, for I can only reply in the same childish manner: they
simply know.

And there is a physical bliss which cannot be compared to
anything. The body is transformed into a gift. And one feels it is a
gift because one is experiencing at source the unmistakable good
fortune of material existence.

In a state of grace, one sometimes perceives the deep beauty,
hitherto unattainable, of another person. And everything ac-
quires a kind of halo which is not imaginary: it comes from the
splendour of the almost mathematical light emanating from
people and things. One starts to feel that everything in existence
– whether people or things – breathes and exhales the subtle
light of energy. The world's truth is impalpable.

It bears no relation to what I vaguely imagine the state of
grace of saints to be. For that is a state of grace I myself have
never experienced and cannot even envisage. No, this is simply
the state of grace of an ordinary person who suddenly becomes
totally real since he is ordinary, human, and recognizable.

The discoveries made in this state of grace cannot be described
or conveyed. So when I find myself in a state of grace, I sit quietly
without uttering a word. As if awaiting an annunciation. But
unheralded by those angels who presumably precede the state of

grace of the saints. As if the angel of life were coming to announce the world.

Then the angel slowly withdraws. Not in a state of trance – for there is no trance – the angel slowly withdraws, sighing, as if already familiar with the world as it is. The angel's sigh is also one of longing. For having tried to acquire a body and a soul and a place on earth, the angel desires these things more and more. It is useless to desire: things only come when desired spontaneously.

I cannot explain it, but I find that animals are more often in an existential state of grace than human beings. Except that animals do not know, while human beings can perceive these things. Human beings come up against obstacles which do not affect the lives of animals, such as reasoning, logic and understanding. While animals enjoy the splendour of that which is direct and proceeds directly.

God knows what He is doing: I do not believe the state of grace should be bestowed on us too often. Otherwise we might pass forever on to the other side of life, which is also real but no one would understand us any more. We should lose our common language.

It is also a good thing that grace should not come as often as I should like. For I might get used to happiness (I forgot to mention that one feels extremely happy when in a state of grace). To get used to happiness could be dangerous. We could become more selfish because happy people are selfish. They are less sensitive to human suffering and we might not feel obliged to try and help those in need – simply because we possess the essence and compensation of life when we are in a state of grace.

No, even if the choice were mine, I should not want to be in a state of grace too often. It would be like becoming addicted to some vice. I should become a contemplative like those who smoke opium. And were that state of grace to occur too often, I feel certain I should abuse it: I should start expecting to live in a permanent state of grace. And this would result in an unforgivable flight from destiny, which is simply human, made up of conflict and suffering, of uncertainties and minor joys.

It is better if the state of grace is short-lived. Should it last too long, as I well know, familiar as I am with my almost childish ambitions. I should end up trying to penetrate the enigmas of Nature. And that would be enough to banish all grace. For grace is a gift which makes no demands, but it would disappear if we were to start demanding answers. We must never forget that the state of grace is only a tiny aperture which allows us to glimpse a sort of tranquil Paradise, but it is not an entrance, nor does it give us the right to eat the fruits of the orchards.

One emerges from a state of grace with clear skin and open, thoughtful eyes. And, even without a trace of happiness, it is as if one's whole body were bathed in a gentle smile. And one comes away a better person than when one entered. To have known grace is to have experienced something which appears to redeem the human condition while accentuating the strict limitations of that condition. After experiencing grace, the human condition is revealed in all its wretched poverty, thereby teaching us to love more, to forgive more, and show greater faith. One begins to have a certain confidence in suffering and its ways, which can so often become unbearable.

Some days are so arid and empty that I would give years of my life in exchange for a few minutes' grace.

E. E. CUMMINGS

thing no is(of
all things which are
who)so alive
quite as one star

kneeling whom to
(which disappear
will in a now)
i say my here

MURIEL SPARK

The Comforters

Chapter 2

A storm, fierce enough to hold up the shipping at the mouth of the Mersey, ranged far enough inland to keep Caroline Rose indoors, where she paced the pale green corridors. Not for exercise but in order to think. A thinking-place of green corridors. The Pilgrim Centre of St Philumena.

"Taking exercise." This was Mrs Hogg tacking on to her, infuriating. Taking exercise. Not a question, a statement.

"Good afternoon," said Caroline.

"And feeling lonely," said Mrs Hogg with her sort of smile. Feeling lonely, taking exercise. Caroline made no answer. The small perfect idea which had been crystallizing in her mind went all to mist. All right, I am at your disposal. Eat me, bloodywell take the lot. I am feeling lonely. Rome has spoken.

"Another time," said Mrs Hogg, "you don't want to make a private Retreat. You want to come in the summer with one of the big pilgrimages for one of the big Feasts."

"Do I?" Caroline said.

"Yes," said Mrs Hogg. "That's what you want to do. Please call me Georgina by the way. I'll call you Caroline. Sometimes we have as many as a hundred and thirty pilgrims to stay. And of course thousands for the day pilgrimages. Sir Edwin and Lady Manders and Father Ingrid had no idea what they started when they started St Philumena's. You must meet the Manders."

"I know them," said Caroline.

"Oh, you do. Are you one of their converts? They are always making converts."

"Converts to what?" said Caroline in the imperative need to be difficult. Caroline vented in her mind her private formula: *You are damned. I condemn you to eternal flames. You are* caput, *as good as finished, you have had it, my dear.* More expressive, and therefore

more satisfying than merely "Go to hell", and only a little less
functional than a small boy's "Bang-bang, you're dead!"

"Converts to the Faith, of course," Mrs Hogg was saying.

During her three days' stay at St Philumena's she had already
observed Mrs Hogg. On her first evening Caroline overheard her:

"You have to take what's put before you here. Sometimes we
have as many as a hundred and thirty pilgrims. Suppose a
hundred and thirty people all wanted tea without milk—"

Her victim, a young lawyer who was recovering from dipsoma-
nia, had replied, "But I only say don't *trouble* to put milk in mine."

"It isn't what you say, it's what you get."

They sat later at a polished oak refectory table silently eating a
suet-laden supper which represented the monastic idea at St Philumena's. Their mouths worked silently, rhythmically, chew-pause-
chew-pause-swallow-pause-chew. A sister from the convent next
door was reading aloud the "holy work" prescribed for mealtimes.
Caroline recognized the Epistle of St John, and listened, fixing her
eyes on the white blouse of Mrs Hogg opposite. Soon her mind was
on Mrs Hogg, and the recent dispute about the tea. She began to
take in the woman's details: an angular face, cropped white hair, no
eyelashes, rimless glasses, a small fat nose of which the tip was
twitching as she ate, very thin neck, a colossal bosom. Caroline
realized that she had been staring at Mrs Hogg's breasts for some
time, and was aware at the same moment that the woman's nipples
were showing dark and prominent through her cotton blouse. The
woman was apparently wearing nothing underneath. Caroline
looked swiftly away, sickened at the sight, for she was prim; her
sins of the flesh had been fastidious always.

That was the first evening.

And this was the third day. At the end of the long corridor they
turned. Caroline looked at her watch. Mrs Hogg did not go away.

"The Manders converted you. They are always converting
somebody."

"No. Not in my case, they didn't."

"The Manders are *very* nice people," said Mrs Hogg defensively.

"Charming people."

"*Very* good people," Mrs Hogg insisted.

"I agree," said Caroline.

"You couldn't possibly disagree. What made you a Catholic then?"

"Many reasons," Caroline said, "which are not too easy to define: and so I prefer not to discuss them."

"Mm . . . I know your type," Mrs Hogg said, "I got your type the first evening you came. There's a lot of the Protestant about you still. You'll have to get rid of it. You're the sort that doesn't mix. Catholics are very good mixers. Why won't you talk about your conversion? Conversion's a wonderful thing. It's not *Catholic* not to talk about it."

The woman was a funny old thing in her way. Caroline suddenly felt light-hearted. She giggled and looked again at her watch.

"I must be going."

"Benediction isn't till three o'clock."

"Oh, but I've come here for rest and quiet."

"But you're not in Retreat."

"Oh yes, you know, I *am* in retreat." Then Caroline remembered that the popular meaning of "retreat" in religious circles was an organized affair, not a private retiring from customary activities, so as to possess one's soul in peace. She added, "I mean, I've retreated from London, and now I'm here for rest and quiet."

"You were speaking plenty to that young lawyer this morning."

In her private neurotic amusement Caroline decided to yield. Ten more minutes of Mrs Hogg. The rain pelted with sudden fury against the windows while she turned to the woman with a patronizing patience.

"Tell me about yourself, Mrs Hogg."

Mrs Hogg had recently been appointed Catering Warden. "If it wasn't for the Faith I couldn't hold down the job. On my feet from six till two, then on again at three and then two hours' break till supper and then there's the breakfast to think about. And I've got a great number of Crosses. That young lawyer you've got in with, the other night he said, 'I don't take milk in my tea' – did you hear him? Sometimes we have as many as a hundred and thirty. Suppose a hundred and thirty people wanted tea without milk—"

"Well, that would be fairly easy," said Caroline.

"Suppose they each wanted something different."

"All at the same time?" said Caroline.

Seeing Mrs Hogg's expression at this moment, Caroline thought. "Now it has struck her that I'm an enemy of the Faith."

But Mrs Hogg righted herself; her mechanism was regulated for a chat.

"I'll tell you how I came here – it was a miracle. Our Lady sent me."

But Caroline's mood had changed again. Her sophisticated forbearance departed and constriction took its place; a pinching irritated sense of being with something abominable, not to be tolerated. She had a sudden intense desire to clean her teeth.

"Oh tell me about the miracle," Caroline said. Her tone was slightly menacing. "Tell me all the details." These scatty women with their miracles. Caroline thought, "I hate all women and of all women Mrs Hogg. My nerves are starting up again. The next few eternal minutes are important. I must mind what I say. Keep aloof. Watch my manners at all costs."

"Well," Mrs Hogg was saying, "I was of two minds whether to take a post in Bristol with a lady who was having her baby at home – I'm a registered midwife, you know, although most of my experience has been as a governess. One time I was housekeeper to a priest for two years. That was in Birmingham. He was sent to Canada in 1935, and when we said good-bye he said, 'Well, Mrs Hogg—' "

"What about the miracle?" said Caroline, and to cover up her testiness overdid it and added, "I can't hear enough about miracles."

And, privately she consoled herself with the words, "Little dear" – for that was how she spoke to herself on occasion – "you will receive letters tomorrow morning from the civilized world."

"Well, you know," Mrs Hogg was saying, "to *me* it was a miracle. I was debating whether to take the job in Bristol or a permanent place in the north with a deaf lady. A letter arrived, it was a Tuesday morning, to say that the lady in Bristol had gone to hospital because of some complications, and was having her baby there. The husband sent me a week's money. Then in the afternoon another letter arrived from the other place. No, I'm wrong, it was the next morning. The deaf lady had died. So there I was without a job. So I said to Our Lady, 'What am I going to do now?' and Our Lady said, 'Go back to St Philumena's and think it over.' I'd already stayed at St Philumena's on one of the big Retreats—"

"Did you actually hear a voice?" Caroline inquired.

"A voice?"

"I mean, when you say, 'Our Lady said', do you mean she spoke audibly to you?"

"Oh no. But that's how Our Lady always speaks to me. I ask a question and she answers."

"How do you hear her answer, then?"

"The words come to me – but of course you won't know much about that. You have to be experienced in the spiritual life."

"How do you know the words come from the Blessed Virgin?" Caroline persisted relentlessly. Mrs Hogg moved her upper lip into an indecent smile. Caroline thought: "She desires the ecstasy of murdering me in some prolonged ritualistic orgy; she sees I am thin, angular, sharp, inquiring; she sees I am grisly about the truth; she sees I am well-dressed and good-looking. Perhaps she senses my weakness, my loathing of human flesh where the bulk outweighs the intelligence."

Mrs Hogg continued: "I know it was Our Lady's message because of what happened. I came to St Philumena's and saw Lady Manders who was here just at that time, When I told her the position she said, 'Now, there *is* a job for you here, if you like to try it. We want to get rid of the Catering Warden, she isn't strong enough for the job. It's hard work, but Our Lady would help you.' So I came for a month's trial. That was in the autumn, and I'm loving it, every minute of it."

"That was the miracle," Caroline said.

"Oh, it *was* a miracle. My arriving here just when Lady Manders wanted to make a change in the staff. I only came, really, to think things over. But I can tell you, I don't have much chance to sit on my behind and think. It's hard work. And I always put duty first, before everything. And I don't mind the work; Our Lady helps me. When the kitchen girls grumble about the work, I always tell them, 'Our Lady will do it for you.' And she does."

"In that case, there's no need for them to do it," Caroline said.

*

DEREK JARMAN

Chroma

White Lies

The first of all simple colours is white, although some would not
admit that black or white are colours, the first being a source or
receiver of colours, and the latter totally deprived of them. But
we can't leave them out, since painting is but an effect of light
and shade, that is chiaroscuro, so white is the first then yellow,
green, blue and red and finally black. White may be said to
represent light without which no colour can be seen.

(Leonardo da Vinci, *Advice to Artists*)

Potters Bar fête 1906. I still have a cherished postcard from
which I painted several pictures as a teenager. Edwardian girls
in long white dresses, lampshade hats and frilly parasols blown
like thistledown out of the nineteenth century. Who were they?
Looking so solemn under the fluttering bunting. Facing the
swings and roundabouts of life. I don't know what I found so
alluring about these girls in white dresses in the parks, piers and
promenades, paddling in the sea with their skirts hitched up in
paintings by Wilson Steer. Turn of the century white, inspired
perhaps by Whistler's monochromatic portrait *The White Girl*.
Throw a paint pot in the public's face and they will catch it. Here
they are again, sitting in the garden on white garden benches,
sipping tea from white porcelain, the gift of China, looking at a
postcard from an elder brother who is climbing Mont Blanc.
Dreaming of white weddings . . .

Ghostly white postcards. As I look at them now, the girls are
blissfully unaware of the wall of death which will change their
Sunday best but not its colour, a few short years ahead. They will
become nurses, factory girls, maybe engineers or even aviators.
Behind the postcard there is white. Behind the painting there is
white ground.

White stretches back. Was white created in the Big Bang? Was the bang itself white?

In the beginning was white. And God made it, of all the colours, and this was a secret until Sir Isaac Newton sat in a darkened room late in the seventeenth century:

THE PROOF BY EXPERIMENTS

Whiteness and all grey Colours between white and black, maybe compounded of all Colours, and the whiteness of the Sun's Light is compounded of all the primary Colours mix'd in a due Proportion. The Sun shining in a dark Chamber through a little round hole in the Window-shut and his Light being there refracted by a Prism to cast his coloured Image upon the opposite Wall: I held a white Paper to that image in such a manner that it might be illuminated by the colour'd Light reflected from thence . . .

(Sir Isaac Newton, *Opticks*)

Looking back through Sir Isaac's prism, is it possible to see Osiris, the God of the White Nile, God of Resurrection and rebirth, in his white crown and white sandals, devoid of colour? Then white was without colour, something which after Newton we can no longer experience. Perhaps the green sceptre that the God holds to herald the return of spring, like the snowdrop, tells us this.

White is the dead mid-winter, pure and chaste, the snowdrop, *Galanthus nivalis* (Candlemas bells), decorated the churches on February the second, the Feast of the Purification of the Virgin . . . but don't bring those snowdrops into your house – they'll bring you bad luck, you might even drop dead: for the snowdrop is the flower of the dead, resembling a corpse in its shroud. White is the colour of mourning except in the Christian West where it is black – but the object of mourning is white. Whoever heard of a corpse in a black shroud?

If you spin a colour wheel fast enough it turns white, but if you mix the pigments, however much you try, you will only get a dirty grey.

That all the colours mixed together produce white, is an
absurdity which people have credulously been accustomed
to repeat for a century, in opposition to the evidence of their
senses.

(Johann von Goethe, *Theory of Colour*)

Light in our darkness.

As the wheel spins a mandala is created. In it you see that the
Gods are white; centuries before Saint John invented the Chris-
tian Heaven, with the Heavenly Host in white worshipping the
Lamb, the Greeks and Romans were celebrating Saturnalia – 17
December. The melancholy Saturn, like Osiris and the coming
Christ, was a white god, worshipped in white with a touch of
Osiris green in the palm leaves his worshippers held in their
hands. The Feast ended on New Year's Day when the Consul,
arrayed in white and riding a white horse, celebrated the tri-
umph of Jupiter on the Capitol.

I'm dreaming of a white Christmas. This song could only be
sung in southern California around a swimming pool. Here, at
the first hint of snow British Rail runs to a standstill, the roads
become impassable, and even the pavements are a danger as
the salt destroys your shoes. Christmas, born of a virgin.
White cotton. Wool beards. And a gross exchange of super-
fluous gifts. The barometer of the mind drops into depression.
A child of good intention who brought the opposite: fear,
loathing, mad American preachers who shout at you. A sa-
viour who saved nothing but the illusions of his own, and
certainly not the white Christmas turkeys boiled alive after
standing in a crowd for a year (yes, they're dreaming of a white
Christmas!).

The entire kingdom was ordered into mourning for Mumtaz
Mahal for two years and a silent gloom spread over Northern
India. There was no public entertainment, and no music, no
jewellery, perfumes and other fineries, brightly coloured
clothes were forbidden, and anyone who dared disrespect
the memory of the Queen was executed. Shah Jehan kept
away from the public eye, the same emperor who once wore

a robe so heavily encrusted with gems that he needed the support of two slaves, now dressed in simple white clothes.

(Shalin Savan, *Shah Jehan, The Taj Mahal*)

White has great covering power. The whitewashed family does not question the bride's blushes beneath the veil.

Desire flaunts itself in the face of pure white, but is buried by the wedding dress. The bride has hidden her scarlet and black fuck-wear, bought in Soho, for the honeymoon. White lace camouflages her pregnancy. The groom's best friend, David, is whispering in his ear, "Cum in my mouth! Cum in my mouth!"

One book opens another. The tears of Saturn form the wide salt sea. Salt is bitter and sad. Salt mines. The salt of the earth is its soul, so precious, if you drop it throw a pinch of it over your shoulder. The wisdom of an old salt. After the salt was blessed it was sprinkled in the baptismal waters. Christ is the salt which makes our earthly bodies incorruptible. Salt is the divine wisdom. So valuable is it, that it is placed in jewelled reliquaries at the High Table. St Hilary said, "Let the world be sprinkled with salt, not deluged with it."

Isn't white that which does away with darkness?

(Wittgenstein)

In my grandmother's living room, my mother and I play Mah-Jong. Building walls with little ivory bricks. On the mantelpiece are two ivory miniatures of the Taj Mahal, its marble funereal white. All the ancient monuments are ghostly white, the statues of Greece and Rome were washed of their colours by time. So, when the Italian artists revived antiquity, they sculpted in white marble unaware that their exemplars were once polychrome – who sculpted the whitest? Canova? A deathly Cupid and Psyche? The Three Ghostly Graces? Ghosts from the antique. The world had become a ghost for artists.

1919. The world is mourning. Kasimir Malevich paints *White On White*. A funeral rite for painting:

I have transformed myself IN THE ZERO OF FORM and dragged myself out of the rubbish-filled pool of academic art. I have torn through the blue lampshade of colour limitations, and come out into the white. I have conquered the lining of the Heavenly, have torn it down and, making a bag, put in colours and tied it with a knot. Sail forth! The white, free chasm, infinity is before us.

(Malevich)

The chemistry of the paint with which Kasimir painted his famous picture was as old as pigment. I doubt that he used titanium, which was only just discovered; perhaps he used zinc oxide, a mere one hundred years old. It's most likely he used lead oxide which stretched back to the antiquity he despised. All the whites with the exception of the chalk-based grounds like gesso are metal oxides. White is metallic.

Flake white. Thin sheets of lead oxidised in the dung-heap produced the heavy white impasto on which Rembrandt balanced the heads of his sitters, leaden ruffs, heavy with starch and propriety.

A colour made alchemically from lead is white. It is called white lead. This white lead is very brilliant, and it comes in little cakes like goblets or drinking glasses. The more you grind this colour the more perfect it will be and it is good on panels – it is even used on walls but avoid it as much as you can for in the course of time it turns black.

(Cennino Cennini, *Il Libro dell'Arte*, translated D V Thompson)

When will Kasimir's *White On White* turn to *Black On Black*? Pliny writes a recipe:
Lead decomposes in jars of vinegar to produce the ground on which we paint.
White lead is very poisonous, and if used unwisely leads to painters' sickness.
Rome poisoned itself with leaden wine vessels. Is the madness of painters like that of hatters? In the chemistry of their art?

Olympiodorus warns us that lead is so possessed by devils and is so shameless, that those who want to learn about it fall into madness and death.

Zinc oxide, Chinese white, originates as a cold white smoke, it is not poisonous and has been used as a pigment since the mid-nineteenth century. Zinc vapour from the molten metal is burned in an oxidising atmosphere at a temperature of 950° centigrade, producing fumes of white oxide. Zinc oxide is a pure cold white.

The whitest of whites is titanium which has the greatest hiding power of any of the whites. It is very stable, unaffected by heat, light or air and is the youngest of the whites, having been introduced after the First World War.

The current price for these pigments from Cornelissen, the artists' colourmen, is:

Flake white	£15.85
Titanium white	£22.50
Zinc white	£26.05
FOR FIVE KILOS	

White shuts out, is opaque, you cannot see through it. Power-crazed white.

In 1942, I was born in Albion, a little white, middle-class boy, behind the great white cliffs of Dover, which defended us against the black-hearted enemy. As I was christened, the white knights fought an aerial battle through the cumulonimbus clouds above Kent. At four, my mother took me to see the sights – the great White Tower of London, no longer limewashed, but grey and sooty. Whitehall, where the Houses of Parliament were even blacker. I learnt quickly that power was white, even our American cousins had their own White House, built like the imperial monuments of antiquity in marble. Marble was expensive, and the living, out of respect for the dead, recorded their passing in marble monuments. One of the most lavish of these is the monument in Rome to Vittorio Emmanuele and the Risorgimento – a building in the worst of taste known by the Romans as the "Wedding Cake". On my fifth birthday I stood in front of this White Elephant awestruck. After a brief sojourn in Italy we returned home. I was six, my education began in earnest at Hordle House on a Hampshire cliff top in sight of the Needles. Behind a Fifties education lay the great White Imperial Burden. Privileged, we of the White Hope were to care, maybe even sacrifice ourselves, for the countries coloured pink in our school atlas.

At seven, I embarrassed my military father asking for a white arum lily as a birthday present, rather than the dead lead soldiers he would have preferred. My childish passion for flowers he thought sissie; he hoped I would grow out of it. I've never had an obsession with white flowers like Vita had at Sissinghurst, though I do have a favourite, the old clove-scented pink, with its shaggy petals, Mrs Sinkins. Gertrude Jekyll, the great Edwardian gardener, loved this flower, though she would have taken me to task for describing it as white:

> Snow white is very vague. There is always so much blue about the colour of snow, from its crystalline surface and partial transparency, and the texture is so unlike that of any kind of flower that the comparison is scarcely permissible. I take it that the use of snow white is like that of golden yellow, more symbolical than descriptive meaning of any white that gives the impression of purity.
>
> Nearly all white flowers are yellowish white and the comparatively few that are bluish white such examples as *Omphalodes linifolia* are of a texture so different from snow that one cannot compare them at all – I should say that most white flowers are near the colour of chalk; for although the words chalky white have been used in a rather contemptuous way, the colour is really a beautiful warm white, but by no means an intense white.
>
> The flower that always looks to me the whitest is that of *Iberis sempervivens*, the white is dead and hard – like a piece of glazed stoneware quite without play or variation, and hence uninteresting.
>
> (Gertrude Jekyll, *Wood and Garden*)

At nine, my Christmas present was the two volumes of Trevelyan's *Illustrated English Social History*. I don't think I read it!

But I'd fallen in love with the pictures – particularly the miniature by Nicholas Hilliard of a young man, who leans lovesick against a tree, his hand on his heart, entwined with white roses. He wears a white ruff, a slashed white and black doublet, white hose and white shoes. Perhaps he lived in one of the black and white timber houses which were also illustrated in the book, and from which I made countless drawings, more fantastical even than None-Such Palace. A world of white turrets, spires and towers . . . above which an aerial battle was fought. I think these drawings reflected my inner turmoil, the battle that had raged throughout my childhood, the bombers and air raid sirens, while down below was a threatened home. Home in black and white.

The advance of white in the twentieth century was delayed by the Second World War. The architect Corbusier's Les Terrasses painted in a cream white – and his Villa Savoie (1930), a pure white, had inspired a thousand imitations which sprang up along the seaside. This pure and domestic modernity had fallen victim to the Final Solution – Hitler's architect Albert Speer's dream of a neo-classical revival was achieved much later in Mrs Thatcher's post-modern 1980s.

In the ruins of the war, colour was reinstated. The pastels of the 1950s, each wall a different shade, pale shades of Mondrian's bright and scintillating *Broadway Boogie Woogie*.

1960. In the white heat of Harold Wilson's Technological Revolution we reinstated white. Out came the white lino paint, and white emulsion covered the browns and greens of our Victorian past and those Fifties pastels. Our rooms were empty, pure and dazzling, though difficult to keep that way as feet soon scuffed the white off the floorboards. In the middle of the room the black Braun fan heater whirred unsteadily – grandfather of the devilish black technology of the Eighties. The black at the centre of the white. At the cinema *The Knack*, with Rita Tushingham painting her room a pure white, art following our lives.

In this white we lived coloured lives. It was a brief moment. By 1967 the jumbled psychedelic rainbow flooded the room.

On the television a battle for purity raged: Persil washes whiter than white, blue-white, Daz, Fairy Snow, Tide, the battle of Dad's white shirt – what a debt we owe to ICI and the chemical factories. Priestly whitewashed whiter, cricket whites, tropical suits, reflecting the sun back at itself. The painter high on his scaffold with his white overalls splashed with white paint, the Carmelite monk and nursing sister. All that dull refinement, bleached white sugar, bleached the sacred grain. I once met an excited Frenchman in a supermarket; he had packed a dozen loaves of white sliced bread for his friends in Paris.

Queer white. Jeans hugging tight arses. Sarah shouts from the garden: "Oh, *that's* how the gay boys recognise each other in the night!" White Nights in Heaven, a gay bar, which would have thrilled Saint John, dazzling T-shirts and boxer shorts achieved after days spent poring over the washing machine's finer programme.

All this white inherited from sport – sportif. The white that contrasted with the green of the pitch. Note that green and white are together again. This white needs self-control . . . you cannot spill a drink or mark the virgin cloth. Now only the foolish or very rich wear white, to wear white you cannot mix with the crowd, white is a lonely colour. It repels the unwashed, has a touch of paranoia, what are we shutting out? It takes hard work whitewashing.

Passing through the Great Salt Lakes of Utah on the Greyhound bus. Shimmering white salt stretched to each horizon, blinding the eyes.

> I am summoned from my bed
> To the Great City of the dead
> Where I have no house or home,
> But in dreams may sometime roam
> Looking for my ancient room.
> (Allen Ginsberg, "White Shroud")

In the first white light of dawn I turn white as a sheet, as I swallow the white pills to keep me alive . . . attacking the virus which is destroying my white blood cells.

The wind has blown without end for five days now, a cold north wind in June. The sea, whipped into a thousand white horses, attacks the shore. Plumes of salt blow in veils coating the windows with brine and burning the flowers. Leaves are blackened and the red poppies too, the roses are wilting, here today and gone tomorrow; but the white perennial pea is untouched. In the distance the white cliffs appear briefly before they are swallowed in the haze. I am shut in, to walk in the garden hurts my tired lungs.

The white seahorses have brought a madness here, irritable, straining at the bit. I hate white.

Then standing in the garden I notice a white flower among the blue viper's bugloss. On closer inspection it turns out to be a single albino sport. No one has ever seen one before. Is it an omen? I mark it to collect the seed, and name it after my friend Howard who has taken the photograph on this book's jacket – *Arvensis sooleyi.*

> Lichtenberg says that very few people have ever seen pure white, so do most people use the word wrong, then? And how did *he* learn the correct use? He constructed an ideal use from an ordinary one and that is not to say a better one, but one that had been refined along "certain" lines and in the process something has been carried to extremes.
>
> (Wittgenstein)

Van Gogh, pale melancholic, haunted in the garret of his mind, his ashen face tinged with green shadows. Child of Saturn. White from long nights in the mind's laboratory. Can you put a face to him?

A snowstorm in a glass globe dropped by a child. The red water in the globe splashes over the white sheets on his bed. "I told you not to play with that!" The sheets, the bloody sheets. A scarlet accident in a snowstorm. Red-faced and angry. The child's sobbing and the red that never washed out, so the sheets remained a witness to the accident.

The blood of a wounded animal shot by hunters stains the clean snow. There is always a tremor when you see pools of blood splattering a street. A fight? A knifing? Maybe a murder?

The snow is blinding, blowing in the face of the winter queen at the battle of the White Mountain. What memories she must have had, moving her one set of furniture from room to room in her ruined palace in the Hague. Elizabeth of Bohemia for whom *The Tempest* was first performed at her marriage ceremony back in 1612.

> Storms beat on the stone walls, snow, the herald of winter, falling thick binds the earth when darkness comes and the night shadow falls, sending bitter hailstones from the North in hatred of men.
>
> *(The Wanderer, c900)*

White and battle – Teutonic Knights sliding to their deaths from icebergs.

We travelled north on an icy February morning on the train from Euston, through a landscape touched by Jack Frost. Woods, fields and hedgerows. A blinding crystalline white etched against a blue sky. The hoar frost shimmered whiter than snow, each leaf and twig, the frozen grass. Motionless white. The hills and valleys hallucinated. I only saw this once, except on post-cards. The beams of the February sun, brighter than midsummer, melted the crystals, and by the time we reached Manchester it was a memory. There is no way we could describe what we saw, it would be as impossible as describing the face of God.

White out in the north, the snow-blind polar bears howling.

DUBRAVKA UGRESIC

Alchemy

This is not a battle to fight.– Graffiti in a New York restaurant

I read in the newspaper that at an auction at Sotheby's in London a small tin of shit sold for £17,250. I see that the word "small" slipped out as I wrote that, as though the news would be more acceptable if it had been a bigger tin of shit. In his day, the Italian artist Piero Manzoni produced ninety tins filled with shit. The tins were numbered and signed, and sold at the current price of gold. An acquaintance of mine, an art dealer, assures me that the price was laughably low.

"If I had a Manzoni tin I could get 150,000 bucks for it without even trying," he assured me.

It turns out that Manzoni's tins are very rare today. Maybe skeptical buyers opened them to check whether they really did contain shit.

"While the price of gold is more or less stable, the price of shit has seen astronomical growth in the last thirty years. And it's still rising," claimed my acquaintance.

The transmutation of shit into gold is nevertheless no simple thing, for if it were we would all be rich. You need institutions, galleries, media, a market, publicity, interpreters (those who will explain the meaning of the artistic gesture), promoters, art dealers, critics, and, of course, consumers. Even when the shit is well packaged there is no guarantee that the transmutation will succeed.

The greatest shock for an East European writer who turned up in the Western literary marketplace was provoked by the absence of aesthetic criteria. Criteria of literary evaluation were the capital which our Easterner assiduously accumulated his whole literary life. And then it turned out that this capital wasn't worth shit.

In the non-commercial East European cultures, there were no divisions into good and bad literature. There was *literature* and there was *trash*. Culture was divided into official culture and underground culture. Underground literature, as a resistance movement, occupied far more space (justifiably or not) on the unofficial scale of literary values. East European writers moved in a world of clear aesthetic coordinates, at least that's what they believed. In their underground literary workshops, they diligently tempered the steel of their literary convictions. In return, they received abundant moral and emotional support from their readership. Both writers and their readers had endless amounts of time at their disposal, both everyday time and "historical" time. And for someone to have any idea at all of what is really good, he needs time.

When East European writers finally began crawling out of their underground, they stepped into the global literary marketplace like self-confident literary arbiters, as unfailing connoisseurs of difference. They brought with them an awareness of their chosen position in this world (the Muses decided, not them), and a conviction that they had an unalienable right to literary art.

Their encounter with the literary market was the biggest shock of their writing lives, a loss of the ground under their feet, a terrible blow to their writers' egos.

"Oh, you're a writer?"

"Yes," our Easterner replies, trying to sound like a modest and well-brought-up person who does not want to humiliate those who have not been chosen.

"What a coincidence! Our ten-year-old daughter is just finishing a novel. We even have a publisher!"

This is merely the first insult that our Easterner has to swallow. He himself does not have a publisher. And he will soon discover that the world of the literary marketplace is densely populated with the "chosen". With his fellow writers. His fellow writers are prostitutes who write their memoirs, sportsmen who describe their sporting lives, girlfriends of renowned murderers who describe the murderer from a more intimate perspective, housewives bored with daily life who have decided to try the creative life; there are lawyer-writers, fisherman-writers, literary critic-writers, innumerable searchers after their own identity, a whole army of those whom someone has offended, raped, or beaten up, or whose toes have been stepped on, and who rush to inform the world in writing of the drama of their long-repressed injury.

Our Easterner is profoundly shaken. He does not believe that all these "colleagues" have the same rights as he does, that in the world of literary democracy everyone is equal, that everyone has the right to a book and to literary success. He does not, however, abandon the hope that (literary-historical) justice will prevail in the end, that the very next day everything will resume its place, that housewife-writers will stay housewives and fisherman-writers fishermen. He has nothing against democracy itself. On the contrary, coming from where he has come from he is the first to recognize its value, but not in literature and art, for God's sake!

Our Easterner is mistaken. The highly exciting life of a fisherman has greater commercial value than an East European's thoughts about what good literature is supposed to be. And the world of the literary marketplace is not only a world of momentary glamour, as our Easterner believes by way of consolation. It is not writers, arbiters of taste, or critics, but the powerful literary marketplace that establishes aesthetic values.

Recently, during a short visit to Moscow, I met a writer. She looked most impressive, covered in sequins and feathers. If I had met her in New York I would have thought she was a transvestite. She gave me two volumes of her book *Notes on Bras (Zapiski na liftchikakh)*. The author was a so-called woman of the people, a former chambermaid or something. She had written a novel about her feminine communist experiences. And the book was selling like hotcakes, she said.

"And what has Solzhenitsyn been doing lately?" I asked stupidly. I really wasn't that interested in Solzhenitsyn at the time.

"Huh?" gawped the author of *Notes on Bras* blankly.

In the world of trash, wrote Vladimir Nabokov, it is not the book that brings success, but the reading public.

Recently, out of curiosity, I visited the website of the author of the iconic book *The Alchemist*. The work, which critics describe as interdenominational, transcendental, and inspirational, is a bag of wind with millions of readers throughout the world. Out of some two hundred enraptured readers on the web, only two expressed mild reservations about the alchemist's talent. The skeptics were immediately pounced upon by *The Alchemist*'s devotees, who asked that Amazon.com deny web access to any such comments.

I wondered why the consumers of victorious products were so fierce and intolerant. I had encountered the same aggressive tone, the same readiness for a fight to the end, each time I had expressed doubt in the value of any work which has millions of devotees. What is it that unites the million-strong army of lovers of *The Alchemist* so firmly and so easily divides the small group of lovers of Bohumil Hrabal? What is it that drives millions of people to shed tears as they watch *Titanic*, and drives a lunatic to deface a well-known painting in a Dutch museum? What is it that drives millions of people all over the world to weep for Lady Di, but to be indifferent when their next-door neighbor dies? I think I know the answer, but I would prefer to keep quiet, for the answer makes me tremble with terror.

"I know perfectly well that the book is shit," said a friend of mine, a teacher of literature at a European university, about some book. "But I looooove it!" he howled, drawing out the "o."

"Americans love junk. It's not the junk that bothers me, it's the love," said George Santayana. He said it at a time when he did not yet know that we were all one day going to become Americans.

But still, there is, presumably, something in the very nature of shit that makes it so loooooved. And however much the theoreticians of popular culture try to explain why shit ought to be loved, the most attractive aspect of shit is nevertheless its availability. Shit is accessible to everyone, shit is what unites us, we can stumble across shit at every moment, step in it, slip on it, shit follows us wherever we go, shit waits patiently on our doorstep ("Like shit in the rain" goes one popular Yugoslav saying). So who wouldn't love it! And love alone is the magic formula that can transform shit into gold.

E. Y. "YIP" HARBURG

It's only a paper moon

Say, it's only a paper moon
Sailing over a cardboard sea
But it wouldn't be make-believe
If you believed in me

Yes, it's only a canvas sky
Hanging over a muslin tree
But it wouldn't be make-believe
If you believed in me

Without your love
It's a honky-tonk parade
Without your love
It's a melody played in a penny arcade

It's a Barnum and Bailey world
Just as phony as it can be
But it wouldn't be make-believe
If you believed in me.

COOKIE MUELLER

Fleeting Happiness

Many years and brain cells ago, I had this belief that everyone would be happy someday. I have since found that this isn't necessarily so.

Happiness is a fictitious feeling. It was created by imaginative story tellers for the purpose of plot building or story resolution. Fortunately most people don't know this. They think the lives they are living are actual screen plays or theater pieces. In earlier times people were convinced their lives were the fantastic tales told at the fireside. Because of this, I have seen people stop in their tracks for a moment and wonder where the plot is, but mostly they just forge on blindly.

Believing that life will someday be wonderful isn't a bad thing, in fact it is absolutely necessary. To know the truth – life is hard, and then you die – isn't a very comfortable thing to live with. If everyone knew the cold facts, the sky would be darkened with falling bodies in suicide leaps.

Most people have been led to believe that their lives would be better if they had money, and usually this isn't wrong. They know it's not impossible to come into money, in fact I've read that every thirty-nine minutes a new millionaire emerges in the world.

But what's the real reason people want lots of money? Food? Clothing? Shelter? Yes, these things are basic, even the poor often have these things in modest amounts. Usually, the more you have of each of these basics, the more complicated life gets. Having too much food makes you fat; you need to diet. Having too many clothes makes it hard to make a decision in the morning; you need to organize. Having too many homes must be really tough; you have to fill them. And why own all these things anyway, if there's no one else to share them with, or no one to hire to help you, or no one to be jealous of you?

I have pondered this and come up with the logical answer.

People want money because they want to be loved. They believe that money will buy them love. OK, we've all heard this.

Now, suppose you had lots of money, thus you had tons of lovers (perhaps it's superficial love but this blossoms), and you had lots of servants who loved you and hung around, and you had lots of friends who were envious. You would expect that everything would be great. Lots of love, lots of money. What else could one want?

Unfortunately, the pitiable human being will still want something else. It is human nature.

The next thing to want would be fame. So you need publicity. That's not difficult; you can buy a newspaper or magazine company and put your own name and picture in the headlines if you want; you can finance films and star yourself. Okay, now you have money, love, and fame. But still people laugh at you behind your back. Then what? The answer is power.

Let's suppose your magazine is successful and your film is a box-office smash. Then you have all four: money, love, fame and power. Would you be happy? No. You would probably go mad.

Look at Howard Hughes. He had all four. In the end he went insane. He was so afraid of germs he was walking around with sanitary Kleenex boxes on his feet.

No one is ever satisfied.

Some people might remind you that the holy men of the East are satisfied, but I don't think so. Even those guys want something. They might want infinite wisdom or they might want to perform miracles to impress followers, or they might want to levitate. It's always something.

Being a human being isn't easy, what with all these insatiable physical, emotional and intellectual desires.

If the ultimate goal in life is to be happy then you have to admit that one-celled creatures have it all over us. Little germs are probably always happy. They are superior, they don't sing the blues. Think about that the next time you bring out the disinfectant bottle and start scrubbing them away.

Look at Howard Hughes again. He must have known that the happiness of germs was something terrifyingly enviable. He must have been jealous.

ITALO CALVINO

Six Memos for the Next Millennium

from Multiplicity

I have come to the end of this apologia for the novel as a vast net. Someone might object that the more the work tends toward the multiplication of possibilities, the further it departs from that unicum which is the *self* of the writer, his inner sincerity and the discovery of his own truth. But I would answer: Who are we, who is each one of us, if not a combinatoria of experiences, information, books we have read, things imagined? Each life is an encyclopedia, a library, an inventory of objects, a series of styles, and everything can be constantly shuffled and reordered in every way conceivable.

But perhaps the answer that stands closest to my heart is something else: Think what it would be to have a work conceived from outside the *self*, a work that would let us escape the limited perspective of the individual ego, not only to enter into selves like our own but to give speech to that which has no language, to the bird perching on the edge of the gutter, to the tree in spring and the tree in fall, to stone, to cement, to plastic. . . .

Was this not perhaps what Ovid was aiming at, when he wrote about the continuity of forms? And what Lucretius was aiming at when he identified himself with that nature common to each and every thing?

RAINER MARIA RILKE

The Ninth Elegy

Why, if this interval of being can be spent serenely
in the form of a laurel, slightly darker than all
other green, with tiny waves on the edges
of every leaf (like the smile of a breeze) –: why then
have to be human – and, escaping from fate,
keep longing for fate? . . .

                  Oh *not* because happiness *exists*,
that too-hasty profit snatched from approaching loss.
Not out of curiosity, not as practice for the heart, which
would exist in the laurel too. . . .

But because *truly* being here is so much; because everything here
apparently needs us, this fleeting world, which in some
   strange way
keeps calling to us. Us, the most fleeting of all.
Once for each thing. Just once; no more. And we too,
just once. And never again. But to have been
this once, completely, even if only once:
to have been at one with the earth, seems beyond undoing.

And so we keep pressing on, trying to achieve it,
trying to hold it firmly in our simple hands,
in our overcrowded gaze, in our speechless heart.
Trying to become it. – Whom can we give it to? We would
hold on to it all, forever . . . Ah, but what can we take along
into that other realm? Not the art of looking,
which is learned so slowly, and nothing that happened here.
   Nothing.
The sufferings, then. And, above all, the heaviness,
and the long experience of love, – just what is wholly
unsayable. But later, among the stars,

what good is it – *they* are *better* as they are: unsayable.
For when the traveler returns from the mountain-slopes into
   the valley,
he brings, not a handful of earth, unsayable to others, but instead
some word he has gained, some pure word, the yellow and blue
gentian. Perhaps we are *here* in order to say: house,
bridge, fountain, gate, pitcher, fruit-tree, window—
at most: column, tower . . . But to *say* them, you must understand,
oh to say them *more* intensely than the Things themselves
ever dreamed of existing. Isn't the secret intent
of this taciturn earth, when it forces lovers together,
that inside their boundless emotion all things may shudder
   with joy?
Threshold: what it means for two lovers
to be wearing down, imperceptibly, the ancient threshold of
   their door—
they too, after the many who came before them
and before those to come. . . . lightly.

Here is the time for the *sayable, here* is its homeland.
Speak and bear witness. More than ever
the Things that we might experience are vanishing, for
what crowds them out and replaces them is an imageless act.
An act under a shell, which easily cracks open as soon as
the business inside outgrows it and seeks new limits.
Between the hammers our heart
endures, just as the tongue does
between the teeth and, despite that,
still is able to praise.

Praise this world to the angel, not the unsayable one,
you can't impress *him* with glorious emotion; in the universe
where he feels more powerfully, you are a novice. So show him
something simple which, formed over generations,
lives as our own, near our hand and within our gaze.
Tell him of Things. He will stand astonished; as *you* stood
by the rope-maker in Rome or the potter along the Nile.
Show him how happy a Thing can be, how innocent and ours,

how even lamenting grief purely decides to take form,
serves as a Thing, or dies into a Thing –, and blissfully
escapes far beyond the violin. – And these Things,
which live by perishing, know you are praising them; transient,
they look to us for deliverance: us, the most transient of all.
They want us to change them, utterly, in our invisible heart,
within – oh endlessly – within us! Whoever we may be at last.

Earth, isn't this what you want: to arise within us,
invisible? Isn't it your dream
to be wholly invisible someday? – O Earth: invisible!
What, if not transformation, is your urgent command?
Earth, my dearest, I will. Oh believe me, you no longer
need your springtimes to win me over – one of them,
ah, even one, is already too much for my blood.
Unspeakably I have belonged to you, from the first.
You were always right, and your holiest inspiration
is our intimate companion, Death.

Look, I am living. On what? Neither childhood nor future
grows any smaller. . . . Superabundant being
wells up in my heart.

ROBERT CREELEY

End

End of page,
end of this

company – wee
notebook kept

my mind in hand,
let the world stay

open to me
day after day,

words to say,
things to be.

ABOUT THE WRITERS

ARMANDO
Armando is a Dutch writer, artist and film-maker who grew up near the Amersfoort concentration camp in The Netherlands. He is the author of over twenty books. *From Berlin* is the first of Armando's literary works to be translated into English. He lives in Berlin.

KATE ATKINSON
Kate Atkinson's first novel, *Behind the Scenes at the Museum*, won the 1995 Whitbread Book of the Year award. She is also the author of the novels *Human Croquet, Emotionally Weird, Case Histories* and *One Good Turn: A Jolly Murder Mystery*, a collection of stories, *Not the End of the World*, and two plays. She lives in Edinburgh.

MARGARET ATWOOD
Margaret Atwood is best known for her novels and poetry but also writes short stories, critical studies, screenplays, radio scripts and books for children. Her works have been translated into over thirty languages and have won prizes worldwide. She lives in Toronto.

PAUL BAILEY
Paul Bailey is the author of six critically acclaimed novels. *An Immaculate Mistake: scenes from childhood and beyond* was the first volume of his memoirs, and his most recent book, *A Dog's Life*, is the second. He lives in London.

NICOLA BARKER
Nicola Barker is the author of three collections of stories and five novels. She has won prizes including the IMPAC Prize, the David Higham Prize for Fiction and the *Mail on Sunday*/John Llewellyn Rhys Prize.

DJUNA BARNES
Djuna Barnes (1892–1982) was a key bohemian figure of the 1920s and 1930s in both Paris and Greenwich Village. Her novel *Nightwood*, with an introduction by T.S. Eliot, became a cult work of modern fiction. She spent the last forty years of her life as a recluse in New York City.

JOHN BERGER
John Berger is a storyteller, essayist, novelist, screenwriter, dramatist and critic and is one of the most influential writers of the last fifty years. His *Ways of Seeing* revolutionized the way that fine art is read and understood; his prizewinning novels include *G, To the Wedding* and *King: A Street Story*.

BERYL THE PERIL
Beryl the Peril was created by David Law, who also brought us Dennis the Menace, for the *Topper* comic in 1953. At that time, she shared several important characteristics with Dennis – the red and black clothes and devilish skill for troublemaking – but not with many other female comic stars. She now appears in the *Dandy*.

XANDRA BINGLEY
Xandra Bingley rode and trained ponies before she started work at seventeen for MI5, and then moved into publishing. *Bertie, May and Mrs Fish* is her first book. She lives in London.

KASIA BODDY
Kasia Boddy lectures in English at University College London. She is a co-editor of *The Virago Book of Twentieth-Century Fiction* (2000) and has just completed a book on the representation of boxing.

JANE BOWLES
In her lifetime, New Yorker Jane Bowles (1917–73) published one novel, *Two Serious Ladies*; one play, *In the Summer House*; and a short story collection, *Plain Pleasures*. She was the wife of Paul Bowles, who credited her for his interest in writing and said he wished he'd written *Two Serious Ladies*.

LOUISE BROOKS
Born in Kansas, Louise Brooks (1906–85) became one of the most famous faces of the silent silver screen. Her performance as the doomed waif Lulu in *Pandora's Box* is now regarded as one of the greatest in film history. She also left us her haircut: the sharp bob.

GEORGE MACKAY BROWN
Poet, short-story writer, novelist and dramatist George Mackay Brown (1921–96) was born in Stromness in the Orkney Islands. Like his fellow Orcadian poet Edwin Muir, his writing celebrates the islands' legend, lore and landscape.

ITALO CALVINO
Italo Calvino (1923–85) was born in Cuba but spent most of his life in his native Italy. A poet, novelist and journalist, he was one of the most important Italian writers of the twentieth century. His works include *If On a Winter's Night a Traveler, Invisible Cities* and *Cosmicomics*.

LEONORA CARRINGTON
Leonora Carrington is a British-born Surrealist painter who has lived and worked in Mexico since leaving Europe during the Second World War. Her books include collections of stories, a novel and an account of a period in an asylum when she was deemed, falsely, incurably insane. Dali called her "the most important female artist".

ANGELA CARTER
Angela Carter (1940–92) was one of the most influential English writers of the twentieth century, perhaps best known for her short stories and novels. She died of cancer when she was only fifty-one.

COLETTE
The French novelist Colette (1873–1954) wrote the Claudine novels, which shocked polite French society, under her husband's pen-name. The author of fifty other novels, including *Gigi*, her private life and loves made her a controversial figure but she also became one of France's most important writers.

ROBERT CREELEY
Robert Creeley (1926–2005) published over sixty works of poetry in the USA and abroad. He was part of the post-war counter-tradition started by Ezra Pound, William Carlos Williams and Louis Zukofsky. He was the New York State Poet Laureate and a Chancellor of the Academy of American Poets.

E.E.CUMMINGS
The popular American poet Edward Estlin Cummings (1894–1962) was born in Cambridge, Massachusetts. His quite radical experiments with form, punctuation and syntax produced work that became loved for its simplicity and playfulness.

FRED D'AGUIAR
Born in London in 1960 to Guyanese parents. His recent writings include the long narrative poems *Bill of Rights*, about the Jonestown massacre in Guyana, and *Bloodlines*, the story of a black slave.

LYDIA DAVIS
Lydia Davis is known for her brilliantly inventive (very) short stories. She has written several collections, including: *Break it Down, Almost No Memory* and *Samuel Johnson is Indignant*, the last of which was published by McSweeney's. She is also a celebrated translator of French literature (including Proust). She lives in upstate New York.

SIMONE DE BEAUVOIR
Simone de Beauvoir (1908–86), the French author and philosopher, is perhaps best known for her groundbreaking treatise *Le Deuxième Sexe (The Second Sex)*. The first volume of her autobiography, *Memoirs of a Dutiful Daughter*, shows her early questioning of the values of her Parisian *bourgeois* background.

H.D. (HILDA DOOLITTLE)
H.D. (1886–1961) was an American poet and novelist who lived most of her life in Europe. She had a romance with Ezra Pound before she settled down with her lifelong partner, Bryher, and her early work has been called the finest of the Imagist poets. However, her later accomplishments in poetry, fiction and non-fiction extended far beyond this.

WILLIAM DOUGLAS
The traditional Scottish song to "Annie Laurie" was originally written by her sweetheart, William Douglas. It was a favourite with Scottish soldiers during the Crimean War.

NELL DUNN
English novelist and dramatist Nell Dunn wrote her first novel, *Up the Junction*, in 1963. This was followed by *Poor Cow*. Both these novels were made into films by Ken Loach. Her most recent work is a play called *Cancer Tales*.

ANNE FRANK
Anne Frank was a German–Jewish teenager who spent over two years hiding with her family and four others in an annexe of rooms in Amsterdam before being deported to Bergen-Belsen. Nine months later, she died of typhus. She was fifteen years old.

LEWIS GRASSIC GIBBON
Lewis Grassic Gibbon (1901–35) was born in a croft in Aberdeenshire. One of Scotland's outstanding writers, he is most famous for his trilogy *A Scots Quair*, which includes the novel *Sunset Song*, a tribute to the Scottish peasant crofters he'd grown up amongst which, in 2005, was voted the Best Scottish Book of All Time. He also wrote short stories and a miscellany with the poet Hugh MacDiarmid. He died in his early thirties.

ALASDAIR GRAY
Alasdair Gray was born in Glasgow and trained as a painter. His highly acclaimed first novel *Lanark* was published in 1981 and is now regarded as a classic. His other books include the novel *Poor Things and* the collections of stories *Ten Tales Tall and True* and *The Ends of Our Tethers: 13 Sorry Stories*. He also edited *The Book of Prefaces*.

LAVINIA GREENLAW
Lavinia Greenlaw was born in London in 1962, where she still lives. She is the author of several prize-winning collections of poetry including *Minsk*, and the novels, *Mary George of Allnorthover* and *An Irresponsible Age*. She also writes for radio and television and reviews both fiction and non-fiction.

E.Y. "YIP" HARBURG
Edgar "Yip" Harburg (1896–1981) was the son of Russian immigrants. He moved from New York to Hollywood in the early 1930s and wrote lyrics for musicals – including *The Wizard of Oz*, for which his "Somewhere Over the Rainbow" won an Academy Award. He was blacklisted from Hollywood during the McCarthy era so turned to Broadway.

RAMONA HERDMAN
Ramona Herdman was born in 1978. She has a BA and an MA in Creative Writing from the University of East Anglia. In 2003 she published her first collection of poems, *Come What You Wished For*, which was called "an auspicious debut" by Hugo Williams.

LAURA HIRD
Laura Hird was born in 1966. She is the author of *Nail and Other Stories* and *Born Free* (1999), a novel set in Edinburgh, where she lives. *Born Free* was shortlisted for both the Orange Prize and the Whitbread First Novel Award.

BILLIE HOLIDAY
Billie Holiday (1915–59) grew up in Maryland. Her difficult childhood has been the subject of much speculation. She moved to New York with her mother in 1928, and started singing in Harlem clubs soon afterwards. She became the outstanding female jazz voice of her day.

A.M.HOMES
A.M. Homes is the author of the novels *The End of Alice, This Book Will Save Your Life, Music for Torching, In a Country of Mothers* and *Jack*, and the short story collections *The Safety of Objects* and *Things You Should Know*. Her fiction has been translated into twelve languages and has received numerous awards. She lives in New York.

ZORA NEALE HURSTON
Zora Neale Hurston (1891–1960) grew up in Eatonville, Florida, the first self-governing black town in America. Her first novel, *Jonah's Gourd Vine*, was published in 1934 and her best-known novel, *Their Eyes Were Watching God*, in 1937. Her autobiography, *Dust Tracks on a Road*, was published in 1942. Once a bright star, Hurston died in poverty before being rediscovered in the 1970s.

KATHLEEN JAMIE
Kathleen Jamie was born in Scotland in 1962. Her poetry has won several prestigious awards and her latest collection, *The Tree House*, won the 2004 Forward Poetry Prize and the 2005 Scottish Arts Council Book of the Year Award. She is also the author of a travel book about northern Pakistan, *Among Muslims*. She lives in Fife.

TOVE JANSSON
Jansson (1914–2001) was a Finnish–Swedish artist, novelist and children's author, most famous for creating the Moomintrolls series in 1945. Her work for adults is gradually gaining attention now – helped by the recent success of *The Summer Book*. She lived much of her life on a small island in the Gulf of Finland with her partner, the graphic artist Tuulikki Pietilä.

DEREK JARMAN
Derek Jarman (1942–94) was a celebrated British film director, stage designer, artist and writer. His films – experimental and influential – include *Jubilee, The Tempest* and *Caravaggio*. During the 1980s Jarman was one of the few openly gay public figures in Britain and was a leading gay rights and AIDS-awareness activist.

JACKIE KAY
Poet, novelist and short-story writer Jackie Kay was born in Edinburgh in 1961 to a Scottish mother and a Nigerian father. She was brought up in Glasgow. Her first novel, *Trumpet*, won the Guardian Fiction Prize. She lives in Manchester.

PHILIP LARKIN
Philip Larkin (1922–85) was an English poet and novelist who worked all his life as a university librarian. He remains one of Britain's most popular poets.

TOM LEONARD
Poet, scholar and essayist Tom Leonard was born in Glasgow in 1944. He is best known for poetry written in Glaswegian vernacular – a radical and innovative approach when his first collection was published in 1969 – and his concern with the politics of language. He is currently Professor of Creative Writing, along with Alasdair Gray and James Kelman, at Glasgow University.

CLARICE LISPECTOR
Clarice Lispector (1920–77) was born in the Ukraine but moved to Brazil when she was two months old. In Brazil she is recognized as one of the most original and influential writers of her time. She wrote novels, stories and non-fiction – including regular newspaper columns.

LIZ LOCHHEAD
Scottish poet Liz Lochhead was born in 1947. Her first collection of poems, *Memo for Spring*, was published in 1972 and later ones include *Bagpipe Muzak*. In the early 1970s she was part of Philip Hobsbaum's writers' group, which included Alasdair Gray, James Kelman and Tom Leonard. She is also one of Scotland's most popular dramatists.

HUGH MACDIARMID
Born in Dumfriesshire, poet Hugh MacDiarmid (1892–1978) spearheaded a revival of the Scots language in poetry, was a founding member of the Scottish National Party and is recognized as the major force in the Scottish Literary Renaissance.

KATHERINE MANSFIELD
Katherine Mansfield (1888–1923) was born in New Zealand and educated in London where she was closely associated with D.H. Lawrence and considered a rival to Virginia Woolf. Her most well-known works are: the story "Prelude", the collection of family memoirs *Bliss* and the highly praised short-story collection, *The Garden Party*.

LEE MILLER
Lee Miller (1907–77) was born in New York and died in England. She started her photographic career as a model but in 1929 went to Paris where she worked with Man Ray. A highly acclaimed fashion and war photographer, her witty pictures also formed an important part of the Surrealist movement.

CZESLAW MILOSZ
Czeslaw Milosz (1911–2004) was born in Lithuania but grew up in Poland. During the Second World War he worked in Warsaw for underground presses but then moved to Europe and the US. Latterly a literature professor at Berkeley, California, he wrote almost all his poems in his native Polish, although his work was banned in Poland until after he won the Nobel Prize for Literature in 1980.

EDWIN MORGAN
Born in 1920 in Glasgow, Edwin Morgan was the city's first Poet Laureate and, in 2004, was also made the first "Scots Makar" – Sco-

tland's national poet. He is one of the foremost and most popular contemporary Scottish poets. He is also acclaimed for his translation work.

COOKIE MUELLER
The US actress and writer Cookie Mueller (1949–89) was born in Baltimore. She is known for her roles in early films by John Waters and her collaborations with Nan Goldin. Her books are cult classics and include the collection *Ask Doctor Mueller*, the memoir *Walking Through Clear Water in a Pool Painted Black* and *Garden of Ashes*.

EDWIN MUIR
Edwin Muir (1887–1959) was born on the Orkney island of Wyre but his family moved to Glasgow in 1901. His poetry and controversial views about the Scots language made him a central figure of the Scottish Renaissance. He also encouraged the early writing of fellow Orcadian George Mackay Brown.

JOYCE CAROL OATES
Joyce Carol Oates is the acclaimed US author of many novels and short stories including *Them, Because it is Bitter, and Because it is My Heart, Blonde* and "Where Are You Going, Where Have You Been?", which inspired both a film and a song. She is currently the Roger S. Berlind Distinguished Professor of the Humanities at Princeton University. She has also written several mystery novels under the pseudonym Rosamond Smith.

MAGGIE O'FARRELL
Maggie O'Farrell was born in Northern Ireland in 1972 and grew up in Wales and Scotland. Her debut novel, *After You'd Gone*, won a Betty Trask Award, and was followed by two further novels: *My Lover's Lover*; and *The Distance Between Us*, winner of a Somerset Maugham Award. Her latest novel is *The Vanishing Act of Esme Lennox*.

ALICE OSWALD
Alice Oswald's first collection of poetry, *The Thing in the Gap-Stone Stile* (1996) won a Forward Poetry Prize and was shortlisted for the T. S. Eliot Prize. In 2004, the Poetry Book Society named her one of its "Next Generation" poets. Her latest collection is *Woods*. She lives in Devon and works as a gardener on the Dartington Estate.

HELEN OYEYEMI
Helen Oyeyemi was born in Nigeria in 1984 and moved to London when she was four. She wrote her much-feted first novel, *The Icarus Girl*, while she was still at school studying for her A-levels. She studied Social and Political Sciences at Cambridge and her second novel, *The Opposite House*, will be out next year.

CYNTHIA OZICK
Cynthia Ozick was born in New York in 1928, to Russian–Jewish parents and is an award-winning author of novels, stories, criticism, poetry and plays. She lives in New York.

GRACE PALEY
Grace Paley is a short-story writer, poet and activist who was born in the Bronx in 1922 to Russian–Jewish immigrants. She is one of America's most revered and well-known short-story writers. Her *Collected Stories* were published in 1994.

SYLVIA PLATH
Sylvia Plath (1932–63) was born in Massachusetts. Most famous as a poet, she is also known for her semi-autobiographical novel *The Bell Jar*. She is considered one of the finest poets of her generation.

DILYS POWELL
Dilys Powell (1901–95) was a British journalist, author and ground-breaking film critic. She also wrote books about film and travel, particularly about Greece, where she spent part of each year.

RAINER MARIA RILKE
Rainer Maria Rilke (1875–1926) is considered the German language's finest twentieth-century poet. He wrote in both verse and prose and his work includes *Sonnets to Orpheus, The Duino Elegies, Letters to a Young Poet* and the semi-autobiographical *The Notebooks of Malte Laurids Brigge*. Born in Prague, he later adopted Switzerland as his homeland.

JACK RILLIE
Jack Rillie taught in the English Department of Glasgow University from 1948 to 1993, where he influenced and inspired generations of students, particularly in the study of poetry. Described by one as "incomparable" and another as a "teacher never to be forgotton", in 2004 he was presented with a book of tributes put together by yet another former student, Alasdair Gray. He lives in Glasgow.

MARILYNNE ROBINSON
Marilynne Robinson was born in 1947 in Idaho. Her first novel, *House-keeping*, won a PEN/Hemingway Award for best first novel, and was nominated for the Pulitzer Prize. Her second novel, *Gilead*, won universal acclaim from critics, as well as the 2005 Pulitzer Prize for Fiction.

JOSEPH ROTH
Joseph Roth (1894–1939) was a Jewish–Austrian writer whose works include *Job* and the family saga *The Radetzky March*. A prominent liberal Jewish journalist, Roth was forced to leave Berlin for Paris during Hitler's rise to power. Much of his writing, only now widely available in English, is concerned with looking back at more tolerant times.

LORNA SAGE
An influential author and literary critic, Lorna Sage (1943–2001) taught at British and American universities and was professor of English at the University of East Anglia. Particularly respected for her studies of women writers, near the end of her life she also published a very successful memoir, *Bad Blood*.

W.G. SEBALD
W.G. Sebald (1944–2001) was a writer and critic who grew up in post-war Germany and later moved to England. His books blend fact, fiction and images, and include *Austerlitz, The Rings of Saturn, The Emigrants* and *Vertigo*. They often deal with the effects of the Second World War on the collective memory of the German people. He died tragically in an accident in 2001.

RACHEL SEIFFERT
Rachel Seiffert was born in 1971 in Oxford to German and Australian parents and now lives in Berlin. Her novel *The Dark Room*, which explores the legacy of Nazi guilt in Germany, was shortlisted for the Booker Prize and won a Betty Trask Award. She is also the author of *Field Studies*, a collection of stories.

NAN SHEPHERD
Anna Shepherd (1893–1981) lived all her life around Aberdeen. She was the author of fiction, poetry and prose – often about the constrained, difficult lives of women in contemporary Scotland. She was a keen hill walker, and both her poetry and non-fiction book *The Living Mountain* express her love of the Grampian mountains.

STEVIE SMITH
Stevie Smith (1902–71) was an English poet and novelist. Her first poetry collection, *A Good Time Was Had By All*, was published in 1937 and her first novel, *Novel on Yellow Paper*, in 1936. She remains one of Britain's best-loved poets.

MURIEL SPARK
Novelist, poet, short-story writer, critic and biographer, Muriel Spark (1918–2006) was born in Edinburgh. Her first novel, *The Comforters*, was published in 1957, but it was with *The Prime of Miss Jean Brodie* that her reputation was established. One of Britain's most important twentieth-century writers, her last novel was *The Finishing School*.

ALAN SPENCE
Alan Spence was born in Glasgow and is the award-winning author of poetry, novels, short stories and plays. His fiction includes *Its Colours They Are Fine, The Magic Flute, Stone Garden* and *Way to Go*. As a poet, he has written three collections of haiku, *Plop! Glasgow Zen* and *Seasons of the Heart*. He lives in Edinburgh.

GERTRUDE STEIN
Gertrude Stein (1874–1946) was an American writer, poet, feminist and playwright who lived most of her life in France. She was a key figure in the development of modernist art, and her salons attracted figures such as Picasso and Hemingway. Her lifelong partner was Alice B. Toklas and her memoir *The Autobiography of Alice B. Toklas* was her first bestseller.

WALLACE STEVENS
Wallace Stevens (1879–1955) was born in Pennsylvania and established himself as a lawyer before starting to write poetry outside office hours.

Now considered one of the major American poets of the century, he did not receive widespread recognition until the publication of his *Collected Poems*, a year before his death.

J.M. SYNGE
John Millington Synge (1871–1909) was an Irish playwright, poet and writer best known for his *Playboy of the Western World*. He died very young, of a form of cancer untreatable at the time. His *Poems and Translations* was published posthumously, with a preface by Yeats, who was one of his great supporters.

MARGARET TAIT
Margaret Tait (1918–99) was born in Kirkwall in the Orkney Islands. Known during her life for her films about Scottish life, both rural and urban, she is a remarkable critical forerunner and figure in the late-twentieth-century renaissance of Scottish writing. She published her poetry herself and most of her films were also self-financed.

EDWARD THOMAS
Edward Thomas (1870–1917) was born in London to Welsh parents. He wrote over thirty books of prose before, encouraged by Robert Frost, he started writing poetry at the age of thirty-six. In just two years, he produced 142 poems. He was killed at Arras.

MARINA TSVETAYEVA
Born in Moscow, Marina Tsvetayeva (1892–1941) was a prolific poet and writer who lived through some of the worst times in Russian history, including the Moscow famine and the Revolution. Her admirers included Anna Akhmatova and Rilke.

AMOS TUTUOLA
Amos Tutuola (1920–97) was a Nigerian writer who wrote *The Palm-Wine Drinkard* in the space of a few days. Published in London and New York in 1952 it was an international hit. He followed this up with *My Life in the Bush of Ghosts*. His last book was *The Village Witch Doctor and Other Stories*.

DUBRAVKA UGRESIC
Dubravka Ugresic was born in Zagreb in 1949. She was a professor of Russian language and literature before she started writing herself. In 1993 she left Yugoslavia for political reasons, and is now based in Amsterdam. The author of internationally acclaimed and prize-winning novels, essays and stories, her books include *The Ministry of Pain, Thank You For Not Reading* and *The Museum of Unconditional Surrender*.

JOY WILLIAMS
Joy Williams was born in 1944 in Massachusetts. She is the author of four novels (including *State of Grace*), two collections of short stories (including *Taking Care*) and a collection of essays, *Ill Nature: Rants and Reflections on Humanity and Other Animals*. Her work has won several prizes.

WILLIAM CARLOS WILLIAMS

William Carlos Williams (1883–1963) was born in New Jersey. An important Imagist poet and a great friend of Ezra Pound, he later turned away from what he saw as essentially a European movement and towards a more American point of view. As a result, he was a great influence on a new generation of American poets – the Beats.

JEANETTE WINTERSON

Jeanette Winterson was born in Manchester and adopted by Pentecostal parents. She was expected to follow a church path, but instead went to Oxford University, where she wrote her groundbreaking first novel, *Oranges Are Not The Only Fruit*. Her novels, stories, poems, criticism and journalism have won international acclaim ever since. Her most recent publication is *Tanglewreck*, a book for children.

VIRGINIA WOOLF

Virginia Woolf (1882–1941) is one of the most important literary figures of the twentieth century. Her most famous works include the novels *Mrs. Dalloway, To the Lighthouse* and *Orlando*, and her essay *A Room of One's Own*.

ACKNOWLEDGEMENTS

For permission to reprint copyright material the publishers gratefully acknowledge the following:

ARMANDO: "Fragments", from *From Berlin* (Reaktion Books, London, 1996), English language translation © Susan Massotty, 1996, reprinted by permission of the publisher.

KATE ATKINSON: "VI: Unseen Translation", from *Not the End of the World* (Doubleday, a division of Transworld Publishers, 2002), © Kate Atkinson 2002, reprinted by permission of the author.

MARGARET ATWOOD: "The Poet Has Come Back . . .", © Margaret Atwood, published by permission of the author and Curtis Brown Ltd.

PAUL BAILEY: "Spunk", from *An Immaculate Mistake: scenes from childhood and beyond* (Bloomsbury Publishing, 1990), © 1990 by Paul Bailey, reprinted by permission of the author.

NICOLA BARKER: "The Butcher's Apprentice", from *Love Your Enemies* (Faber & Faber, 1993), reprinted by permission of the publisher.

DJUNA BARNES: "The Terrible Peacock", from *Smoke and Other Early Stories* (Virago Press, in association with Sun & Moon Press, Maryland, 1985), © Sun & Moon Press 1982, reprinted by permission of Green Integer Books, www.greeninteger.com.

JOHN BERGER: "Between Two Colmars", from *About Looking* (Vintage International, 1991), © 1980 by John Berger, reprinted by permission of Pantheon Books, a division of Random House Inc.

BERYL THE PERIL: "Double Act" (D. C. Thomson & Co., 1972), reprinted by permission of the publisher.

XANDRA BINGLEY: "Mrs Fish", from *Bernie, May and Mrs Fish. A Wartime Country Memoir* (HarperCollins Publishers, 2005), © Xandra Bingley 2005, reprinted by permission of the author c/o David Godwin Associates.

KASIA BODDY: "On the Ward with TV, iPod and Telephone", © 2006 Kasia Boddy, published by permission of the author.

JANE BOWLES: "Everything Is Nice", from *Plain Pleasures*, in *My Sister's Hand in Mine, An Expanded Edition of The Collected Works of Jane Bowles* (The Ecco Press, 1978), © 1970, 1972, 1976, 1977, 1978 by Paul Bowles.

LOUISE BROOKS: "Kansas to New York", from *Lulu in Hollywood* (Arena, 1987), © 1974, 1982 by Louise Brooks, reprinted by permission of Alfred A. Knopf, a division of Random House Inc.

GEORGE MACKAY BROWN: "Witch", from *A Calendar of Love and other stories* (Triad/Panther Books, 1978), © George Mackay Brown 1967, reprinted by permission of John Murray (Publishers) Ltd.

ITALO CALVINO: from "Multiplicity", from *Six Memos for the Next Millennium*, translated by Patrick Creagh (Vintage, 1996), © The Estate of Italo Calvino 1988, reprinted by permission of The Wylie Agency Inc.

LEONORA CARRINGTON: "The Happy Corpse Story", from *The Seventh Horse and Other Stories* (Virago Press, in association with E. P. Dutton, 1989), © 1988 Leonora Carrington.

ANGELA CARTER: from *Wise Children* (Chatto & Windus), © Angela Carter 1991. Reprinted by permission of Rogers, Coleridge & White Ltd, 20 Powis Mews, London W11 1JN, on behalf of the author.

COLETTE: "Mae West", from *Colette at the Movies. Criticism and Screenplays*, edited and introduced by Alain and Odette Virmaux, translated by Sarah W. R. Smith (Frederick Ungar Publishing Co., 1980), © 1980 Frederick Ungar Publishing Co., Inc., reprinted by permission of The Continuum International Publishing Group.

ROBERT CREELEY: "End", from *Later* (Marion Boyars, 1980), reprinted by permission of the publisher.

E.E.CUMMINGS: "thing no is (of", from *Complete Poems 1904–1962* by e.e. cummings, edited by George J. Firmage (Liveright Publishing Corporation, 1991), © 1991 by the Trustees for the e.e.cummings Trust and George James Firmage, reprinted by permission of W.W.Norton & Company.

FRED D'AGUIAR: "Bring Back, Bring Back", from *The Times Literary Supplement* (December 17, 2005), reprinted by permission of the author.

LYDIA DAVIS: "In the Garment District", from *Almost No Memory* (Picador, New York, 2001), © 1997 by Lydia Davis, reprinted by permission of Farrar, Straus & Giroux LLC.

SIMONE DE BEAUVOIR: from *Memoirs of a Dutiful Daughter*, translated by James Kirkup (Penguin Books, 1980), © Librairie Gallimard, 1958; translation © The World Publishing Company, 1959, reprinted by permission of Penguin Books Ltd.

H.D. (HILDA DOOLITTLE): "The Cinema and the Classics. I: Beauty", from *Close Up*, Volume 1, No.1 (July 1927), in *Close Up 1927–1933: Cinema and Modernism*, edited by James Donald, Anne Friedberg and Laura Marcus (Cassell, 1998), © 2005 by The Schaffner Family Foundation, reprinted by permission of New Directions Publishing Corporation, agents.

NELL DUNN: "The Deserted House", from *Up the Junction* (Virago Press, 1988), © Nell Dunn, 1963, reprinted by permission of Alan Brodie Representation Ltd.

ANNE FRANK: "Saturday, 8 July 1944", from *The Diary of A Young Girl: The Definitive Edition* by Anne Frank, edited by Otto H. Frank and Mirjam Pressler, translated by Susan Massotty (Viking, 1997), ©

The Anne Frank-Fonds, Basle, Switzerland, 1991, English translation © Doubleday, a division of Random House Inc., by permission of Liepman Agency on behalf of The Anne Frank-Fonds and Penguin Books Ltd.

ALASDAIR GRAY: "Houses and Small Labour Parties", from *Ten Tales Tall & True* (Bloomsbury Publishing, 1993), © Alasdair Gray 1993, reprinted by permission of the publisher.

LAVINIA GREENLAW: "The Falling City", from *Minsk* (Faber & Faber, 2003), © Lavinia Greenlaw, 2003, reprinted by permission of the publisher.

E. Y. "YIP" HARBURG: from "It's only a paper moon", © Harms, Inc., 1933 (Warner Chappell Music).

RAMONA HERDMAN: "He died on Friday", from *Come What You Wished For* (Egg Box Publishing, 2003), © Ramona Herdman, 2003, reprinted by permission of the publisher.

LAURA HIRD: "Joni", from *Born Free* (Rebel Inc., 1999), © 1999, Laura Hird, reprinted by permission of Canongate Books.

BILLIE HOLIDAY with WILLIAM DUFTY: from *Lady Sings the Blues* (Penguin Books by arrangement with Doubleday & Company, Inc., 1984), © Eleonora Fagan and William F. Dufty, 1956, reprinted by permission of Doubleday, a division of Random House Inc.

A.M.HOMES: "Remedy", from *Things You Should Know. A Collection of Stories* (HarperCollins Publishers, 1998), © 1998 by A.M.Homes, reprinted by permission of HarperCollins Publishers and Granta Publications.

ZORA NEALE HURSTON: from *Their Eyes Were Watching God* (Harper Perennial Modern Classics, 1998), © 1937 by Zora Neale Hurston, renewed 1965 by John C. Hurston and Joel Hurston.

KATHLEEN JAMIE: "Meadowsweet", from *Jizzen* (Picador, 1999), © Kathleen Jamie 1999, reprinted by permission of Macmillan London Ltd.

TOVE JANSSON: "Art in Nature", from *Dockskapet* ("The doll's house", 1978), reprinted in *Books from Finland* (2001), translated by David McDuff, © Tove Jansson, 1978. First published by Schildts Förlags Ab, Finland, reprinted by permission of Schildts Forlags and the translator.

DEREK JARMAN: "White Lies", from *Chroma. A Book of Colour – June '93* (Century, 1994), © Derek Jarman 1994, reprinted by permission of The Random House Group Ltd and the Overlook Press.

JACKIE KAY: "Old Aberdeen", from *Life Mask* (Bloodaxe Books, 2005), © Jackie Kay 2005, reprinted by permission of the author.

PHILIP LARKIN: "The Trees", from *High Windows* (Faber & Faber, 1983), © 1974 by Philip Larkin, reprinted by permission of the publisher.

TOM LEONARD: "baa baa black sheep", from *Intimate Voices: Poems 1965–1983* (Etruscan Books, 2003), © Tom Leonard, reprinted by permission of the author.

CLARICE LISPECTOR: from *State of Grace*, from *Selected Crônicas* (Carcanet Press, 1992), © 1984 Editora Nova Fronteiro, translation © 1992 Giovanni Pontiero, reprinted by permission of Carcanet Press and New Directions Publishing Corporation.

LIZ LOCHHEAD: "On Midsummer Common", from *Memo for Spring* (Reprographia, 1972), © Liz Lochhead 1972, reprinted by permission of Polygon, an imprint of Birlinn Ltd.

HUGH MACDIARMID: "Bairns Arena Frightened", from *The Revolutionary Art of the Future. Rediscovered Poems*, edited by John Manson, Dorian Grieve and Alan Riach (Carcanet Press, 2003), © the Estate of Hugh MacDiarmid 2003, reprinted by permission of the publisher.

LEE MILLER: "Colette", from *Lee Miller's War. Photographer and Correspondent with the Allies in Europe 1944–45,* edited by Antony Penrose (Thames & Hudson, 2005); "Colette" text © Lee Miller Archives, England, 2006. All rights reserved. www.leemiller.co.uk.

CZESLAW MILOSZ: "Ars Poetica?" and "On Angels", from *The Collected Poems 1931–1987* (Penguin Books by arrangement with The Ecco Press, 1988), © Czeslaw Milosz Royalties, Inc., 1988, reprinted by permission of Penguin Books Ltd.

EDWIN MORGAN: "More Questions than Answers", from *Virtual and Other Realities* (Carcanet Press, 1997), © Edwin Morgan 1997, and "Instructions to an Actor", from *New Selected Poems* (Carcanet Press, 2000), © Edwin Morgan 2000, both reprinted by permission of the publisher.

COOKIE MUELLER: "Fleeting Happiness", from *Garden of Ashes* (Hanuman Books, 1990), © 1990 The Estate of Cookie Mueller, © Hanuman Books, 1990.

EDWIN MUIR: "The Child Dying", from *Selected Poems* (Faber & Faber, 1981), © this selection Faber & Faber, 1965, reprinted by permission of the publisher.

JOYCE CAROL OATES: "Small Avalanches", from *Where Are You Going, Where Have You Been? Selected Early Stories* (Ontario Review Press/Princeton, 1993), © 1993 by Joyce Carol Oates, reprinted by permission of the author.

MAGGIE O'FARRELL: "The House I Live In", © 2006 by Maggie O'Farrell, published by permission of the author.

ALICE OSWALD: "Hymn to Iris", from *Woods etc.* (Faber & Faber, 2005), © Alice Oswald, 2005, reprinted by permission of the publisher.

HELEN OYEYEMI: "Independence", © 2006 by Helen Oyeyemi, published by permission of the author.

CYNTHIA OZICK: from the preface to *Bloodshed and Three Novellas* (E. P. Dutton, by arrangement with Alfred A. Knopf, 1983), © 1976 by Cynthia Ozick, reprinted by permission of Alfred A. Knopf, a division of Random House Inc.

GRACE PALEY: "Wants", from *The Collected Stories* (Virago Press, 1999), © Grace Paley 1994, reprinted by permission of Farrar, Straus & Giroux LLC.

SYLVIA PLATH: "Black Rook in Rainy Weather", from *The Colossus* (Faber & Faber, 1977), © 1960 by Sylvia Plath; this edition © 1967 by Ted Hughes, reprinted by permission of the publisher.

DILYS POWELL: "Reconciliation", from *An Affair of the Heart* (Efstathiadis, 1983), © 1983 by P. Efstathiadis & Sons S.A.

RAINER MARIA RILKE: "The Ninth Elegy", from *The Selected Poetry of Rainer Maria Rilke*, edited and translated by Stephen Mitchell (Picador, 1987), © Stephen Mitchell 1980, 1981, 1982, reprinted by permission of Macmillan London Ltd and The Bob Cornfield Agency on behalf of the translator.

JACK RILLIE: "Call-girls" © Jack Rillie 2006 and reprinted by permission of the author.

MARILYNNE ROBINSON: from *Housekeeping* (Faber & Faber, 1981), © Marilynne Robinson, 1981, reprinted by permission of the publisher.

JOSEPH ROTH: "Passengers with Heavy Loads", from *What I Saw: Reports from Berlin 1920–33*, translated with an introduction by Michael Hofmann (Granta Books, 2003), © 1996 by Verlag Kiepenheuer & Witsch; translation © 2003 by Michael Hofmann, reprinted by permission of Granta Publications.

LORNA SAGE: "Our Lady of the Accident", from *Good As Her Word. Selected Journalism* (Fourth Estate, 2003), © Lorna Sage 1972–2001, reprinted by permission of Sharon Toliani-Sage.

W. G. SEBALD: "Whoever closes the wings", from *After Nature*, translated by Michael Hamburger (Hamish Hamilton, 2002), © The estate of W.G. Sebald, 2002; translation © Michael Hamburger, 2002.

RACHEL SEIFFERT: "Field Study", from *Field Study* (William Heinemann, 2004), © Rachel Seiffert 2004, reprinted by permission of The Random House Group Ltd.

NAN SHEPHERD: "Frost and Snow", from *The Living Mountain*, in *The Grampian Quartet* (Canongate Classics, 2001), reprinted by permission of the publisher.

STEVIE SMITH: "This Englishwoman", from *The Collected Poems of Stevie Smith*, edited by James MacGibbon (Penguin Modern Classics, 1985), this arrangement © James MacGibbon, 1975, reprinted by permission of the Estate of James MacGibbon c/o James & James (Publishers) Ltd.

MURIEL SPARK: from *The Comforters* (Macmillan, 1957), © Muriel Spark, 1957, reprinted by permission of the publisher.

ALAN SPENCE: "into the sea I launch", from *Seasons of the Heart. Haiku* (Canongate Books, 2000), © Alan Spence, 2000, reprinted by permission of the publisher.

GERTRUDE STEIN: "On the Meaning of 'rose is a rose is a rose'", from *Look At Me Now and Here I Am* (Peter Owen, 1967), selection © Peter Owen Ltd., 1967, reprinted by permission of the publisher.

WALLACE STEVENS: "Earthy Anecdote", from *Collected Poems* (Faber & Faber, 1984), © 1984 by the Estate of Wallace Stevens, reprinted by permission of the publisher.

J. M. SYNGE: "Prelude" and "In May", from *Collected Works. Volume 1: Poems*, edited by Robin Skelton (Colin Smythe, 1982), © 1962 Oxford University Press, reprinted by permission of Oxford University Press.

MARGARET TAIT: "Elasticity" and "To Anybody At All", from *origins and elements* (privately printed, 1959), © Margaret Caroline Tait 1959, reprinted by permission of Alexander Pirie.

MARINA TSVETAYEVA: "We shall not escape Hell", from *Selected Poems*, translated by Elaine Feinstein (Penguin Books, 1974), translation © Elaine Feinstein, 1971, reprinted by permission of Carcanet Press.

AMOS TUTUOLA: from *The Palm-Wine Drinkard*, in *The Palm-Wine Drinkard and My Life in the Bush of Ghosts* (Grove Press, 1954), *The Palm-Wine Drinkard* © 1953 by George Braziller.

DUBRAVKA UGRESIC: "Alchemy", from *Thank You for Not Reading: Essays on Literary Trivia*, translated by Celia Hawkesworth with the assistance of Damion Searles (Dalkey Archive Press, 2003), © 2001, 2003 by Dubravka Ugresic; translation © 2003 Celia Hawkesworth, reprinted by permission of the publisher.

JOY WILLIAMS: "Lu-Lu", from *Escapes and Other Stories* (Flamingo, 1991), © Joy Williams 1990.

WILLIAM CARLOS WILLIAMS: "Pastoral", from *The Collected Poems of William Carlos Williams. Volume 1: 1909–1939*, edited by A. Walton Litz and Christopher MacGowan (Carcanet Press, 1987), © 1938 by New Directions Publishing Corporation, reprinted by permission of Carcanet Press and New Directions Publishing Corporation.

JEANETTE WINTERSON: "The 24-Hour Dog", from *The World and Other Places* (Jonathan Cape, 1998), © Jeanette Winterson 1998, reprinted by permission of the author c/o The William Morris Agency.

VIRGINIA WOOLF: from *Orlando* (The Hogarth Press, 1978), © Quentin Bell and Angelica Garnett 1928. "Sunday, July 25th 1926", from *A Writer's Diary*, edited by Leonard Woolf (The Hogarth Press, 1953), © Quentin Bell and Angelica Garnett 1953, reprinted by permission of The Random House Group Ltd and Harcourt, Inc.

W.B.YEATS: "The Song Of Wandering Aengus", from *Selected Poetry*, edited by A. Norman Jeffares (Pan Books in association with Macmillan London, 1976), © A. Norman Jeffares and Macmillan & Co Ltd 1962, reprinted by permission of A. P. Watt Ltd on behalf of Michael B. Yeats, and Scribner, an imprint of Simon & Schuster Adult Publishing Group.

Every effort has been made to contact and acknowledge all copyright holders prior to going to press, but in some cases this has not been possible. Constable & Robinson Ltd therefore wish

to thank all copyright holders who are included without ac-
knowledgement, and apologize for any errors or omissions in the
above list. If contacted, the publisher will be pleased to rectify
these at the earliest opportunity.

INDEX OF WRITERS

Armando 358–61
Atkinson, Kate 148–63
Atwood, Margaret 8
Austen, Jane 7

Bailey, Paul 51–6
Barker, Nicola 377–84
Barnes, Djuna 9–16
Berger, John 102–7
Beryl the Peril 68–9
Bingley, Xandra 233–44
Blake, William 271, 272
Boddy, Kasia 89–93
Bowles, Jane 78–84
Brooks, Louise 170–86
Brown, George Mackay 34–47

Calvino, Italo 446
Carrington, Leonora 1–2, 387–90
Carter, Angela 70–5
Colette 119–21
Creeley, Robert 450
cummings, e.e. 422

D'Aguiar, Fred 219
Davis, Lydia 88
De Beauvoir, Simone 402–11
Donne, John 139
Doolittle, Hilda (H.D.) 111–18
Douglas, William 62–3
Dufty, William 17–21
Dunn, Nell 57–61

Frank, Anne 350–2

Gibbon, Lewis Grassic 2, 273–87
Gray, Alasdair 288–301
Greenlaw, Lavinia 169

Harburg, E.Y. "Yip" 443
Hardy, Thomas 221–2
H.D. see Doolittle, Hilda
Herdman, Ramona 310–11
Hird, Laura 22–33
Holiday, Billie 17–21
Homes, A.M. 189–218
Hurston, Zora Neale 64–7

Jamie, Kathleen 49
Jansson, Tove 224–9
Jarman, Derek 428–38

Kay, Jackie 246
Keats, John 87

Larkin, Philip 257
Leonard, Tom 412
Lispector, Clarice 419–21
Lochhead, Liz 5–6, 187–8

MacDiarmid, Hugh 245
Mansfield, Katherine 147
Miller, Lee 1, 122–8
Milosz, Czeslaw 99, 100–1

Morgan, Edwin 136, 137–8
Mueller, Cookie 444–5
Muir, Edwin 312

Oates, Joyce Carol 337–49
O'Farrell, Maggie 313–36
Oswald, Alice 223
Oyeyemi, Helen 302–9
Ozick, Cynthia 129

Paley, Grace 96–8
Plath, Sylvia 4, 231–2
Powell, Dilys 353–7

Rilke, Rainer Maria 447–9
Rillie, Jack 94
Robinson, Marilynne 76–7
Roth, Joseph 166–8

Sage, Lorna 413–18
Sebald, W.G. 108–10
Seiffert, Rachel 362–76

Shakespeare, William 385–6
Shepherd, Nan 2, 258–66
Smith, Stevie 4, 50
Spark, Muriel 4, 423–7
Spence, Alan 267
Stein, Gertrude 269
Stevens, Wallace 230
Synge, J.M. 268

Tait, Margaret 5, 95
Thomas, Edward 164
Tsvetayeva, Marina 48
Tutuola, Amos 391–401

Ugresic, Dubravka 439–42

Williams, Joy 140–6
Williams, William Carlos 256
Winterson, Jeanette 247–55
Woolf, Virginia ix, 1, 85, 130–5

Yeats, W.B. 165